DATE DUE

FEB 1 0 2012	
JUN 1 0 2013	

BRODART, CO.   Cat. No. 23-221-003

Racism, Xenophobia, and Distribution

Racism, Xenophobia, and Distribution

Multi-Issue Politics in Advanced Democracies

John E. Roemer

Woojin Lee

Karine Van der Straeten

Russell Sage Foundation

New York

Harvard University Press

Cambridge, Massachusetts

London, England

2007

Library of Congress Cataloging-in-Publication Data

Roemer, John E.
Racism, xenophobia, and distribution : multi-issue politics in advanced democracies / by John E. Roemer, Woojin Lee, and Karine Van der Straeten.
p. cm.
Includes bibliographical references and index.
ISBN-13: 978-0-674-02495-3 (alk. paper)
ISBN-10: 0-674-02495-8 (alk. paper)
1. Income distribution—Mathematical models. 2. Racism—Mathematical models.
3. Xenophobia—Mathematical models. 4. Political science—Mathematical models.
5. Income distribution—Case studies.
I. Lee, Woojin. II. Straeten, Karine Van der. 1. Title.

HB523.R623 2007
305.8001/5195 22   2006052027

to Natasha

to Jihyun

à Pierre, Jean, et Marguerite

Contents

Acknowledgments   *xi*

1 Introduction   *1*

2 Political Equilibrium: Theory and Application   *14*
   2.1 The Data   *14*
   2.2 Characterization of PUNE as a System of Equations   *17*
   2.3 The Probability-of-Victory Function   *20*
   2.4 Factional Bargaining Powers   *22*
   2.5 The Three-Party Model   *27*
   2.6 First Application: The Logarithmic Utility Function   *28*
   2.7 Second Application: The Euclidean Utility Function   *36*
   2.8 Conclusion   *39*

3 History of Racial Politics in the United States   *41*
   3.1 Introduction   *41*
   3.2 Race and American Exceptionalism   *44*
   3.3 Issue Evolution   *46*
   3.4 The Dixiecrats   *49*
   3.5 The Presidential Election of 1964 and Its Aftermath   *56*
   3.6 The Reagan Democrats   *61*
   3.7 Race, Class, and Welfare Reform in the 1990s   *64*
   3.8 Conclusion   *66*

Contents

4   United States: Quantitative Analysis   68

    4.1   Introduction   68
    4.2   Recovering Voter Racism from Survey Data   69
    4.3   Estimation of the Model's Parameters   92
    4.4   Numerical Solution of the Log Utility Model   113
    4.5   The Euclidean Function Approach   123
    4.6   Conclusion   127

5   History of Racism and Xenophobia in the United Kingdom   130

    5.1   Introduction   130
    5.2   Immigration in Britain   135
    5.3   An Issue of "High Potential"   138
    5.4   From Powell to Thatcher: Challenging the Consensus   148
    5.5   The Rise of Thatcher and the Breakdown of the
          Consensus of Silence   153
    5.6   Immigration in the 1990s and Beyond   159
    5.7   Conclusion   164

6   United Kingdom: Quantitative Analysis   166

    6.1   Introduction   166
    6.2   Minorities, Race, and Class Politics in the UK   168
    6.3   Estimation of Parameters   173
    6.4   The PBE and ASE: Computation   180
    6.5   Conclusion   190

7   Immigration: A Challenge to Tolerant Denmark   191

    7.1   Introduction   191
    7.2   The Early Years: Guest Workers and Their Families   192
    7.3   The Eighties: The Emergence of Refugees   195
    7.4   The Nineties: Xenophobia Emerges, Front and Center   197
    7.5   No Longer Marginal: The Far Right and the Election of 2001   202

8   Denmark: Quantitative Analysis   205

    8.1   Parties and Issues   205
    8.2   Estimation of the Model's Parameters   210
    8.3   Political Equilibrium: Observation and Prediction   226
    8.4   The Policy-Bundle and Antisolidarity Effects: Computation   230
    8.5   Conclusion   235

Contents

9   Immigration and the Political Institutionalization of Xenophobia
    in France   *237*

    9.1   Introduction   *237*
    9.2   Immigration in France: A Brief Sketch   *238*
    9.3   The Politicization of Immigration   *243*
    9.4   The Rise of Le Pen   *246*
    9.5   The Mainstreaming of Xenophobia   *247*
    9.6   The 1988 Presidential Election   *250*
    9.7   Xenophobia Remains in the Headlines   *252*
    9.8   Conventional Politics Return as a New Cleavage Is Born   *254*
    9.9   Conclusion   *263*

10   France: Quantitative Analysis   *265*

    10.1   Parties and Voter Opinion   *265*
    10.2   Political Equilibrium with Three Parties   *268*
    10.3   Estimation of Model Parameters   *273*
    10.4   Political Equilibrium: Observation and Prediction   *289*
    10.5   The Policy-Bundle and Antisolidarity Effects: Computation   *303*

11   Conclusion   *307*

    11.1   The Rise of the New Right Movement   *307*
    11.2   Recapitulation   *308*
    11.3   The Log Utility Function Approach   *312*
    11.4   The Euclidean Utility Function Approach   *314*
    11.5   Limitations   *318*
    11.6   Final Remark   *320*

    Appendix A: Statistical Methods   *323*

    Appendix B: Additional Tables   *327*

    Notes   *359*

    References   *381*

    Index   *395*

Acknowledgments

This project has been financed mainly by two grants from the Russell Sage Foundation: the first to Lee and Roemer, with which the initial analysis of the United States that now appears in Chapter 4 was carried out, and the second to all three authors. The project was initially conceived during Van der Straeten's visit to Yale University, during the fall of 2001. We thank the Economics Department and the Cowles Foundation at Yale for supporting her visit. The Yale Center for International and Area Studies (YCIAS) provided some support during the final preparation of the manuscript.

We are most grateful to three graduate students in political science at Yale, who researched and wrote the four historical chapters in this book: Stephen Engel (Chapter 3), Rafaela Dancygier (Chapters 5 and 9), and Daniel Doherty (Chapter 7). We thank Dancygier, in addition, for her comments on the entire manuscript.

We are grateful to Thomas Piketty for providing us with his data set for France, which eventually we did not use, and to Nonna Mayer for pointing us to the French data sets that we did, finally, use; to the CEVIPOF and CIDSP for providing us with French data; and to the Danish Statistical Archive for providing us with Danish data. The U.S. and UK data are available from public sources.

We have presented parts of this work, over the past several years, at many seminars and conferences, and we are indebted to the participants and discussants who gave us their comments and advice. We apologize for not having

Acknowledgments

kept a proper list of the names of these generous colleagues, but we mention the following venues: Boston University, University of Copenhagen, École Polytechnique, University of Graz, Harvard University, University of Heidelberg, the Juan March Institute and Carlos III University (Madrid), University of Marseilles, University of Massachusetts at Amherst, Paris-Jourdan Sciences Économiques, University of Pompeu Fabra, University of Rochester, Stanford University, Yale University, the World Bank, and the University of Toulouse.

Material in some chapters is presented in modified form from previously published articles: in Chapter 4, from the article by Woojin Lee and John Roemer, "Racism and redistribution in the US: A solution to the problem of American exceptionalism," *Journal of Public Economics* 90 (2006): 1027–1052, copyright 2005 Elsevier BV, used with permission of Elsevier; in Chapter 8, from the article by John Roemer and Karine Van der Straeten, "The political economy of xenophobia and distribution: The case of Denmark," *Scandinavian Journal of Economics* 108, no. 2 (2006): 251–277, used with permission of Blackwell Publishers; in Chapter 10, from the article by John Roemer and Karine Van der Straeten, "Xenophobia and the size of the public sector in France: A politico-economic analysis," *Journal of Economics* 86 (2005): 95–114, used with permission of SpringerWien New York.

Finally, we thank two anonymous referees for their reviews of the manuscript, and Elizabeth Gilbert for her acute editorial eye.

Racism, Xenophobia, and Distribution

1

Introduction

In at least the advanced democracies, and perhaps in all democracies, and perhaps in all countries regardless of the nature of their political institutions, the primary struggle among citizens is and has been over the distribution of economic resources. The advent of universal suffrage in the advanced democracies caused many parties of the Left to alter the focus of the struggle over the distribution of income from the trade union movement and labor action of the strike and the boycott to the ballot box. Marx and Engels believed that universal (male) suffrage would be quickly followed by the victory of socialism through the ballot box: "Universal suffrage is the equivalent of political power for the working class of England, where the proletariat forms the large majority of the population . . . The carrying of universal suffrage in England would, therefore, be a far more socialistic measure than anything which has been honoured with that name in the Continent. Its inevitable result, here, is the political supremacy of the working class."[1] Thus elections were to bring about a peaceful revolution from a society based on the exploitation of workers to one that would provide conditions for universal liberation. Marx and Engels probably could not have imagined what would transpire, that between one-third and one-half the national incomes of the European democracies would be controlled by the state, yet economic competition through markets, among firms that are privately owned, would remain the central institution of economic organization.

Although matters of economic distribution have been the primary focus of the Left, politics have hardly been unidimensional. Important secondary issues have always existed, and at times have become primary: issues relating to foreign policy, region, religion, gender, ethnicity, and race. Przeworski and Sprague (1986) provide a convincing argument that, at least in the period of 1880–1940, both redistribution and religion were important dimensions in European politics. In his study of nine European democracies over the 1970s and 1980s, Kitschelt (1994) argues that politics can be understood as being two-dimensional, over a socialist-capitalist dimension and a libertarian-authoritarian dimension. Laver and Hunt (1992) present empirical evidence that democratic politics are multidimensional in a set of over twenty countries. Kalyvas (1996) investigates under what conditions Western European confessional parties were able to establish religion as a central cleavage structuring party competition.

In this book, we choose race or immigration as the important secondary issue and study the effect of racism or xenophobia on redistribution in four advanced democracies: the United States, the United Kingdom, France, and Denmark.

The issue of race has been a prominent secondary issue in the United States since its founding, first around slavery, and then, after the Civil War, concerning the rights of African-Americans and their integration into mainstream American society. Although the racial caste system, which lasted for 350 years, was almost entirely dismantled in the first twenty-six years following World War II, racially tinged issues, such as welfare, crime, permissive judges, prison funding, and government regulation, have been the subject of strenuous political debate and strong legislation for the last three decades.

It has long been recognized that racism divides the American working class, thus blocking its attempt to redistribute national income away from capital toward labor.[2] Traditionally the theory has been that racism among workers weakens unions, which shifts revenues of firms toward profits and away from wages, but a second mechanism, which operates through electoral politics, has also been discussed. Racism reduces "compassion" among citizens; some whites consequently vote against the redistributive party (in the United States, the Democrats), because blacks are prominent beneficiaries of redistributive taxation.

In Europe, with the exception of the UK, the influx of people of color has, in large part, been a phenomenon of the last forty years, via immigration from Asia, Asia Minor, and Africa. There have recently emerged, in several countries, politically significant movements and parties that are anti-immigrant and xenophobic: Le Pen's in France is the best known, but one must also mention Austria, Belgium, the Netherlands, Denmark, and Switzerland. Indeed, the phenomenon of ethnocentrism or xenophobia is "realigning" voters in these countries; many who used to vote Left are now voting for the New Right. In particular, many unskilled white workers, who feel most threatened by immigration, globalization, and skill-biased technological change, have switched their allegiance.

Historically, emigration was far more important than immigration in Europe, as people of colonial mother countries migrated overseas to their colonies. European governments believed that emigration would assist the economic development of their empires, strengthen ties between colonies and mother countries, and increase the power of the mother countries in the world. Since 1960, the tables have turned. In almost all Western European countries, immigration has become an important issue, with large influxes of immigrants from the former colonies who directly compete for jobs with indigenous unskilled workers. Immigration was initially encouraged by governments and firms, especially by those faced with a major shortage of labor, in industries such as textiles, or those facing strong unions, such as steel. When the rapid economic expansion of the postwar years came to an end, however, rising unemployment and declining growth rates meant that immigrant populations were no longer needed or welcomed. Soon the immigrants and their children became the scapegoats for many of the economic and social ills in these countries.

There is a direct economic effect on real incomes of natives from the immigration of unskilled workers from other countries. One would expect the real incomes of those whose income comes primarily from capital to increase, because the price of unskilled labor falls due both to its increased supply and to the lower reservation wages that immigrants from poor countries have. The effect on the real incomes of the working class is not so obvious: on the one hand, increased labor supply will tend to lower the wages of those with whom immigrants compete for jobs, but on the other hand, some or many goods in workers' consumption baskets will become cheaper, due to the use of cheaper immigrant labor.

Our purpose in this book is to study one effect of the existence of a class of primarily poor workers whose races or ethnicities differ from that of the majority of natives, on the distribution of income in the country. We will not, however, be concerned with the general-equilibrium economic effects alluded to in the previous paragraph, important as they may be, but rather with the distributional effects whose origins are in political competition. When racism toward a class of natives, as in the United States, or racism toward immigrants, as in many advanced European democracies, becomes significant, issues directly related to race or immigration can become political issues in their own right, and competition between political parties can occur both regarding economic distribution or redistribution and regarding the race/immigration issue. Formally, political competition is, in this case, properly modeled as one taking place on a two-dimensional policy space. Of course there are many other dimensions of political competition, but if the race issue is the second most important one, parsimony suggests a model with two policy dimensions. Typically the political parties in the country will propose, in their platforms and manifestos, positions on both distributive issues (such as tax policy and the financing of the public sector) and positions on the race or immigration issue (in the United States, at various times, on civil rights, integration, law and order; in Europe, on immigration law and the treatment of immigrants). Here we are interested in the effect that the existence of a race/immigration issue has on what parties propose on the primary issue of fiscal redistribution.

As an example, consider the present political equilibrium in the United States. For the last twenty-five years at least, the Republican Party has taken a conservative position on the economic issue (antiregulation, antitax, laissez-faire) and a conservative position on the race issue (often using the code words of "law and order"). The details are found in Chapter 3 below. The Democratic Party, in contrast, has taken a pro-redistribution position and a liberal position on the race issue. Among the polity, there is a distribution of views on these two issues. Denote, schematically, a voter's position on these two issues as (θ, ρ), where θ and ρ each lie in the interval $[0, 1]$, a large value of θ means pro-redistribution, and a large value of ρ means racist. (See Figure 1.1.)

A voter with characteristics $(1, 0)$ should clearly vote Democratic, and a voter with characteristics $(0, 1)$ should likewise clearly vote Republican, assuming that the above encapsulation of the parties' positions is accurate. But what about a voter with characteristics $(0, 0)$ or $(1, 1)$? That voter has a problem: neither party offers the political portfolio she desires. The $(1, 1)$ voter is (typically) a poor, white racist, and the $(0, 0)$ voter might be an economic libertarian with liberal racial views. If the race issue is sufficiently salient for the $(1, 1)$ voter, he will vote Republican, although that party does not represent his economic interests; and if the $(0, 0)$ voter is sufficiently concerned with the race issue, she will vote Democratic, despite the Democratic Party's

4

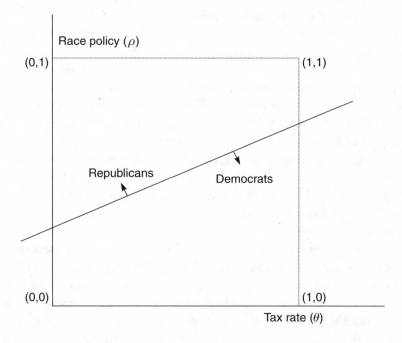

Figure 1.1 Hypothetical voter separation.

position on big government, which she deplores. This is the case shown in Figure 1.1.[3]

Conceptually, it is useful to decompose the effect of the race issue on the equilibrium position of parties on the distributive issue into two subeffects, which we call the *antisolidarity effect* (ASE) and the *policy-bundle effect* (PBE). Typically, a section of natives believes that the poor minority is lazy, exploits the welfare state, and is generally undeserving, and that individuals among the minority or immigrant group are poor by virtue of bad habits and lack of effort rather than by virtue of bad luck (including the bad luck of being uneducated for reasons beyond the individual's control). For specificity's sake, let us think again of the United States. The feeling just described, if it is widespread, will cause both political parties to call for less redistribution than they otherwise would, because that redistribution would aid a group that many voters consider to be undeserving. Solidarity exists when citizens identify with the plight of other citizens, and so we call this effect on the equilibrium positions on the distributive issue the antisolidarity effect.

In addition, there may be a significant contingent of (1, 1) voters who vote for the Republican Party, despite their preferences for redistribution, because they abhor the Democrats' position on the race issue. This contingent strengthens the Republican Party and hence the antiredistributive position. In political equilibrium, it allows the Republicans to compromise less on the distributive issue than they otherwise might have to, and also pulls the Democrats to the right on the redistributive issue, in order to compete. This phenomenon is the policy-bundle effect. Of course, if a sufficiently large number of (0, 0) voters vote for the Democratic Party, the policy-bundle effect could go the other way, strengthening the Democrats and hence the redistributive platform. We will see, however, that in the United States, the net effect of policy bundling is to reduce the degree of redistribution from what would otherwise occur.

Before the 1960s, the southern racist senators, primary among whom was Strom Thurmond, were Democrats. Their political position was (1, 1)—redistributive and racist. Hence for southern white racist voters, it was possible, at least at the congressional level, to vote both redistributive and racist. The Republican Party was still identified with Abraham Lincoln, and attracted the votes of many black citizens. This situation changed after the civil rights movement: the Democratic Party could no longer tolerate racism in its ranks, and the Dixiecrats, led by Thurmond, switched to the Republican Party, which eventually adopted the so-called southern strategy, of "playing the race card" in order to retain some working-class voters—principally white racists.[4] In the period 1970–1990, the majority of southern whites voted Republican, not because they were economic libertarians, but because of their preference for the Republican position on the race issue. (See Chapter 4 for econometric evidence.)

We speculate that the exit of the Dixiecrats from the Democratic Party pushed redistributive politics to the right in the United States, because it enabled the Republicans to remain a viable party without compromising their position on the economic issue. This is the consequence of the policy-bundle effect.

Of course, the policy-bundle effect need not be linked to the race issue: in contemporary American politics, since 1990, in particular, the issue of religiosity and/or "family values" has perhaps become the most important secondary issue, which allows the Republicans to remain a viable party despite their economic views. And in many European countries, the law-and-order issue is probably the most important noneconomic issue. Indeed, the George W.

Bush administration has emphasized the religious issue a great deal, and appears to be, at least superficially, antiracist (with two African Americans in the heart of its first administration and an African American secretary of state in the second). But in the period that we study here (1976–1992), we maintain that the principal secondary issue in the United States was race, not religion or family values.

In the United States, those in the minority against whom racism is directed are citizens, and hence it is impossible to discriminate against them in a targeted way. Laws that effectively reduce the welfare of black Americans must be laws that apply to all citizens (regarding affirmative action, busing, prison sentences for drug possession, payments from the welfare system, and so on). In continental Europe, however, where immigrants against whom racism is directed are not citizens (for the most part), it is possible to target policies against them, by passing laws that refer specifically to the rights of and benefits accruing to noncitizens. We might therefore expect the political consequence of voter racism to reduce the size of the welfare state in the United States, while in Europe, it might only reduce benefits accruing to immigrants. The United Kingdom would be an intermediate case, where racism is directed against both citizens and immigrants. We will discuss this further in the chapters pertaining to European countries.

We have been referring to the effect on *political equilibrium* of racism or xenophobia among voters. This supposes that we have a model of political competition, with respect to which we can speak of equilibrium. Indeed, our strategy in this study is to exploit heavily the equilibrium apparatus. Our way of estimating the ASE and the PBE will be to calibrate a game-theoretic model of party competition to the country at hand, and then to conduct counterfactual thought experiments in which we calculate how the equilibrium would change, were voters to be less racist or xenophobic. The change in the size of the tax rate or the size of the public sector that we thus compute is the effect of voter racism on the redistributive issue. Indeed, computing the two effects will require running two counterfactual experiments, which we describe in Chapter 2.

Thus the approach adopted in this book is that of calibration and counterfactual experiment. There is an emerging econometric literature measuring the significance of voter racism on redistribution (Alesina, Glaeser, and Sacerdote 2001; Luttmer 2001). Purely econometric exercises, however, do not identify mechanisms; there could be many causes for the observed correlations. Unlike Alesina and colleagues (2001) and Luttmer (2001), we will propose a formal model of political competition between parties. Observations on voting behavior and fiscal policy will be, however, used to estimate the model's parameters and to construct their confidence intervals.

The model of party competition that we employ must postulate (at least) a two-dimensional policy or issue space, because our analysis involves understanding the interaction of the race issue and the distributive issue. The classical Hotelling-Downs model and the associated median-voter theorem are therefore of no use, because, as is well known, equilibrium in that model only exists when the policy space is unidimensional.[5] Moreover, it is necessary that our model be such that, in equilibrium, parties propose *different* policies, or else the policy-bundle effect would have no bite. Therefore modified Downsian models, like that of Coughlin (1992) and Lindbeck and Weibull (1987), which do possess equilibria with multidimensional policy spaces, but in which both parties play the same policy, will not do either.

We use the party-unanimity Nash equilibrium (PUNE) model introduced in Roemer (1999, 2001), which conceptualizes parties as consisting of factions with different interests. We will define the model precisely in the next chapter; here we introduce it in a nonmathematical way. The model is a generalization of the two standard models of unidimensional political competition, those of Downs (1957) and of Wittman (1973). To avoid complexities at this point, we consider the two-party version.

In the Downs model, each party wishes to maximize its vote share, or, in a model with uncertainty, its probability of victory.[6] This is easily formulated as a game. The payoff function of a party is simply the probability that it wins the election, which is a function of the policies played by both parties. A Downsian equilibrium is a Nash equilibrium of this game. Under standard assumptions (single-peakedness of voters' utility functions over policies), a unique equilibrium exists: both parties play the policy that maximizes the utility of the voter whose "ideal policy" is the median among all ideal policies in the polity. Thus in the Downs model, we can think of parties as being unabashedly *opportunist*—they are concerned only with winning office and do not represent constituencies in any way.

In the Wittman model, parties are in a sense of the opposite kind—they are only interested in the welfare of their constituencies. Imagine that each party has, exogenously specified, a constituency whose interests can be summarized with a single utility function defined on the policy space. Indeed, suppose that the constituencies have preferences over lotteries on policies, and that these preferences satisfy the von Neumann–Morgenstern (vNM) axioms. Each party's payoff function is now the expected utility of its constituency. For example, if the Left party's utility function is v^L and the policy space is T, and the probability that Left wins if Left and Right play the policies τ^L and τ^R, respectively, is $\pi(\tau^L, \tau^R)$, then the Left party's payoff function is:

$$\Pi^L(\tau^L, \tau^R) = \pi(\tau^L, \tau^R)v^L(\tau^L) + (1 - \pi(\tau^L, \tau^R))v^L(\tau^R). \qquad (1.1)$$

In words, the payoff to the L party at a policy pair is the probability that it wins multiplied by the utility its constituents receive at its policy plus the probability that the Right party wins multiplied by the utility of its constituents at the Right's policy. The Right party has a similar utility function:

$$\Pi^R(\tau^L, \tau^R) = \pi(\tau^L, \tau^R)v^R(\tau^L) + (1 - \pi(\tau^L, \tau^R))v^R(\tau^R). \qquad (1.2)$$

A Wittman equilibrium is a Nash equilibrium of the game played between the parties equipped with these two payoff functions. Under standard assumptions on the underlying functions, Wittman equilibrium exists if the policy space is unidimensional; in it, parties play differentiated policies. Thus the Wittman concept escapes the tyranny of the median voter and produces a somewhat more satisfactory result that conforms to the reality of differentiated policies.[7]

Unfortunately the Wittman model does not generalize in a satisfactory way to multidimensional policy spaces either: we have no guarantee that, on such spaces, Wittman equilibrium exists.

The PUNE model generalizes both the Downs and the Wittman models in supposing that party entrepreneurs comprise both opportunist and constituency-representing types. To be precise, we will suppose that each party consists of three factions among its organizers or entrepreneurs: Opportunists, who wish only to maximize the party's probability of victory; Reformists, who are the players of the Wittman model, and wish to maximize the *expected utility* of the party's constituency; and Militants, principled characters, who wish to use the party as a vehicle for advertising the constituency's interests—their desire is to play the *ideal* policy of their constituency. We conceive of these three factions as bargaining with each other to arrive at a policy platform: in this bargaining situation, they face the policy announcement of the opposition party. An equilibrium in the game of party competition will be a pair of policies (which, in our application, will each be two-dimensional), each of which is a solution to one party's internal bargaining game, when facing the policy proposal of the other party. Thus the equilibrium is Nash, in the sense that each party responds optimally to what the other party is proposing, *but* that optimal response is itself the solution of an internal party bargaining game, not the maximizer of a (traditional single) payoff function. In fact, three payoff functions (those of the internal factions) are taken into account.

This approach might seem unnecessarily complex: but the payoff is that the model possesses equilibria even when the policy space is multidimensional. Furthermore, the model is tractable: it is possible to compute these equilibria when the data are specified.

Indeed, the data of the (two-party) model are: a set of voter types H, a probability distribution of these voter types in the population, $\mathbf{F}$, a policy space T, a function $v : T \times H \to \mathbb{R}$ which specifies the utility that a type h voter receives from a policy t, and a probability-of-victory function $\pi : T \times T \to \mathbb{R}$: thus, the tuple $(H, \mathbf{F}, T, v, \pi)$. Given these data, the model produces a set of equilibria, each of which consists in:

- a partition of the polity into two party constituencies, L and R;
- a pair of policies, (τ^L, τ^R), each of which is proposed by a party which represents one of the constituencies; and
- a probability $\pi(\tau^L, \tau^R)$ that τ^L wins the election.

Thus an equilibrium consists not only in the policy pair but in an *endogenously determined* partition of the polity into two constituencies.

We have said that the benefit derived from this equilibrium concept is that it produces equilibria on multidimensional policy spaces, in which parties play differentiated policies, and in which (we now add) party constituencies are endogenously determined. The cost we bear for using this concept is that it produces many equilibria, not just one. Indeed, the equilibria form what is called a two-dimensional manifold in the space $T \times T$ (roughly, we can specify two parameters somewhat arbitrarily, which will determine one equilibrium). We can think of this multiplicity of equilibria as due to there being *missing data* that we have not specified: indeed, we will show in Chapter 2 that the missing data can be construed to be the relative powers of the party factions in the internal bargaining game. If we knew those relative powers, we could settle upon one equilibrium in the manifold (there is, however, a danger that *no* equilibrium will exist with a given prespecified pair of relative bargaining powers). In our application, however, we are unable to calibrate the relative powers of the internal factions, and hence we will settle for examining the entire manifold of equilibria. It turns out, fortunately, that this manifold is often quite concentrated in the space $T \times T$, so we do not lose much precision because of multiplicity.

Let us explain our choice of the four countries: the United States, the United Kingdom, France, and Denmark. The United States is an obvious choice: racism has been an important issue for over two hundred years and has played an important role in politics. In the UK, racism has been significant, both re-garding West Indian immigrants and, more recently, immigrants from South Asia. These two countries have the longest histories of politically salient racism in our four. We choose France because of the importance of the Front National movement, initiated by Jean-Marie Le Pen in 1972. In 2002, Le Pen's party came in second in the first ballot of the presidential elections, with almost 17 percent of the vote. Indeed, because of its colonial relationship with North Africa, France has experienced immigrants of color for some time. We select Denmark as the fourth country, because it is the first Nordic social democracy where a right-wing coalition has come to power (in 2001) because of the immigration issue.[8]

Our study concentrates on racism, in the United States and the UK, and anti-immigrant feeling, what we call xenophobia for lack of a better word, in Denmark and France. We do not believe that racism and xenophobia are identical phenomena: racism is often based on *incorrect* views about a racial minority (for example, that they are biologically inferior), while xenophobia may be based on correct views (for example, that Islam oppresses women).

Although racism and xenophobia are not identical, we believe that they have much in common. In present-day Europe, for instance, anti-immigrant sentiment and opposition to asylum seekers combine racist language with a rhetoric of defending (the purity of) the nation-state, which is said to be under threat from corrupting foreign influences.[9]

Indeed, since the 1960s, extreme right-wing parties in Western Europe have tended to refer to themselves as nationalist rather than racist. In the UK, for instance, in contrast to John Tyndall's "old" British National Party, which was closely associated with a British variant of Nazi Aryanism, Nick Griffin's "new" British National Party argues that it is committed to a "new, modernist nationalism" based upon the sophisticated discourse of "differentialist" racism and ethnic ecumenicalism, originally evolved by Nouvelle Droite and taken up enthusiastically by Le Pen's Front National in France. Thus Griffin argues: "The British National Party is not a race supremacist party. It does not claim that any one race is superior to any other, simply that they are different. The party merely wishes to preserve those differences which make up the rich tapestry of human kind" (cited from Griffin 2001).[10]

We focus our discussion mainly on racism against "colored" minorities and their children, because the most disadvantaged and discriminated groups in the four countries are those people with dark skin. This is not to deny that some "white" migrant groups have been subject to a process of racialization in some countries in certain periods: the Irish and Jewish experiences during the nineteenth century, the Cypriot and Jewish experiences in the twentieth century, and the Eastern European experience recently. Most of postwar immigration control was, however, intended to curb "nonwhite" migrants to "keep the social fabric and cohesion of the country undamaged" (Virdee 1999).

Some scholars understand racism as a combination of prejudice and white domination over colored people. Racism is a prejudice, but we do not endorse the view that associates racism with the white possession of power. Among some sections of the white working class, racist beliefs and sympathy for New Right politics appear to be a response to their powerlessness.

Finally, a note about the incidence and evolution of racism in the United States. The "end of racism" in American politics is often asserted from what surveys say about whites' attitudes toward blacks on a few old-fashioned racial issues. It is, however, well documented that there is a large gulf between whites and blacks in the perception of racial inequality and its causes. No matter what national surveys say about whites' attitudes toward blacks, most blacks still see racism as persisting among whites. Sigelman and Welch (1991) document striking facts. As of 1989, when only 4 percent of whites characterized most whites as sharing the Ku Klux Klan's extreme racial views, almost one black in four claimed that more than half of all white Americans accepted the Klan's views. Approximately 50 percent of blacks perceive discrimination in the market for unskilled and skilled labor, while only 10–15 percent of whites perceive it.

The book proceeds as follows. In the next chapter, we present the formal definition of our equilibrium concept, PUNE, and describe the counterfactual experiments by which we compute the antisolidarity and policy-bundle effects. We then present four country sections. For each country, we use election studies and other surveys to estimate the preferences of the polity, and we calibrate the PUNE model to that country. The model specifications are slightly different for each country, because of the way the data come to us. We begin each of these four sections with a historical chapter that examines the political role of racism or xenophobia in the country; we then proceed to a chapter that employs the election-study data to estimate the preferences of the polity over the two issues of distribution and race, fits the PUNE model to the observed political equilibrium in several elections in the country (this involves choosing some free parameters in our model which we cannot estimate), and finally computes the ASE and PBE. A final chapter concludes with a brief summary, some intercountry comparisons, and some caveats. Some statistical details are presented in Appendix A; additional tables (referenced in the text as, for example, Appendix Table B.1) will be found in Appendix B.

2

Political Equilibrium: Theory and Application

2.1 The Data

In Chapter 1, we described the data in the context of the two-party model. We describe our model here in a more general context; thus we slightly modify what we wrote in Chapter 1. The data of the model are the components of the 6-tuple $e = (H, \mathbf{F}, T, v, \pi, n)$, where H is a set of voter types, $\mathbf{F}$ is the probability distribution of voter types in the polity, T is the policy or issue space, $v : T \times H \to \mathbb{R}$ is the profile of utility functions of types over policies, n is the number of parties, and $\pi = (\pi_1, \ldots, \pi_{n-1})$ is a vector of probability functions, where $\pi_j : T^n \to [0, 1]$ gives the probability that party j wins the election, as a function of the vector of all party platforms, for $j = 1, \ldots, n - 1$. (T^n is the n-fold cross-product of the policy space T.) We define the probability that party n wins as $1 - \sum_{j=1}^{n-1} \pi_j$.

Thus the number of parties is exogenous. The constituencies of parties will be endogenous, but we present no theory to determine the number of parties. In our applications, we will model the United States, United Kingdom, and Denmark as having two parties, and France as having three. Although in fact Denmark and France have many parties, we will argue that political competition can be approximated in these countries with two and three parties, respectively. Until section 2.5 below, we will assume that $n = 2$, in order to simplify the discussion.

We conceive of a party as a complex organization, with several aims; each aim is the goal of a set of party entrepreneurs or activists, who together determine the party's platform in the election. We call these sets of activists *factions,* and we characterize the goal of a faction by a payoff function, which describes the "utility" derived by the faction's members as a function of the policies played by *all* competing parties.

As we wrote earlier, the Opportunists in a party wish to maximize the probability of victory. Thus in the two-party model, we can write the payoff function of party 1 as:

$$\Pi_1^{Opp}(\tau^1, \tau^2) = \pi_1(\tau^1, \tau^2). \tag{2.1}$$

We will henceforth delete the subscript on π_1 because there is only one such function in the two-party model.

Suppose now that the polity is partitioned into two sets, H_1 and H_2, such that $H_1 \cup H_2 = H$ and $H_1 \cap H_2 = \varnothing$. Each of these sets will be represented by one of the parties. We can represent the average utility function of the coalition H_1 as:

$$v^1(\tau) = \frac{\displaystyle\int_{h \in H_1} v(\tau, h)d\mathbf{F}(h)}{\mathbf{F}(H_1)}. \tag{2.2}$$

We say that the Reformists in party 1 aim to maximize the average expected utility of their constituents, and so their payoff function is:

$$\Pi_1^{Ref}(\tau^1, \tau^2) = \pi(\tau^1, \tau^2)v^1(\tau^1) + (1 - \pi(\tau^1, \tau^2))v^1(\tau^2), \tag{2.3}$$

as we discussed in Chapter 1.

Finally we introduce the Militants, whose payoff function (in party 1) is:

$$\Pi_1^{Mil}(\tau^1, \tau^2) = v^1(\tau^1); \tag{2.4}$$

in other words, the Militants do not care about winning (as the Reformists do), but only about the party's being faithful to its members' interests. They are best conceived of as a group who wish to use the party as a pulpit to advertise the constituency's interests: perhaps, in a dynamic model, this would play a role in changing preferences of voters, or in developing consciousness among constituents of their "true" interests. We will below offer another interpretation of the Militants (section 2.4.2).

Party 2 possesses the analogous three factions, whose payoff functions are given by:

$$\Pi_2^{Opp}(\tau^1, \tau^2) = 1 - \pi(\tau^1, \tau^2)$$

$$\Pi_2^{Ref}(\tau^1, \tau^2) = \pi(\tau^1, \tau^2)v^2(\tau^1) + (1 - \pi(\tau^1, \tau^2))v^2(\tau^2) \qquad (2.5)$$

$$\Pi_2^{Mil}(\tau^1, \tau^2) = v^2(\tau^2)$$

We now state how we model the outcome of bargaining among the three factions of party 1, when facing a policy τ^2 proposed by party 2. The problem for party 1's factions is to come up with a proposal τ^1. We require only a minimal condition: that the proposal of party 1 be *Pareto efficient* with respect to the goals of its three factions. Thus a policy τ^1 is an admissible outcome of the bargaining process (in party 1) if there is no policy τ^* such that all three factions of party 1 are at least as well off at τ^* as they are at τ^1, and at least one faction is better off. That is to say: there is no τ^* such that:

$$\Pi_1^J(\tau^*, \tau^2) \geq \Pi_1^J(\tau^1, \tau^2), \quad \text{for } J = Opp, Ref, Mil \qquad (2.6)$$

with at least one of the three inequalities strict. This is the only characteristic of the internal bargaining game that we employ—that it exhausts the possibilities of gains from bargaining, in the sense of reaching a point on the Pareto frontier of the payoff functions of the three factions.

We can now state fully the definition of an equilibrium.

Definition A *party-unanimity Nash equilibrium* (PUNE) is:

(a) a partition of $H = H_1 \cup H_2$, $H_1 \cap H_2 = \varnothing$ and
(b) a pair of policies (τ^1, τ^2),
  such that:
  (b-1) there is no $\tau^* \in T$ such that for $J = Opp, Ref, Mil$, $\Pi_1^J(\tau^*, \tau^2) \geq \Pi_1^J(\tau^1, \tau^2)$, with at least one inequality strict;
  (b-2) there is no $\tau^* \in T$ such that for $J = Opp, Ref, Mil$, $\Pi_2^J(\tau^1, \tau^*) \geq \Pi_2^J(\tau^1, \tau^2)$, with at least one inequality strict;
  (b-3) $h \in H_1 \Rightarrow v(\tau^1, h) \geq v(\tau^2, h)$

$$h \in H_2 \Rightarrow v(\tau^2, h) \geq v(\tau^1, h).$$

Only the last condition has not been discussed: it states that the party memberships (constituencies) are *stable*, in the sense that no member of either party is better represented by the other party.

Thus we speak of constituencies and members interchangeably, and party entrepreneurs and activists interchangeably. But activists should not be thought of as voters of particular types: they are professional politicians, who have various goals, which we take as given. Party entrepreneurs are not citizens of certain types; they are of a different breed.

The definition makes precise the claim stated in Chapter 1, that the solution concept is Nash equilibrium—each party plays a "best response" to its opponent—but best responses are the outcome of a bargaining process; they cannot be represented as the consequence of maximizing a single payoff function.

We can now provide some intuition to explain why conceptualizing party competition in this way generates existence of equilibrium even when policy spaces are multidimensional. Consider a pair of policies (τ^1, τ^2); we will test to see if it is a PUNE. To do so, we first consider possible deviations by party 1. A successful deviation from τ^1 must satisfy *three* tests—it must make each of three payoff functions at least as large as τ^1 does (and one strictly larger). It is harder to satisfy this condition than to increase the value of one payoff function. The problem with Downsian equilibrium (and Wittman equilibrium, too) is that only one payoff function has to be increased for a deviation to succeed, and with more than one policy dimension, this can (almost) always be accomplished. But the payoff functions of our three factions are sufficiently different (one might say orthogonal) that it is relatively difficult for a deviation to succeed. Thus there are many policy pairs that will pass the deviation test for both parties. Condition (b-3) places another restriction on equilibrium, but it turns out we nevertheless will have many PUNEs.

2.2 Characterization of PUNE as a System of Equations

To calculate PUNEs, we must be able to characterize them as solutions to a system of equations. We first note that it turns out that the Reformist faction is gratuitous! By this we mean that the set of PUNEs is exactly the set of equilibria that would arise if only the Opportunist and Militant factions existed. Although this is not difficult to prove, we will not do so here, but refer the

interested reader to Roemer (2001, theorem 8.1) for the argument. Therefore, from the mathematical viewpoint, it is parsimonious to eliminate the
Reformist faction. A comment is in order. It is not difficult to find historical
examples of parties with factions that look like the Opportunists, Reformists,
and Militants. We are saying that, as long as the Opportunists and Militants
exist, the existence of Reformists will not alter the *set* of equilibria that are
possible. Nevertheless, Reformists may be important in determining which
equilibrium (in the manifold) is realized. Because we shall have no interest
in such a determination, we do not need to consider further the Reformists.

What does it mean for condition (b-1) of the definition of PUNE to hold
for the two factions $J = Opp, Mil$? Consider the indifference curve of the
Opportunists in party 1 at a PUNE (τ^1, τ^2): this is the set of policies $\{\tau \in T \mid$
$\Pi_1^{Opp}(\tau, \tau^2) = \Pi_1^{Opp}(\tau^1, \tau^2)\}$. Likewise, the indifference curve of the Militants
in party 1 is $\{\tau \in T \mid \Pi_1^{Mil}(\tau, \tau^2) = \Pi_1^{Mil}(\tau^1, \tau^2)\}$. The fact that τ^1 satisfies
condition (b-1) means that these two indifference curves are tangent at the
point (τ^1, τ^2): in other words, there is no direction in the policy space at
(τ^1, τ^2) in which a small movement would increase the value of both payoff
functions (or increase one payoff function and not decrease the other). This
means that the gradients of the two payoff functions with respect to the first
policy must point in opposite directions: see Figure 2.1, in which the policy
space is three-dimensional.

The gradient is the vector of first partial derivatives of the function. Denote
the generic policy by $\tau = (\tau_1, \tau_2)$. (For policy variables, superscripts refer to
parties, subscripts to single issues.) In our applications below, τ_1 is the tax
policy and τ_2 is the racial policy. Thus the gradient of $\Pi_1^{Opp}(\cdot, \tau^2)$ is the vector
$(\frac{\partial \pi}{\partial \tau_1^1}, \frac{\partial \pi}{\partial \tau_2^1})$ evaluated at (τ^1, τ^2); we write this, using conventional notation, as
$\nabla_1 \pi(\tau^1, \tau^2)$. Similarly, the gradient of $\Pi_1^{Mil}(\cdot, \tau^2)$ is just

$$\left(\frac{\partial v^1}{\partial \tau_1^1}(\tau^1), \frac{\partial v^1}{\partial \tau_2^1}(\tau^1) \right) = \nabla v^1(\tau^1).$$

The requirement that these two gradients point in opposite directions is stated:

- There exists a number $x \geq 0$ such that $x \nabla v^1(\tau^1) = -\nabla_1 \pi(\tau^1, \tau^2)$;   (2.7)

in other words, one gradient should be a negative multiple of the other one.

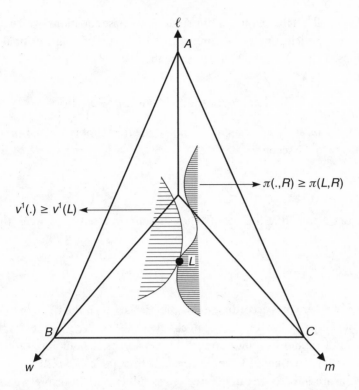

Figure 2.1 A policy space with policies (w, m, ℓ). Illustrated are the probability isoquant for party 1 when the other party is playing a policy R, and the indifference curve of the Militants of party 1. At the policy L, the indifference curves are tangent: there is no feasible policy (in the simplex) which can increase the welfare of both Opportunists and Militants. If policy R satisfies the analogous tangency condition, given policy L, than (L, R) constitute a PUNE.

Now let us consider the same condition for party 2. For party 2's Opportunists, we have: $\nabla_2 \Pi_2^{Opp}(\tau^1, \tau^2) = -\nabla_2 \pi(\tau^1, \tau^2)$. Therefore the condition for tangency of the indifference curves of the Opportunists and Militants in party 2 is:

- There exists a number $y \geq 0$ such that $y \nabla v^2(\tau^2) = \nabla_2 \pi(\tau^1, \tau^2)$.   (2.8)

We now note that equations (2.7) and (2.8) comprise four equations in six unknowns—the four policy parameters and the two "Lagrangian multipliers,"

x and y. It follows that if there is one solution to these equations, we can expect (from the implicit function theorem) that there is a two-dimensional set of solutions. This will indeed turn out to be the case.

2.3   The Probability-of-Victory Function

Let (τ^1, τ^2) be any pair of policies, and define the set of types that prefer the first policy to the second:

$$\Omega(\tau^1, \tau^2) = \{h \in H \mid v(\tau^1, h) > v(\tau^2, h)\}.$$

We can also define the set of types that are indifferent between the two policies:

$$I(\tau^1, \tau^2) = \{h \in H \mid v(\tau^1, h) = v(\tau^2, h)\}.$$

If every voter votes according to his preferences, then the fraction of voters who vote for party 1 at this party pair should be $\mathbf{F}(\Omega(\tau^1, \tau^2)) + \frac{1}{2}\mathbf{F}(I(\tau^1, \tau^2))$. (We assume random voting among indifferent types.) In our applications, the set of voters who are indifferent between distinct policies will always be a set of $\mathbf{F}$-measure zero, so we can ignore the second term in this expression.

We now introduce uncertainty about voter behavior in an extremely simple way. We say that there is some noise in the model's representation of the polity, and so the *true* vote for party 1 will be $\mathbf{F}(\Omega(\tau^1, \tau^2)) + X$ where X is a random variable—say, X is distributed uniformly on an interval $[-\beta, \beta]$ for some positive number β. The idea is that not all voters vote according to their preferences; or perhaps there are other tertiary issues that we have failed to model; or perhaps there will be a scandal exposed in one campaign, or a faux pas committed by one candidate. Note that the kinds of uncertainty modeled by the random variable X may well have a correlated effect across voters: thus X models not individual stochastic behavior of voters, which will cancel out in a large polity, but deviations of reality from the model that are caused by correlated deviations of voters. So uncertainty about vote share will exist even with a large polity.

Furthermore, note that the uncertainty in question may not be small, for it is the uncertainty that parties face at the time that they publish their manifestos, or announce their platforms, and this may be several months before the election takes place.

We can now compute the probability of victory in the two-party model. The probability that party 1 wins the election at the pair (τ^1, τ^2) is

$$\Pr(\mathbf{F}(\Omega(\tau^1, \tau^2) + X > 0.5)$$

$$= \Pr(X > 0.5 - \mathbf{F}(\Omega(\tau^1, \tau^2)))$$

$$= \begin{cases} 0, & \text{if } 0.5 - \mathbf{F}(\Omega(\tau^1, \tau^2)) \geq \beta \qquad (2.9) \\ \dfrac{\beta - 0.5 + \mathbf{F}(\Omega(\tau^1, \tau^2))}{2\beta}, & \text{if } -\beta < 0.5 - \mathbf{F}(\Omega(\tau^1, \tau^2)) < \beta \\ 1, & \text{if } 0.5 - \mathbf{F}(\Omega(\tau^1, \tau^2)) \leq -\beta \end{cases}$$

Thus we define

$$\pi(\tau^1, \tau^2) = \frac{\beta - 0.5 + \mathbf{F}(\Omega(\tau^1, \tau^2))}{2\beta} \qquad (2.10)$$

in the standard case when both parties win with positive probability. (The formula expressed in (2.9) is easily computed by drawing a picture of the interval $[-\beta, \beta]$, and computing the probability that a uniformly distributed random variable X on this support is greater than some constant k. Here $k = 0.5 - \mathbf{F}(\Omega(\tau^1, \tau^2))$.)

Given our definition of the probability of victory, we now note that maximizing that probability is equivalent to maximizing the expected vote share (which, for party 1, is $\mathbf{F}(\Omega(\tau, \tau^2))$).[1] Therefore we may further simplify the PUNE statement to:

- There exists a partition $H_1 \cup H_2 = H$, associated average utility functions v^1 and v^2, and policies τ^1 and τ^2 such that:

$$x \nabla v^1(\tau^1) = -\nabla_1 \mathbf{F}(\Omega(\tau^1, \tau^2))$$

$$y \nabla v^2(\tau^2) = \nabla_2 \mathbf{F}(\Omega(\tau^1, \tau^2)). \qquad (2.11)$$

Thus the parameter β has fallen away, and so we need not worry about what the degree of uncertainty is. (This tells us that the *set* of PUNEs is invariant with respect to the degree of uncertainty. It again may be the case that which PUNE in the equilibrium manifold is realized will depend upon β; more on this below.)

2.4 Factional Bargaining Powers

2.4.1 Nash's Bargaining Solution

We can construct a specific bargaining game between the Opportunist and Militant factions at a PUNE, which allows us to associate particular bargaining powers of factions at that PUNE. We use John Nash's (1950) theory of bargaining.

Nash's theory proposes the following set-up. Let two bargainers be denoted O and M (to remind us of our two factions), and let them possess von Neumann–Morgenstern utility functions P^O and P^M defined on a set of possible bargaining outcomes, T. Suppose that if a bargain fails to be made, an outcome τ^* will obtain, in which case the bargainers receive utilities $P^O(\tau^*)$ and $P^M(\tau^*)$. Suppose further that the relative powers of these bargainers are α and $1 - \alpha$, for O and M, respectively. Then, Nash argues, the bargaining outcome will maximize the product

$$(P^O(\tau) - P^O(\tau^*))^\alpha (P^M(\tau) - P^M(\tau^*))^{1-\alpha}. \qquad (2.12)$$

The arguments inside the parentheses are the utility gains of each bargainer from the "threat point," or from their impasse utilities.

We apply this bargaining solution to our problem. Suppose that the default outcome, should the O and M factions in party 1 fail to agree on a proposal, is that party 2 wins the election for sure. Then party 1 receives zero vote share, and its constituents must live under the policy τ^2. Let us take the vNM utility function of the O faction to be its expected vote share—that is, $\mathbf{F}(\Omega(\tau, \tau^2))$—and the vNM utility function of the M faction to be $v^1(\tau)$. We will also say that, in the event that a bargain fails to materialize, the "utility" of the M faction is $v^1(\tau^2)$, because the only policy that is put forth in the public arena is τ^2. Then the solution to the internal bargaining game between the O and M factions in party 1 is

$$\arg\max_{\tau \in T} (\mathbf{F}(\Omega(\tau, \tau^2)) - 0)^{\alpha_1}(v^1(\tau) - v^1(\tau^2))^{1-\alpha_1}, \qquad (2.13)$$

where α_1 is the bargaining power of faction O in party 1.

To find this solution, we first note that it is equivalent to maximize the logarithm of the expression in (2.13):

$$\alpha_1 \log \mathbf{F}(\Omega(\tau, \tau^2)) + (1 - \alpha_1) \log(v^1(\tau) - v^1(\tau^2)). \qquad (2.14)$$

The first-order necessary conditions for the solution to this problem are given by setting the gradient of the expression with respect to τ equal to the zero vector, that is:

$$\alpha_1 \frac{\nabla_1 \mathbf{F}(\Omega(\tau, \tau^2))}{\mathbf{F}(\Omega(\tau, \tau^2))} + (1 - \alpha_1) \frac{\nabla v^1(\tau)}{(v^1(\tau) - v^1(\tau^2))} = (0, 0). \tag{2.15}$$

If τ^1 is the solution of this bargaining game—because (τ^1, τ^2) is the PUNE at hand—then we know that $x\nabla v^1(\tau^1) = -\nabla_1 \mathbf{F}(\Omega(\tau^1, \tau^2))$ (from equation (2.11)); we can substitute this into equation (2.15) and solve for α_1:

$$\alpha_1 = \frac{\mathbf{F}(\Omega(\tau^1, \tau^2))}{\mathbf{F}(\Omega(\tau^1, \tau^2)) + x(v^1(\tau^1) - v^1(\tau^2))}. \tag{2.16}$$

Note that α_1 is a positive number between zero and one, as it should be. (We know that $v^1(\tau^1) - v^1(\tau^2) \geq 0$ by condition (b-3) of the definition of PUNE.) Note that if the Opportunists are indeed maximizing their vote share, and $\nabla_1 F(\Omega(\tau^1, \tau^2)) = (0, 0)$, then from equation (2.11) we must have $x = 0$, and from (2.16) $\alpha_1 = 1$.

In like manner, we can solve for the relative bargaining power, call it α_2, of the Opportunists in party 2:

$$\alpha_2 = \frac{1 - \mathbf{F}(\Omega(\tau^1, \tau^2))}{1 - \mathbf{F}(\Omega(\tau^1, \tau^2)) + y(v^2(\tau^2) - v^2(\tau^1))}. \tag{2.17}$$

We now make a point that will play an important role in our study: at a PUNE, we know, as well as the policies, the Lagrangian multipliers x and y, and so we can compute the relative bargaining powers α_1 and α_2. Thus each PUNE will be associated with a pair of relative bargaining powers, each expressing the relative bargaining power of the Opportunists and the Militants in one party.

In other words, we can parameterize the elements in the PUNE manifold by the relative bargaining powers (α_1, α_2) of the Opportunists in the two parties. This is why we wrote, earlier on, that we could view the multiplicity of equilibria as due to missing data about the relative bargaining powers of the factions. If we knew from observed data the ordered pair (α_1, α_2), then we could append equations (2.16) and (2.17) to the four PUNE equations, giving us six equations in six unknowns. We would then expect to find a unique PUNE. The problem, however, is that PUNEs generally do not exist for *all* pairs (α_1, α_2) in the square $[0, 1] \times [0, 1]$. Thus a particular political economy may only support certain possible pairs of relative bargaining powers. We will use this calculation of bargaining powers in the following chapters.

We decided, above, to endow the Opportunists in party 1 with a vNM utility function $F(\Omega(\cdot, \tau^2))$, which they employ in the bargaining game. This is not the same thing as endowing them with the vNM utility function $\pi(\cdot, \tau^2)$, because these two functions are not positive affine transformations of each other. They *are* related by positive affine transformation in the region where the probability is *strictly* between zero and one, but they are not so related over the entire policy domain (see expression (2.9)). This may seem to be a picayune point; however, it turns out not to be, because the threat point of the game involves a situation in which the party's probability of victory is zero. If we were to use the function $\pi(\cdot, \tau^2)$ as the Opportunists' vNM utility, then equation (2.16) would be replaced by:

$$\alpha_1 = \frac{\pi(\tau^1, \tau^2)}{\pi(\tau^1, \tau^2) + x(v^1(\tau^1) - v^1(\tau^2))}, \tag{2.18}$$

with an analogous change in (2.17).

In our applications, we will use (2.16) to compute the bargaining powers at PUNEs. This allows us to avoid having to propose a value for the uncertainty parameter β, which enters into (2.18), but not into (2.16).

2.4.2   An Alternative Interpretation of the Militants

It is often the case that a formal model has several interpretations, and this is the case with PUNE. Here, we offer a second interpretation of the Militant faction, which may be more appealing in some cases.

Let us now rechristen the Militants as the Guardians: their role is to guard the interests of the constituents of the party. Thus the Opportunists are ceaselessly pushing for policy compromise, in order to win more votes, and the Guardians insist upon not proposing policies that are unacceptable for the constituency. We can then model what happens in party 1 as the solution to the following optimization program:

$$\max_{\tau \in T} F(\Omega(\tau, \tau^2))$$

$$\text{s.t.} \quad v^1(\tau) \geq k^1 \tag{2.19}$$

That is, the Opportunists choose the policy that maximizes expected vote share subject to the requirement, imposed by the Guardians, that average utility of the constituents not fall below some value k^1.

In like manner, the policy in party 2 is determined by

$$\max_{\tau \in T}(1 - \mathbf{F}(\Omega(\tau^1, \tau)))$$

$$\text{s.t.} \quad v^2(\tau) \geq k^2 \tag{2.20}$$

Now we know that the solution to (2.19) is given by a pair $(\tau^1, x) \in T \times \mathbb{R}_+$ such that

$$\nabla_1 \mathbf{F}(\Omega(\tau^1, \tau^2) + x\nabla v^1(\tau^1) = 0, \tag{2.21}$$

$$v^1(\tau^1) = k^1, \tag{2.22}$$

by invoking the Lagrange method of constrained optimization. In like manner, the solution to (2.20) is given by a pair $(\tau^2, y) \in T \times \mathbb{R}_+$ such that:

$$-\nabla_2 \mathbf{F}(\Omega(\tau^1, \tau^2) + y\nabla v^2(\tau^2) = 0, \tag{2.23}$$

$$v^2(\tau^2) = k^2. \tag{2.24}$$

But notice that equations (2.21) and (2.23) are identical to our PUNE equations (2.11). Therefore every PUNE is also an Opportunist-Guardian equilibrium, and conversely.

Note that equations (2.21)–(2.24) comprise six equations in six unknowns. There may be no solution to (2.21) and (2.23) that also satisfies (2.22) and (2.24). But there will be solutions for some two-dimensional manifold of ordered pairs (k^1, k^2).

Of course, in the Opportunist-Guardian interpretation, the numbers k^1 and k^2 are playing the role that the bargaining powers α_1 and α_2 play in PUNE— the larger is k^1, the tougher are the Guardians in party 1, which corresponds to a low value of α. We could thus also parameterize the manifold of PUNEs by the ordered pairs (k^1, k^2).

The Opportunist-Guardian account places into quite sharp relief the basic insight that political parties must deal with two conflicting goals: attracting votes and representing their constituencies. In our model, we have modeled these goals as the unitary interests of different factions. One must realize that this is simply a device. The critical point about our construction is that parties do not possess a *complete order* of pairs of policies (τ^1, τ^2) in $T \times T$ that might appear in political competition. Perhaps the pair (τ^1, τ^2) dominates the pair $(\hat{\tau}^1, \tau^2)$ for party 1 as far as expected vote share is concerned, but $(\hat{\tau}^1, \tau^2)$ dominates (τ^1, τ^2) as far as the welfare of the party's constituency at the party's policy is concerned. If the party had a complete order over all pairs of policies, it could choose one of these over the other; but in our model, either pair could be a stable point, because the Opportunists would veto moving from $(\hat{\tau}^1, \tau^2)$ to (τ^1, τ^2) and the Militants would veto moving from (τ^1, τ^2) to $(\hat{\tau}^1, \tau^2)$.

2.4.3   Reenter the Reformists

Let us now suppose, as in the beginning, that Reformists exist as well, and that bargaining occurs among the three factions. We consider the bargaining in party 1. Note that the Reformists' payoff function can be written as:

$$\Pi_1^{Ref}(\tau, \tau^2) = \pi(\tau, \tau^2)(v^1(\tau) - v^1(\tau^2)) + v^1(\tau^2).$$

If the factions fail to propose a policy, then the default utility for the Reformists is what their constituents receive at party 2's policy, which is $v^1(\tau^2)$. Thus the Reformists' utility gain from the impasse point, gotten by subtracting this value from the payoff, is $\pi(\tau, \tau^2)(v^1(\tau) - v^1(\tau^2))$. Therefore we may write the bargaining game among the *three* factions in party 1 as the solution of some problem of the form:[2]

$$\pi(\tau, \tau^2)^\alpha (\pi(\tau, \tau^2)(v^1(\tau) - v^1(\tau^2)))^{1-\alpha-\delta}(v^1(\tau) - v^1(\tau^2))^\delta, \tag{2.25}$$

where the powers of the O, M, and R factions are, respectively, α, δ, and $1 - \alpha - \delta$. But this can be written as

$$\max_{\tau \in T} \pi(\tau, \tau^2)^{1-\delta}(v^1(\tau) - v^1(\tau^2))^{1-\alpha}. \tag{2.26}$$

Using expression (2.26), we could re-do the calculation of section 2.4.1 and calculate the value of $(1 - \alpha)/(1 - \delta)$ at a PUNE, as in equation (2.16). We cannot, however, determine α and δ without further information.

This demonstrates how a particular PUNE can be viewed as *either* the result of a bargaining game with all three factions, *or* as a result of the game with only the two factions O and M. Expression (2.26) also clarifies our statement, made in Chapter 1, that the existence of Reformists, though not altering the set of PUNEs, can alter which PUNE is chosen, because that choice is associated with what the relative bargaining powers of the factions are and, in particular, how many factions there are.

We finally note, for the sake of completeness, how Wittman equilibrium and Downs equilibrium appear as special cases of PUNE. A Downs equilibrium is one where the Opportunists have all the power in each party: that is, $\alpha = 1$, $\delta = 0$ in both parties. In this case, the Opportunists' payoff function simply becomes the payoff function of the party. A Wittman equilibrium is where the Opportunists and Militants have the *same degree* of power in both parties, that is, $\alpha = \delta$ in both parties. In this case, notice that maximizing the expression (2.26) is equivalent to maximizing $\pi(\tau, \tau^2)(v^1(\tau) - v^1(\tau^2))$, which is equivalent to maximizing $\Pi_1^{Ref}(\tau, \tau^2)$. If both parties do this at a PUNE, the result is a Wittman equilibrium, that is, a Nash equilibrium where each player is maximizing the Reformists' payoff function.

However, just as Downsian equilibrium generally fails to exist when the policy space has dimension greater than one, so there is no guarantee that a Wittman equilibrium exists in general: there may be no PUNE where the Militants and Opportunists have equal bargaining powers.

We will see, however, that in our application of PUNE to our study of the politics of race and distribution, a two-dimensional manifold of PUNEs always exists.

2.5   The Three-Party Model

We model France as having three parties: a Left, a Right, and an Extreme Right. To do this, we require a definition of political equilibrium with three parties.

The serious complication that arises in political competition with more than two parties is that, if no party wins a majority, then, in a parliamentary system, a coalition government must form. Thus the political game should be modeled as having two stages: first, a general election, and second, a coalition-formation game and a choice of policy. There is, in the literature, much recent work on this topic, but no canonical model has yet emerged. As our project is sufficiently complicated without worrying about coalition formation, we choose simply to ignore it.

When coalition formation exists, the rational voter, in the general election, should not necessarily vote for the party she favors, for she must take into account how she wishes to influence the coalition-formation subgame with her vote. Thus voters should be strategic and not sincere. We ignore this, and assume that all voters, in the three-party model, are sincere. Clearly we will have to remember this assumption when we interpret our empirical results.

There is no conceptual complication in writing down the definition of PUNE with three parties. A PUNE consists of a partition of the type space into three elements, each of which is represented by a party. Each party has Opportunist, Militant, and Reformist factions, and each party proposes a policy that is Pareto efficient for its three factions, given the policies of the other two parties.

Because we will use the three-party model only once in our study, in the case of France, we will present the formal statement of it in section 10.2.

2.6   First Application: The Logarithmic Utility Function

We now discuss our application of the model in more detail. We will describe two somewhat specific models, one using a logarithmic utility function and the other a Euclidean utility function. Each approach has its own strengths and weaknesses. In both approaches, the policy space will consist of ordered pairs (t, r) where t is now a number standing for a *tax rate* or a *size of the public sector*, and r is the party's position on the *race* or *immigration* issue.

We prefer the log utility function approach. But except for the United States and the UK, the data are not available to use this approach. Hence we use the Euclidean function approach as well. This section describes the log utility function approach, and the next section explains the Euclidean utility function approach.

2.6.1   Voter Types and Preferences

In the log utility function approach, the voter *type* is characterized by a pair $h = (\hat{w}, \rho) \in H$ where $\hat{w}$ is the voter's family head's real wage rate, called the *representative wage* of the voter family, and ρ is the voter's racial/immigration position. The representative wage is an individual wage except for wives. It coincides with his/her own wage for singles and married males but corresponds to the husband's wage for a married female. The racial/immigration position of voter h is, in contrast, completely individualistic; a wife's position is allowed to differ from her husband's.

The distribution of voter types is given by a joint density function $g(\rho \mid \hat{w})f(\hat{w})$. We find that the racial view is uncorrelated with the wage rate in the United States and the UK. (See Chapters 4 and 6 below.) Thus we will assume that $g(\rho \mid \hat{w}) = g(\hat{w})$. The distribution function for $f(.)$ is $F(.)$ and the distribution function for $g(.)$ is $G(.)$. (Do not confuse marginal distributions $F(.)$ and $G(.)$ with the (joint) probability distribution $\mathbf{F}(.)$ that we used in sections 2.1–2.5.)

The justification for our model specification—that is, that a voter's economic position is characterized by his/her representative wage while his/her racial position is individualistic—is threefold:

First, many tax-benefit policies are applied at the family level. Consumption and labor participation behavior of an individual can be properly understood only within the family framework.

Second, labor supply behavior may be different for males and females, in particular for married couples.

Third, voting behavior on the tax rate will typically depend on family income, not individual income, but voting behavior on the racial issue can be quite different among the members of the same family (although there may be a strong correlation among family members). For instance, although her actual earned income is zero, a nonworking housewife living with a rich husband may vote like a rich individual on tax rates. She may, however, be more liberal than her husband on the racial issue. Our utility function will permit this possibility.

A voter has direct preferences over vectors (x_h, L_h^f, E, r), where x_h is the consumption of goods and services of voter h *at the family level*, L_h^f is the vector of working hours of the voter's family members (hence $L_h^f = L_h$ if h is single, and $L_h^f = (L_{M(h)}, L_{F(h)})$ if he/she is married, where $M(h)$ $(F(h))$ stands for the male (female) member of h's family), E is a measure of equality in the distribution of family consumption (called solidarity), and r is the position of the elected government on racial issues. More specifically, the direct utility function of an individual h is of the form:

$$U(x_h, L_h^f, E, r; \hat{w}, \rho) = \phi(x_h, L_h^f) - \frac{\gamma}{2}(r - \rho)^2 + (\delta_0 - \delta_2\rho)E, \qquad (2.27)$$

where

$$\phi(x_h, L_h^f) = \begin{cases} \text{Log}(x_h) + \beta_M \, \text{Log}(\lambda_M - L_{M(h)}) + \beta_F \, \text{Log}(\lambda_F - L_{F(h)}) \\ \qquad\qquad\qquad\qquad\qquad\qquad\qquad\qquad \text{if } h \text{ is married} \\ \text{Log}(x_h) + \beta_S \, \text{Log}(\lambda_S - L_h) \qquad\qquad\qquad \text{if } h \text{ is single} \end{cases}$$

and

$$E = \text{Log} \left(\frac{x_{0.25}}{x_{0.75}} \right)$$

is the log ratio of the consumption of the family at the 25th percentile of the income distribution to that at the 75th percentile.

Thus the utility function consists of three parts: the subutility function $\phi(.)$ defined over consumption and labor participation of family members, the preferences over the race/immigration issue, and preferences for equality.

It is assumed that the β's and λ's, which affect the shape of labor supply functions, differ across sexes and marital statuses but do not differ among individuals in each subgroup. The parameter γ measures the *relative salience* of the race issue. The coefficient of the equality term E, in contrast, measures the extent to which voters value equality in the distribution of consumption. In this approach, the antisolidarity effect of racism is embodied in the parameter δ_2 (the more positive the coefficient δ_2, the stronger the antisolidarity effect); note that we have modeled a voter's desire for equality as declining in his degree of racism (ρ), assuming that $\delta_2 > 0$. The policy-bundle effect, however, will depend on the parameter γ.

Each political party proposes an affine fiscal policy (t, b), applied to family income, where the after-tax income of a family with gross income y will be $(1 - t)y + b$, and a racial/immigration policy, r. The policy vector is applied to all individuals, once it is determined through political competition.

Empirical estimation of the affine fiscal policy is a tricky issue. For the United States, we compute only federal income taxes while ignoring sales and state taxes; in the UK, however, indirect taxes, which usually make up more than 30 percent of government revenue, cannot be ignored. We take the indirect taxes into account by asking: what would be the effective affine tax policy were its indirect taxes transformed into equivalent income taxes? We will explain the procedure used in the UK. (The U.S. procedure is a special case of this.)

Suppose W_h is the pretax family income of individual h, which consists of an earned income (Y_h) and an asset income (O_h). Suppose also that the total amount of government transfers, b, can be divided into "cash transfers," $b_1 = \alpha b$, and "noncash transfers" (that is, benefits in kind), $b_2 = (1 - \alpha)b$, where $\alpha \in [0, 1]$ is the proportion of cash transfers in total transfers. Then the disposable family income of individual h is $DI_h = (1 - t_W)W_h + b_1$, and the post-fisc family income x_h (which we call "consumption") is obtained by subtracting indirect taxes paid (IT_h) from and adding noncash transfers to the disposable income; thus $x_h = (1 - t_W)W_h + b_1 - IT_h + b_2$.

If we approximate indirect taxes by $IT_h = d \times DI_h$, then the post-fisc income is

$$x_h = (1 - t_W)(1 - d)W_h + (1 - d)b_1 + b_2$$

$$= (1 - t_W - d + t_W d)W_h + (1 - d\alpha)b. \tag{2.28}$$

Thus the effective income tax rate is $t_W + d - t_W d$ and the effective amount of transfer payments is $b' = (1 - d\alpha)b$. (Alternatively speaking, each household pays taxes of $(t_W + d - t_W d)W_h + d\alpha b$ and receives transfer payments of b. The U.S. case is equivalent to setting $d = 0$.) It would be desirable to compute the income tax rate and the indirect tax rate separately at PUNEs; to reduce the dimensionality of a policy space, we chose to compute only the effective tax rate. Because $t_W d$ is usually small, we will approximate the effective tax rate by $t = t_W + d$.

The optimality conditions for labor supply of married couples are

$$\frac{(1 - t)w_s}{x} = \frac{\beta_s}{\lambda_s - L_s}, \tag{2.29}$$

where $s = M, F$, and $x = (1 - t)(w_M L_M + w_F L_F + O) + b'$. (To avoid cluttering the notation, we drop h here. Notational remark: We use the capital letter S to denote "singles," and the small letter s as an index for "sexes.") Rearranging terms for both sexes, we have the following two equations:

$$L_M = \frac{\lambda_M}{1 + \beta_M} - \frac{\beta_M}{1 + \beta_M}\left(\frac{b'}{1 - t} + w_F L_F + O\right)\frac{1}{w_M} \quad \text{for males,} \tag{2.30}$$

and

$$L_F = \frac{\lambda_F}{1 + \beta_F} - \frac{\beta_F}{1 + \beta_F}\left(\frac{b'}{1 - t} + w_M L_M + O\right)\frac{1}{w_F} \quad \text{for females.} \tag{2.31}$$

Note that for an individual of either sex, the labor supply function is negatively correlated with (effective) taxes, (effective) transfers, and the labor income of his/her spouse, and positively correlated with his/her own wage.

To maintain the two-dimensional type space, we assume that female wage rates are proportional to male wage rates: $w_F = k_1 w_M$ for married couples. Empirically, the female wage rate is represented quite accurately as a proportion of the male wage rate. For a nonworking housewife, w_F is her imputed wage rate, which is positive if her husband is working.[3]

Solving equations (2.30) and (2.31) simultaneously and using the facts that $w_F = k_1 w_M$ and $\hat{w} = w_M$ for married couples, we compute the optimal labor supply for both sexes:

$$\hat{L}_M(t, b', \hat{w}) = \frac{\lambda_M(1 + \beta_F) - k_1 \lambda_F \beta_M}{1 + \beta_M + \beta_F}$$

$$- \frac{\beta_M}{1 + \beta_M + \beta_F} \left(\frac{b'}{(1 - t)} + O \right) \frac{1}{\hat{w}}, \tag{2.32}$$

and

$$\hat{L}_F(t, b', \hat{w}) = \frac{\lambda_F(1 + \beta_M) - \frac{1}{k_1} \beta_F \lambda_M}{1 + \beta_M + \beta_F}$$

$$- \frac{\beta_F}{1 + \beta_M + \beta_F} \left(\frac{b'}{(1 - t)} + O \right) \frac{1}{k_1 \hat{w}}. \tag{2.33}$$

We derived the labor supply functions for married couples. For singles, we do not have to consider the simultaneous decision problem. Hence for singles

$$\hat{L}_S(t, b', \hat{w}) = \frac{\lambda_S}{1 + \beta_S} - \frac{\beta_S}{1 + \beta_S} \left(\frac{b'}{1 - t} + O \right) \frac{1}{\hat{w}}, \tag{2.34}$$

where $\hat{w}$ is his/her own wage.

Using (2.32)–(2.34), we obtain household labor income of an individual

$$Y = \begin{cases} w_M \hat{L}_M(t, b', \hat{w}) + k_1 w_M \hat{L}_F(t, b', \hat{w}) & \text{for a married} \\ w_S \hat{L}_S(t, b', \hat{w}) & \text{for a single} \end{cases} \tag{2.35}$$

$$= A^* \hat{w} - B^* \left(\frac{b'}{1 - t} + O \right),$$

where

$$A^* = \begin{cases} \dfrac{\lambda_M + k_1 \lambda_F}{1 + \beta_M + \beta_F} & \text{for a married} \\[2mm] \dfrac{\lambda_S}{1 + \beta_S} & \text{for a single} \end{cases}$$

and

$$B^* = \begin{cases} \dfrac{\beta_M + \beta_F}{1 + \beta_M + \beta_F} & \text{for a married} \\[2mm] \dfrac{\beta_S}{1 + \beta_S} & \text{for a single} \end{cases}$$

Hence pretax family income, as the sum of labor income and other nonlabor income, is given by

$$W = A^*\hat{w} - B^* \left(\frac{b'}{1-t} + O \right) + O$$

$$= A^*\hat{w} - B^* \frac{b'}{1-t} + (1 - B^*)O. \tag{2.36}$$

"Other nonwage income" is usually generated from savings, the source of which is past labor income or past other income (that is, the past pre-fisc income). We assume that "other income" is proportional to the current pre-fisc income: $O = k_3 W$. Past pre-fisc income is highly correlated with current pre-fisc earned income. Then pre-fisc family income is

$$W = \frac{1}{1 - k_3(1 - B^*)} \left(A^*\hat{w} - B^* \frac{b'}{1-t} \right). \tag{2.37}$$

Equation (2.37) simply states that the pre-fisc income W is proportional to labor income, where the proportion coefficient is greater than 1, due to the existence of other nonwage income.[4]

Therefore family consumption is given by

$$x(t, b', \hat{w}) = (1 - t)W + b'$$

$$= \frac{(1 - t)A^*\hat{w} + (1 - k_3)(1 - B^*)b'}{1 - k_3(1 - B^*)}. \tag{2.38}$$

Dropping constant terms we thus have:

$$\phi(x(t, b', \hat{w}), L^f(t, b', \hat{w})) \tag{2.39}$$

$$= \begin{cases} \text{Log}((1-t)A^*\hat{w} + (1-k_3)(1-B^*)b')^{1+\beta_M+\beta_F} \\ \quad - \text{Log}((1-t)\hat{w})^{\beta_M+\beta_F} & \text{for a married} \\ \text{Log}((1-t)A^*\hat{w} + (1-k_3)(1-B^*)b')^{1+\beta_S} \\ \quad - \text{Log}((1-t)\hat{w})^{\beta_S} & \text{for a single} \end{cases}$$

To reduce our computation time we will estimate β's and λ's for married couples only and then simply impute $\beta_S = \beta_M + \beta_F$ and $\lambda_S = \lambda_M + k_1\lambda_F$ for singles.[5] (In other words, it is assumed that the indirect subutility functions are identical for both married couples and singles.)

It remains to derive the government budget equation. In this approach, it is assumed that government revenues are used to finance lump-sum redistribution, b, and to finance publicly provided goods, C, where the per capita spending on publicly provided goods is given and exogenous.

Note from equation (2.37) that taxable income W is positive only for individuals with $\hat{w} > \frac{B^*}{A^*}\frac{b'}{1-t}$. This is because labor income is zero for individuals with low wages, given a positive tax rate and government transfers. Hence the government's budget constraint is

$$b' + C = t \int_{\frac{B^*b'}{A^*(1-t)}}^{\infty} \left(\frac{1}{1-k_3(1-B^*)} \left(A^*\hat{w} - B^*\frac{b'}{1-t} \right) \right) dF(\hat{w}). \tag{2.40}$$

The amount of the effective transfer, b', is determined by solving the integral equation (2.40). The budget constraint will enable us to solve for b' as a function of t, and we therefore write $b' = b'(t)$. (This defines the Laffer curve in our model.) Consequently, we now write policies as ordered pairs $(t, r) \in \mathbb{R}^2$. The policy space is two-dimensional.

The indirect utility function, after substituting $b'(t)$, is given by

$$v(t, r; \hat{w}, \rho) = \tilde{\phi}(t; \hat{w}) - \frac{\gamma}{2}(r - \rho)^2 + (\delta_0 - \delta_2\rho)\tilde{E}(t), \tag{2.41}$$

where

$$\tilde{\phi}(t; \hat{w}) = \phi(x(t, b'(t), \hat{w}), L^f(t, b'(t), \hat{w}))$$

and

$$\tilde{E}(t) = \text{Log} \left(\frac{x(t, b'(t), \hat{w}_{0.25})}{x(t, b'(t), \hat{w}_{0.75})} \right).$$

The function v, so defined, is the function $v : T \times H \rightarrow \mathbb{R}$ of the formal definition in sections 2.1–2.5.

The ideal tax policy of a voter is derived by maximizing $v(t, r; \hat{w}, \rho)$ with respect to t. We denote the ideal tax policy by $\theta(\hat{w}, \rho)$. Note that the ideal tax policy depends upon not only the voter's economic position ($\hat{w}$) but also her racial view (ρ), because of the presence of the antisolidarity effect. Because the utility function is single-peaked, a voter's utility decreases as the actual tax policy moves away from her ideal policy.

Let $\tau = (t, r)$ be a policy vector. The set of types that prefer a policy $\tau^L = (t^L, r^L)$ to a policy $\tau^R = (t^R, r^R)$ is then

$$\Omega(\tau^L, \tau^R) = \{(\hat{w}, \rho) : v(t^L, r^L; \hat{w}, \rho) > v(t^R, r^R; \hat{w}, \rho)\}. \qquad (2.42)$$

The fraction voting for party L is thus defined by

$$\varphi(\tau^L, \tau^R) = \iint\limits_{\Omega(\tau^L, \tau^R)} dG(\rho)dF(w). \qquad (2.43)$$

2.6.2 The Policy-Bundle Effect and the Antisolidarity Effect

The two counterfactual experiments are performed in the following way. First, we simulate an election in which taxation is the only policy. Thus we assume that the government's racial/immigration policy is exogenously fixed at some $r = \bar{r}$. (This is equivalent to assuming that $\gamma = 0$.) In this experiment, the phenomenon of poor, racially conservative voters voting Conservative because the Conservatives put forth racially conservative positions— that is, the policy-bundle effect—*will not exist*, because neither party offers a position on race/immigration.[6] However, voters will still be equipped with their antisolidaristic preferences, which are in part a consequence of racism/xenophobia, and those continue to influence the equilibrium tax rate. The difference between the tax rates in the equilibria of this counterfactual and the tax policy in the full model is the policy-bundle effect of racism.

We next run a second experiment in which we continue to assume that the race/immigration issue is not a policy issue; we also now assume that all voters have nonracist preferences—that is, we assign the lowest possible value of ρ, that is, $\rho_{\min}$, to all voters. We again compute PUNEs. The tax policies in these PUNEs are what we predict taxes would be if *neither* were racial attitudes reducing solidarity among citizens *nor* were the policy-bundle effect active.

Schematically, our decomposition procedure is as follows. Let t^J be equilibrium tax policy for party J. Then for each party J the total effect of voter racism on the tax rate can be decomposed into:[7]

$$t^J(\text{full model}) - t^J(r = \bar{r}, \rho = \rho_{\min}) \quad \text{total effect}$$

$$= t^J(\text{full model}) - t^J(r = \bar{r}) \qquad \text{policy-bundle effect} \quad (2.44)$$

$$+ t^J(r = \bar{r}) - t^J(r = \bar{r}, \rho = \rho_{\min}) \quad \text{antisolidarity effect.}$$

2.7 Second Application: The Euclidean Utility Function

2.7.1 Voter Types and Preferences

In the Euclidean utility function approach, a voter's type is given by a pair $h = (\theta, \rho)$ where θ is the voter's ideal public sector size (which we call, for short, her ideal "tax rate") and ρ is her position on the race/immigration issue. The voter's type is distributed by a bivariate distribution function, $\Phi(\theta, \rho)$. We denote the two marginal distributions of $\Phi(\theta, \rho)$ by Φ_θ and Φ_ρ. The policy space T is a set of ordered pairs (t, r), which we may take to be the real plane, where t is a party's policy on the size of the public sector and r is its policy on race/immigration.

In the log utility function approach, the ideal tax rate is theoretically derived and shown to depend on income and racism/xenophobia. There is no such micro-foundation in the present approach. We empirically find that the voter's ideal public sector size in France and Denmark is negatively correlated with both her income and degree of xenophobia. We find similar negative relationships in the UK and the United States. Thus in this approach, it is assumed that the ideal tax rate is negatively correlated with income and racism. The voter type distribution function $\Phi(\theta, \rho)$ in the Euclidean utility function approach can be viewed as an analog of the distribution function which can be induced in the log utility function approach from a pair of variables (ϑ, ρ), where $\vartheta = \theta(\hat{w}, \rho)$, and the joint distribution of $\hat{w}$ and ρ.

In this approach, we do not assume that θ and ρ are independently distributed. (Even if incomes and racial views are not correlated in the logarithmic utility approach, the ideal tax rate, which is induced by both incomes and racial views, and the racial view would correlated.)

The utility function of the polity in the current approach is given by a Euclidean utility function $v : T \times H \to \mathbb{R}$:

$$v(t, r; \theta, \rho) = -(t - \theta)^2 - \frac{\gamma}{2}(r - \rho)^2. \tag{2.45}$$

This utility function can be considered a shortcut to the indirect utility function derived in the log utility function approach; a voter's utility decreases as the actual tax policy moves away from her ideal policy. As in the log utility function approach, γ represents the salience of the race/immigration issue, although its value does not have to be identical to the value of γ in the log utility function approach. (We abuse the notation for the sake of analogy.)

The set of types that prefer a policy $\tau^L = (t^L, r^L)$ to a policy $\tau^R = (t^R, r^R)$ is

$$\Omega(\tau^L, \tau^R) = \{(\theta, \rho) : v(t^L, r^L; \theta, \rho) > v(t^R, r^R; \theta, \rho)\}, \tag{2.46}$$

and the voting fraction for party L is defined by

$$\varphi(\tau^L, \tau^R) = \iint\limits_{\Omega(\tau^L, \tau^R)} d\Phi(\theta, \rho). \tag{2.47}$$

2.7.2 The Policy-Bundle Effect and the Antisolidarity Effect

The two counterfactual experiments are carried out in the following way. The first counterfactual experiment is done exactly in the same way as in the log utility function approach: that is, we assume that *race/immigration policy* (r) *is not an issue* in the election. Parties compete over the single issue of public sector size, t. Voters, however, continue to possess exactly the distribution of preferences on public-sector size as described by a marginal distribution, Φ_θ. Since those preferences are influenced by their views on race/immigration, it continues to be the case, in this counterfactual contest, that voters' views on race/immigration will *indirectly* affect the political equilibrium, via their effect on preferences over size of the public sector. If we call t^J an equilibrium tax policy for party J in the full model and t_1^J an equilibrium tax policy for party J

in this counterfactual, then the difference $t_I^J - t^J$ is exactly a measure of the policy-bundle effect, for in this counterfactual election, there is no race issue.

The second counterfactual is then carried out by estimating a distribution of *racism-free demands for the public sector*. We estimate what the distribution of preferences over public-sector size would be, were all voters nonxenophobic or nonracist. Call this distribution Φ'_θ. We now run a second unidimensional election, on public-sector size, where we assume that the distribution of voter preferences on the tax issue is given by Φ'_θ. The results of this election will be sterilized of both the policy-bundle and the antisolidarity effects. If we summarize the policy of the PUNEs here calculated by t_{II}^J then we say that the total effect of xenophobia is $t_{II}^J - t^J$, and the antisolidarity effect is $t_{II}^J - t_I^J$.

Counterfactual racism-free economic preferences are estimated as follows. We first select a reference level of *racism* ρ_{ref} that will be considered as the nonracist, nonxenophobic threshold. Then we postulate that racism-free demand for public sector is given by:

$$\theta' = \theta + \delta \max(0, \rho - \rho_{ref}), \tag{2.48}$$

where δ is the decrease in the support for public sector generated by an increase of one point on the racism/xenophobia scale. Thus it is presumed that for all individuals with racism less than or equal to this reference level ρ_{ref}, there is no antisolidarity effect in play, and thus their observed preferences for the public sector are also the ASE-free economic preferences. On the other hand, for all individuals with racism greater than this critical level ρ_{ref}, we assume that there is some ASE at play, and define their ASE-free economic preferences as those that they would have, were their racism preferences the critical value specified.

As we noted at the end of section 2.6, in running the counterfactual elections, we control for the relative bargaining powers of the party factions, by fixing them to the powers that were observed in the relevant PUNEs of the full model. We now add one complication to this explanation. When we fit the full PUNE model to the election data of a particular country, we seek to compute enough equilibria to provide a picture of the entire two-dimensional equilibrium manifold. However, we then restrict our choice of PUNEs by targeting on the vote shares. That is, we know the vote share in the actual election, and so we limit ourselves to PUNEs that deliver approximately this vote share. This is a (small) subset of the set of PUNEs. Now associated with the PUNEs in this subset are relative bargaining powers of the factions. We compute the average relative bargaining power of the Militants in each party in these PUNEs. When we run the counterfactual elections, we choose those PUNEs with bargaining powers that are close to the estimated ones. Of course, we do not know what the bargaining strengths of the two factions would be in the counterfactual world. We have not proposed a theory of the endogenous determination of bargaining strengths of factions. We choose to examine only counterfactual PUNEs with the "correct" bargaining strengths—ones that match the average bargaining strengths of the factions in the PUNEs of the full model—for otherwise—if, for instance, we took an average of *all* counterfactual PUNEs— we would introduce a second effect into the counterfactual, namely, one on the equilibrium tax rate due to a change in the relative bargaining strengths of the factions from what is estimated in the full model. The bargaining strengths of the factions in the PUNEs are not randomly distributed, and so our results would be biased if we ignored this fact. Thus our method is an attempt to control for the bargaining strengths of the factions in the two parties.

2.8   Conclusion

Thus we may summarize our strategy as follows:

1. Estimate parameters of the distribution of voter types and the utility function of voter types from the data;
2. Compute PUNEs for the two-dimensional model;
3. Select those PUNEs in which the vote share is close to the observed vote share in the election under study;
4. Compute the relative bargaining powers of the factions in the two parties in these PUNEs;
5. Run the first counterfactual election, in which race is not an issue, selecting only those counterfactual PUNEs for which the bargaining powers of the factions approximate the ones calculated in step 4; then compute the policy-bundle effect;
6. Run the second counterfactual, in which the distribution of voter types is modified to eliminate racism; then compute the total effect of racism or xenophobia on the tax rate/size of public sector.

As we wrote, the log utility function approach is superior to the Euclidean approach, because it models economic preferences in a precise way. We apply it only for the United States and the UK, where we have access to data sets that enable us to estimate the relevant economic parameters. We use the Euclidean utility function approach for Denmark and France—and we also compute the Euclidean model for the United States and the UK, for purposes of comparison.

As we justify in the country chapters, we assume a two-party model in all countries except France, where we use a three-party model.

3

History of Racial Politics in the United States

Appealing to the racial divide in [U.S.] society attracts more opprobrium than any other political tactic. "Playing the race card" is the strongest pejorative in modern political parlance, because of the sense that race should be viewed as a moral issue. That appeals to racial fears or tensions persist despite the prospect of harsh criticism illustrates the effectiveness of these tactics, as well as the enduring nature of America's racial divide.

—Jeremy D. Mayer (2002, 7)

3.1 Introduction

On December 5, 2002, Senate majority leader Trent Lott (R-MS) offered some words of praise to his colleague Strom Thurmond (R-SC), to commemorate Thurmond's hundredth birthday: "I want to say this about my state: When Strom Thurmond ran for president, we voted for him. We're proud of it. And if the rest of the country had followed our lead, we wouldn't have had all these problems over all these years."[1] Lott's statement reads as an endorsement of Thurmond's 1948 "Dixiecrat" run for the presidency, which reeked of racist appeals and supported racial segregation outright. With that comment, Lott provoked a torrent of castigating rebukes from fellow senators on both the left and the right, members of the House of Representatives, and various conservative and liberal media outlets. Even President George W. Bush distanced himself from the implications of Lott's statements.

Conservative commentator Andrew Sullivan summarized the decision that confronted the Republican Party in the aftermath of Lott's comments: "After his disgusting remarks at Strom Thurmond's 100th-birthday party, it seems to me that the Republican Party has a simple choice. Either they get rid of Lott as majority leader; or they should come out formally as a party that regrets desegregation and civil rights for African-Americans."[2] Ultimately the Republican Party opted to oust Lott from his position on December 20, 2002. In an age when the norm of racial equality is so widely accepted, to come out in favor of segregation is political suicide.

This chapter was written by Stephen Engel.

Ousting Lott did not necessarily imply that the Republican Party embraced or was reaching out to the African American electorate. What exactly were the implications of Lott's misstep that led to his resignation as majority leader? By expressing support for Thurmond's 1948 racist ideology, masked by a coded appeal to states' rights, was Lott exposing the "dirty little secret" of the Republican Party itself (Crespino 2002), namely its repeated use of race-based appeals at least since 1964 to divide the electorate, abandon its formerly loyal black constituency, and attract white voters, especially from the South, in an effort to gain and maintain majority status in national government?

Accusations of widespread racism within the ranks of the Republican Party are not merited. Yet the party may have criticized and then forced Lott to step down as political cover, to portray outwardly a belief in equality while continuing to employ implicit racial appeals as campaign strategy.

One of the Democratic candidates for president in the 2004 race, Howard Dean, accused the Republican Party of employing these tactics. A year after Lott's remarks, in a speech delivered on December 7, 2003, Dean accused the Republican Party of dividing the electorate along racial lines and seeking to inspire a white backlash in order to capture the vote and obfuscate the party's classist intentions:

> In 1968, Richard Nixon won the White House. He did it in a shameful way—by dividing Americans against one another, stirring up racial prejudices and bringing out the worst in people. They called it the 'Southern Strategy,' and the Republicans have been using it ever since. Nixon pioneered it, and Ronald Reagan perfected it, using phrases like 'racial quotas' and 'welfare queens' to convince white Americans that minorities were to blame for all of America's problems. The Republican Party would never win elections if they came out and said their core agenda was about selling America piece by piece to their campaign contributors and making sure that the wealth and power is concentrated in the hands of a few. To distract people from their real agenda, they run elections based on race, dividing us, instead of uniting us.[3]

Dean's claim is not that the Republican Party is a racist party; rather he articulates the powerful strategy that Lott's comment exposed. Perceiving the possibilities of white backlash toward the civil rights advances of African Americans, Republicans have exploited this reaction by adopting a racial conservatism that has potential to appeal to race-based fears.

Carmines and Stimson (1989) identify the election of 1964 as a critical flash-point in the reemergence of race as a major cleavage in American politics: "The issue has a long political life cycle; it has been a recurring theme in American politics since the nation's founding. Most of that time it has been submerged, too contentious for the party system. But it . . . reemerged as a partisan conflict in the early 1960s and has remained prominent since then . . . if a significant issue evolution is occurring in American politics, it is most likely to revolve around the issue of race" (14).

The role of race in the American political system and the use of the racial cleavage as a wedge issue during elections has a highly complex history. Racial tension permeates the American political party structure, and as such, to identify one particular election as pivotal for greater racial equality or inequality is not sufficient. Certain elections act as critical moments, and the presidential contest of 1964 between Lyndon Johnson and Barry Goldwater in the wake of the passage of the Civil Rights Act earlier that year was one such moment. Yet to view race as salient only at specific points underestimates the depth of that cleavage in the United States as well as the way in which it has fundamentally shaped the development of the two major political parties.[4] Racial tensions, while not at the forefront of every election, lurk at some point in all of them. As Tali Mendelberg (2001) posits: "Egalitarian norms, a racial party system, and white voters' racial stereotypes and resentments jointly explain why race is virtually absent from the surface of campaigns but very much present underneath" (19).

Thus while the immediate relevance of race may have subsided after the 1964 election, racial issues are still present, and emotions regarding them can be stirred up by campaigns through coded language that appeals to voter racism. Hence to grapple with how race and racial appeals have affected and been used in American elections is to identify an issue that has structured the political party system itself, served as the basis for massive party realignment—first with the Republicans in the more liberal position and then the Democrats—led to the breakup of the so-called solid South, and been masked by a series of code words implying a racial conservatism in order to attract voters who may be put off by identifying with outright racism.

This use of racial politics may have prevented a more comprehensive redistributive economic policy in the United States, as racial positions and economic liberalism represent two competing and distinct axes on a two-dimensional issue space. Because there is now no party that is both pro-redistribution and anti–civil rights (though southern Democrats prior to 1964 might have fit this description), voters' position on the race issue may compete with and outweigh their choices regarding redistributive policy.

This chapter traces the history of race in the American political system, focusing on how the racial cleavage structured the political party system, the position shift and seeming reversal of Republican and Democratic stances on civil rights and federal support of African American equality, the move from explicit racism to implicit racial appeals or racial conservatism, and ultimately the effects of race-based campaign strategy on the representative capability of the Democratic and Republican parties. While this chapter chronicles the long historical significance of the racial dimension in American politics into the present day, the following chapter takes advantage of more recent data to show what effects the racial cleavage and voter racism have had not only on partisan alignments but also on tax policy and redistribution in the last quarter of the twentieth century.

3.2   Race and American Exceptionalism

Although many scholars focus on the election of 1964 as representing the strongest reemergence of racial issues in American political discourse since the Civil War, other scholars have suggested that racial concerns were significant much before then and led to a fundamental cleavage in the American political structure. Indeed, the salience of racial divisions in the United States is often cited as one reason why a class-based political party system never took shape, as well as why socialism never gained secure footing in the country (Lipset and Marks 1997). For example, characterizing the cleavage structure in the United States during the second industrial revolution, Domhoff (1995) writes, "the primary producers in the United States—those who work with their hands in factories and fields—were more seriously divided among themselves until the 1930s than was the case in most other countries. The deepest and most important of these divisions was between whites and African-Americans" (45). On a similar point, Glaser (1996) argues:

> One of the important consequences of this partisan situation was that class issues were, for the most part, kept off the political agenda. Appeals to racial hatred were designed to distract lower-class whites from challenging the prevailing economic order. By keeping emotions high on racial issues, elites were able to minimize the possibility of a class-based political movement emerging . . . Class-based politics was largely sub-

ordinated to race-based politics in the South, and southern Democrats worked hard to keep it that way. (3–4)

In short, the race-based cleavage was and perhaps remains the predominant division in the United States, trumping other forms of collective identity, including class.

That race is so critical to understanding the American political system should not be surprising given that in the debates surrounding the nation's establishment, compromise was already necessary on the "peculiar institution" of slavery. Written into the Constitution was the quantification of each African American slave as three-fifths of a human being in order to determine the population on which to base representation in the House of Representatives.[5] As Frymer (1999) notes, the subject of race in early America was predicated on compromise and silence regarding the fundamental contradiction that slavery posed into the ideologies of equality and freedom that were the nation's founding pillars. Frymer argues that the racial cleavage "was a central factor in the initial design of the nation's two-party system," which developed when the need to ignore the divisive tensions stemming from slavery in order to maintain the Union was high. Because dissension over slavery was perceived as a sectional conflict, coming to the fore with the possible admission of Missouri as a state in 1819, there existed a need to refocus political parties on issues that were unrelated to slavery. Frymer credits Martin Van Buren with developing an ideological base for the Democratic Party that muted the regional tensions over slavery in favor of the promotion of decentralized power, or states' rights.[6]

The avoidance of slavery as a politically divisive issue was institutionalized by the so-called two-thirds rule that structured the nomination process for the Democratic presidential candidate. Representation at the nominating convention was proportional to seating within the Electoral College, which would have left the South weakened with only 40 percent of the vote. However, the South was shielded from Northern domination by the two-thirds rule, mandating that the party nominee must receive at least a two-thirds majority vote. This rule translated into the repeated nomination of moderate candidates who would alienate neither southern plantation owners nor northern abolitionists (Frymer 1999, 37–38). It was further agreed that no statement regarding slavery would be made in the party platforms. The Democratic Party never explicitly condoned slavery as an institution; however, rather than actually avoiding the issue, "the repeated insistence by Democrats that slavery should be kept off the political agenda constituted more than implicit defense of the institution" (Gerring 1998, 163–165). Gerring (1998) suggests that explicit racism was rampant within the Democratic Party in the antebellum period and during the Civil War, Reconstruction, and the Gilded Age, and this racism was eventually translated into the question of whether and how the federal government could intervene in the states to protect the rights of the new class of freedmen. The ideological base of the nineteenth-century Democratic Party, according to Gerring (1998), rested securely on the virtue of white supremacy:

> Its opposition to federal voting rights laws, its all-pervasive anti-statism, its constitutional fundamentalism (centered on the Tenth Amendment), its "minoritarian" view of democracy and general distrust of power, its defense of property rights, its praise for the virtues of tolerance and a pluralistic society, its proto-Marxist critique of capitalism, and its embrace of the interests of agriculture—all bolstered the legitimacy of the increasingly peculiar institution and thereafter, of Jim Crow. (165)

Whether or not the Democratic Party could be characterized as predominantly pro-slavery, it seems that tension along this issue demanded that Van Buren—along with many other Democrats—take contradictory positions on matters related to slavery, such as opposing the admission of Texas as a slave state while promoting three pro-slavery judges to the Supreme Court, and all the while supporting a gag rule that prevented slavery from being discussed in congressional debates. If the issue were not recognized as such, Democrats believed, then it would not manifest as a threat to the coherence and stability of their party. However, just because slavery was not always at the surface of debate does not mean that it did not act to become a more divisive wedge, ultimately spelling the demise of the Whigs, the rise of the Republicans, and the plunging of the nation into civil war.

3.3 Issue Evolution

In their work *Congress: A Political-Economic History of Roll Call Voting*, Poole and Rosenthal (1997) provide a model to account for patterns in the ways that members of Congress make choices during roll-call voting. Their model provides an account of how the nation's racial cleavage gained increasing importance throughout the first half of the nineteenth century, ultimately fostering a realignment along the racial issue dimension. Although their evidence suggests that representatives and senators' stances on issues can be placed upon an ideological continuum of liberal to conservative that corresponds predominantly to economic concerns (that is, redistributive policy),[7] they also provide evidence of the salience of race as a critical cleavage that has shaped American history, hinting at a correlation between economic redistribution and voter racism.

They attempt to refute more complex models that take into account various issue dimensions—for example, government management, agriculture, foreign policy, civil liberties—by claiming that these issues do not constitute dimensions in and of themselves, but merely map onto a continuum of liberal-conservative, which corresponds to a tendency to support redistributive policy. In other words, a model of low dimensionality accounts highly effectively for roll-call voting patterns throughout American history. This finding leads them to posit a historical trend given only a primary and secondary issue dimension: "One way of interpreting the dynamics of the spaces is that the horizontal axis usually picks up the conflict between, roughly speaking, rich and poor (or, more accurately, rich and less rich). Other issues (slavery, civil rights, currency inflation) cross-cut this basic conflict. If . . . one of these other issues becomes too intense, dimensional alignments break down and a reorganization of the party system results" (46).

Poole and Rosenthal (1997) show that the debate over slavery in the 1820s through the 1850s leading to the Civil War corresponds to this notion that a secondary issue dimension can replace the primary economic one. In doing so, they provide evidence that the traditional classification of this period as a realignment—the breakdown of the Whigs and the solidification of the shift with the establishment of the antislavery Republicans—is correct. They write: "As the conflict within the country grew, the Whig and Democratic parties split along North-South lines along the second dimension, and the first dimension continued to divide the Whigs from the Democrats on the traditional economic issues (for example, tariffs, internal improvements, the national bank, and public lands). By 1853, this economic dimension collapsed and was replaced by the slavery dimension" (95).

Before and in the immediate aftermath of the Civil War, as well as during Reconstruction, when race remained a prominent cleavage defining the positions of political parties—with Republicans espousing liberalism and Democrats taking a conservative position—campaign appeals could be *explicitly* racial in content. Mendelberg (2001) defines an explicit appeal as "a racial appeal . . . [that] uses nouns or adjectives to endorse white prerogatives, to express anti-black sentiment, to represent racial stereotypes, or to portray a threat from African Americans" (8).

Such appeals acquired increasing salience as the national party system cleaved along racial lines, but the positioning of the parties along this issue dimension did not necessarily require that campaign rhetoric be explicitly racial. As Mendelberg (2001) notes, "the Democrats could have, for example, appealed exclusively to the idea of states' rights . . . But they chose to appeal not only to states' rights but also to derogatory views about blacks. Their position against extending citizenship rights to African Americans was communicated with explicitly racial messages that derogated African Americans in a direct and overt way" (29). Mendelberg's insight derives from the contention that issue positions do not solely guide rhetoric; rather, they respond to social norms. Because the norm of inequality was more prevalent during the nineteenth century and the early part of the twentieth, it could be exploited more readily as a campaign strategy.[8]

During this time when explicit racial appeals could be made, negative perceptions of African Americans were prevalent on both sides of the cleavage. Stereotypes of dangerous sexuality and the dangers of so-called racial amalgamation or "miscegenation," black laziness, and black criminality were common and inspired calls by Democrats to limit black suffrage and ban racial intermarriage (Mendelberg 2001, 43–45). Furthermore, claims of Republican progressiveness on race should not be exaggerated. Mendelberg finds that since social constraints on supporting racial inequality were so minimal, Republicans also were not bound by them: "a large number of Republicans saw full equality as unthinkable and abhorrent; they hated slavery in part because it required the presence of many blacks; and they planned to permanently separate whites from blacks should emancipation come about . . . Republicans were not sympathetic to full equality with blacks more than anyone else" (ibid., 36).

With the passage of the Thirteenth, Fourteenth, and Fifteenth amendments, however, Democrats refrained from using explicitly racial appeals, recognizing that such a strategy might have an electoral cost. Consequently, by 1872 campaign rhetoric shifted to other predominant issues, primarily tax policy,[9] and the explicit messages were masked within positions taken on seemingly unrelated economic issues. Democratic rhetoric shifted from emphasizing the claims regarding black inferiority to stressing the importance of maintaining white superiority, a stance that, given the prevalent norm of inequality in both the North and the South, was amenable to whites in both parties (Mendelberg 2001, 49–53).

As Reconstruction came to an end with the Compromise of 1876 in which Rutherford B. Hayes gained southern electoral votes in exchange for agreeing to withdraw troops from the South, the two parties seemed to move beyond the issue of race for both political and ideological reasons. Mendelberg (2001) notes that "each party had decided that abandoning the issue of race best served its electoral purpose. Republicans abandoned the issue from a lack of will and sense of futility. Democrats abandoned it because their position on the issue had acquired a strong association with their position in favor of southern whites . . . The parties moved away from race and sectionalism, and toward class and economic issues" (56). The Democrats, having been discredited by their association with the Confederacy, thus sought to broaden their appeal beyond the South. The Republicans retreated from racial equality in order to mend the schism that it had produced between the Radical and the Liberal Republicans. Furthermore, the Republican Party could abandon its previous support for racial equality because the African American voting population—which substantially fell with the establishment of Jim Crow— became an essentially captured group. With freedmen tied to the party of Lincoln as their emancipators, there was little to no danger that the black constituency of the Republican Party would bolt to support the Democrats.[10] Because African Americans had no other electoral option, the Republican agenda could move beyond racial equality, with party leaders secure that they would not jeopardize black support. Hence, as Reconstruction ended, the Republicans were able to advocate a "let alone" policy toward the South and to define their differences with the Democratic opponents in terms of economic matters (Frymer 1999, 63–65). The political cleavage re-formed along the primary economic issue dimension, and would not resurface prominently until the 1960s.

3.4 The Dixiecrats

Carmines and Stimson (1989) identify the election of 1948 as a missed opportunity, or in the language of their issue evolution model, an "aborted critical moment" (37) in that it was the first election in which the Democrats, under the influence of the northern wing of the party, wrote strong support for the civil rights of African Americans into the party platform (34–35). This move confirmed the schism between northern and southern Democrats, for despite the increasing acceptance of racial equality as a norm by the late 1940s, the southern wing of the Democratic Party remained grounded in the ideology of white supremacy. As Earl and Merle Black (1992) note, "of all the ties that bound the South to the Democratic party in the first half of the twentieth century, by far the most compelling and sacrosanct was the shared understanding that the Democratic party was the party of white supremacy. This belief was the essence of the traditional southern political culture" (141).

The adoption of a strong civil rights plank by the Truman ticket therefore alienated much of the southern constituency; the entire Alabama delegation, nine-tenths of the Mississippi delegation, just under three-fourths of the South Carolinian delegation, and half of the Louisiana delegation defected to form a third party, the States' Rights Democrats, or "Dixiecrats," nominating Strom Thurmond for president on a blatantly segregationist platform (Sundquist 1983, 293). This election is treated as a missed opportunity to foster broader acceptance of civil rights within the Democratic Party precisely because the elections of 1952, 1956, and 1960 illustrate a return to the normalcy of Republican racial liberalism and Democratic silence on racial matters. Hence, according to Carmines and Stimson, the election of 1964 functions as the critical turning point on race; in this election Democrats stake their claim on the left of the racial question, while the Republicans chart out new territory on the right, supporting the issue evolution of racial conservatism by attracting Southern whites, beginning the fracture of the formerly Democratic "solid South" while pushing blacks to abandon the party of Lincoln for the party of Johnson and the Civil Rights Act of 1964 and the Voting Rights Act of 1965 (Carmines and Stimson 1989, 35–47, 190–191).

While this assessment is accurate, to move from the end of Reconstruction to the pivotal Johnson-versus-Goldwater campaign of 1964 without taking account of the development of Jim Crow or Democratic domination of the South—at least in presidential contests—until 1948 is to ignore how racial politics structured the South and gradually fractured the Democratic Party along sectional interests. As detailed above, it is common to understand the end of Reconstruction as heralding the end of sectional politics; race—a sectional issue as defined by Poole and Rosenthal, Frymer, and Mendelberg—retreats into the background while the more common economic cleavage reasserts itself. However, as Earl and Merle Black argue in their work *The Rise of the Southern Republicans,* the racial cleavage is the defining one, at least for the South. Indeed Republicans continued to have a "southern problem" at least until 1964. Their party failed to attract any kind of significant support in the former Confederacy, as it could not and would not escape its connection with Lincoln and the emancipation of the slaves (Black and Black 2002, 13–16). As Earl and Merle Black (2002) note, sectional politics defined the American party system from the establishment of the Republican Party until at least 1932:

> The revolutionary insight of the politicians who invented the Republican party—that a major party deliberately founded on sectional rather than national interests could dominate national politics—was generally borne out by subsequent events. For seven decades the Lincoln Strategy was the Lincoln Solution . . . From 1860 through 1930 the Republican party controlled the Senate in thirty-one of thirty-six Congresses. In twenty-three Congresses—almost two-thirds—it won national majorities in the House of Representatives. (14)

Essentially, the Civil War produced what Black and Black refer to as "battlefield sectionalism" in which the geographic division between the North and South translated into an abnormal political situation. While the war had ended by 1865, the regional animosity played itself out in the voting booth. The artificially southern Republican state governments that characterized Reconstruction were replaced by Democrats; this party utilized white supremacy as "the undisguised political theory and the standard practice of the racist white Democrats who ended Reconstruction" (Black and Black 2002, 11). Earl and Merle Black refuse to acknowledge this kind of politics as the normal national politics that other political scientists have termed it: "There was nothing 'normal' or 'constitutional' about the relentlessly undemocratic and morally corrosive mechanisms that restored white Democrats to their preeminence in the southern House delegation." During this period, with the effective disenfranchisement of African Americans, white racially conservative Democrats dominated the South, eliminating any meaningful competition by Republicans and earning the moniker of the "solid South." Glaser's analysis of the regional character of the political parties supports the thesis of sectionalism between the end of the Reconstruction and the election of 1932: "the Solid South was white supremacist and solidly Democratic, two tendencies that reinforced each other. Given this status quo, Republicans, as 'the party of Lincoln,' were unable to gain a foothold in the electorate . . . In a party system whose genesis lay in the Civil War and Reconstruction, they had no natural constituency to appeal to, particularly as blacks were disenfranchised" (Glaser 1996, 2–3). In other words, the sectional divide of the Civil War brought on by racial politics continued to color the political field until some other shock might reconfigure electoral allegiance. That shock was the Great Depression.

Thus for Earl and Merle Black (2002), the critical turning point in American elections and the national dominance of the racially liberal Republicans was the onset of the Great Depression and the election of Franklin Roosevelt in 1932 (15). While not triggering any kind of reformulation of racial strategies by the parties, the election signaled the beginning of the Democratic coalition of liberal northerners and conservative southerners. Southerners remained in the party out of sheer animosity toward Lincoln. Northerners were reacting to the failure of the Hoover administration to combat the Great Depression and supported the more aggressive economic recovery package offered by Roosevelt. This realignment of the electorate dramatically pushed the Republicans into minority status. The Republicans' Lincoln strategy of writing off the South as not winnable and relying on the support of the North, West, and Midwest had to change. The party could maintain national dominance without the South, but it could not do so without the North. The rise of Roosevelt and the New Deal coalition left the Republicans without any geographically determined base (ibid., 16–20).

While the campaign of 1932 may have laid the roots for the breakup of the solid South by linking northern liberals with southern conservatives, the election and the Roosevelt administration in general did little to change the political status of African Americans. The New Deal's economic policies began to restructure the South, altering its traditional socioeconomic relations between whites and blacks, but it did not include a civil rights agenda out of fear of fissuring the coalition (Frederickson 2001, 11–16). The Great Depression and New Deal policies provided a shock to the southern political system that threatened to permanently destabilize this pattern, ultimately chopping away at the racial norms and eventually cracking the one-party South. The election of 1936 reveals the first defections of African Americans from the Republican Party to the Democratic Party; Roosevelt received 75 percent of the black vote. Yet this realignment had little to do with any kind of civil rights reforms taken by Roosevelt (ibid., 20), who had remained silent on the failed attempts to pass a federal antilynching law, for example, precisely because he did not want to alienate his southern constituency.

In short, the 1932 election is critical only in terms of the Republican Party's losing its base and foreshadowing the need to develop a new campaign strategy to attract voters; however, in terms of racial politics, the Democrats remained on the right and Republicans held true to Lincoln's ideals. Even by 1944, the Democrats continued to compromise on the issue of race. The acceptance of Truman as Roosevelt's running mate illustrates this. Increasingly anxious about the socioeconomic upheavals that the New Deal had wrought upon the South as well as the shift of the national party's ideology to reflect that of the northern and urban wing, southern Democrats attempted to block the nomination of Roosevelt for a fourth term (Frederickson 2001, 37–38). When this tactic proved unsuccessful, southern conservatives banded together to block the selection of racially liberal Henry Wallace as the vice presidential candidate. Again, the conflict over race produced avoidance and compromise:

> Wallace's support for the rights of organized labor and African Americans was anathema to Dixie conservatives. Fearful of antagonizing the party's disparate factions, Democratic National Committee (DNC) chairman Robert F. Hannigan was determined to find an uncontroversial, inoffensive vice-presidential candidate who could foster party unity . . . Above all else, Truman's ability to avoid seriously offending any critical party constituency assured him the second spot on the ticket . . . White southerners . . . were pleased with Truman . . . Truman charted a tentative course on civil rights and in general pursued a policy agenda that increasingly alienated his party's left wing. Unwilling to antagonize the conservative bloc in Congress, Truman expended little political capital to save the FEPC [Fair Employment Practices Committee] from the political axe wielded by Dixie congressmen, and he retreated from his earlier opposition to the poll tax, stating that it "was a matter for the Southern states to work out." (Ibid., 38–39)

The racial ideological gap between the Republicans and the Democrats by 1944 could not have been wider. Whereas the Democratic platform weakly asserted a belief in the right of racial and religious minorities to an equal vote and to live as free citizens as guaranteed by the Constitution, the Republican platform called for aggressive civil rights protections, including the desegregation of the military, the permanent institutionalization of the FEPC, a constitutional amendment banning the poll tax, and a strong federal antilynching law

(Carmines and Stimson 1997, 32). In stark contrast to the position of the parties by 1964, the Democrats remained firmly beholden to their southern wing, preventing any kind of movement on civil rights. This positioning on the racial political spectrum shifted, to some degree, in 1948 with the Democrats moving left while the Republicans remained on the left.

The election of 1948 marks the first attempts by the Democrats to move toward embracing racial equality, and the subsequent defection of some of the southern delegates and their support of the segregationist Dixiecrat Thurmond-Wright ticket led V. O. Key (1950) to comment that "in its grand outlines the politics of the south revolves around the position of the Negro." The irony of southern support for Truman in 1944 was that by 1946, Truman started to make serious advances to support civil rights. Impelled by the widespread contention that the Republican success in the 1946 midterm elections was attributable to the black vote, in December of that year, Truman established the President's Committee on Civil Rights (Frederickson 2001, 57). The report of that committee, *To Secure These Rights,* revealed widespread violations of civil rights and advocated what was essentially the 1944 Republican platform on racial equality, namely an antilynching law, an anti–poll tax law, greater support of fair employment practices, and desegregation of the armed forces (ibid., 65). By the 1948 Democratic National Convention, the party was fairly splintered on regional lines; the northern liberals demanded a strong civil rights plank that was abhorred by the southern contingent. Southerners called for a series of states' rights resolutions that were soundly defeated; instead the Humphrey-Biemiller resolution, which called for the securing of full and equal political participation and equal treatment in terms of services and armed forces—that is, the civil rights committee's recommendations— was overwhelmingly approved (ibid., 129). Given that southern power in the party had also been diminished by the revocation of the two-thirds rule in 1936 (Carmines and Stimson 1997, 34), part of the southern delegation bolted to establish its own States' Rights, or Dixiecrat, Party.

Despite evidence that Dixiecrat Strom Thurmond had the legislative record of a racial moderate,[11] his rhetoric during the campaign illustrates perhaps one of the last times that explicit racial appeals were utilized in a presidential contest. At one point during the campaign, Thurmond stated, "There's not enough troops in the Army to force the southern people to break down segregation and admit the Negro race into our theaters, into our swimming pools, into schools, and into our homes."[12] However, much of this inflammatory language was only designed to attract southern candidates. Thurmond attempted to steer his campaign on the legitimate constitutional question of states' rights. Hence, while explicit racial appeals may have been common in the South, the rhetoric aimed at the North bowed to the increasing norm of equality (Frederickson 2001, 140; Mendelberg 2001, 72–73). Indeed, given the support for racial equality among Republicans and northern Democrats, the South's racial conservatism appeared increasingly isolated. The changing perception toward support of the civil rights of black Americans was brought about not only by the increasing political mobilization of blacks and the mobilization of blacks during World War II, but by the fact that the de jure racism of segregation in the South and the de facto racism of the North proved to be a public relations problem for the United States at the beginning of the cold war (Mendelberg 2001, 72). The United States could not be an effective advocate for human rights and democracy when it failed to demonstrate these qualities among its own population.

The Dixiecrats failed to receive any popular support beyond the South, and Truman returned to the presidency. However, the Dixiecrat revolt was the first manifestation of a crack within the New Deal coalition. Seeing that the Dixiecrats had succumbed to the common fate of third parties in the United States' two-party majoritarian system, by 1952, southern Democrats, feeling betrayed by the racially liberal turn of the national party, began to split their tickets, voting for Democratic members of Congress but for Republican presidential candidates (Frederickson 2001, 217–218). The critical importance of the Dixiecrat revolt is not that it steered the Democrats toward racial equality—in fact the party backpedaled from its 1948 racial liberalism throughout the 1950s with its nomination of racial moderate Adlai Stevenson in a failed effort to mend the sectional rift—but rather that it pushed racist or at least racially conservative southern whites toward the Republican Party. In 1952 Eisenhower took Florida, Oklahoma, Tennessee, Texas, and Virginia from the Democrats (ibid., 230–231). Party identification has taken a dramatic turn in the South since then. Glaser finds that in the early 1950s, 85 percent of southerners considered themselves Democratic, and only 13 percent identified themselves as Republican. By 1992, 43 percent of white southerners were Republicans while only 42 percent still identified as Democrats, illustrating a tremendous degree of "white flight" from the Democratic Party (Glaser 1996, 9).[13] Furthermore, southern presidential votes demonstrate a dramatic swing toward the Republican candidate from at least 1960 onward with the exception of Jimmy Carter's election of 1976 (ibid., 11). This shift in partisan identification and support for Republican presidential candidates is attributable to the recasting of the Republican Party less as the party of Lincoln and more as the party of Goldwater and Reagan, a party that has used the ideological stance of racial conservatism and the rhetoric of code words to appeal to former southern Democrats, peeling them away from their party and finally shattering the solid South.

3.5   The Presidential Election of 1964 and Its Aftermath

The presidential election of 1964 between Lyndon Johnson and Barry Goldwater established the positions of the Democratic and Republican parties along the racial political dimension that we recognize today, that is, the Democrats on the left and the Republicans on the right, essentially reversing the parties' predominant positions to that point. The parties' positions on racial equality and civil rights for blacks had been essentially identical in 1960 (Carmines and Stimson 1989, 39). Republican nominee Richard Nixon held fast to his party's identification with Lincoln and racial progressivism while Democratic nominee John Kennedy sought to bring the ideological beliefs of the party's northern wing to the fore. Kennedy had overtaken the more racially liberal contender, Hubert Humphrey, in the primaries, and the selection of Johnson as Kennedy's running mate is commonly perceived as "explicitly about returning the once solid South to the Democratic fold" (J. Mayer 2002, 22). The pairing of the racially moderate senator from Massachusetts with the racially conservative senator from Texas is emblematic of the compromise positions that the Democrats had been forced to make to maintain the New Deal coalition: "The selection of Johnson dovetailed nicely with a strong Democratic platform on civil rights. The South was given a familiar face and accent to go along with a northerner with a reputation for racial moderation; blacks were given a progressive platform and a northerner atop the ticket" (ibid., 38). The parties' positions on civil rights were thus nearly identical in 1960, yet blacks continued to defect to the Democratic Party as Kennedy improved on Stevenson's levels of black support. This was true despite the fact that Nixon and his running mate, Henry Cabot Lodge, had a much more racially liberal record than Kennedy-Johnson. The impact of Nixon's loss was dramatic for the racial politics of the Republican party. As Jeremy Mayer notes, the Republicans "had put their strongest civil rights ticket forward, along with a platform that was at least competitive with the Democrats, and lost significant ground among blacks. The Nixon campaign of 1960 was the high tide for racial liberalism in the Republican Party, which they have never approached since" (ibid., 39).

The most dramatic turn came in 1964, which has been characterized as the last electoral realignment of the political parties.[14] With the passage of the Civil Rights Act and, the next year, the Voting Rights Act, the Democratic Party was planted firmly on the side of racial liberalism, thereby disaffecting much of its southern white constituency. Barry Goldwater's nomination as Republican candidate signaled the ascendancy of conservatism within that party, as civil rights liberals such as Nelson Rockefeller split state delegations with Goldwater while the latter won the entire southern region (Carmines and Stimson 1997, 44). Yet Goldwater's conservatism was not necessarily concerned with racial matters; rather, he advocated a minimalist perspective on national government involvement in domestic issues. In their work *Divided by Color: Racial Politics and Democratic Ideals,* Donald Kinder and Lynn Sanders (1996) note that while Goldwater's ideology was not racist in nature, its implications for minimalist federal intervention appealed to the racial bias of the South:

> If read literally, the Goldwater campaign was not racist. Goldwater's vote against the Civil Rights Bill should probably be understood as a principled expression of his general conservatism, a complaint lodged against what he took to be inappropriate encroachments of the federal government . . . As pure or careful as the original intentions might have been, however, the Goldwater campaign obviously appealed to racism. In the South especially, the rhetoric of states' rights was, in part, familiar code for keeping blacks in their place. (203)

Since Goldwater voted against the Civil Rights Bill, his ideological standing could be misconstrued as racist; however, "Goldwater's appeal to states' rights had no references to 'blacks,' 'whites,' or 'race'" (Mendelberg 2001, 86). And thus while Goldwater was not a racist or a segregationist, "his racial conservatism had a powerful appeal to anti–civil rights forces that had been deserted by the national Democratic party"(Carmines and Stimson 1997, 45). Regardless, Goldwater's use of race was critical to winning the nomination. He made specific comments in the South, using coded references to law and order and "the distinct cultural loss" brought about in the South by federal intervention (J. Mayer 2002, 54–55). In the end, Johnson won a landslide victory as Goldwater's racial conservatism proved too alienating beyond the deep South; however, Goldwater took the entire deep South, winning by large margins in Alabama, Georgia, Louisiana, Mississippi, and South Carolina, the region characterized by Mendelberg (2001) as "most intent on maintaining racial hierarchy" (86). Furthermore, African American voters abandoned the Republican Party. While Republicans won the white South, Democrats took the black South. By 1964, 86 percent of southern blacks aligned with the Democrats (Glaser 1996, 8–9). The message of the election to the Republicans was clear. As Mayer (2002) says, "the open racism practiced by Goldwater's southern supporters must be decried, denied, and denounced. Yet Goldwater's strong showing in the South and in parts of the North contained the broader import of the election for Republicans. If racial politics could draw white voters into the camp of a candidate as extreme and unelectable as Barry Goldwater, then it was indeed among the most powerful forces in American politics" (68).

Thus, in 1964, the party of Lincoln embarked on a strategy of alienating its black support and forgetting its history of racial progressivism, while the Democrats, having lost hold of the solid South, became further dependent on the black vote, leading, in part, to electoral disasters in the presidential contests of the 1970s and 1980s. The 1964 election represents a racial realignment of the political parties as we know them today: "Before 1964, most Americans saw no difference between the parties on civil rights, while afterward, most were able to correctly point to the Democratic party as the champion of civil rights and the Republican party as the opposition" (Mendelberg 2001, 86). Furthermore, the 1964 election was perceived as an overwhelming endorsement of the civil rights advances of the Johnson administration. But the end of segregation in no way spelled the end of race as a divisive campaign issue. Given that the norm of equality had taken hold, however, any further appeals to racist tendencies had to be masked through coded language.

After 1964, campaigns were marked by two strategies on race, not necessarily mutually exclusive. The strategy of "benign neglect" refers to candidates' avoidance of the race question: "they neither defended nor attacked segregation and they said as little as possible about the racial caste system" (Kinder and Sanders 1996, 222). This strategy was highly effective in the southern gubernatorial races by the 1970s, and the Ford, Reagan, and George H. W. Bush campaigns used it as well. (See Kinder and Sanders 1996, 222, and Mendelberg 2001, 75–76.) The alternative tactic of "code words"[15] or implicit racial appeals, defined by Mendelberg (2001, 9) as "present[ing] an ostensibly race-free conservative position on an issue while incidentally alluding to racial stereotypes or to a perceived threat from African Americans," appealed to white backlash as implementation of the civil rights agenda became identified with the divisive policies of busing, quotas, welfare, and affirmative action. The lack of support for these policies did not derive from the foundering of the norm of equality itself, but rather from the impact of civil rights legislation on both the South and the North (ibid., 93–94); it was one thing for the Civil Rights and Voting Rights acts to target the racist behavior believed to be endemic to the South, but it was quite another when achieving the goal of racial equality meant busing students in Boston or Detroit. The success of George Wallace's racial appeals in the 1968 campaign highlighted that white backlash had moved north: "As school-desegregation decisions, antidiscrimination housing ordinances, and race riots moved north in the mid-1960s, Americans soon discovered there was a bit of redneck in Grand Rapids as well as in Birmingham" (Carter 1996, 9). Following the surprising success of George Wallace in 1968 and 1972, the Republican strategy devised by Nixon and carried forward by Reagan and later George H. W. Bush made increasing use of implicit racial appeals to exploit white fears in the wake of riots and lawlessness and white beliefs that affirmative action and other government policies gave racial minorities an "unfair" advantage.

Given that the social norm of equality was so strong, the trick to winning elections by 1968 was to appeal to fears that were at the foundation of white backlash in a way that would not appear extremist or alienate more moderate voters. The use of the implicit appeal in elections from 1968 onward persists for two reasons: (1) voters do not want to acknowledge their own racial prejudices, since such opinions are frowned upon, and (2) politicians perceive a wide audience for such appeals. For example, on the first point, Kuklinski, Cobb, and Gilens (1997) contend that the claim of a "New South" free of the racism that characterized its history is a myth, supported by flawed opinion surveys unable to move beneath so-called desirability effects: "Validly measuring racial attitudes is one of the most difficult tasks that social scientists face. As long as people know they are being asked to express their beliefs and feelings about race, the investigator cannot dismiss the possibility of desirability effects—people giving an insincere, 'right' answer" (ibid.). Hence there may exist a level of racism that coded racial appeals tap into while enabling the voter to still plausibly deny racial prejudice, because the conservatism of the message masks its racial undertones. Furthermore, Frymer (1999) contends that beyond social norms, implicit appeals remain prevalent because politicians perceive the electorate as divided on racial lines and exploit that cleavage for electoral gain: "the behavior of party leaders reflects their belief that the nation is divided along racial lines . . . Sometimes, party leaders are clearly right in their perception that the median voter is racist. Other times, it is not so clear" (34).

While one would be hard-pressed to suggest that the electorate was racist in 1972 or even 1968, it would be easier to identify beliefs that the civil rights movement was moving too fast or that whites were uncomfortable with the fact that Martin Luther King Jr.'s call for a color-blind society had translated into race-conscious policies of quotas, busing, and affirmative action. Nixon employed implicit appeals in 1968 and 1972 precisely because of the success of George Wallace's unabashedly racist third-party run in the North. Commenting on a 1968 campaign commercial that highlighted Nixon's promise to reestablish "law and order," Nixon is quoted as remarking that the commercial "hits it right on the nose . . . it's all about law and order and the damn Negro–Puerto Rican groups out there."[16] His comment illustrates how the use of certain phrases such as "law and order"—or in later Reagan campaigns, the phrase "welfare queens"—could subtly refer to race and foment white racial fears while remaining disconnected from any overt sense of racism.

Even Wallace attempted to moderate his own racist record by claiming a mantle of states' rights and law and order, and thus he presented a populist persona at the national level (Mendelberg 2001, 91–92; J. Mayer 2002, 75), but his rhetoric on crime amounted to "nothing more than code words" (J. Mayer 2002, 85) and occasionally overt racism would slip into his speeches. At one point, Wallace claimed in response to the epidemic race riots of 1968, "We don't have riots in Alabama . . . They start a riot down there, first one of 'em to pick up a brick gets a bullet in their brain, that's all."[17] While Wallace's rhetoric condemned him to a free fall in the polls as the election neared, the impact of his presence should not be underestimated. That he was able to muster support in the North was highly influential on the evolution of Republican campaign strategy from that point forward. Mayer (2002) summarizes this impact on Nixon's victory in 1968:

> That a candidate in a three-way race, and in the face of extraordinary expansion in black suffrage, could surrender the black vote and win validated the Republican strategy of "the hell with them." For the rest of the century, Republicans would not reach out to blacks and would never lose the white vote to the Democrats . . . The election of 1968 showed how race and war had destroyed the Democratic coalition. Wallace, a former Democrat, had been much closer to the Republican rhetoric on race,

federalism, crime, and war . . . If the Republican Party could bring Wallace voters in their coalition, they would have a virtual lock on the White House. Moreover, such a coalition would have no need of black support. (94–95)

And cater to Wallace supporters is just what Nixon did in 1972 when his so-called southern strategy contributed to a massive landslide victory over Democrat George McGovern, which was interpreted as a mandate to travel much more cautiously on the road to racial equality. The 1972 election revolved, in part, around the issues of busing and quotas, and while the Nixon campaign was able to capture Wallace supporters by coming out against the policy, McGovern was forced to stake a position in favor of it in order to maintain the Democratic hold on the black vote. Indeed Wallace—fervently against both busing and quotas—won the Democratic primaries in Michigan and Maryland, but withdrew from the race after being shot in an assassination attempt (J. Mayer 2002, 105). With McGovern forced to take unpopular stances on these racial issues, not only was Nixon able to capture the South, but he broadened his appeal among the staple of Democratic ethnic white voters in the North—Italian Americans, Irish Americans, and Jews—who perceived quotas as offering unfair advantages (Carter 1996, 51; J. Mayer 2002, 110). Nearing the end of the campaign, McGovern embarked on a full assault of the Nixon strategy, branding Nixon not merely racially conservative but outrightly racist; in one speech McGovern claimed "the Nixon Administration has put down black people every chance it has had."[18] By 1972, the racial divide had transformed the parties. Republicans had dropped their racial progressivism, abandoned the black vote, and made massive inroads in the South and the traditionally Democratic constituency of ethnic and blue-collar workers by utilizing coded rhetoric to appeal to white backlash. Meanwhile Democrats were increasingly perceived as out of touch with mainstream voters, too far to the left, and captured by the "special interests" of minority voters.

3.6 The Reagan Democrats

Reagan's exploitation of the racial cleavage in the United States was, in some sense, incorporated into his supply-side economic policy, which hit lower-income Americans, especially African Americans, hard. The rhetoric of tax cuts was belied by the facts that the top 10 percent income bracket enjoyed most cuts whereas those between the 50th and 90th percentile saw marginal tax relief (Carter 1996, 62). While much is often made of Reagan's use of code words such as "welfare queen," this language was more prominent in his failed 1976 bid against Carter than in his 1980 and 1984 campaigns. Reagan's poor record on civil rights—he did not support the Civil Rights Act of 1964 and he attacked the Voting Rights Act of 1965 as unnecessarily humiliating toward southerners (ibid., 55–56; J. Mayer 2002, 152–155)—could not be overcome by his outreach to the black vote by speaking to the NAACP, traveling through the South Bronx, and receiving the endorsement of former King aide Ralph Abernathy (J. Mayer 2002, 165–172). Reagan's poor record on race and his calling forth the mantle of states' rights and the legacy of Goldwater led the Carter campaign to inspire fear of a Reagan presidency and called for the electorate not to be fooled by the use of code words that masked racism.

However, by the elections of 1980 and 1984, race was treated by Reagan through the use of anecdotes befitting the sunny disposition of the former actor. Speeches on race relations would invoke warped stories of how desegregation of the armed forces was attributable to the heroic acts of a black naval colonel at Pearl Harbor rather than to Truman's executive order (Carter 1996, 65). Such stories, which were symbolically appealing but factually inaccurate, fit with Reagan's own fervent ideological individualism. However, the importance of Reagan's defeat in 1976 and his use of such individualist symbolism during his administrations lies in the fact that Reagan never intended to court the black vote. He merely attempted to portray himself as not antiblack (J. Mayer 2002, 172). Thus he was able to achieve far more racially conservative policies than Nixon without suffering the opprobrium associated with racial appeals. The combined effects of Reagan's fiscal and racial conservatism were to drastically reduce taxes while at the same time consolidating and expanding the Republicans' white working-class electorate, who resented government largesse perceived to benefit African Americans. As the analysis in the next chapter shows, had voter racism been absent during the Reagan years, both parties would have proposed considerably higher tax rates.

The Republican Party continued to draw on racist support during George H. W. Bush's presidency. That one of the strongest examples of an implicit racial appeal would be made in 1988 by George H. W. Bush, who was widely perceived as a racial moderate, is ironic; Bush had a much better record on civil rights than Reagan, and he seemed, in some sense, to hearken back to the moderate Republicans, whose last stand in presidential politics came in the third-party run of John Anderson in 1980. While Bush's early attempts to win a Senate seat in Texas in 1964 are clouded by Goldwater-like coded calls for states' rights as he sought to overcome criticisms of his Yankee background and prove himself a southerner, he moderated his tone on civil rights in a subsequently successful bid for the House in 1966. While serving in Congress in 1968 he was a vocal proponent of housing integration, and he apologized for his earlier opposition to the Civil Rights Act of 1964. When he left Congress in 1970 to pursue positions as the Republican National Committee chair, ambassador to China, and later director of the CIA, he rarely had a forum to make known his position on racial issues (Carter 1996, 73–74; J. Mayer 2002, 203–205). But his racial appeals during the 1988 campaign did not involve merely the benign neglect of his predecessor or repeated attempts to link his competitor, Michael Dukakis, with the racially divisive 1984 and 1988 Democratic presidential runs of Jesse Jackson. Rather Bush exploited the racial cleavages dividing the American electorate much more explicitly than Reagan or Ford by highlighting the case of Willie Horton (Kinder and Sanders 1996, 232–233).[19]

Willie Horton was an African American convicted of murder and imprisoned in Massachusetts who, during a forty-eight-hour weekend furlough, broke into a home in Maryland, tied, beat, and stabbed a white man, Clifford Barnes, and then repeatedly raped his fiancée, Angela Miller. The fact that Horton committed this crime while taking part in the Massachusetts furlough program left Bush's Democratic contender, Massachusetts governor Michael Dukakis, open to criticism as being soft on crime. Bush initially vacillated on exploiting the Horton story precisely because furlough programs were not uncommon in many parts of the United States, and he feared that focusing on the crime would lead to accusations of racism that would sink his campaign. However, after his campaign advisor, Lee Atwater, conducted a test highlighting the effect that the Horton story had on thirty Dukakis supporters, half of whom reversed their position and supported Bush, the campaign ran a series of the most racially charged advertisements in recent memory (Carter 1996, 72–76; J. Mayer 2002, 211–214).

One such ad depicted obviously African American men walking through a revolving door in which "by carefully juxtaposing words and pictures, the ad invited the false inference that 268 first-degree murderers were furloughed by Dukakis to rape and kidnap" (Jamieson 1996, 471). Another ad invoking the Horton case contrasted the positions of Bush and Dukakis on the death penalty, noting that while the Republican candidate supported the penalty, Dukakis not only opposed it, but also was in favor of releasing convicted murderers for weekend furloughs (ibid., 471–473). During the campaign, the Horton story became synonymous with Dukakis's position on crime, and for a party that already appeared too beholden to racial minorities and out of step with the American public, weakness on crime was further damaging. Yet the critical point of the Horton ad was that it invoked a racial appeal more dramatic, and perhaps more powerful, than any strategy employed by Bush's predecessor:

> Certainly, the case of Horton conflated issues of race and crime. Just as Nixon's law-and-order slogans of 1968 appealed to legitimate concerns about expansions in the rights of the accused and the spiraling rate of crime, Bush's rhetoric on Horton and the death penalty did highlight a partisan difference in attitude toward crime . . . Yet Bush's use of Horton remains a classic example of "coded racism," intended to activate white hostilities to blacks. In the end, Bush and his associates must be held culpable for the nature of the white response. Even if some voters were merely responding to the crime element in the Horton story, the postelection surveys suggested that the final two months of relentless emphasis on black crime pushed racism among white voters to a twenty-year high. (J. Mayer 2002, 225–226)

Bush won the 1988 election, and by the entrance of Democratic candidates into the campaign fray by 1992, Republicans were clearly the party of the racial right, while Democrats, given the prominent position of Jesse Jackson in the 1984 and 1988 campaigns, appeared to be out of touch with the demands of white America. Bill Clinton was able to alter this perception dramatically when he utilized the 1992 Los Angeles riots as a moment to distance himself from Jesse Jackson and to attack the racist comments of rap artist Sister Souljah (Frymer 1999, 119).[20]

3.7   Race, Class, and Welfare Reform in the 1990s

Indeed, Clinton's rhetoric adopted a seemingly Republican tone as he called for massive welfare reform including cutbacks on "excessive" unemployment benefits and other areas of government spending widely perceived as benefiting "undeserving" African American citizens. Perhaps more telling of the Democrats' reorientation on race in 1992 was that the party platform made no statement on rectifying racial injustices. The race issue had divided the Democratic Party for far too long and had cost the party too many presidencies. The

Clinton-Gore ticket's relative silence on race reflected the belief that by further speaking to the aims of blacks, the party would inevitably alienate further portions of its white constituency. Since the bids of Jackson had proved unsuccessful in the 1980s, and given the racially conservative rhetoric and strategies of the Republicans—a party that included a legacy of Goldwater, Nixon, Reagan, Bush, and Patrick Buchanan that seemed to overshadow any resemblance to the party of Lincoln—the African American vote was viewed as functionally captured. Hence, like the Republicans of the nineteenth century, Democrats of the late twentieth and early twenty-first century can retreat from their racially liberal rhetoric because they do not fear losing the black vote, for it has nowhere else to turn.[21] Discussions of race were abandoned and the Democrats took a page from the Republican playbook by focusing attention on a "new Democratic" call to reform welfare, a call that, as history demonstrates, had the potential to be interpreted in a racial manner. Given the racial undertones of the politics of welfare reform, it is not surprising that, as we will see in the next chapter, racial attitudes continue to exert a substantial influence on the party identification of the American electorate—even when race ceases to be explicitly salient.

The rise of the Republicans to majority status in Congress after the 1994 midterm elections confirms the long realignment[22] of the South from the Democratic to the Republican Party. The trend continued throughout the last decade of the twentieth century: "While the southern Republicans increased their lead over southern Democrats from three seats in 1994 to seventeen in 1996, in the North the Republican surplus fell from twenty-three in 1994 to three in 1996 and dropped to a five-seat deficit two years later. After 1998, southern surpluses alone accounted for the Republicans' tiny majorities in the House of Representatives" (Black and Black 2002, 9). In short, the Republican Party has taken on a decidedly southern tinge, evidenced by the fact that during the late 1990s, the three most powerful positions in Congress—the Speaker of the House, the majority whip, and the Senate majority leader—were all held by southern Republicans—Newt Gingrich, Tom DeLay, and Trent Lott, respectively. While this alignment of the South toward the Republican Party, along with the inroads that Republicans have made among ethnic Americans and blue-collar workers, cannot be solely attributed to their increasing use of racially conservative rhetoric and positions, it can be attributed to conservative policies on cultural flashpoints that incorporate, in part, implicit racial appeals. Indeed, while it might be claimed that the success of Gingrich's Contract with America rested on the electorate's call to end big government and welfare, the undercurrent of racial politics cannot be denied. As Dan Carter (1996) notes:

> Class fears and moral outrage played a critical role in demonizing wel-
> fare mothers; the hostility of middle- and upper-income taxpayers to-
> ward welfare recipients was far more complicated than a dressed-up
> version of the old southern demagogue's cry of "nigger, nigger, nigger."
> But surely it was not simply a coincidence that the issue that resonated
> most powerfully during the 1994 political ad wars was the call for end-
> ing welfare . . . Although whites, by a narrow margin, constituted the
> majority of those individuals on the nation's welfare rolls, almost ev-
> ery American knew that, statistically, African Americans were far more
> likely to end up "on welfare." Almost every American knew that, statis-
> tically, the rate of illegitimacy and welfare dependency was higher in the
> African American community than among whites . . . Republicans were
> exploiting the anger of middle-class taxpayers who believed that their tax
> dollars were going to the undeserving poor . . . The unspoken subtext of
> this outlook was the belief that "these women are inner-city substance-
> abusing blacks spawning a criminal class." (110–111)[23]

By 1994, welfare had become the ultimate code word to carry out an agenda of conservative racial politics.

3.8   Conclusion

The story of race in American politics is a highly complex tale of avoidance and volatile confrontation that shapes the foundation of the political party system and the identities of the parties themselves. This circumstance is not surprising, in that the parties that exist today are the same parties that were born out of the Civil War, a conflict that at its very core was fought over states' rights to impose a racial hierarchy. Yet the Democrats and the Republicans of today bear little resemblance to their nineteenth-century counterparts, es-sentially swapping positions on the continuum of racial politics. The formerly white supremacist Democrats are now the racial liberals following the passage of the Civil Rights Act of 1964 and the Voting Rights Act of 1965 under Lyndon Johnson's guidance. The Republicans, the former racial liberals who utilized the Lincoln strategy of ignoring the South through much of the late nineteenth and early twentieth centuries in order to maintain their dominance in national government, are now reliant upon the South and upon racial conservatism in general to maintain the recent majorities that they have held since 1994. This modern transformation of racial politics revolves around a series of pivotal elections—1932, 1948, 1964, 1968, 1988, and 1992—that showcase how politicians have used both explicit and implicit racial appeals to foment white backlash and/or black fear to muster electoral support. While Glaser (1996) might comment that "Republican campaign managers vigorously deny that they are trying to appeal to racist attitudes with their campaign tactics, and candidates take great offense when they or their tactics are labeled by others as racist" (69), it is clear that playing with race remains a critical and delicate strategy to attain votes. In the following chapter we will see that this tactic has come not only at great moral but also at great fiscal cost.

4

United States: Quantitative Analysis

4.1 Introduction

In this chapter we will quantify the antisolidarity and policy-bundle effects of voter racism on redistribution in the United States during the period from 1976 to 1992, which covers four years of Democratic government (Jimmy Carter) and twelve years of Republican government (Ronald Reagan and George H. W. Bush). We describe U.S. politics in this period with a model of political competition between the two major U.S. parties, as we elaborated in Chapters 1 and 2. In applying the theory to the United States, we will use both approaches (the log utility function approach and the Euclidean function approach) that we described in Chapter 2, although the main emphasis will be upon the log utility function approach.

In the U.S. case we denote by *voter racism* an affirmation of what are conventionally viewed as conservative policies on the race issue, induced by *antiblack affect* and *the belief that blacks are pushing too fast*. (See below for the precise operational definition of voter racism.) This is not the old-fashioned, blatant Jim Crow racism. We leave open the question of *why* the voter in question has the affect and the belief he/she does.

We use two sources of micro data for the U.S. analysis, the Panel Study of Income Dynamics (PSID) and the National Election Studies (NES).

In section 4.2, we start by considering the data, and present our operational definition of voter racism in the United States. We shall argue that the racial

68

dimension has been important (and often more important than the income dimension) in electoral politics of the United States. In section 4.3, we estimate the values of the underlying parameters as well as the distribution of voter types according to the log utility function approach. In section 4.4, we calculate the equilibrium platforms of the two parties using the model described in Chapter 2, with parameter values and functions estimated in section 4.3, and decompose the total effect of voter racism on redistribution into its two separate effects. We find that both the policy-bundle and the antisolidarity effects of racism on fiscal policy are significant and positive in the United States in the 1976–1992 period. The total effect of racism is, we estimate, to reduce the marginal tax rate between 11 and 18 percentage points, and this decomposes about equally into the two effects. We show that the time trend of computed equilibrium platforms traces very closely that of actual historical data.

To facilitate the comparison of the U.S. results with those of other countries, section 4.5 studies the effect of racism using the Euclidean utility function approach.

4.2   Recovering Voter Racism from Survey Data

Various polls and many scholarly works show that Americans have rapidly rejected the blatant "biological" racism, so common half a century ago, that asserts the natural inferiority of minorities and calls for strict segregation. But race as a political issue has hardly disappeared, as we discussed in Chapter 3. Although Americans now overwhelmingly endorse formal racial equality, and much progress in the economic and social position of African Americans has been made in the last half century, significant inequality in the quality of life continues to exist, and American society is highly polarized about it; debates are fierce when "race-conscious" remedies such as affirmative action are on the table, as seen in the cases *Bakke v. Regents of the University of California* (1978) and *Hopwood v. Texas* (1996).

We have reviewed in Chapter 3 the views that race as a political issue has led to party and voter realignment in American politics; see Table 4.1 and Figure 4.1 for the vote share details.

According to the National Election Studies, the support for the Democratic Party in the presidential elections of 1960 and 1964 (the Kennedy-Johnson era) was 60.48 percent. In particular, 61.76 percent of nonrich white voters

Table 4.1 Voting fractions (percentage) in the United States

	Period	Fraction voting for				Net change from 1960 to 1964		
		D	R	Third	Total	D	R	Third
A. Entire population (whites and blacks)								
All	1960–64	60.48	39.11	0.4	100			
	1968–72	37.24	57.83	4.92	100	−23.24	18.72	4.52
	1980–88	43.78	53.06	3.17	100	−16.7	13.95	2.77
	1992–96	47.9	37.85	14.26	100	−12.58	−1.26	13.86
Whites	1960–64	57.86	41.7	0.44	100			
	1968–72	32.22	62.51	5.27	100	−25.64	20.81	4.83
	1980–88	38.19	58.4	3.41	100	−19.67	16.7	2.97
	1992–96	42.68	41.6	15.72	100	−15.18	−0.1	15.28
Blacks	1960–64	93.06	6.94	0	100			
	1968–72	89.09	10.00	0.91	100	−3.97	3.06	0.91
	1980–88	91.16	7.18	1.66	100	−1.9	0.24	1.66
	1992–96	91.72	4.46	3.82	100	−1.34	−2.48	3.82
B. Whites only								
Nonrich	1960–64	61.76	37.83	0.41	100			
whites	1968–72	33.43	60.39	6.19	100	−28.33	22.56	5.78
	1980–88	42.32	54.63	3.05	100	−19.44	16.8	2.64
	1992–96	47.85	38.8	13.34	100	−13.91	0.97	12.93
Rich	1960–64	52.97	46.53	0.5	100			
whites	1968–72	30.11	65.84	4.04	100	−22.86	19.31	3.54
	1980–88	32.26	64.02	3.72	100	−20.71	17.49	3.22
	1992–96	35.34	44.4	20.26	100	−17.63	−2.13	19.76
Uneduca-	1960–64	59.7	39.8	0.49	100			
ted whites	1968–72	32.52	61.7	5.78	100	−27.18	21.9	5.29
	1980–88	38.36	58.88	2.76	100	−21.34	19.08	2.27
	1992–96	45.3	37.44	17.26	100	−14.4	−2.36	16.77
Educated	1960–64	42.31	57.69	0	100			
whites	1968–72	30.92	66.18	2.9	100	−11.39	8.49	2.9
	1980–88	37.62	57.04	5.34	100	−4.69	−0.65	5.34
	1992–96	38.52	48.98	12.5	100	−3.79	−8.71	12.5

Source: NES.

Note: D = Democrats; R = Republicans; Third = Third candidates. *Nonrich whites* are those whose incomes are below the 67th percentile of the national income distribution. Other white people are classified as *rich whites*. *Uneducated whites* are those whose degrees are less than a bachelor's. Other white people are classified as *educated whites*.

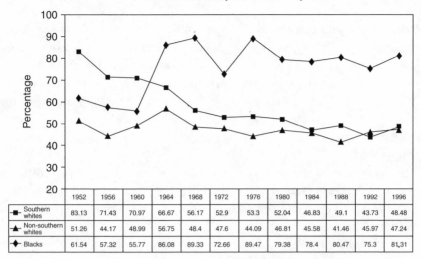

	1952	1956	1960	1964	1968	1972	1976	1980	1984	1988	1992	1996
Southern whites	83.13	71.43	70.97	66.67	56.17	52.9	53.3	52.04	46.83	49.1	43.73	48.48
Non-southern whites	51.26	44.17	48.99	56.75	48.4	47.6	44.09	46.81	45.58	41.46	45.97	47.24
Blacks	61.54	57.32	55.77	86.08	89.33	72.66	89.47	79.38	78.4	80.47	75.3	81.31

Year

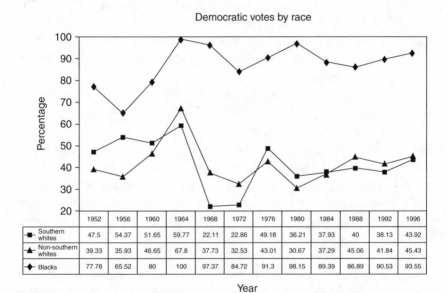

	1952	1956	1960	1964	1968	1972	1976	1980	1984	1988	1992	1996
Southern whites	47.5	54.37	51.65	59.77	22.11	22.86	49.18	36.21	37.93	40	38.13	43.92
Non-southern whites	39.33	35.93	46.65	67.8	37.73	32.53	43.01	30.67	37.29	45.06	41.84	45.43
Blacks	77.78	65.52	80	100	97.37	84.72	91.3	98.15	89.39	86.89	90.53	93.55

Year

Figure 4.1 U.S. voter realignment since 1952. Source: NES.

(whose incomes are below the 67th percentile of the national income distribution) and 59.7 percent of the less-educated white voters (whose degrees are less than a bachelor's) voted for the Democratic Party. The fall in the support for the Democratic Party, in particular among white voters, is dramatic in the 1968 and 1972 elections, a fall that is 23.24 percentage points in total, but 25.64 percentage points among white voters, 28.33 percentage points among nonrich whites, and 27.18 percentage points among less-educated white voters.

In contrast to the percentage of white Democratic votes, the percentage of blacks voting Democratic has since the 1960s been greater than 90 percent. Indeed the black vote is a pivotal factor for the Democratic Party in presidential elections.[1]

This pattern of voting differences across races tells us little about voter racism; whites may have turned away from the Democratic Party because they oppose big government and the welfare state. (Abramowitz 1994 expresses one such view; but see below.) There is a significant variation in racial views among white voters, and trends of racial views shown in surveys differ greatly depending on the kind of question asked. How then do we understand white racism in American politics?

Explaining whites' opposition to liberal racial policies has been the subject of extensive research by American social scientists over the past quarter century. Although details of this research are quite nuanced, the debates have mainly centered around the relative importance of two factors underlying American racial attitudes: (1) psychological antipathy/resentment, prejudice, and negative beliefs (including stereotyping) against minorities; and (2) political ideology and values such as individualism and libertarianism. Scholars have disputed which of these factors is the principal source of the public's opposition to race-related policies, such as affirmative action programs.[2]

We cannot engage in this debate here; we make only two remarks.

First, political ideology is not *unidimensional.* One can, for example, be liberal in one dimension (say, pro-choice on abortion issues) but conservative in another dimension (say, opposition to redistribution).[3] Thus voters' responses on specific racial issues might be a reflection of various ideological components, not just racism. Consider, for instance, the NES variable "7 point aid-to-blacks score," which ranges between 1 ("governments should help blacks to improve their socio-economic position") and 7 ("blacks should help themselves"). One might legitimately argue that the voter position on this variable is shaped not by racism but by libertarianism. As we will see below, both racism and libertarianism play a role in explaining this variable, although a much larger effect is due to the former.

Second, racism is a *latent* variable. It is useful to distinguish between attitude and behavior. Racial prejudice is *attitudinal and covert* while racial discrimination is *behavioral and overt*. One can easily imagine a person who holds prejudices about blacks but does not act generally on the basis of these attitudes. This prejudice might be revealed through his voting pattern at election time, however, when he punishes the party that he believes overrepresents blacks.

To address these issues, we decompose "political ideology" (liberal-conservative) of whites into four *orthogonal* latent factors—racism, libertarianism, feminism, and compassion for the poor—which we believe constitute core components of American political ideology, by carrying out factor analyses on ten variables in the NES for each presidential election year.

These ten variables are: (1) *antiblack affect,* measured by the difference between a white respondent's thermometer rating of blacks and his rating of his own ethnic group; (2) the belief that *blacks are pushing too hard,* measured by the responses on the question of whether the civil rights movement is pushing too fast; (3) the thermometer rating toward *the poor;* (4) the thermometer rating toward *people on welfare;* (5) the thermometer rating toward *trade unions;* (6) the belief that *government is too strong* to be able to respect individual responsibility and liberty; (7) the *lack of trust* in government; (8) the thermometer rating toward the *women's liberation movement;* (9) the perception about *an equal role for women;* and (10) the scale of *political ideology* (a conservative-libertarian scale).[4]

Racism is defined as a factor loading highly on (1) and (2), compassion toward the poor loads highly on (3)–(5), libertarianism loads highly on (6)–(7), and feminism loads highly on (8)–(9). All factors load on political ideology.[5] We believe that our definition of racism is minimal and conservative. Antiblack affect and the perception that blacks are pushing too hard are the "least common denominators" in almost all recent research on racism.

Four primary orthogonal factors emerge from our factor analysis. Which factor becomes the first component (that is, the one that explains the most of the variation of these ten variables) differs across years; nevertheless, four factors came out consistently from our factor analysis across all years (with eigenvalues ranging from 1.00 to 2.5), and these explain about 60 percent of the total variation of the ten variables in each year. By construction, these factors are uncorrelated with each other and each has mean zero and standard deviation 1.

Factor loadings for white respondents in the two end years (1976 and 1992) after varimax rotation are reported in Table 4.2. In 1992, for instance, the first factor loads very highly on the women's liberty thermometer and the women's equal role while loading very weakly on all other variables except political ideology. We name this factor *feminism*. The second factor loads highly on the poor thermometer, the welfare thermometer, and the union thermometer. This factor therefore measures *compassion for the poor*. The third factor loads highly on the questions about whether the government is strong and about trust in government. In 1992, a lower value in this component is positively correlated with the belief that the government is too strong and the government cannot be trusted. We reverted the factor scores of this component (around 0) to get the *libertarianism* scores. (Recall that each factor has mean zero and standard deviation 1.) The fourth component is *racism;* it loads very highly on antiblack affect and the belief that the civil rights movement is moving too fast.[6]

We also decompose the political ideology of black respondents into three factors (libertarianism, compassion, and feminism) using only (3)–(10) (we define blacks to be racism-free), but the discussion in this section will mainly focus on white voters.

Figure 4.2 shows the average factor scores for whites across regions and various demographic factors.[7] (See the graphs in the first four panels.)

For both racism and feminism, the regional gap appears to be more important than the gender gap. Although women are more liberal than men on both racism and feminism, the bigger difference lies across regions, not genders; the West and the Northeast are racially liberal and feminist, while the Midwest and the South are racially conservative and antifeminist. The pattern is different for compassion and libertarianism. In all regions, women are less libertarian and more compassionate than men.

Figure 4.2 also shows how these four factors are correlated with education and marital status. (See the graphs in the last two panels.) Note that education is negatively correlated with racism and positively correlated with feminism. As many authors argue, this finding is mainly because prejudice (toward

Table 4.2 Varimax-rotated factor loadings: Whites only

1976 (obs. = 497)	Variable				
	1 Feminism	2 Compassion	3 Libertarianism	4 Racism	Uniqueness
Antiblack affect	0.01822	−0.07963	−0.07387	**0.82937**	0.30001
Civil rights push too fast	−0.20691	0.0181	0.19432	**0.69206**	0.44015
Poor thermometer	−0.05059	**0.74197**	0.12747	0.01666	0.43039
Welfare thermometer	0.07812	**0.77161**	−0.08294	−0.19544	0.35343
Union thermometer	0.06135	**0.58147**	−0.40796	0.18032	0.45918
Strong government	0.08319	−0.05828	**0.7398**	0.07416	0.43688
Trust government	0.07357	−0.01298	**−0.70663**	0.00232	0.49509
Women equal	**−0.80756**	0.25927	0.0293	0.08598	0.27238
Women liberty thermometer	**0.81714**	0.24631	0.05921	0.02117	0.26766
Political ideology	−0.54612	−0.19377	0.10397	0.22827	0.60128
Eigenvalues	2.03891	1.59067	1.1905	1.12346	
Difference	0.44824	0.40017	0.06704	0.23372	
Proportion	0.2039	0.1591	0.1191	0.1123	
Cumulative	0.2039	0.363	0.482	0.5944	

1992 (obs. = 608)	1 Feminism	2 Compassion	3 Antiliber- tarianism	4 Racism	Uniqueness
Antiblack affect	0.03785	−0.06921	0.01671	**0.86212**	0.25024
Civil rights push too fast	−0.37889	0.02574	−0.07252	**0.62184**	0.46384
Poor thermometer	−0.02324	**0.7910**	−0.05156	0.05249	0.36837
Welfare thermometer	0.09675	**0.7356**	−0.02186	−0.31366	0.35067
Union thermometer	0.13894	**0.68017**	0.20075	0.10673	0.46637
Strong government	−0.23476	−0.19503	**−0.67365**	0.04696	0.45084
Trust government	−0.06428	−0.05826	**0.85737**	0.01266	0.25723
Women equal	**−0.80464**	0.08237	0.01048	−0.08149	0.33902
Women liberty thermometer	**0.63397**	0.42618	0.10187	−0.13395	0.38814
Political ideology	−0.71939	−0.13268	−0.03531	0.18314	0.43009
Eigenvalue	2.57095	1.39317	1.21693	1.05412	
Difference	1.17777	0.17624	0.16281	0.30858	
Proportion	0.2571	0.1393	0.1217	0.1054	
Cumulative	0.2571	0.3964	0.5181	0.6235	

Source: NES.

Note: See Appendix Table B.3 for definitions of the variables. The bold cells indicate the questions upon which the named factor loads highly.

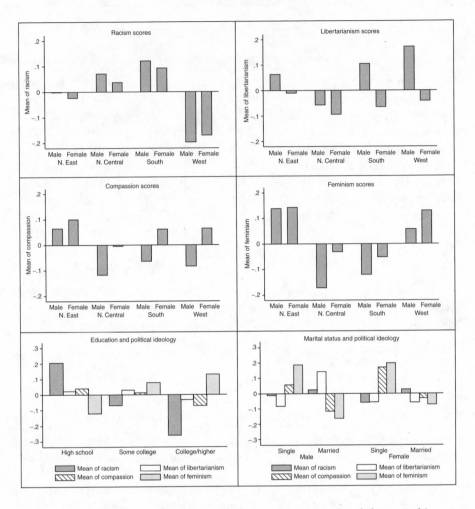

Figure 4.2   Comparison of political ideology across regional and demographic factors: Whites only (1976–1992). Source: NES.

minorities and women) is negatively correlated with the level of education. In the cases of compassion and libertarianism, in contrast, the relationship between education and political ideology is either nil or nonexistent. Marital status matters for compassion and feminism (singles are more liberal in both sexes) but not for racism and libertarianism.[8]

To see how these four factors affect various social attitudes of white voters, we ran a series of multivariate regressions. First, we ran regressions with six dependent variables tapping various aspects of racial attitude. Table 4.3 reports the regression results.[9]

Table 4.3 shows that in all cases, racism is the single most important factor in explaining various racial attitudes, in terms of both the size of the coefficient and statistical significance. We learn that, in contrast to the popular political rhetoric, libertarianism plays very little role in explaining racial attitudes, except for aid-to-blacks. Consider, for example, column (4), which takes as the dependent variable the question asking whether "blacks can become better off if they try harder." A majority of white voters provide positive answers to this question, and on the basis of this observation, it is often argued that whites oppose racially liberal policies because they believe that blacks lack an individualistic work ethic, a belief that is considered *race-neutral*. If this contention were true, we would expect that libertarianism, which is racism-free by construction, would have a highly significant coefficient; but it does not. This point is clearer in column (6). Racists are more likely to believe that the position of blacks has changed a lot, while racism-free libertarians, like feminists, say that it has not changed much. Thus Table 4.3 appears to show that it is not racism-free libertarianism but racism camouflaged behind libertarian rhetoric that explains much of the white opposition to various racial policies in the United States. This type of covert racism parallels conservative politicians' expressed dislike of "racial quotas" or "welfare queens," discussed in Chapter 3—policy positions that simultaneously imply libertarianism as well as racial prejudice.

Our result is consistent with findings of other scholars. In measuring individualism or libertarianism, many scholars warn against treating positive answers to *race-referring* questions—such as "*blacks* can become better off if they try harder"—as a direct expression of individualism or libertarianism. Kinder and Sanders (1996) approach the issue by making use of a set of six questions in the NES that attempt to tap individualism in a race-neutral way (for example, "any *person* who is willing to work hard has a good chance at succeeding"); it could be expected that those high on individualism measured in this way would be those most likely to oppose government action to help blacks. They find that controlling for social backgrounds, there is little evidence of a relationship between these two views.[10]

Table 4.3 also shows that the income variable is very weakly associated with racial views.[11] In most cases, the coefficients are not significant, and even in the significant cases the size of the coefficient is very small. One popular contention is that whites oppose racially liberal policies because whites are richer

Table 4.3 Determinants of whites' racial attitudes

	(1) OLS	(2) OLS	(3) OLS	(4) OLS	(5) OLS	(6) OPROB
	Aid-to-blacks scale	Conditions make it difficult for blacks	Blacks should not have special favors	Blacks must try harder	Blacks gotten less than they deserve	How much has position of negro changed
	1 = pro ... 7 = con	1 = agree ... 5 = disagree	1 = agree ... 5 = disagree	1 = agree ... 5 = disagree	1 = agree ... 5 = disagree	1 = not much ... 3 = a lot
Racism	0.539** (15.93)	0.423** (10.89)	−0.425** (13.32)	−0.436** (12.88)	0.468** (13.38)	0.293** (9.17)
Libertarianism	0.192** (5.71)	0.027 (0.67)	−0.031 (0.93)	0.027 (0.74)	−0.003 (0.10)	−0.051+ (1.74)
Compassion	−0.344** (9.39)	−0.189** (4.53)	0.163** (4.87)	0.137** (3.74)	−0.199** (5.45)	−0.012 (0.40)
Feminism	−0.343** (9.80)	−0.272** (6.46)	0.261** (7.58)	0.240** (6.37)	−0.255** (6.99)	−0.066* (2.16)
Incomevalue10k	0.001* (2.20)	0.001+ (1.81)	−0.002** (3.08)	−0.000 (0.68)	0.001* (2.45)	−0.001 (1.19)
Education1-1	0.380+ (1.81)	0.625** (2.65)	−0.942** (6.36)	−0.971** (4.66)	0.468* (2.28)	0.253 (1.61)
Education1-2	0.375** (4.47)	0.366** (3.61)	−0.625** (7.42)	−0.648** (7.30)	0.309** (3.58)	0.283** (3.75)

	(1)	(2)	(3)	(4)	(5)	(6)
Education1–3	0.289** (3.54)	0.386** (3.78)	−0.431** (4.74)	−0.322** (3.42)	0.288** (3.19)	0.121 (1.57)
Upmobile	0.039 (0.46)	0.012 (0.12)	−0.017 (0.20)	0.003 (0.03)	−0.029 (0.34)	0.035 (0.48)
Downmobile	0.192 (1.27)	0.174 (0.69)	−0.094 (0.60)	0.207 (1.14)	0.186 (0.97)	−0.004 (0.03)
Respondent age	0.000 (0.07)	−0.002 (0.31)	0.006 (1.28)	0.004 (0.69)	−0.009$^+$ (1.77)	0.004 (0.95)
Pre_crm_cohort	−0.195 (1.47)	−0.258 (1.55)	−0.416** (3.17)	−0.151 (1.02)	0.112 (0.79)	0.069 (0.57)
Post_crm_cohort	−0.083 (0.76)	−0.243$^+$ (1.69)	−0.003 (0.02)	0.027 (0.22)	−0.167 (1.36)	−0.080 (0.81)
Femaledummy	−0.064 (0.96)	−0.034 (0.43)	0.000 (0.00)	−0.019 (0.27)	−0.053 (0.77)	−0.101$^+$ (1.72)
Marrieddummy	−0.059 (0.81)	−0.061 (0.73)	0.026 (0.37)	−0.043 (0.59)	0.026 (0.35)	0.016 (0.25)
Unemployeddummy	0.011 (0.07)	0.146 (0.81)	−0.211 (1.35)	−0.185 (1.23)	−0.033 (0.21)	−0.169 (1.36)

Table 4.3 (continued)

	(1) OLS	(2) OLS	(3) OLS	(4) OLS	(5) OLS	(6) OPROB
	Aid-to-blacks scale	Conditions make it difficult for blacks	Blacks should not have special favors	Blacks must try harder	Blacks gotten less than they deserve	How much has position of negro changed
	1 = pro ... 7 = con	1 = agree ... 5 = disagree	1 = agree ... 5 = disagree	1 = agree ... 5 = disagree	1 = agree ... 5 = disagree	1 = not much ... 3 = a lot
Unionmemdummy	0.058 (0.71)	0.022 (0.22)	0.019 (0.23)	-0.155+ (1.77)	0.041 (0.47)	-0.040 (0.55)
Protestantism	-0.004 (0.10)	-0.040 (0.75)	-0.055 (1.27)	0.045 (1.00)	-0.066 (1.41)	-0.019 (0.48)
Region–2 (Midwest)	0.118 (1.29)	-0.075 (0.66)	0.019 (0.20)	0.112 (1.18)	0.028 (0.30)	0.060 (0.73)
Region–3 (South)	0.206* (2.09)	0.022 (0.18)	0.042 (0.43)	0.006 (0.06)	0.070 (0.68)	0.288** (3.23)
Region–4 (West)	0.018 (0.18)	-0.256* (2.23)	0.110 (1.07)	0.293** (2.80)	-0.013 (0.13)	0.097 (1.10)
Observations	1,905	989	989	986	986	1,697
Covered years	All	88, 92	88, 92	88, 92	88, 92	76, 84, 88, 92
R-squared	0.25	0.20	0.30	0.28	0.26	

+ significant at 10%; * significant at 5%; ** significant at 1%.

Source: NES.

Note: Robust t-statistics for OLS and z-statistics for OPROB (Ordered Probit) in parentheses. Year dummies and constant are controlled but not reported here. See Appendix Table B.3 for definitions of the variables.

than minorities on average and these policies benefit only poor minorities at the cost of whites. But our results suggest that whites do not see racial policies as redistributive ones that are costly to them.

Next, we examined how important these four components are in explaining positions on various policy issues; see the regression results reported in Table 4.4. Other control variables in these regressions are exactly the same as those in Table 4.3, but to save space, we report only the coefficients on the four core components.

Rows (1)–(6) report the results when the dependent variables are various measures of government spending. The dependent variable in row (1) is the question about general government spending. Both libertarians and racists are against increasing spending, but the coefficient on libertarianism is not significant statistically.

Results derived from the question on *general* government spending might be misleading, because government spending consists of various components and people have varying opinions about different spending programs. The results in rows (2)–(6) support this claim. Libertarians and racists differ in several ways. Note that libertarians are strongly against increasing public school spending, but the effect of racism is much weaker. Also libertarians want to increase environmental spending while racists want to decrease it; in the case of environmental spending, libertarianism is in line with feminism and compassion. Finally, although libertarians strongly believe that the government wastes tax money, this belief is not strongly correlated with the racism variable (row (10)).

Thus it appears that racism-free libertarians are consistent in opposing any kind of government spending (except environmental), although coefficients are insignificant in many cases. Racists, in contrast, exhibit different attitudes to different spending programs. It appears that racism negatively affects preference for government spending mainly when the spending program is perceived to target "minorities" (such as welfare, food stamps, and so on).

Coefficients in the remaining rows are self-explanatory; we make four observations.

1. The seven-point "government-guaranteed job" scale in the NES (row (7)) is often regarded as a variable tapping the libertarian dimension of policy attitude. But our regression result indicates that it is a conflation of all four components. Furthermore, the most important characteristics in explaining the responses to this question are compassion and feminism rather than libertarianism.

Table 4.4 Influence of four factors on whites' attitude on various social issues

	Racism	Libertarianism	Compassion	Feminism	Obs.	Covered years	R^2
(1) Govt services/ spending: 1 = decrease . . . 7 = increase (OLS)	-0.205** (4.22)	-0.061 (1.56)	0.234** (5.16)	0.338** (7.5)	1,156	84, 88, 92	0.19
(2) Govt health insurance: 1 = pro . . . 7 = con (OLS)	0.226** (4.25)	0.056 (1.14)	-0.326** (6.22)	-0.376** (7.28)	1,541	76, 84, 88, 92	0.17
(3) Food stamps spending–federal budget: 1 = increase . . . 3 = decrease (OPROB)	0.196** (5.33)	0.024 (0.71)	-0.375** (10.16)	-0.236** (6.56)	1,193	84, 88, 92	
(4) Public schools spending–federal budget: 1 = increase . . . 3 = decrease (OPROB)	0.067+ (1.74)	0.108** (2.92)	-0.083* (2.2)	-0.264** (7.07)	1,225	84, 88, 92	
(5) Social security–federal budget: 1 = increase . . . 3 = decrease (OPROB)	-0.029 (0.76)	0.03 (0.85)	-0.111** (3.01)	-0.126** (3.41)	1,216	84, 88, 92	
(6) Environment spending–federal budget: 1 = increase . . . 3 = decrease (OPROB)	0.157** (4.02)	-0.061+ (1.67)	-0.056 (1.48)	-0.279** (7.31)	1,216	84, 88, 92	
(7) Guaranteed job scale: 1 = pro . . . 7 = con (OLS)	0.160** (3.67)	0.200** (5.57)	-0.310** (7.65)	-0.318** (7.72)	1,863	All	0.16

Variable					N	Years	R^2
(8) Should worry less about equality: 1 = agree . . . 5 = disagree (OLS)	−0.310** (7.64)	−0.086* (2.29)	0.200** (5.23)	0.364** (9.59)	1,232	84, 88, 92	0.22
(9) Poor-welfare-union thermometer: 0–100 (OLS)	−0.627** (4.97)	−1.499** (13.9)	13.163** (104.77)	2.560** (17.55)	2,010	All	0.90
(10) Does govt waste tax money: 1 = a lot . . . 3 = not much (OPROB)	−0.029 (0.89)	−0.346** (11.26)	0.068* (2.1)	0.064* (1.99)	2,005	All	
(11) Will people take advantage of someone: 0 = no, 1 = yes (PROBIT)	0.273** (4.03)	0.179** (2.71)	0.015 (0.21)	−0.087 (1.29)	463	76	
(12) Are people helpful: 0 = no, 1 = yes (PROBIT)	−0.266** (5.81)	−0.174** (3.86)	0.016 (0.35)	0.079 + (1.72)	1,000	76, 92	
(13) Defense spending: 1 = decrease . . . 7 = increase (OLS)	0.325** (7.82)	−0.031 (0.83)	−0.003 (0.06)	−0.223** (5.45)	1,473	80, 84, 88, 92	0.26
(14) Urban unrest: 1 = solve by helping poor . . . 7 = solve by force (OLS)	0.447** (7.31)	0.100 + (1.78)	−0.263** (4.11)	−0.333** (5.15)	916	76, 92	0.20

Table 4.4 (continued)

(15) Authority of Bible:	−0.099**	0.032	−0.052*	0.075**	951	80, 84, 88	0.23
1 = agree . . . 4 = disagree (OLS)	(4.65)	(1.6)	(2.52)	(3.6)			
(16) Should prayer be allowed in schools:	−0.166**	−0.061	0.01	0.268**	543	80, 84	
1 = agree . . . 3 = disagree(OPROB)	(2.93)	(1.1)	(0.18)	(4.44)			
(17) When should abortion be allowed by law:	−0.081**	0.018	−0.108**	0.277**	1,511	80, 84, 88, 92	0.20
1 = never . . . 4 = always (OLS)	(2.93)	(0.72)	(3.93)	(10.83)			

[+] significant at 10%; * significant at 5%; ** significant at 1%.

Source: NES.

Note: Robust t-statistics for OLS and z-statistics for Probit and OPROBIT are reported in parentheses. Other regressors are exactly the same as those in Table 4.3. See Appendix Table B.3 for definitions of the variables.

2. Racism appears to be positively correlated with authoritarian and traditionalist values, which true libertarians might oppose.[12] For instance, racism is positively correlated with support for defense spending (row (13)), while libertarianism is negatively correlated with it. Racists strongly prefer to solve the urban unrest problem by force, while libertarians' support for force is much weaker (row (14)). Libertarians are neutral about the authority of the Bible, school prayer, and abortion, but racists are strongly in favor of school prayer, hold firm beliefs regarding the Bible's authority, and take a strong antiabortion position, even after we control for a religion effect (rows (15)–(17)).

3. Racism is also negatively correlated with variables tapping "trust." Racism is positively correlated with the view that "people take advantage of someone" (row (11)) and negatively with the view that "people are helpful" (row (12)). The finding that racism underlies both the perception that "blacks are lazy" and the view that "people take advantage of others" therefore suggests that more careful work is needed on reciprocal altruism, which postulates that people feel altruistic toward others who are good to them and vengeful toward those who take advantage of them.

4. Some authors, including Alesina, Glaeser, and Sacerdote (2001), often find a positive effect for a religion variable, in particular Protestantism, on the "blacks are lazy" variable, or on variables capturing demand for redistribution, and interpret this as an indication of a Protestant work ethic. Compared with citizens of other nations, Americans are certainly religious (in terms of religious preference, 64 percent of Americans are Protestant) and since the time of Max Weber, a Protestant ethic has been an important explanatory variable for American exceptionalism.

This interpretation, however, appears to be too hasty. First, it implicitly assumes that a variable such as "blacks are lazy" is an indication of individualism. Second, it also assumes that members of a certain religious group, like Protestants, are more oriented toward the work ethic than those of other religious groups.

Regarding the first assumption, we have already shown that a variable such as "blacks are lazy" is an indication of racial prejudice rather than of individualism. Thus a proper interpretation of a result like regression (5) in Table 4.3 is that religiosity has nothing to do with prejudice, once ideological and demographic factors are controlled for.

Regarding the second assumption, we emphasize that Protestants are a pluralistic group and on most issues there is greater disagreement among

Protestants of various persuasions than between Protestants and other religious groups. In particular, mainline Protestants and more secular groups significantly differ from evangelical Protestants and fundamentalist groups. Particularly important since the early 1980s are evangelical groups, which now make up 48 percent of all Protestants and about 22 percent of the population. Overall, these groups are very conservative, in particular on school prayer, civil rights, homosexuality, and women's issues, and have always been a mainstay of the Republican Party, except in 1976 when a "born-again" Democratic candidate, Jimmy Carter, ran for election.[13]

Figure 4.3 examines how religion is associated with different social attitudes. The graphs in the first four panels correspond to the average scores of the four components across religious denominations; the graphs in the last two panels show the attitude toward abortion law and the mean scores of trust across religious denominations.

If identification of Protestantism with the "work ethic" were correct, we would expect Protestants to be the most libertarian. What is clear from Figure 4.3 is that it is not Protestants (including both mainline and evangelical Protestants) who are the most libertarian; rather it is nontraditional orthodox Christians, people with non-Christian–non-Jewish religion, and people without religion. (On the other hand, both Jews and Catholics are antilibertarian.) At the same time the figure shows that evangelical Protestants are the most racist, the least compassionate, and the most antifeminist; this attitude is sharply in contrast with mainline Protestants.[14]

Thus the positive coefficient of the Protestantism variable reported in some empirical analyses, in particular when these regressions do not control for ideological components, may be only a reflection of ideological components, such as racial conservatism or authoritarianism. Our results show that once ideological components are controlled for, religiosity is correlated with only religious issues, such as school prayer and abortion, and has nothing to do with either individualism/libertarianism or racial prejudice.

Finally, we examine the importance of these factors in shaping party preferences; see Table 4.5. Columns (1) and (2) report the determinants of party affect, and they show that racism, together with compassion and feminism, is an important factor in determining a voter's party affect. Libertarians do not like the Democratic Party, but the effect of racism is stronger than that of libertarianism; also libertarianism is not significant as a determinant of the Republican Party affect, once racism has been controlled for.

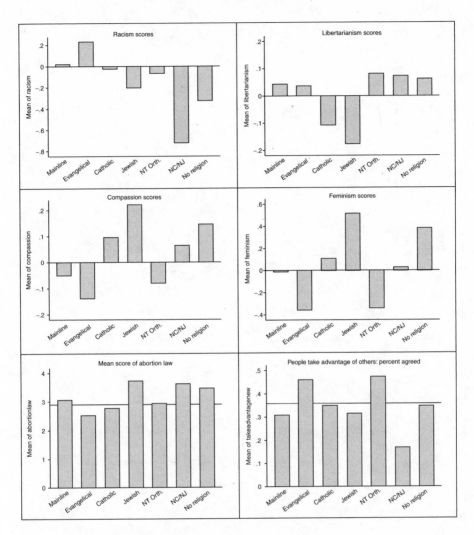

Figure 4.3 Religion and political ideology: Whites only (1976–1992). NT = Non-traditional; NC/NJ = non-Christian/non-Jewish. Source: NES.

At the beginning of this section, we documented the large-scale white flight from the Democratic Party in the past three decades (see Table 4.2). For most people, party identification is a central aspect of political identity. Compared with ordinary political opinions, a person's party identification is quite stable

Table 4.5 Determinants of whites' attitude on political parties

	(1) OLS Democratic Party affect	(2) OLS Republican Party affect	(3) PROB DefectionD	(4) PROB DefectionR	(5) PROB PresvoteR
Racism	-0.214**	0.298**	0.256**	-0.122[+]	0.311**
	(4.86)	(6.82)	(3.34)	(1.69)	(6.90)
Libertarianism	-0.060	-0.047	-0.003	-0.069	0.023
	(1.43)	(1.14)	(0.04)	(1.10)	(0.56)
Compassion	0.216**	-0.155**	-0.192*	0.069	-0.240**
	(4.95)	(3.60)	(2.54)	(0.98)	(5.52)
Feminism	0.513**	-0.541**	-0.303**	0.206**	-0.415**
	(11.79)	(12.52)	(4.11)	(2.61)	(9.17)
Incomevalue10k	-0.001	0.002*	0.003[+]	-0.001	0.002**
	(1.64)	(2.04)	(1.94)	(0.55)	(3.05)
Education1-1	0.744**	0.166	-0.029	0.018	-0.258
	(3.12)	(0.71)	(0.08)	(0.03)	(1.05)
Education1-2	0.067	0.033	0.089	0.294[+]	-0.045
	(0.62)	(0.31)	(0.48)	(1.74)	(0.42)
Education1-3	-0.203[+]	0.249*	0.233	0.122	0.133
	(1.82)	(2.25)	(1.26)	(0.74)	(1.26)
Upmobile	-0.208[+]	0.365**	0.519**	0.095	0.189[+]
	(1.94)	(3.41)	(2.84)	(0.59)	(1.75)
Downmobile	-0.406*	0.091	0.057	0.342	0.294
	(2.13)	(0.48)	(0.16)	(1.26)	(1.56)
Pasteconomy*incumbentisD	-0.230*		0.096		
	(2.25)		(0.88)		
Pasteconomy*incumbentisR		-0.225**		0.199**	-0.244**
		(6.30)		(3.40)	(6.79)

Femaledummy	0.191*	0.059	0.243+	−0.006	0.115
	(2.25)	(0.70)	(1.75)	(0.04)	(1.38)
Marrieddummy	−0.147	0.094	−0.003	−0.137	0.109
	(1.63)	(1.05)	(0.02)	(0.94)	(1.23)
Unemployeddummy	−0.312+	−0.006	−1.033+	0.201	−0.285
	(1.69)	(0.03)	(1.85)	(0.59)	(1.29)
Unionmemdummy	0.180+	−0.337**	−0.300+	−0.118	−0.276**
	(1.66)	(3.14)	(1.80)	(0.64)	(2.67)
Protestantism	−0.109+	0.153**	−0.037	−0.227**	0.203**
	(1.94)	(2.74)	(0.39)	(2.66)	(3.78)
Respondent age	0.000	−0.015*	−0.018+	−0.004	−0.005
	(0.01)	(2.43)	(1.78)	(0.41)	(0.76)
Pre_crm_cohort	−0.008	0.289+	0.227	−0.025	0.053
	(0.04)	(1.65)	(0.83)	(0.09)	(0.32)
Post_crm_cohort	−0.067	−0.145	−0.362	−0.005	−0.168
	(0.46)	(1.00)	(1.56)	(0.02)	(1.19)
Region–2 (Midwest)	−0.055	−0.037	−0.285	0.160	0.074
	(0.45)	(0.30)	(1.43)	(0.80)	(0.62)
Region–3 (South)	−0.062	−0.011	−0.052	−0.195	0.127
	(0.49)	(0.09)	(0.26)	(0.89)	(1.01)
Region–4 (West)	0.135	−0.096	−0.096	0.113	−0.031
	(1.07)	(0.76)	(0.50)	(0.55)	(0.25)
Observations	1,527	1,527	537	595	1,234
Covered years	80, 84, 88, 92	80, 84, 88, 92	80, 84, 88, 92	80, 84, 88, 92	80, 84, 88, 92
R-squared	0.17	0.22			

+ significant at 10%; * significant at 5%; ** significant at 1%.

Source: NES.

Note: Robust *t*-statistics for OLS and *z*-statistics for Probit in parentheses. Year dummies and constant are controlled but not reported here. See Appendix Table B.3 for definitions of the variables.

over time, both before and after adjustment for measurement error. What drove such a large-scale white flight?

To estimate the effects of different types of issues on white flight from the Democratic Party, we conducted probit analyses of voting behavior separately for those who declare that they are Democrats and for those who declare that they are Republicans. The dependent variable in this analysis is party defection: among the self-declared Democrats, those who vote Democratic (D) are coded 0; those who had defected from the Democratic Party (that is, those who voted for either the Republican (R) or a third candidate) are coded 1. Similarly, among the self-declared Republicans, those who voted R are coded 0; those who defected are coded 1.

Columns (3) and (4) in Table 4.5 show that the defection of Democrats was largely due to their dissatisfaction with the Democratic Party's racial liberalism, whereas the defection of Republicans was mainly due to their dissatisfaction with the Republican Party's conservatism on the gender/family issue. Poor economic performance under a party's incumbency is also an important factor explaining the defection from that party. In contrast to Abramowitz's (1994) argument that the large-scale defection of whites from the Democratic Party is mainly due to traditional Democrats' becoming increasingly fed up with big government and the welfare state, the libertarianism variable is statistically insignificant and carries a negative coefficient.[15]

Column (5) shows the result of our probit regression on voting pattern. Because there are only two parties, we report only the R vote share. Again racism, compassion, and feminism show up as important explanatory variables, but libertarianism does not. Figure 4.4 shows the slope of the regression equation with respect to each component of political ideology, together with 95 percent asymptotic confidence intervals; the graph is almost flat with respect to libertarianism.

We have seen the importance of voter racism in various ways; what matters for our purposes is the voter's position on politically salient racial issues, such as affirmative action or the government's aid to minorities. One variable that measures the voter position on racial issues is the "7 point aid-to-blacks score." Complications of interpretation arise, however, because the voter position on aid-to-blacks could be shaped by many factors, not just by racism. For instance, as we have seen in Table 4.3, libertarianism plays some role in explaining this variable, although a much larger effect is due to racism. Simply treating voters who are not in favor of aid to blacks as racist would overestimate the extent of racial conservatism in the United States; we need to

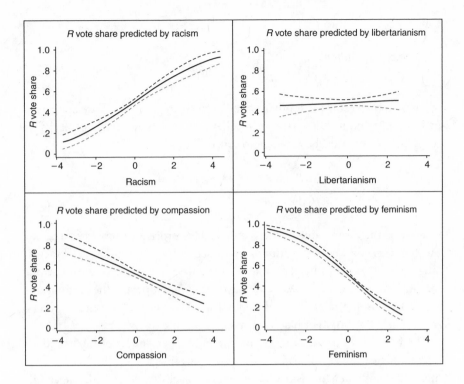

Figure 4.4 Changes in the predicted R vote share with respect to changes in four core ideologies based on a probit regression of Table 4.5. Graphs are based on the estimated coefficients reported in column (5) of Table 4.5. We fixed all other variables at their mean values. Thin dashed lines around the thick solid lines are upper and lower bounds of 95% asymptotic confidence intervals. The asymptotic standard errors of the predicted R vote shares are computed using a delta method (see Greene (2000), 824).

extract from the "aid-to-blacks" answers the effect of other factors that may have nothing to do with racism.

We therefore construct the *aid-to-blacks score induced only by voter racism* as follows. The aid-to-blacks variable runs from 1 to 7, but let us assume that voters' true attitudinal value on aid-to-blacks lies continuously in the interval $[0.5, 7.5]$.[16] For the samples consisting of white respondents, we ran the following regression in each year,

$$Aidtoblacks = \frac{7 * \exp\left(\alpha_1 Racism + \alpha_2 \mathbf{Z} + v\right)}{1 + \exp\left(\alpha_1 Racism + \alpha_2 \mathbf{Z} + v\right)} + 0.5, \tag{4.1}$$

which is equivalent to

$$\log \left(\frac{Aidtoblacks - 0.5}{7.5 - Aidtoblacks} \right) = \alpha_1 Racism + \alpha_2 \mathbf{Z} + v, \tag{4.2}$$

where $\mathbf{Z}$ is the vector of all other variables in the regression (those appearing in Table 4.3) and v is the error term. Then "racism-induced aid-to-blacks" is constructed from the above regression by the equation

$$\rho = \frac{7 * \exp \left(\hat{\alpha}_1 Racism + \hat{\alpha}_2 \bar{\mathbf{Z}} \right)}{1 + \exp \left(\hat{\alpha}_1 Racism + \hat{\alpha}_2 \bar{\mathbf{Z}} \right)} + 0.5,$$

where $\bar{\mathbf{Z}}$ is the mean value of the vector $\mathbf{Z}$. This procedure generates a policy position variable whose variation is explained only by the variation of racism after controlling for other explanatory variables. It also guarantees that our racism-induced aid-to-blacks scores have the same support as the original aid-to-blacks scores. The racism-induced aid-to-blacks is our measure of voters' racial policy position. For blacks we assign the score of 1.[17]

The NES provides information on the public perception of the presidential candidates' positions on aid-to-blacks. Figure 4.5 graphically illustrates the mean score of voters' racism-induced aid-to-blacks together with the candidate positions perceived by the public.

As is clear from Figure 4.5, the racial positions of the two parties' candidates have always been somewhat different, at least in the eyes of the public. If citizens are correctly perceptive, this picture clearly challenges the convergence thesis of Downsian models.

4.3 Estimation of the Model's Parameters

In this section, we estimate the parameter values of the utility function, the joint distribution of voter traits, and the observed policies of the two parties according to the log utility function approach using two sources of microdata: the Panel Study of Income Dynamics (PSID) and the National Election Studies (NES). The estimation is carried out for each presidential election year between 1976 and 1992. We briefly describe our estimation procedure below. The estimated values of the model parameters are summarized in Table 4.6. Panel (a) summarizes those parameter values for the log utility function approach; panel (b) summarizes those values for the Euclidean function ap-

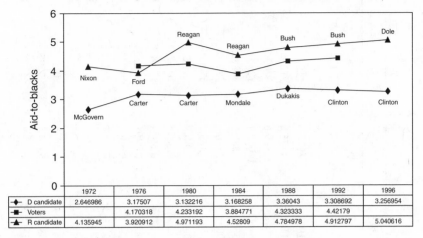

Mean ratings by voters of their own position and candidate positions

	1972	1976	1980	1984	1988	1992	1996
D candidate	2.646986	3.17507	3.132216	3.168258	3.36043	3.308692	3.256954
Voters		4.170318	4.233192	3.884771	4.323333	4.42179	
R candidate	4.135945	3.920912	4.971193	4.52809	4.784978	4.912797	5.040616

Year

Figure 4.5 Mean ratings of position on the racial issue: Voters' racism-induced position and candidate positions. Voters' racial policy position is computed by the mean score of racism-induced aid-to-blacks. Candidate positions are computed by the mean scores of aid-to-blacks of candidates perceived by voters. Source: NES.

proach, which will be discussed in section 4.5; and panel (c) summarizes observed Democratic Party membership (see section 4.3.4.4).

Parameter values will be estimated for each year, but densities and thus our numerical computation will be based upon four sets of data pooled over two adjacent election years: 1976–1980, 1980–1984, 1984–1988, and 1988–1992. The reason for this is twofold.

First, having accurate density estimates for the distribution of voter types is very important for improving the fit of our model; a small number of samples will increase the bias of our density estimates significantly. The sample-size problem is particularly serious for estimating "racism-induced aid-to-blacks." The number of sample points for the racism-induced aid-to-blacks is only about 350 per year. By pooling samples of adjacent years, we double the sample size.

Second, by pooling samples in two adjacent election years, we have relatively stable results that will not be driven by year-specific political issues (for example, candidate personality), which we did not model.

93

Table 4.6a Estimated parameter values of the log utility model (Summary)

	1976	1980	1984	1988	1992[a]	Source
cpi multiplier (1984=1)	1.826	1.2609	1	0.8783	0.7949	ERP
w_M: Male hourly wage (nominal $)	6.18	8.65	10.75	12.79	13.46	PSID
w_F: Female hourly wage (nominal $)	2.72	3.95	5.26	6.78	7.77	PSID
L_M: Male annual working hours	1951.2	1919.8	1925.7	1973.6	1974.5	PSID
L_F: Female annual working hours	850.3	966.0	1101.0	1176.9	1208.1	PSID
Y_M: Male labor income (nominal $)	12790.2	17790.8	23049.4	27769.6	30099.3	PSID
Y_F: Female labor income (nominal $)	3563.7	5542.5	8160.6	11009.1	12703.3	PSID
O: Other family income (nominal $)	1504.3	2124.0	3557.6	4381.5	4331.9	PSID
W: Pre-fisc family income (nominal $)	14978.0	21217.7	29085.3	36310.3	39320.5	PSID
X: Post-fisc family income (nominal $)	13361.7	11357.3	25574.0	32385.9	35000.9	PSID
Gini: Pre-fisc family income (nominal)	0.4211	0.4206	0.4351	0.4489	0.4627	PSID
Gini: Post-fisc family income (nominal)	0.3273	0.3237	0.3471	0.3633	0.3734	PSID
Theil: Pre-fisc family income (nominal)	0.3097	0.3034	0.3435	0.3654	0.3878	PSID
Theil: Post-fisc family income (nominal)	0.1792	0.1734	0.2155	0.2401	0.2534	PSID
$k_1 = w_F/w_M$	0.4397	0.4562	0.4889	0.5301	0.5772	PSID
$k_3 = O/W$	0.1004	0.1001	0.1223	0.1207	0.1238	PSID
Uncompensated elasticity (male)	0.03		0.05			HT
Uncompensated elasticity (female)	0.99		0.97			HT
t_{obs}: observed tax rate	0.3496	0.3722	0.3204	0.2808	0.2793	PSID
b_{abs}: observed per capita transfer (real $)	6609.9	6555.0	5807.7	5509.8	5295.6	PSID
C: per capita public good (nominal $)	1616.3	2697.8	3511.3	3924.4	4319.6	PSID

t^D_{obs}	0.3496	0.3496	0.3496	0.3496	0.3496	PSID
t^R_{obs}	0.2793	0.2793	0.2793	0.2793	0.2793	PSID
b^D_{obs} (real $)	6609.9	6609.9	6609.9	6609.9	6609.9	PSID
b^R_{obs} (real $)	5295.6	5295.6	5295.6	5295.6	5295.6	PSID
r^D_{obs}	3.1751	3.1322	3.1683	3.3604	3.3087	NES
r^R_{obs}	3.9209	4.9712	4.5281	4.7850	4.9128	NES
White population ratio	0.880	0.879	0.877	0.874	0.870	SAUS
Observed D vote share	0.511	0.447	0.408	0.461	0.535	SAUS
Self-reported D vote share	0.49	0.43	0.43	0.49	0.57	NES
Observed R vote share	0.489	0.553	0.592	0.539	0.465	SAUS

Note: PSID = Panel Study of Income Dynamics; NES = National Election Studies; ERP = Economic Report of the President; SAUS = Statistical Abstracts of the United States; HT = Hausman (1981) and Triest (1990); cpi = Consumer Price Index.

a. Parameter values for 1992 estimated from the PSID are based on the 1991 PSID.

Table 4.6b Estimated parameter values of the Euclidean utility model (Summary)

	1984–1988	1988–1992	Source
t_{obs} ($= \mu_\theta$: mean of θ)	2.81849	2.85327	NES
r_{obs} ($= \mu_\rho$: mean of ρ)	2.30252	3.83746	NES
t_{obs}^{L} of militants	3.40906	3.41891	NES
t_{obs}^{R} of militants	2.34848	2.25378	NES
r_{obs}^{L} of militants	2.47445	3.05883	NES
r_{obs}^{R} of militants	4.15815	4.60149	NES
σ_θ (standard deviation of θ)	1.26449	1.25443	NES
σ_ρ (standard deviation of ρ)	1.83933	1.89494	NES
$\rho_{\theta\rho}$ (correlation between θ and ρ)	−0.400	−0.396	NES
μ_θ in the racism-free environment			
(option 1)	3.22246	3.50851	NES
(option 2)	3.08989	3.32441	NES
σ_θ in the racism-free environment			
(option 1)	1.27516	1.23886	NES
(option 2)	1.25029	1.21946	NES
δ	−0.2664	−0.2665	NES

Table 4.6c Observed Democratic Party membership

	Racism					
Publicsize	0–1.99	2–2.99	3–3.99	4–4.99	5–5.99	Total
1984–1988						
0–1.99	0.0000	0.0000	0.2000	0.0435	0.1750	0.1333
2–2.99	1.0000	0.2500	0.2963	0.3000	0.2245	0.3099
3–3.99	0.8182	0.7778	0.6170	0.3500	0.3220	0.4915
4–4.99	0.8718	0.8000	0.6486	0.3684	0.4138	0.6013
5–5.99	0.9189	0.8750	1.0000	0.8333	0.4286	0.8767
Total	0.8785	0.6667	0.5735	0.3121	0.2826	0.4790
1988–1992						
0–1.99	0.6667	0.0000	0.3333	0.0588	0.1744	0.1696
2–2.99	1.0000	0.3636	0.1429	0.3137	0.1905	0.2535
3–3.99	0.8421	0.8000	0.6190	0.3800	0.3885	0.4530
4–4.99	0.9333	0.6667	0.6538	0.5833	0.5402	0.6512
5–5.99	0.9400	1.0000	0.8750	0.8235	0.7200	0.8696
Total	0.9200	0.6000	0.5517	0.4262	0.3413	0.4703

4.3.1 Distribution of Voter Types

In our model, voters are characterized by a trait vector $(\hat{w}, \rho)$. We define ρ to be the racism-induced aid-to-blacks that we constructed in section 4.2. Recall from section 4.2 that racial attitudes are not significantly influenced by income in the United States. This suggests that we can estimate the joint distribution of voter traits by estimating $f(w)$ and $g(\rho)$ separately.

When we examine the conditional densities $g(\rho \mid w)$, we do not find a significant difference across income groups. (See Figure 4.6.) We formally tested the independence assumption using two nonparametric test statistics. First, we compute the Kolmogorov-Smirnov similarity statistic for each pair of conditional densities to see whether they differ across income groups. Except in a few cases, we were unable to reject the hypothesis that a pair of two conditional densities is identical. Second, we calculate the T_1 statistic suggested

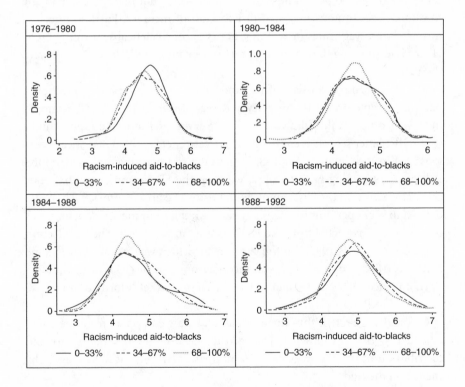

Figure 4.6 Racism-induced aid-to-blacks across income levels: Whites only. Source: NES.

by Ahmad and Li (see Pagan and Ullah 1999, 71, and Appendix A below); we were again unable to reject the null hypothesis of independence against the alternative of dependence.[18]

We estimate the distribution of ρ for whites nonparametrically using the Rosenblatt-Parzen kernel density estimation method. (See Appendix A for details.) We assigned $\rho = 1$ to all blacks in section 4.2, but for the sake of numerical computation which needs a continuous density function, we assigned the normal distribution with mean 1 and small variance that makes the actual support for blacks become [0.5, 1.5). The entire distribution of the variable ρ is constructed as the weighted sum of the two races' density functions, where weights are given by population fractions reported in Table 4.6a.

Next we turn to the estimation of the real wage rate. In the NES, voters are classified into five income groups according to their percentile pre-fisc family incomes: 0–16 percentile, 17–33 percentile, 34–67 percentile, 68–95 percentile, and 96–100 percentile. This classification is not fine-grained enough to estimate continuous marginal distribution of incomes. Furthermore, information on wage rates or working hours is completely absent in the NES. Hence in estimating the real wage rates, we rely upon an independent source: the PSID.

The PSID sample consists of two independent samples: a cross-sectional national sample drawn by the Survey Research Center (SRC) and a sample of low-income families drawn from the Survey of Economic Opportunity (SEO); the latter sample is confined to Standard Metropolitan Statistical Areas (SMSAs) in the North and non-SMSAs in the southern region. To avoid the risk of oversampling poor families, we drop the SEO sample, and base our calculation only on the SRC sample with positive taxable incomes.[19] The PSID data set in year s pertains to calendar year $s - 1$; the labor market data for year s below were constructed from the PSID data set in year $s + 1$. The last election year in our study is 1992. But the last year for which we can calculate income taxes, post-fisc income, and pre-fisc income from PSID is 1990 (using the 1991 PSID). Hence for 1992, we had to use the labor market information in 1990 contained in PSID 1991.[20]

Our real wage rate is thus the nominal wage rate computed from the PSID, adjusted by the CPI index (normalized to the 1984 level). The density and distribution of the real wage rates are nonparametrically estimated, again by the kernel method.

After estimating the two marginal densities separately, we take the joint density to be their product.[21]

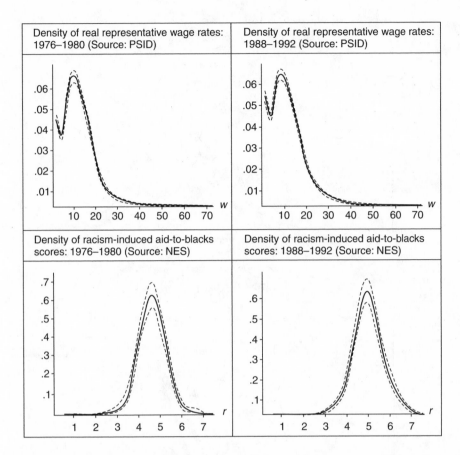

| Density of real representative wage rates: 1976–1980 (Source: PSID) | Density of real representative wage rates: 1988–1992 (Source: PSID) |
| Density of racism-induced aid-to-blacks scores: 1976–1980 (Source: NES) | Density of racism-induced aid-to-blacks scores: 1988–1992 (Source: NES) |

Figure 4.7 Kernel density estimates of voter types and their 95% asymptotic confidence intervals: 1976–1980 and 1988–1992, Whites only. Thick solid lines are density estimates, and thin dashed lines are upper and lower bounds of 95% confidence intervals. Kernel = Gaussian, bandwidth = $h = 0.9 * n^{-1/5}$Min[Var, $(IQR/1.349)$], where n is the number of samples, Var is the variance, and IQR is the inter-quartile range.

Figure 4.7 shows the estimated densities together with their 95% asymptotic confidence intervals for two periods (see Appendix A again for the formula). It turns out that the marginal densities are quite tightly estimated.

Figure 4.8 shows the estimated distribution of racism-induced aid-to-blacks for several years; the first panel shows the densities and the second panel the distribution functions. Note that the distribution of racism-induced aid-to-blacks has changed over time. Racial conservatism, so measured, decreased

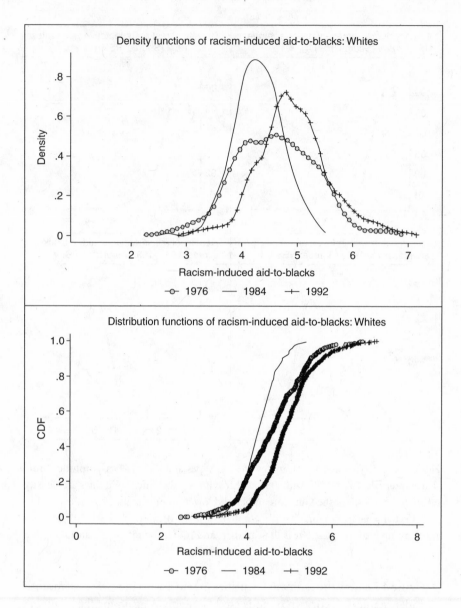

Figure 4.8 Distribution of racial policy attitude: Whites only. Source: NES.

from 1976 to 1984 but increased in 1992. Another interpretation is that attitudes did not change, but the degree to which voters perceived the government's aiding blacks did.

4.3.2 Estimation of Observed Tax Rates and Transfer Payments (t_{obs} and b_{obs})

To calculate the observed marginal tax rates and transfer payments consistent with the affine tax scheme of our model, we regress post-fisc family income on pre-fisc family income with a constant term; then the slope coefficient is $1 - t$ and the constant corresponds to b.

To run the regressions, we need to estimate post-fisc incomes. To calculate post-fisc family income, we first subtracted federal income taxes, social security taxes (paid by employees), and Medicare taxes (paid by employees) from the taxable (that is, pre-fisc) family income, and then added government transfer payments received by each family.

Federal income taxes paid by each household are already provided in the PSID, but the other two taxes are not. We calculated them using the social security and Medicare tax rate table. Since an individual's retirement benefits are linked to past social security tax payments, treating all social security taxes as pure taxes is problematic. We treated the employee contribution as a pure tax, and ignored the employer contribution as in Triest (1990).

For government transfers, we included the following: AFDC, SSI (Supplemental Security Income), other welfare, VAP (Veterans Administration Pension), other retirement benefit, unemployment benefit, worker's compensation, child benefit, government subsidy for heating costs, and monetary value of food stamps.[22] The regression results are reported in Table 4.7 and Figure 4.9.

Several remarks can be made from Table 4.7 and Figure 4.9. First, one might conjecture that the linear regression is problematic because fiscal policies in the United States are progressive. But Figure 4.9 shows that the linear fit is extremely good. The R^2 is higher than 0.90 in almost all years, and the regression with the quadratic or cubic terms does not add much explanatory power. Indeed Figure 4.9 compares our linear fit with nonparametric fits based on locally weighted smoothing (lowess) with two different bandwidths. Although post-fisc income is slightly concave in pre-fisc income in 1976 and slightly convex in 1990, the linear fit does an excellent job. One cannot tell the difference

Table 4.7 Estimation of marginal tax rates and transfer payments

Year	Source	b	$(1 - t)$	R^2	Obs.	Marginal tax rate	CPI-adjusted transfers (1984 = 100)
1971	PSID 1972	2230.54 (42.41)	0.6927 (172.95)	0.9174	2,695	0.3073	5953.1
1972	PSID 1973	2341.2 (44.94)	0.6926 (185.7)	0.9268	2,725	0.3074	5819.3
1975	PSID 1976	3379.2 (51.63)	0.6481 (175.98)	0.9119	2,995	0.3519	6525.9
1976	PSID 1977	3619.9 (52.33)	0.6504 (183.22)	0.9161	3,077	0.3496	6609.9
1979	PSID 1980	4938.8 (48.72)	0.6246 (157.33)	0.8828	3,288	0.3754	7067.9
1980	**PSID 1981**	**5198.7 (50.81)**	**0.6278 (167.26)**	**0.8955**	**3,268**	**0.3722**	**6555.0**
1983	PSID 1984	5643.9 (44.38)	0.6820 (197.5)	0.9202	3,386	0.3180	5887.7
1984	**PSID 1985**	**5807.7 (45.97)**	**0.6796 (219.06)**	**0.9338**	**3,405**	**0.3204**	**5807.7**
1987	PSID 1988	5920.1 (39.24)	0.7102 (229.18)	0.9378	3,485	0.2898	5414.5
1988	**PSID 1989**	**6273.3 (39.44)**	**0.7192 (233.07)**	**0.9398**	**3,479**	**0.2808**	**5509.8**
1990	PSID 1991	6661.1 (38.21)	0.7207 (234.08)	0.9397	3,518	0.2793	5295.6

Source: PSID.

Note: The estimation is based on the following linear regression: (Post-fisc income) $= b + (1 - t)$ (Pre-fisc income), where t is the marginal tax rate and b is the transfer amount. Numbers in parentheses are t-values. Bold rows indicate election years. CPI = Consumer Price Index.

between them except in the range where very few high income samples exist as outliers.

Second, the marginal tax rates increase until 1980, and then decline gradually. The decline was especially remarkable in 1984 and 1988, a consequence of two tax reforms introduced by the Reagan administration, the Economic Recovery Tax Act of 1981 and the Tax Reform Act of 1986.

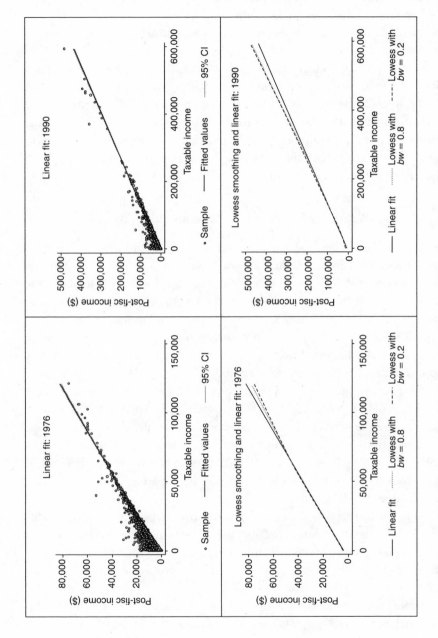

Figure 4.9 Goodness-of-fit of the regression line estimating the marginal tax rate. CI = confidence intervals. Source: PSID.

Third, as the marginal tax rates decline over time, the transfer payments also decline in real terms. As the last column of Table 4.7 indicates, the transfer payments calculated in real terms using the Consumer Price Index (1984 = 100) declined from $6609.9 in 1976 to $5295.6 in 1990.

Finally, one may wonder whether the time variation in estimated tax rates is due either to varying sample sizes or sample units, not to real changes in fiscal policy. To see whether our estimation is driven purely by different samples, we also estimated the tax-transfer in adjacent years. As reported in Table 4.7, the observed tax rates are almost identical in adjacent years. Hence the changes in tax rates over time in Table 4.7 can be considered to reflect real changes in fiscal policies in the United States.

4.3.3 Parameter Values of the Economic Subutility Function

In Table 4.6a, we also report the wage rates of males and females, labor incomes, and other incomes. They are used in calculating the ratios of female wage rates to male wage rates (k_1) and of nonwage incomes to total pre-fisc incomes (k_3). In 1984, for example, k_1 is about 0.49, and k_3 is about 0.12. The ratio of the female wage rate to the male wage rate has gradually increased from 0.44 in 1976 to 0.58.[23] The proportion of asset income in total taxable income has also increased over time but that increase is not significant; it is approximately 10–12 percent for all years.

Using an average ratio, such as k_1, to convert the female wage rate to the wage rate of males may hide the wide dispersion between them. But when we compare the density of male wage rates with the density of female wage rates multiplied by $1/k_1$, for samples with positive wage rates, the two densities are strikingly similar (not reported). Hence converting the three-dimensional type space (w_M, w_F, ρ) into the two-dimensional space (w_M, ρ) for married couples does not discard much information.

Table 4.6 also reports the estimated value of C, which is equal to the difference between the mean of pre-fisc and post-fisc incomes. (If tax revenues are completely redistributed, then C must equal zero, because in that case, the sum of pre-fisc incomes across families is equal to the sum of post-fisc incomes.)

It remains to estimate the parameter vector that characterizes the labor supply functions, (β_M, β_F, λ_M, λ_F). Hausman (1981) and Triest (1990) estimated uncompensated wage elasticities of labor supply for both males and females for 1976 (Hausman) and 1984 (Triest) using nonreduced form labor supply functions, which correspond to equations (2.36) and (2.37) in our model, and using the same methodology and the same data set, PSID. These elasticities are reported in Table 4.6.[24]

Their estimates are based upon the assumption that husbands do not take into account the labor income of wives (that is, $Y_F = w_F L_F$ in our model) in making their labor supply decision, while wives do take into account the labor income of husbands. In the context of our model, the elasticities computed from nonreduced form equations are:

$$\zeta_M = \frac{\partial \log L_M}{\partial \log w_M} = \frac{\dfrac{\beta_M}{1+\beta_M}\left(\dfrac{b}{1-t}+Y_F+O\right)\dfrac{1}{w_M}}{L_M}, \qquad (4.3)$$

$$\zeta_F = \frac{\partial \log L_F}{\partial \log w_F} = \frac{\dfrac{\beta_F}{1+\beta_F}\left(\dfrac{b}{1-t}+Y_M+O\right)\dfrac{1}{w_F}}{L_F}, \qquad (4.4)$$

where

$$L_M = \frac{\lambda_M}{1+\beta_M} - \frac{\beta_M}{1+\beta_M}\left(\frac{b}{1-t}+Y_F+O\right)\frac{1}{w_M}, \qquad (4.5)$$

$$L_F = \frac{\lambda_F}{1+\beta_F} - \frac{\beta_F}{1+\beta_F}\left(\frac{b}{1-t}+Y_M+O\right)\frac{1}{w_F}. \qquad (4.6)$$

We use the Triest estimates for all years since 1984 and the Hausman estimates for 1976 and 1980 (assuming that the elasticity of labor supply does not change much over time). We estimate the four parameters (β_M, β_F, λ_M, λ_F) by solving the above four equations simultaneously while setting $Y_F = 0$ and substituting yearly estimated values of t and b and the mean values of working hours, O, Y_M, w_M, and w_F into the equations.

Once the distribution of voter types and parameter values for the economic subutility function are estimated, we can estimate the Laffer curve in the model. Figure 4.10 shows the estimated Laffer curves together with the observed policy pair (t_{obs}, b_{obs}) (estimated by the average value of two years).

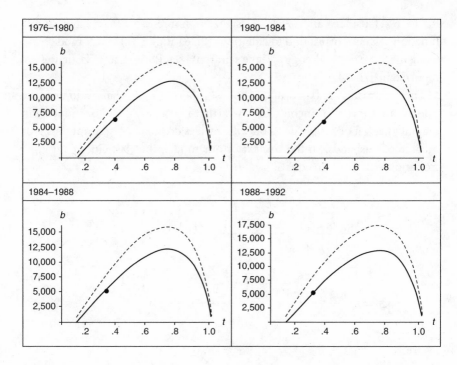

Figure 4.10 The estimated transfer function (Laffer curve), the function $b(t)$. The solid line represents the estimated Laffer curve when the wage distribution is estimated nonparametrically. The dashed line represents the estimated Laffer curve when the wage distribution is assumed to be lognormal and its two parameters are estimated by minimizing the L_2-norm of the difference betweeen the lognormal density and the kernel density. The big black dot in the graph represents (t_{obs}, b_{obs}), estimated from the data in section 4.3 (see Table 4.6). The precise values of b_{obs} and $b(t_{obs})$, and t_{max} for other years are as follows.

	1976–1980	1980–1984	1984–1988	1988–1992
b_{obs}	6582.45	6181.35	5685.75	5402.70
$b(t_{obs})$	6815.52	6353.38	5860.17	5459.48
t_{max}	0.745	0.732	0.714	0.711

The solid line represents the Laffer curve based on our nonparametric estimation of the wage distribution. The fit of our model is remarkably accurate; the observed fiscal policy (the large dot) lies very close to the estimated Laffer curve for all periods. For the sake of comparison, we also estimated the Laffer curve based on the lognormal wage distribution function, two parameters of which are estimated from the data (the dotted curve). (The two parameters are estimated by minimizing the L_2-norm of the difference between the lognormal density and the kernel density.) Superiority of the nonparametric estimation method is clear.[25]

4.3.4   Observed Vote Share, Observed Policies, and Observed Party Membership

Observed vote share, observed policies of the two parties, and observed party membership are also estimated using both the PSID and the NES.

4.3.4.1   Observed Vote Share

Observed vote share is taken from two sources: the Statistical Abstracts of the United States and the NES. In both cases, we take as the population citizens voting for either party D or party R. The former source provides the exact historical vote share whereas the latter provides the vote share based upon respondents' report. Both are summarized in Table 4.6, which shows that the NES vote share is quite close to the actual vote share.

4.3.4.2   Observed Racial Policy (r_{obs}^D and r_{obs}^R)

The NES provides information on the public perception about the presidential candidates' position on aid-to-blacks, which we have seen in section 4.2 (see Figure 4.5). Assuming that voters are perceptive, we took the mean values as the candidates' positions on the racial issue.

4.3.4.3   Observed Fiscal Policy (t_{obs}^D and t_{obs}^R)

Estimating the tax policy of the two political parties is the most difficult part. Tax rates "announced" by parties are rarely observable.

We simply assume that the observed fiscal policy vector before the enactments of the two major Reagan tax reforms is the policy vector close to the announced policy of party D, whereas the policy vector after the reforms is close to the announced policy of party R. Indeed, the fiscal system in the United States was basically unchanged between the New Deal and the early 1980s.

Hence we take the viewpoint that party D's announced policy vector is (no less than) the observed policy vector in 1980 in Table 4.7 (with the marginal tax rate of 37.2 percent) and party R's observed policy vector is (no higher than) the observed policy vector in 1990 (with the marginal tax rate of 27.9 percent).

4.3.4.4   Observed Party Membership

Our model identifies those who vote for a party with its membership, in equilibrium. It is useful to look at how party membership is distributed over voter types. We calculate the party membership probabilistically from the NES by looking at the fraction of citizens voting for party J, $J = D, R$, in each of the 25 discrete voter types. The observed party membership for party D calculated in that way (see Table 4.6c) will be compared with the equilibrium party membership later (see Figure 4.13, for instance). As is clear from Figure 4.13, the more liberal on the racial issue and the poorer a citizen is, the more likely he/she belongs to party D.

4.3.5   The Weight Function

We must explain one feature that is particularly relevant to the case of the United States: the influence of campaign contributions. Consider equation (2.2) of Chapter 2, which represents the average utility of members of party 1, and a similar equation for party 2. In the ideal case of perfectly representative democracy, each member should receive equal weight in both parties. In reality, however, party platforms may be disproportionately influenced by the wealthy via, for example, campaign contributions. Bartels (2002) examines the differential responsiveness of U.S. senators to the preferences of rich and poor constituents, including broad summary measures of senators' roll-call voting behavior as well as specific votes on the minimum wage, civil rights, government spending, and abortion. In every instance, he finds that on average, constituents at the 75th percentile of the income distribution have almost three times as much influence on senators' general voting patterns as those at the 25th percentile, and several times as much influence on specific salient roll-call votes.

We thus introduce a weight function as a shortcut to capture the unequal influence of constituents on party policy. Then the average utility function of coalition H_J is modified to:

$$v^J(\tau) = \frac{\int_{h \in H_J} q^J(h) v(\tau; h) dF(h)}{F(H_J)},$$

(4.7)

where $q(\cdot)$ is the weight function.

Because the rich contribute disproportionately more than the poor, we take the weight functions to be convex up to a cap. In particular, we specify that for both parties the weight function is given by:

$$q^J(h) = \begin{cases} \hat{q}(w) = q_0 + q_1 \exp(q_2 w) & w \leq w_{cap} \\ 1 & w > w_{cap} \end{cases},$$

(4.8)

where $\hat{q}(w)$ satisfies $\hat{q}(0) = 0$ and $\hat{q}(w_{cap}) = 1$, which implies that

$$q_1 = \frac{1}{\exp(q_2 w_{cap}) - 1} \quad \text{and} \quad q_0 = -q_1.$$

We set w_{cap} as the 99th centile of the wage rate distribution. (So all individuals whose incomes are above the 99th centile have equal weights.) The value of q_2 is estimated using Bartels's (2002) result that constituents at the 75th percentile of the income distribution have three times as much influence as those at the 25th percentile.

4.3.6 Remaining Parameters

There remain three unestimated parameters in the utility function related to the equality term and the salience of the racial issue: $(\delta_0, \delta_2, \gamma)$. To estimate these parameters, we proceed as follows.

Consider the utility function (2.30) and suppose that an individual derives from the policy of party J the random utility of

$$v_J = \tilde{\phi}(t^J, w) - \frac{\gamma}{2}(r^J - \rho)^2 + (\delta_0 - \delta_2 \rho)\tilde{E}(t^J) + \varepsilon^J,$$

(4.9)

where $J = D, R$ is an index for a party, and ε^J is a random error term. Then at the observed vector of platforms $(t^D_{obs}, t^R_{obs}, r^D_{obs}, r^R_{obs})$, the individual will vote party R if and only if

$$
\begin{aligned}
\varepsilon^D - \varepsilon^R < &- \left[\tilde{\phi}(t^D_{obs}, w) - \tilde{\phi}(t^R_{obs}, w) \right] \\
&+ \frac{\gamma}{2} \left[(r^D_{obs} - \rho)^2 - (r^R_{obs} - \rho)^2 \right] \\
&- \delta_0 \left[\tilde{E}(t^D_{obs}) - \tilde{E}(t^R_{obs}) \right] \\
&+ \delta_2 \rho \left[\tilde{E}(t^D_{obs}) - \tilde{E}(t^R_{obs}) \right].
\end{aligned}
\tag{4.10}
$$

Note that $(r^D_{obs} - \rho)^2 - (r^R_{obs} - \rho)^2$ can be expanded into

$$
2(r^D_{obs} - r^R_{obs}) \left(\frac{r^D_{obs} + r^R_{obs}}{2} - \rho \right).
$$

Rearranging terms of (4.10) while using this expansion, we have

$$
\begin{aligned}
\varepsilon^D - \varepsilon^R < &\left[\tilde{\phi}(t^R_{obs}, w) - \tilde{\phi}(t^D_{obs}, w) \right] \\
&+ \left[\delta_2 \left(\tilde{E}(t^D_{obs}) - \tilde{E}(t^R_{obs}) \right) - \gamma (r^D_{obs} - r^R_{obs}) \right] \rho \\
&+ \text{constant}.
\end{aligned}
\tag{4.11}
$$

The first term on the right-hand side of expression (4.11) is a function of w while the second term is a function of ρ. If one assumes that the term $\left[\tilde{\phi}(t^R_{obs}, w) - \tilde{\phi}(t^D_{obs}, w) \right]$ can be approximated by a linear (or log-linear) function of income and other demographic variables such as education, and $\varepsilon^* \equiv \varepsilon^D - \varepsilon^R$ is distributed by a distribution function Φ, one may be able to run a binary choice regression model with variables measuring income, racial position, and other controls.

But as is clear from equation (4.11), what can be estimated is the size of $\delta_2 \left(E(t^D_{obs}) - E(t^R_{obs}) \right) - \gamma (r^D_{obs} - r^R_{obs})$. This is an identification problem in econometrics, but it points out an important issue in empirical studies on the politics of race. Many empirical researchers set specifications similar to those of (4.11) to determine the effect of "racism" on voting behavior, and our regression (5) in Table 4.3 is also of this type. But as equation (4.11) shows, the coefficient of ρ combines two effects (the policy-bundle effect and the antisolidarity effect), because it involves both δ_2, associated with the antisolidarity effect, and γ, associated with the policy-bundle effect. Without an equilibrium theory like ours, one cannot distinguish these two effects.

Because of the identification problem, we cannot estimate all these parameters with regression techniques. First, we can only estimate the size of $\delta_2 \left(E(t_{obs}^D) - E(t_{obs}^R) \right) - \gamma (r_{obs}^D - r_{obs}^R)$, which gives a linear relationship between δ_2 and γ. Second, we cannot estimate δ_0 because it is absorbed into the constant term.

This procedure reduces the dimension of the remaining parameter space to two. To further reduce the dimension of the parameter space, we impose the following condition:

$$\varphi(t_{obs}^D, t_{obs}^R, r_{obs}^D, r_{obs}^R; \delta_0, \delta_2, \gamma) = \varphi_{obs}; \tag{4.12}$$

that is, we require the model to produce equilibrium vote shares that correspond to observation.

Thus we have left one degree of freedom in the choice of parameters.[26] The justification for constraint (4.12) is that our full model must be correctly specified at least in one aspect to make our counterfactual experiments meaningful. As we have seen earlier through the tight fit of the Laffer curve (Figure 4.10), our model is well specified on the economic side.

We ran probit regressions to estimate the size of $\delta_2 \left(E(t_{obs}^D) - E(t_{obs}^R) \right) - \gamma (r_{obs}^D - r_{obs}^R)$, which appears as the size of the coefficient on the racism-induced aid-to-blacks. The results are reported in Table 4.8.

Perception about the performance of the economy in the past is an important explanatory variable for vote shares of all years. Dropping this variable will cause some bias for the estimated coefficient. Unfortunately, information on this variable is not available for 1976. We ran two regressions, one with the past-economy variable as a regressor (except 1976–1980) and the other without it. The coefficients are slightly different. We use the estimated coefficients from the regressions with the past-economy variable included, except for 1976–1980.[27]

Table 4.8 Republican vote share weighted probit regression

	(1) 1976–1980	(2) 1980–1984	(3) 1984–1988	(4) 1988–1992
Racism_induced_aidtoblacks	0.193[+] (1.94)	0.695** (3.98)	0.741** (6.41)	0.584** (6.06)
Libertarianism	0.144* (2.42)	0.134[+] (1.83)	−0.146* (2.19)	−0.032 (0.58)
Compassion	−0.300** (4.88)	−0.253** (3.38)	−0.142* (2.03)	−0.270** (4.38)
Feminism	−0.234** (3.77)	−0.217** (2.79)	−0.430** (5.71)	−0.658** (9.70)
Logrealwage	0.104 (1.25)	0.219* (2.24)	0.283** (3.29)	0.160* (2.14)
Education1	−0.796** (2.98)	−0.030 (0.08)	−0.184 (0.49)	−0.589[+] (1.66)
Education2	−0.399* (2.53)	0.173 (0.89)	0.033 (0.19)	−0.282[+] (1.91)
Education3	−0.236 (1.47)	0.153 (0.81)	0.329* (1.97)	0.154 (1.04)
Upmobile	0.076 (0.48)	0.272 (1.38)	0.266[+] (1.65)	0.205 (1.33)
Downmobile	0.132 (0.66)	0.398 (1.42)	−0.537 (1.02)	0.005 (0.02)
Pasteconomy*incumbentisR		−0.218** (2.98)	−0.237** (4.97)	−0.239** (5.06)
Blackdummy	−1.237** (2.67)	0.375 (0.54)	1.005* (2.07)	0.691 (1.56)
Femaledummy	−0.054 (0.46)	0.011 (0.08)	0.080 (0.60)	0.003 (0.03)
Marrieddummy	0.202 (1.48)	0.106 (0.64)	0.002 (0.01)	0.159 (1.26)
Unemployeddummy	0.178 (0.62)	−0.011 (0.03)	−0.354 (0.98)	−0.391 (1.37)
Unionmemdummy	−0.352** (2.59)	−0.536** (3.08)	−0.530** (3.31)	−0.188 (1.31)

Table 4.8 (continued)

	(1) 1976–1980	(2) 1980–1984	(3) 1984–1988	(4) 1988–1992
Protestantism	0.096	0.129	0.126	0.214**
	(1.23)	(1.34)	(1.50)	(2.81)
Respondent age	−0.002	−0.023*	−0.006	0.006
	(0.21)	(2.12)	(0.61)	(0.70)
Pre_crm_cohort	0.107	0.384	0.079	−0.093
	(0.48)	(1.27)	(0.30)	(0.40)
Post_crm_cohort	0.110	−0.422+	−0.267	0.079
	(0.58)	(1.79)	(1.17)	(0.38)
Region–2 (Midwest)	−0.011	−0.108	0.085	0.127
	(0.07)	(0.49)	(0.44)	(0.77)
Region–3 (South)	−0.203	0.123	0.168	−0.146
	(1.19)	(0.57)	(0.79)	(0.82)
Region–4 (West)	0.028	0.128	0.055	−0.209
	(0.16)	(0.58)	(0.27)	(1.17)
Observations	623	448	580	781

+significant at 10%; *significant at 5%; **significant at 1%.
Source: NES.
Note: Absolute value of z-statistics in parentheses. Year dummies and constant are controlled but not reported here. See Appendix Table B.3 for definitions of the variables.

4.4 Numerical Solution of the Log Utility Model

We carry out the computation separately for four periods: 1976–1980, 1980–1984, 1984–1988, and 1988–1992. Finding equilibrium values for all three models (the full model and the ones for the two counterfactuals) requires about 1000 iterations for each set of parameter values in each period.

The full model forms a system of four equations in six unknowns (the four policy variables and the two Lagrangian multipliers; see equations 2.11). Consequently, we can expect to find a two-dimensional manifold of solutions in the full model if there are any solutions, as we discussed in Chapter 2. We formed fine grids of the relevant domain $[t_{min}, t_{max}] \times [t_{min}, t_{max}]$ and started the computation by (randomly) choosing a pair of tax rates from a grid corresponding to the lowest possible values of t^D and t^R (with $t^D > t^R = t_{\min}$); we solve the four equations for r^D, r^R, x, and y for the chosen values of t^D and t^R. In the computation we checked whether (1) the root found by the computer satisfies the four first-order conditions, (2) the indifference curves of party factions are indeed tangent to each other for both parties, and (3) x and y are nonnegative. We gradually increased the values of t^D and t^R and solved the four equations repeatedly, until we covered the relevant domain $[t_{\min}, t_{\max}] \times [t_{\min}, t_{\max}]$. Each run with one set of parameter values requires about 300–330 iterations. The two counterfactual models are calculated then.

In the calibrations, we use the parameters and density functions estimated in section 4.3. Because there is one degree of freedom, we varied δ_0 and determined δ_2 and γ by the two estimated equations:

$$\delta_2 \left(E(t_{obs}^D) - E(t_{obs}^R) \right) - \gamma (r_{obs}^D - r_{obs}^R)$$

(4.13)

$$= \text{regression coefficient on } \rho,$$

and

$$\varphi(t_{obs}^D, t_{obs}^R, r_{obs}^D, r_{obs}^R; \delta_0, \delta_2, \gamma) = \varphi_{obs}.$$

(4.12)

We found that the *admissible* range of δ_0 is not wide. If δ_0 is too small, γ or δ_2 becomes negative. When δ_0 is too large, equilibria fail to exist. (Recall that we have to find equilibria for all three models.) The admissible range of δ_0 that allows us to obtain the equilibrium for *all* years and for all *three* models is approximately between 0.85 and 1.1. We admit that the value of the parameter δ_0 is crucial for our equilibrium computation; unfortunately, we have no way of estimating it. We carry out numerical computations with two parameter values: $\delta_0 = 0.9$ and $\delta_0 = 1$. We discuss the results for $\delta_0 = 1$. The results for $\delta_0 = 0.9$ are reported in Appendix Table B.1.

As predicted by our model, we find many PUNEs. In Figure 4.11, we report the equilibrium values of PUNEs in 1984–1988, the period in which we obtain the largest number of PUNEs for the full model, in several different ways. The first cell in Figure 4.11 shows the equilibrium values of (t, b, r) in a cube to illustrate how PUNEs are distributed. The second cell presents the equilibrium values of (t, r) in the two-dimensional policy space. In both cells, we use black

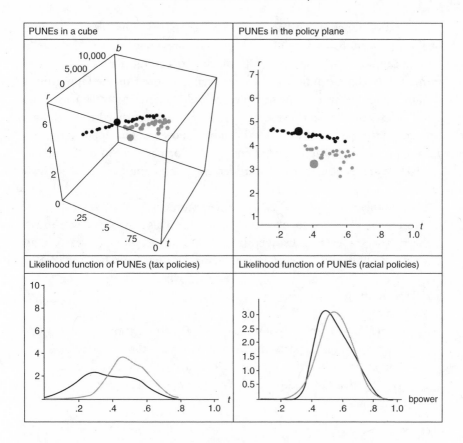

Figure 4.11   PUNEs in 1984–1988. Parameter values for these graphs are: $\delta_0 = 1$, $\delta_2 = 0.1508$, $\gamma = 0.3559$. Black = Republicans; gray = Democrats.

dots to denote the equilibrium policy vectors for party R and gray dots to denote those for party D. The big black dot represents the observed policy vector for party R and the big gray dot represents the observed policy vector for party D.

The first and second panels of Figure 4.11 might give an impression that PUNEs are scattered, which they are. The equilibrium tax rate proposed by party D, for instance, ranges from 32 percent to 61 percent and that for party R ranges from 11 percent to 56 percent in the period of 1984–1988. But they are not uniformly scattered.

To see whether they appear *equally likely* and what the likelihood of PUNEs would be if the same computation were carried out many times, we examined the likelihood functions of PUNEs for both parties. The likelihood function of the equilibrium tax rate for each party is presented in the third panel. As one can see from the graph, PUNEs are concentrated rather than uniform. The likelihood function of the bargaining power of the Opportunist faction, presented in the fourth panel, reveals a clearer picture. This panel clearly shows that the bargaining power is highly concentrated for both parties. The mean values of the relative bargaining power of the Opportunists are approximately 0.5545 for party D and 0.4909 for party R. So in the period of 1984–1988, factions have almost identical bargaining powers in the two parties.[28]

Because there are many PUNEs, we need summary statistics. One way of presenting the PUNEs is to take a simple average. This may be problematic in some instances; a few PUNEs, at both ends of the distribution, can exercise an unduly large influence in determining the mean value. Thus, because PUNEs are concentrated, we take a weighted average, where weights are computed according to the following rule:

1. For each year, we first compute the likelihood function of the bargaining power in each party and identify its mode (that is, the value of the bargaining power that is most likely to appear).

2. For the ith equilibrium, we then compute its weight for each party, ω_i^J, as follows:

$$\omega_i^J = W \left(\frac{\left| \alpha_i^J - \alpha_{\text{mod}}^J \right|}{\max_i \left| \alpha_i^J - \alpha_{\text{mod}}^J \right|} \right),$$

where $W(.)$ is a weight function and α_i^J is the bargaining power of the Opportunist in party J at the ith equilibrium. We chose the popular tricube weight function $W(z) \equiv (1 - z^3)^3 \mathbf{I}_{[0, 1]}(z)$.[29] Thus if α_i^J is identical to the mode, the platform of party J in the ith equilibrium gets the weight of 1; it is penalized as α_i^J moves away from the mode.

3. Finally, we apply the computed weights to calculate the weighted average of each party's platform vector.

Table 4.9 shows the results obtained by this procedure when $\delta_0 = 1$ for all periods. The expected tax rate is the average of the tax rates of the two parties, weighted by the vote share that each party gets.

Table 4.9 PUNEs and the decomposition of racism effect, United States ($\delta_0 = 1$)

	Full	$r = $ rbar	$r = $ rbar, $\rho = \rho$min	Total effect	PBE	ASE	PBE (%)	ASE (%)
1976–1980								
α_D (mode)	0.5421							
α_R (mode)	0.1940							
t^D	0.3473	0.3791	0.4824	0.1351	0.0318	0.1033	23.54	76.46
t^R	0.2212	0.3432	0.4450	0.2238	0.1220	0.1018	54.51	45.49
r^D	2.7663							
r^R	4.1144							
t^{exp}	**0.2927**	**0.3696**	**0.4742**	**0.1815**	0.0769	0.1046	42.36	57.64
D vote share	0.5166	0.7351	0.7814	0.2648	0.2185	0.0463	82.52	17.48
No. of PUNEs	9	45	26					
1980–1984								
α_D (mode)	0.5932							
α_R (mode)	0.2214							
t^D	0.4025	0.4137	0.4666	0.0641	0.0112	0.0529	17.47	82.53
t^R	0.2129	0.3638	0.4391	0.2262	0.1509	0.0753	66.71	33.29
r^D	3.4307							
r^R	3.7914							
t^{exp}	**0.3465**	**0.4011**	**0.4567**	**0.1102**	0.0546	0.0557	49.48	50.52
D vote share	0.5609	0.7466	0.6417	0.0808	0.1857	−0.1049	229.83	−129.83
No. of PUNEs	11	42	19					
1984–1988								
α_D (mode)	0.5545							
α_R (mode)	0.4909							
t^D	0.3709	0.3859	0.4993	0.1284	0.0150	0.1134	11.68	88.32
t^R	0.2392	0.3234	0.4042	0.1650	0.0842	0.0808	51.03	48.97
r^D	2.7771							
r^R	3.6483							
t^{exp}	**0.3109**	**0.3659**	**0.4699**	**0.1590**	0.0550	0.1040	34.61	65.39
D vote share	0.4049	0.6804	0.7906	0.3857	0.2755	0.1102	71.43	28.57
No. of PUNEs	23	52	15					
1988–1992								
α_D (mode)	0.5529							
α_R (mode)	0.0705							
t^D	0.3154	0.3320	0.4409	0.1255	0.0166	0.1089	13.23	86.77
t^R	0.1504	0.3004	0.4030	0.2526	0.1500	0.1026	59.38	40.62
r^D	2.8738							
r^R	4.1953							
t^{exp}	**0.2870**	**0.3241**	**0.4270**	**0.1400**	0.0371	0.1028	26.53	73.47
D vote share	0.5797	0.7508	0.6320	0.0523	0.1711	−0.1188	327.15	−227.15
No. of PUNEs	15	36	11					

First, we remark that the equilibrium prediction in the full model is very close to the observed values; in addition, the time series pattern is close to the historical trend reported in Table 4.7. For instance, the expected tax rate at the equilibrium changes from 29.3 percent in 1976–1980 to 34.65 percent in 1980–1984, and then declines afterward up to 28.7 percent in 1988–1992. This is remarkable, because we only imposed the specification condition that the vote share predicted by our model at the observed platforms be equal to the observed vote share.

Because the expected tax rate is determined by three factors—the vote share, the tax rate proposed by party D, and the tax rate proposed by party R—looking only at the expected tax rate may not be enough. So we examined each of these factors separately.

The equilibrium tax rates are differentiated between the two parties. The tax rate proposed by the Democratic Party is usually 12–16 percent higher than that proposed by the Republican Party. In 1984–1988, for instance, the Democratic Party proposes a marginal tax rate of 37 percent while the Republican Party proposes a tax rate of 23.9 percent, which is also close to the observed tax rates that we postulated in section 4.3.

The equilibrium vote share of party D is also close to the historical vote share, although its prediction is poor in 1980–1984. Our equilibrium prediction is that the vote share for the Democratic Party in that period is greater than 50 percent, although the Republican Party won that election.

One reason for inaccuracy in some years is because the true value of δ_0, which we are unable to identify, may not be equal to 1 for these years. Nevertheless, we believe that the level of prediction accuracy achieved by a model that controls only two dimensions of American political life is high.

The second (third) column in Table 4.9 reports the results of the first (second) counterfactual election; see section 2.6.2. The effect of racism on redistribution in the United States is large. We predict that the Republican Party would have proposed a marginal tax rate of 40 percent in 1984–1988, absent racism. Because of the existence of racism, however, the Republicans were able to propose a tax rate of 23.9 percent in this period; thus the effect of racism on the tax rate is about 16.5 percent in 1984–1988 for the Republican Party. The effect of racism on the tax rate of the Democratic Party is also large. Absent racism, we predict party D would have proposed a marginal tax rate of 49.9 percent; due to the existence of racism, it proposed 37 percent. Similar effects operate in the period 1988–1992. This is consistent with our discussion in the previous chapter, especially with the

Clinton-Gore campaign's conservative stance on public expenditures and welfare.

The fact that the total effect of racism appears to be large for both parties implies that voter racism pushes both parties in the United States *significantly to the right* on the economic issue. Absent race as an issue in American politics, fiscal policy in the United States would look quite similar to fiscal policies in northern Europe.

Although the total effect is large for both parties, the composition of the total effect differs between the two parties; see Table 4.9. In terms of the tax policy, the policy-bundle effect is bigger than the antisolidarity effect for the Republican Party, whereas the antisolidarity effect is bigger for the Democratic Party. In 1980–1984, for example, for party D, 82 percent of the total effect of racism on the tax rate is attributed to the antisolidarity effect.

The effect of racism on redistribution varies across time, reflecting changes in the distribution of voter traits. In terms of the expected tax rate, the smallest effect is in 1980–1984, where the distribution of racial views among citizens is least skewed and has the lowest mean.

The effect of voter racism on the vote share for party D is also large. The biggest effect occurred in 1984–1988 when the Democrats lost about 38 percent of vote share because of racism. This party realignment reflects the Republicans' successful strategy in the 1980s: the transformation of working-class whites into "Reagan Democrats." (Note that during the same period, British prime minister Margaret Thatcher was also able to court blue-collar whites through her use of racial politics; see Chapters 5 and 6.) We note that for some years (1980–1984 and 1988–1992), the antisolidarity effect of voter racism on vote share is positive rather than negative. Recall that the vote shares are affected through two channels: the direct channel mediated through changes in parameter values and the indirect channel through changes in equilibrium platforms. Indeed when we compute the vote share while fixing the platform at the value obtained from the full model, the two effects of voter racism on D vote share are always negative; the indirect effect induced by the platform change has a large influence on the vote share.

Another way of looking at the significance of the policy-bundle effect is to examine the equilibrium party membership. (Recall that our model determines party memberships endogenously, together with the equilibrium policy vectors.) In Figure 4.12, we have drawn the party membership separation hyper-space, together with the observed membership distribution of voter types, for three models: the full model and the two counterfactual models.

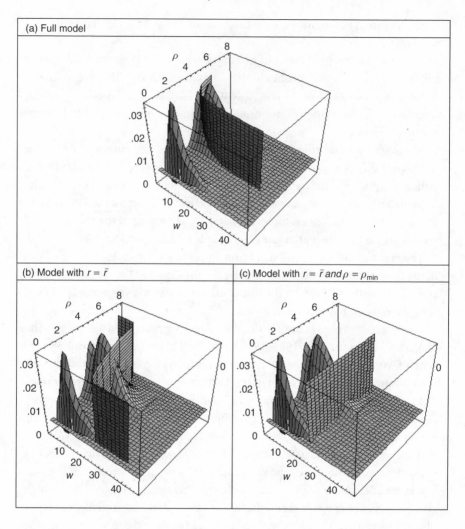

Figure 4.12 Equilibrium party membership at PUNEs: 1984–1988. Voter separation hyperplanes are drawn at the mean value of equilibrium policy vectors. Parameter values for these graphs are: $\delta_0 = 1$, $\delta_2 = 0.1508$, $\gamma = 0.3559$.

Figure 4.12a shows that party membership is more sensitive to voters' racial positions than to their economic positions. The hyper-space that separates the type space into the two parties is negatively sloped in the full model, but the slope is small. Figures 4.12b and 4.12c indicate that, were the race issue not a dimension of political competition, citizens would be partitioned into parties more according to their economic position rather than according to their racial position.

Alternatively phrased, our model predicts an alignment of political parties in the United States primarily along the racial issue, in the sense that party membership for a large portion of the income distribution is best characterized by a partition of the space of voter types that differentiates citizens according to their racial views, not their incomes. If, somehow, the race issue were to disappear from politics, there would be realignment so that membership would be defined primarily by differentiation of voters along the economic dimension. We take this difference between party identification in the multi- and unidimensional policy problems to be quite significant.

We next compare the equilibrium separation of citizens into the two parties, determined by the model, with the real party identification estimated from the actual data; Figure 4.13 shows the graph.

Each panel in Figure 4.13 represents the type space, with the citizen's wage on the abscissa and racial view in the ordinate. In the graph we represent different densities of *observed* Democratic Party membership across 25 discrete cells with different shades of gray; the darker the cell is, the higher the observed Democratic membership. Shown together with the density plots is the party separation graph $\rho = \Psi(w, \tau^D, \tau^D)$, the cutoff hyper-space for party membership in the model. Since there are many PUNEs, there are as many Ψ graphs as there are PUNEs. The graph of Ψ drawn in Figure 4.13 is based on the (weighted) mean value of the platform vector (τ^D, τ^R). If reality conformed perfectly to the model, then each of these graphs would be all black below the curve and all white above the curve. Albeit imperfect, the separation of party membership by the hyper-space is quite close to the actual separation of party membership.

Figure 4.13 shows the historical voter realignment more clearly than Figure 4.12. In 1976–1980 and 1980–1984, the model predicts that many poor racist voters should have voted for the Democratic Party. But these voters are shown to defect from the Democrats to the Republicans gradually, and in 1984–1988, poor racist voters no longer vote Democratic. In 1988–1992, poor voters again should vote Democratic, but this is not because the slope of the voter separation curve has changed; the slope of the curve is quite similar. Rather it is mainly because the curve itself has shifted up.

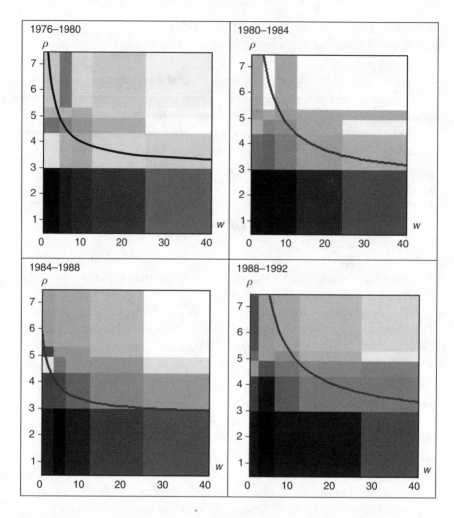

Figure 4.13 Equilibrium and observed party membership. Shades of gray represent the density plot of observed D party membership computed from actual data; the darker the cell is, the higher the observed membership. The downward-sloping curves represent the equilibrium party separation graph in the model. Parameter values for these graphs are as follows.

	1976–1980	1980–1984	1984–1988	1988–1992
δ_0	1	1	1	1
δ_2	0.0640	0.0955	0.1508	0.0787
γ	0.1584	0.2999	0.3559	0.1632

4.5   The Euclidean Function Approach

In Chapter 2, we explained an alternative approach to the log utility function approach. This section studies the effect of racism using this approach.

4.5.1   Estimation of Parameters

Estimation of parameters for the Euclidean function approach is simpler. The racism variable is the same as the one used in the log utility function approach: the racism-induced aid-to-blacks. It is rescaled from 1–7 to 0–6. The size of the public sector, on the other hand, is constructed from the average of the following three variables chosen from the NES: (1) Govt Spending, (2) Job Guarantee, (3) Less equality. (See Appendix Table B.3 for their definitions.) These variables have been scaled differently; for all years and all variables, we converted the original scales into the scales of 0 (conservative) to 6 (liberal). As is clear from the regression results reported in Table 4.4, responses to all these variables reflect respondents' racism at least in part. The variables Govt Spending and Less Equality are available only for 1984–1992. Thus our analysis in this approach is restricted to two pooled data sets: 1984–1988 and 1988–1992.

The marginal densities for the ideal size of the public sector and racism-free preferences for the public sector are depicted in Figure 4.14. We approximate the joint distribution by a bivariate normal distribution with estimated parameter values reported in Table 4.6, panel (b). Almost all the support of a bivariate normal falls on the square $[-2, 8]^2$. (For instance, for 1997, 99.1 percent of the support lies on this square.)

We estimate δ by running a regression of θ against ρ and a constant. Then we estimate the racism-free demand for two different values of ρ_{ref}: $\rho_{ref} = 1$ (option 1) and $\rho_{ref} = 2$ (option 2).

4.5.2   Numerical Results

Figure 4.15 shows the results. Panels in the first row show PUNEs, while those in the second row show the graph of party partition. The support of the density function is $[-2, 8] \times [-2, 9]$. We require this support to get at least 99 percent of the mass of the normal distribution. As in the case of the log utility function approach, the race issue appears to be more salient than the economic issue.

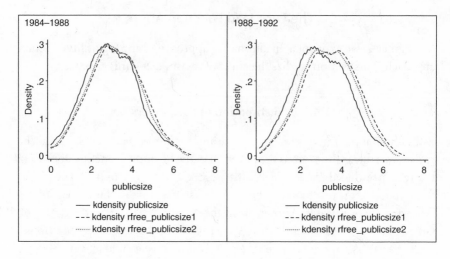

Figure 4.14 The distribution of the preferred size of the public sector and the counterfactual distribution of racism-free preferences. kdensity publicsize: the kernel density estimate of the preferred size of the public sector. kdensity rfree_publicsize1: the kernel density estimate of racism-free preferences for the size of the public sector, taking $\rho_{ref} = 1$. kdensity rfree_publicsize2: the kernel density estimate of racism-free preferences for the size of the public sector, taking $\rho_{ref} = 2$.

Table 4.10a–b reports the numerical results for two periods, 1984–1988 and 1988–1992. For each period, the first table reports values of the bargaining powers, the tax rate, and the race policies of the two parties for the full model, the first counterfactual, and the two second counterfactuals. The second table shows the policy-bundle effect and the antisolidarity effect separately for Democrats and Republicans, together with the average effect (the average weighted by vote shares).

We actually computed PUNEs with two different methods: (1) with no restriction on the bargaining powers in the counterfactuals; and (2) restricting the bargaining powers in the counterfactual PUNEs so that the bargaining power of the Militants in *each* party is within .05 of the average bargaining power of the Militants of that party in the PUNEs of the full model.

The qualitative results are largely similar between the two methods; Tables 4.10 and 4.11 report the results with the bargaining power restriction. (The results without restriction are reported in Appendix Table B.2a–b.)

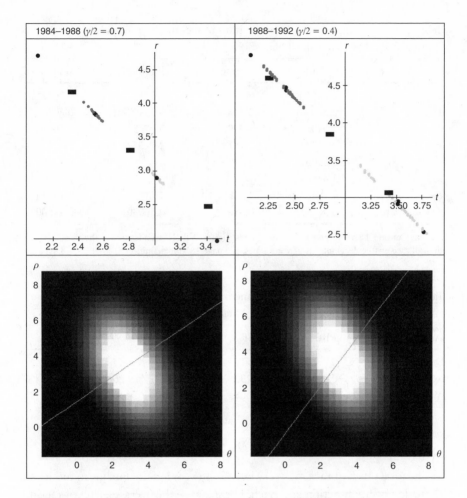

Figure 4.15   PUNEs according to the Euclidean function approach. The space of the two upper graphs is (t, r). The small dots are PUNEs: light gray for Democrats (scattered in the southeast), dark gray for Republicans (scattered in the northwest). The large rectangular symbols indicate the average ideal points of the entire sample (middle), and the average ideal points of those who voted D and R. The circular dots toward the middle are the average PUNE values for D and R parties. The circular dots toward the extremes are the average ideal points of the types who identify with D and R in PUNEs. The space of the bottom two graphs is (θ, ρ). The straight lines are the party partition of types of the average PUNE. These lines are superimposed over a density plot of the distribution of types.

Table 4.10a   PUNEs and the decomposition of racism effect, Euclidean function approach, United States, 1984–1988

	Full	Counter 1	Counter 2i	Counter 2ii
$1-\alpha^D$	0.245104	0.231614	0.248427	0.26727
$1-\alpha^R$	0.26025	0.24313	0.249035	0.263644
t^D	3.02084	3.09978	3.05654	3.46608
t^R	2.5324	2.44143	2.87072	2.73933
r^D	2.8905			
r^R	3.83879			
t^{exp}	2.78408	2.77881	3.21958	3.10014
D vote share	0.515018	0.512387	0.500301	0.496007

Note: Counter 1 are P-PUNEs; Counters 2i and 2ii are Q-PUNEs under two of the three hypothetical racism-free distributions of voter types. See page 185 for definition of P- and Q-PUNEs.

Table 4.10b   The policy-bundle (PB) and antisolidarity (AS) effects, Euclidean function approach, United States, 1984–1988 ($\gamma = 0.8$)

Party	PBE	ASE_i	ASE_{ii}	$\dfrac{TOT_i}{std.\ dev.}$	$\dfrac{TOT_{ii}}{std.\ dev.}$
Democratic	0.0789	0.4677	0.3663	43.3%	35.3%
Republican	−0.0910	0.4293	0.2979	26.9%	16.4%
Average	−0.0053	0.4408	0.3213	34.6%	25.1%

Note: TOT_i is ($PBE + ASE_i$). Std. dev. is the standard deviation of the observed distribution of views on the racism issue.

The total effect of racism is very large in the case of the Euclidean model as in the log utility function approach. For instance the average effect of racism ranges between 25 and 34 percent of one standard deviation in the period 1984–1988.

But there is an important difference between the two models. In contrast to the log utility function approach, the policy-bundle effect of the Republican Party is generally negative, although the policy-bundle effect for the Democratic Party is positive. The size of the policy-bundle effect is also small relative to the antisolidarity effect whether it is positive or negative. In particular, the fact that the policy-bundle effect for the Republican Party is negative is puzzling.

We do not have a good explanation for this different pattern, except to say that these two models are quite different in many ways. The Euclidean

Table 4.11a PUNEs and the decomposition of racism effect, Euclidean function approach, United States, 1988–1992

	Full	Counter 1	Counter 2i	Counter 2ii
$1-\alpha^D$	0.439624	0.417365	0.414733	0.430561
$1-\alpha^R$	0.416716	0.438313	0.436186	0.421754
t^D	3.3263	3.35046	3.99958	3.85993
t^R	2.4131	2.2747	2.93667	2.81256
r^D	3.1669			
r^R	4.45699			
t^{exp}	2.85792	2.82566	3.48233	3.33067
D vote share	0.492704	0.511914	0.513446	0.494685

Note: For explanation of column heads, see note, Table 4.10a.

Table 4.11b The policy-bundle (PB) and antisolidarity (AS) effects, Euclidean function approach, United States, 1988–1992

Party	PBE	ASE_i	ASE_{ii}	$\dfrac{TOT_i}{std.\ dev.}$	$\dfrac{TOT_{ii}}{std.\ dev.}$
Democratic	0.0242	0.6491	0.5095	53.9%	42.7%
Republican	−0.1384	0.6620	0.5379	41.9%	31.9%
Average	−0.0323	0.6567	0.5050	49.9%	37.8%

Note: See note, Table 4.10b.

utility function, which has only one degree of freedom in its parameters and assumes a symmetric (normal) distribution function, may be too simplistic as a description of U.S. politics.

4.6 Conclusion

We conclude that both the policy-bundle effect and antisolidarity effect of racism on fiscal policy are significant in the period under study. Judging from the log utility function approach, it appears that the total effect of racism is to reduce the marginal tax rate by between 11 and 18 percentage points. In terms of the expected tax rate, the antisolidarity effect is approximately similar to the policy-bundle effect, and both effects operate in the same direction. In other words, voter racism pushes both parties in the United States significantly to the right on economic issues. We are skeptical, however, that

U.S. tax rates would increase by 11–18 percentage points, absent racism. The large effects here are probably the consequence of modeling only two dimensions of voter type and two dimensions of policy. See section 11.5 for discussion.

Our analysis provides a very different perspective on the importance of the race issue in American politics from that of Poole and Rosenthal (1997), who argue that, although race has sometimes been a significant second issue, it is of only marginal significance. McCarty, Poole, and Rosenthal (2003) go one step further; they argue that the income dimension has become increasingly important. The Poole-Rosenthal-McCarty analysis, as it is not based on an equilibrium model, is unable to postulate counterfactual histories. Indeed Figures 4.12 and 4.13 show how radically the partition of the set of types into two parties would change were race to cease to be an issue. With the race issue present, the D–R party partition is defined very sharply with respect to racial views, and much less sharply with respect to income class. We thus believe that a unidimensional (economic) model of American politics gravely mischaracterizes the nature of political competition.

Indeed the historical observation that the United States has experienced increasing income inequality *and* significant tax cuts since the 1980s raises one puzzle to the well-known claim of unidimensional Downsian models, which states that the equilibrium tax rate is positively correlated with inequality. If the dimension of income had become more and more important in determining the voting pattern, how could one explain that the equilibrium tax rates have been declining in the period of rising inequality?[30] This chapter provides an answer: the existence of a noneconomic dimension, such as race, changes the alignment of voters in a way significantly different from that predicted by unidimensional models.

Our analysis also provides a different perspective on the importance of the race issue in American politics than that of Alesina et al. (2001) and other work cited in our introductory chapter. These authors attribute the effect of racism largely to what we call antisolidarity, but we have shown that the policy-bundle effect is nonnegligible. As we indicated in section 4.3, running simple regressions with a racism variable as a regressor cannot identify the two separate effects. Attributing the magnitude of the coefficient on the racism variable to the antisolidarity effect alone significantly overestimates its importance.

There are many factors not captured in our model that may affect electoral outcomes; our model captures only two dimensions of politics and two dimensions of voter type. Our results nevertheless indicate that the explanatory power of the 2×2 model is superior to that of the traditional 1×1 model.

5

History of Racism and Xenophobia
in the United Kingdom

Here is the means of showing that the immigrant communities can or-
ganise to consolidate their members, to agitate and campaign against
their fellow citizens, and to overawe and dominate the rest with the legal weapons which the ignorant and the ill-informed have provided. As
I look ahead, I am filled with foreboding. Like the Roman, I seem to see
'the River Tiber foaming with much blood.' The tragic and intractable
phenomenon which we watch with horror on the other side of the At-
lantic, but which there is interwoven with the history and existence of the
State itself, is coming upon us here by our own volition and our own neglect . . . [Britons] found their wives unable to obtain hospital beds in
childbirth, their children unable to obtain school places, their homes and
neighborhoods changed beyond recognition, their plans and prospects for
the future defeated.

—J. Enoch Powell (Conservative MP), *The Observer*, April 21, 1968

5.1 Introduction

In the UK local elections of 2003, when asylum and race relations ranked
just after education and health as issues most concerning British voters,[1] the
British National Party (BNP)—a racist party born in 1982 and led at this

---

This chapter was written by Rafaela Dancygier.

writing by Cambridge University–educated Nick Griffin—fielded a record number of candidates across Britain, mostly in communities plagued by economic decline and high unemployment. The BNP played upon fears that ethnic minorities and asylum seekers received preferential treatment over white natives in the allocation of state resources and threatened to destroy the identity of the British nation.

As Table 5.1 shows, the number of asylum applications increased dramatically in the 1990s, although only a handful were granted asylum. Most applications came from the continents of "people of color" (Asia and Africa) (see also Figure 5.1).

The British National Party, as well as the British National Front, is very much like Le Pen's Front National in France, the Austrian Freedom Party (Freiheitliche Partei Österreichs), and the Italian Social Movement/National Alliance. Thanks to the British electoral system (first-past-the-post elections in single-member districts), which generally produces two-party competition, the BNP and the National Front have never been a significant numerical force in British national politics. However, both parties have been effective in establishing racism and xenophobia as important wedge issues that compete with conventional class-based politics.

The fact that a substantial share of Britain's electorate now identifies with racist populism and ethno-nationalism has had a major effect on the country's mainstream parties. The Conservative Party in particular has tried to court the racist vote. Enoch Powell's "Rivers of Blood" speech of 1968 (cited in the epigraph) is exemplary. The most publicized example, however, is Margaret Thatcher's comment of 1978. When the British National Front fielded ninety-three candidates in that year's general election, Thatcher, as new leader of the Conservatives, deliberately signaled toughness on immigration by expressing her "sympathy" for those who feared the country was being "swamped by immigrants." The dramatic collapse of the British National Front in that year was directly due to the way the Conservatives were perceived by racist British voters. More recently, in March 2001, just a few months before the general election, the Conservatives' leader, William Hague, warned that a return of Labour to office would transform Britain into a "foreign land," in a speech that made the fight against "bogus" asylum seekers one of the Tories' central campaign themes.[2]

For the last three decades, the British electorate has perceived the Conservatives as the more consistent xenophobe of the two major parties. This has not always been the case. This chapter illustrates how Britain's two

Table 5.1 UK asylum applications and granted asylums by region of origin

Year	All regions	Europe	Americas	Africa	Middle East	Asia	Unknown
1986	4,300	200		1,100	1,200	1,800	
1990	26,205	2,200	245	13,870	2,650	6,890	350
	910 (3.5%)	255 (11.6%)	20 (8.2%)	450 (3.2%)	105 (4.0%)	75 (1.1%)	5 (1.4%)
1991	44,840	3,685	210	27,500	2,540	10,495	410
	505 (1.1%)	115 (3.1%)	20 (9.5%)	175 (0.6%)	110 (4.3%)	75 (0.7%)	10 (2.4%)
1992	24,610	8,435	465	7,630	1,980	6,100	
	1,115 (4.5%)	470 (5.6%)	5 (1.1%)	225 (2.9%)	350 (17.7%)	65 (1.1%)	
1993	22,370	4,535	745	10,295	1,520	5,175	100
	1,590 (7.1%)	345 (7.6%)	5 (0.7%)	865 (8.4%)	340 (22.4%)	35 (0.7%)	
1994	32,835	5,360	890	16,960	1,985	7,515	125
	825 (2.5%)	130 (2.4%)	10 (1.1%)	115 (0.7%)	520 (2.6%)	50 (0.7%)	

Year							
1995	43,965	7,050	1,340	22,545	2,295	10,685	50
	1,290 (2.9%)	355 (5.0%)	10 (0.8%)	80 (0.4%)	785 (3.4%)	60 (0.6%)	
1996	29,645	6,475	1,765	11,290	2,150	7,885	80
	2,240 (7.6%)	1,220 (18.8%)	15 (0.9%)	210 (1.9%)	745 (34.7%)	50 (0.6%)	
1997	32,495	9,145	2,825	9,515	2,335	8,570	105
	3,990 (12.3%)	1,870 (20.5%)	35 (1.2%)	1,460 (15.3%)	510 (21.8%)	115 (1.3%)	
1998	46,015	17,745	975	12,380	2,785	11,940	190
	5,345 (11.6%)	1,060 (6.0%)	175 (18.0%)	3,315 (26.8%)	695 (25.0%)	100 (0.8%)	
1999	71,155	28,280	2,025	18,435	4,165	17,465	785
	7,815 (11.0%)	6,480 (22.9%)	5 (0.3%)	785 (4.3%)	415 (10.0%)	65 (0.4%)	65 (8.3%)
2000	80,315	22,880	1,420	17,920	14,415	23,230	450
	10,370 (12.9%)	790 (3.5%)	120 (8.5%)	6,340 (35.4%)	1,350 (9.4%)	1,545 (6.6%)	225 (50%)

Source: 1986: Office for National Statistics, Social Trends 30—Asylum applications, by region of origin, 1986 to 1998; *1990–1993*: Office for National Statistics, 1998, Asylum Statistics United Kingdom 1997; *1994–2001*: Office for National Statistics, 2003, Asylum Statistics United Kingdom 2002.

Note: For each year, first row is number of applications; second row is number granted and approval rate. Typical countries of origin are, for *Europe*, Bulgaria, Czech Republic, Cyprus, Macedonia, Moldova, Poland, Romania, Russia, Turkey, Ukraine, and Yugoslavia; for the *Americas*, Colombia, Ecuador, and Jamaica; for *Africa*, Algeria, Angola, Burundi, Cameroon, Congo, Ethiopia, Gambia, Ghana, Ivory Coast, Kenya, Liberia, Nigeria, Rwanda, Sierra Leone, Somalia, Sudan, Tanzania, Togo, Uganda, Zimbabwe, and Zaire; for the *Middle East*, Iran, Iraq, and Lebanon; and for *Asia*, Afghanistan, Bangladesh, China, India, Pakistan, Sri Lanka, and Vietnam.

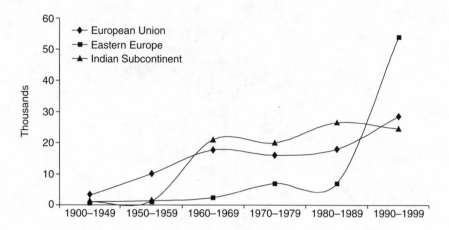

Figure 5.1   Time of arrival in the UK. Source: Russel Haque, "Migrants in the UK: A descriptive analysis of their characteristics and labour market performance, based on the Labour Force Survey," Technical Report, Department for Work and Pensions, 2002, Chart 6.

major parties have treated the issues of immigration and race relations since the postwar years. We begin by presenting a brief overview of immigration to Britain, a process that was set in motion rather accidentally, eluding careful political and economic planning. When the first waves of immigrants arrived after World War II, the two main parties' initial approach was one of issue containment. Early on, intraparty divisions between those who favored immigration for economic and ideological reasons and those who hoped to garner votes by fomenting xenophobia immobilized Labour and Tories alike. Unprepared and unwilling to let immigration disturb the precarious two-party balance and the class-based partisan cleavage structure, the two mainstream parties made joint efforts to keep the issue out of the national political agenda. However, a series of developments challenged and ultimately brought down this bipartisan commitment and ushered in a more adversarial political climate. In an electoral setting where hostility against foreign newcomers cuts across demographic, socioeconomic, and partisan lines and where anti-immigrant third parties threaten to be vote spoilers, the Conservative Party has occasionally flirted with extremism for electoral gains. Because several election campaigns have apparently demonstrated that pandering to xenophobic prejudices can bring in pivotal profits at the polls, playing the race card is likely to remain a common weapon in the Conservatives' arsenal.

5.2   Immigration in Britain

Migration has long formed an integral part of Britain's national experience. For Britain, as a colonial power, emigration of Englishmen throughout the Commonwealth was a cornerstone of the mother country's economic, political, and foreign policy. On balance, emigrants have outnumbered immigrants over the past two centuries. Most went to Canada, Australia, New Zealand, and increasingly to the United States, in particular, after the discovery of gold in California.

Meanwhile, colonial ties also contributed to large inflows of immigrants, initially coming predominantly from Ireland and later from the West Indies, the Indian subcontinent, and Africa. While migrant labor was often crucial for furthering Britain's economic expansion, native Britons generally did not extend a friendly welcome to these newcomers. In the twentieth century, anti-immigrant sentiment often took on a racial dimension. Britain's first "race riots" occurred in 1919, when white mobs in several port cities attacked black workers who had come to Britain from West Africa and the West Indies to help in the war effort. Once the war ended, returning white soldiers, often unskilled and jobless, refused to work alongside black workers, whose labor was in any case no longer needed (Fryer 1984, 298–316).

The majority of today's immigrant population and its descendants arrived in Britain after World War II, in search of economic opportunity and prosperity. After the war, Britain, like most other European countries, was faced with a major shortage of labor, in particular in industries such as manufacturing and textiles. The expanding demand for labor was met by a variety of sources, including 500,000 refugees, displaced persons, and ex-prisoners of war from Europe between 1946 and 1951, and a further 350,000 European nationals between 1945 and 1957 (Solomos 1993). However, the overwhelming majority of immigrants came to Britain from Ireland and the New Commonwealth, or NCW, countries (a code word for "colored" in the UK), primarily from the West Indies and the Indian subcontinent (Miles and Brown 2003).

Despite confronting severe labor shortages, however, British governments were wary of the prospect of expansive immigration from the colonies to Britain. In its report on the United Kingdom's demographic development, the

1949 Royal Commission on Population advised against large-scale immigration from Britain's colonies even as its gloomy forecasts warned of massive population declines and critical labor shortages. Instead, the commission promoted pro-natalist policies that would help maintain the "Britishness" of the United Kingdom. In particular, the commission's report ruled out immigration of nonwhite colonists, for British society could only be expected to receive migrants who were of "good human stock and were not prevented by their religion or race from intermarrying with the host population and becoming merged in it" (Paul 1997, 128, quoting the 1949 Report of the Royal Commission on Population). Indeed the British government had reservations about the absorption of "colored" workers into British society and feared that West Indian immigrants would prefer to live off unemployment benefits in Britain than to seek employment (Layton-Henry 1992, 12, 29). These fears were not voiced in regard to white European foreign workers, mostly soldiers, displaced persons, and former prisoners of war from Eastern Europe and Germany, whom the committee welcomed (Paul 1997, 78–79, 87–88).

Over the next four decades, successive governments enacted a series of immigration restrictions. These controls ultimately failed to prevent Britain from becoming the multicultural country it is today. Half a century after the Royal Commission advised against immigration, Britain's ethnic minority population numbers 4.64 million, or 7.6 percent of the population (see Table 5.2).[3]

While policymakers had been preoccupied with preserving and promoting the (white) British empire, they did not anticipate that their vision of the British Commonwealth, in which all subjects traveled, worked, and set-

Table 5.2   Ethnic minorities in Great Britain

Year	Nonwhites (percent)	Composition of minorities (percent)			
		South Asian	Black	Chinese	Other
1961	0.73				
1971	2.16				
1981	3.73				
1991	5.50	49.1	29.1	5.5	16.4
2001	7.60	44.5	27.1	4.2	24.1

Source: Spencer (1997); Commission for Racial Equality, "Ethnic Minorities in Britain," CRE Factsheets, 1999; White (2002).

tled freely as British citizens, would facilitate extensive, permanent settlement of New Commonwealth colonists in Britain. The 1948 Nationality Act, which granted all Commonwealth subjects full citizenship rights in the United Kingdom by creating one common definition of British nationality, was born out of an attachment to the ideology of the Old Commonwealth of Canada, New Zealand, Australia, and South Africa. A bipartisan consensus supported the maintenance of free movement throughout the Commonwealth, for it was widely assumed that the main population transfers would consist of English emigration. The major side effect of the act—large-scale immigration from the West Indies, Africa, and the Indian subcontinent—was not even conceived of when the uncontroversial act passed through Parliament (Hansen 2000, 17). Thus, while the British government had decided against a policy of organized labor recruitment from abroad, the legal framework of Commonwealth citizenship made it possible for hundreds of thousands of immigrants to enter and settle in Britain.

Between 1948 and the first half of 1962 (the year of the first immigration controls, see below), net migration from the New Commonwealth and colonies had reached half a million. The majority of these newcomers hailed from the West Indies (55 percent), followed by immigrants from India (16 percent) and Pakistan (13 percent) (see Table 5.3a, own calculations and

Table 5.3a   Net immigration from colonies and New Commonwealth: January 1, 1948, to June 30, 1962

Year	West Indies	India	Pakistan	Others	Total
1948–1953	14,000	2,500	1,500	10,000	28,000
1954	11,000	800	500	6,000	18,300
1955	27,550	5,800	1,850	7,500	42,700
1956	29,800	5,600	2,050	9,400	46,850
1957	23,000	6,600	5,200	7,600	42,400
1958	15,000	6,200	4,700	3,950	29,850
1959	16,400	2,950	850	1,400	21,600
1960	49,650	5,900	2,500	−350	57,700
1961	66,300	23,750	25,100	21,250	136,400
June 30, 1962	27,037	19,245	23,837	13,652	83,771

Source: Hiro (1991), app. 2.
Note: The 1962 Commonwealth Immigrants Act went into effect on July 1, 1962.

Table 5.3b Number of citizens of colonies and New Commonwealth allowed to settle in Britain: July 1, 1962, to December 31, 1972

Year	West Indies	India	Pakistan	UK passport holders from East Africa	Others	Total
July–Dec. 1962	7,004	2,855	1,106		7,849	18,814
1963	7,928	17,498	16,336		15,287	57,049
1964	14,848	15,513	10,980		20,776	62,117
1965	14,828	17,086	9,401		12,336	53,651
1966	10,928	16,708	10,245		8,721	46,602
1967	12,424	19,067	18,644		7,513	57,648
1968	7,013	23,147	13,426		12,617	56,203
1969	4,531	10,958	12,658	6,249	5,795	40,191
1970	3,934	7,158	9,863	6,839	5,707	33,501
1971	2,774	6,874	6,957	11,564	5,006	33,175
1972	2,453	7,589	5,399	34,825[a]	9,584	59,850

Source: Hiro (1991), app. 2.
Note: The 1971 Immigration Act went into effect on July 1, 1973.
a. This figure includes about 27,000 Ugandan Asians.

Table 5.3b–c for later years). These migrants were eager to fill job vacancies and generally took up employment in declining or less profitable sectors of the economy—manufacturing, mining, textiles, and transport, for example—that had become undesirable to the native workforce. With the exception of those working in the health sector, these foreign workers tended to take jobs that required skills well below their qualifications and training (Fryer 1984, 374).

The process of mass migration was thus set in motion. Supply and demand dynamics were embedded in a liberal legal framework that allowed for expansive immigration. Ill-equipped for this almost accidental inflow of migrants, the British political elite had no well-conceived policy blueprint to follow and instead opted for a strategy of issue containment.

5.3 An Issue of "High Potential"

British politicians, policymakers, and, most of all, the British public had not been prepared for the influx of immigrants and the establishment of im-

Table 5.3c   Number of citizens of colonies and New Commonwealth allowed to settle in Britain: July 1, 1973, to December 31, 1988

	West Indies	India	Pakistan	Bangladesh	UK passport holders from East Africa	Others	Total
1973	2,685	6,240	3,638	1,753	10,443	7,488	32,247
1974	3,198	6,654	4,401	1,022	13,436	13,820	42,531
1975	3,698	10,195	7,724	3,276	13,792	14,580	53,265
1976	2,697	11,021	11,699	3,975	11,655	13,966	55,013
1977	2,237	7,339	13,331	3,306	6,401	11,541	44,155
1978	1,753	9,886	12,425	4,385	5,350	9,140	42,939
1979	1,282	9,268	10,945	3,915	4,038	7,599	37,047
1980	1,080	7,930	9,080	5,210	3,030[a]	7,290	33,620
1981	980	6,590	8,970	5,810	2,780	6,240	31,370
1982	770	5,410	7,750	7,020	2,720	6,710	30,380
1983	750	5,380	6,440	4,870	3,280	6,830	27,550
1984	680	5,140	5,510	4,180	2,690	6,600	24,800
1985	770	5,500	6,680	5,330	2,180	6,590	27,050
1986	830	4,210	5,580	4,760	1,680	5,600	22,660
1987	890	4,610	3,930	3,080	1,860	6,460	20,830
1988	1,030	5,020	4,280	2,890	1,910	7,670	22,800

Source: Hiro (1991), app. 2.
a. The classification was changed from "UK passport holders from East Africa" to "British Overseas Citizens."

migrant communities in their neighborhoods. Having ruled out organized immigration as an official policy, British government leaders at the time nevertheless did not put a stop to immigration and also did next to nothing to assist in the accommodation or employment of their fellow immigrant citizens (Castles and Kosack 1973, 275). A similar attitude of "benign neglect" pervaded government strategy in tackling the issue of immigration politically. From the inception of mass immigration, Labour and Conservative leaders tacitly agreed that it would be most advantageous to both parties if immigration were kept under the political radar, for not only would politicization of the issue prove internally divisive for the two parties but the electoral gains to be collected from such politicization were also far from certain. Notwithstanding these reservations, immigration controls soon received utmost political publicity. As anti-immigrant sentiment grew and intensified among a large share of the British public, anti-immigrant factions within the Conservative Party gained momentum. The Conservative government decided to impose immigration controls in 1961, which would be further tightened by the following Labour government in 1965 and 1968.

5.3.1 Between Imposed Silence and Outspoken Racism

Most observers attribute the bipartisan conspiratorial silence on immigration to two related variables: the inflexibility of the British political system to address issues that cut across traditional cleavage structures in general and the internal divisions within the two parties on the specific matter of immigration in particular. With regard to the first constraint, Miller writes:

> A two-party system must treat one issue as the basis for political division and the other [cross-cutting issue] as a dangerously misleading distraction that would erode party discipline if not suppressed. The parties can choose, and must choose, those subjects on which they will fight and those on which they will present a united front, for the alternative is to retreat from party government itself. As long as the parties are in collusion on policies which are generally popular . . . the situation is stable. (Miller 1980, 17)

In the 1950s and 1960s, the Labour and Tory leadership consensus to suppress public discussion about immigration in the face of growing public interest in the subject was an open secret and commented on by contemporary observers. Deakin (1965) notes that "the tacit agreement of central party headquarters prevents the twin issues of immigration and colour from becoming a major feature of the national [1964] election campaign" (10). In concluding, he blames protest votes and abstentions in this election on the intransigent electoral configuration: "Where an issue cuts across the established lines in this way the British electoral system severely limits the way in which a voter can register his discontent" (158). This tacit consensus also had much to do with the internal divisions on the issues of immigration and race that deadlocked constructive policymaking.

Regarding the second constraint, the two parties were split into several factions. The Conservative Party was roughly split into three. The first faction, the "Tory Radicals," was steadfastly opposed to discrimination and committed to racial integration. However, "this group is distinguished not so much by its general bias towards philanthropy, nor for its racial drive, but for its understanding of modern economics" (Foot 1965, 153). Recognizing the vital need for immigrant labor in economic reconstruction and expansion, the Tory Radicals sought to copy the guestworker schemes that many West European countries had adopted. The "Traditional Right" represented a second opinion on the matter. Dedicated to the ideals of the Commonwealth, this group viewed free movement of its subjects as an essential foundation of the British Empire, which it hoped to preserve. A final faction, labeled the "New Right," was vehemently opposed to immigration and drew most of its support from the Tory middle class. Fearing that immigrant communities would dilute the British character of the nation, they lobbied for immigration controls as the only way to prevent this type of "mongrelization" (Foot 1965, 153–157; Messina 1989, 24–25).

The Labour Party was equally split. In fact, two Labour factions had views on immigration and race very similar to those of the Tory Radicals and Traditionalists, endorsing continued immigration for commitments to economic and Commonwealth principles, respectively. Contending that an immigrant invasion would eat away the privileges of the British working class, a third faction stoked anxieties and anti-immigrant hostility among its lower-class supporters in the hopes of attractive electoral returns (Foot 1965, 189–190; Messina 1989, 28–29).

Given this constellation of interests, the respective party leaderships calculated that addressing the issue of immigration would have risked fractious infighting within the parties and upset the traditional balance of Britain's political system. However, while the alliance of the Radicals and the Traditionalists, both within and across parties, had helped to keep Britain's borders open to nonwhite migrants and the topic closed for discussion, public sentiment against continued immigration hardened and events unfolded that would force the issue to the center of national attention.

5.3.2 The Local Impact of Immigration: Competition and Discontent

Beneath the veneer of principled acceptance of immigration fostered at the level of national politics, tensions in the localities where immigrants actually settled soon made themselves felt. Immigrants predominantly settled in urban areas where the labor shortages were most severe, particularly in Greater London and the West Midlands conurbations (Birmingham), but also in the Greater Manchester area and West Yorkshire (Layton-Henry 1992, 14). Once the newcomers were settled, a process of chain migration set in that contributed to the further concentration of the immigrant population in certain areas. The uneven geographical distribution of the migrant communities was quite visible early on.[4] By the mid-1960s, many of the 630 parliamentary constituencies housed no NCW immigrants and in more than half, these immigrants constituted less than 1 percent of the resident population. However, in 51 constituencies NCW immigrants made up between 5 and 15 percent of the resident population (Money 1997, 700–701).

The spatial concentration of immigrants exacerbated an already critical housing situation in many cities and towns. While tight labor markets muted the competition in the employment sector in the early years of immigrant arrival, the situation on the overcrowded housing market was quite different. In the 1960s, England and Wales faced severe housing shortages; millions of houses were old and dilapidated and in need of replacement, and households were often forced to share accommodations with other families. In light of this adverse set-up, the entry of migrant workers into the housing market was often greeted with resentment and discrimination. Landlords regularly put up "No Coloured" and "Europeans Only" signs, and local newspaper advertisements did not refrain from specifying that immigrants "of colour" need not apply (Daniel 1968, 154; Hiro 1991, 50). Constrained in their accommodation choices, immigrants often settled for the purchase of cheap, run-down houses, abandoned by the native population, which were occupied by several households at a time. This overcrowding brought about unsanitary conditions and inevitable further property damage, and soon many immigrant neighborhoods were associated with urban decay and ghettoization in the public's mind (Moore 1975, 11). When immigrants became eligible for state-subsidized council housing, their accommodations did not always improve and the resentment by the local population—who often felt that they were more entitled to these government benefits than the migrant newcomers—only intensified.[5] Many reports that studied immigration at the time concluded that "housing [was] both the greatest problem that [confronted] the immigrants themselves and the sphere in which the greatest tensions [were] likely to arise between immigrants and the local people" (Patterson 1969, 194).

As these poor housing conditions turned many working-class neighborhoods into slums, the white residents that had remained became particularly prone to anti-immigrant hostility. Before long, this antagonism escalated into violence directed against the newcomers. Isolated street disturbances had become routine in some areas, but nothing had prepared the country for the antiblack rioting that took place in the summer of 1958 in Nottingham and Notting Hill. Following a series of altercations between West Indian immigrants and white youths in Nottingham, the latter went on what they referred to as "nigger hunts." Thousands of white males, predominantly lower-class youths, ganged up to attack West Indian immigrants in fighting that lasted several days. The political reaction was swift: the local MPs (one Conservative, one Labour) immediately called for a complete stop of immigration and endorsed aggressive repatriation measures (Fryer 1984, 377). About a week later, Notting Hill, a London neighborhood that was then predominantly West Indian, witnessed similar civil unrest. Hundreds participated in racially inspired violent attacks, resulting in the arrest of 140 rioters, most of whom were white. The violent gangs were spurred on by racist propaganda materials that put the entire blame for the squalid living conditions in the neighborhood on the immigrant population. When some West Indian immigrants decided to fight back in self-defense, some accused the police of failing to protect the immigrants because the officers themselves were harboring racist resentments (Fryer 1984, 378–380; Hansen 2000, 80–81; Hiro 1991, 38–40; Layton-Henry 1992, 38–39).

The effects of the riots were far-reaching. Helped by extensive press and television coverage and public debate, they succeeded in transforming immigration from a local issue into a persistent national headline that reached even the most remote, rural, all-white areas. The riots put a dramatic end to the prepolitical "Age of Innocence" (Hiro 1991, 40) and ushered in a more conflictual state of affairs. Prior to the 1958 violence, the political elite had managed to keep the lid on issues related to immigration and race relations, allowing pressures to simmer at the local level and on the back benches. Although the riots were widely condemned by the mainstream political establishment, some MPs sought to understand and even sympathize with the white rioters, whom they pitied as victims of an immigrant invasion. This show of understanding was most likely also motivated by the first opinion polls on immigration and interracial relations, conducted as a result of the riots. According to most surveys, the vast majority of the British public rejected unrestricted migration by the early 1960s, and it soon became clear that opposition to liberal immigration laws cut across partisan lines (Messina 1989, 26–27). In 1961, a Gallup poll found that 67 percent favored controls and a further 6 percent endorsed a complete ban (Deakin 1965, 5). The first reaction of shock, disgust, and condemnation thus soon gave way to a more hostile climate and the Conservative Macmillan government felt increased pressure to heed the public's calls for immigration controls.

5.3.3 The Politics of Appeasement: The First Immigration Controls

Several institutional channels helped mobilize the opposition to Britain's liberal immigration regime within the Conservative Party. Conservative activists relayed their constituencies' hostility to the party leadership by issuing thirty-nine resolutions at the 1961 Annual Conservative Party Conference, calling for an immediate halt to unrestricted immigration. These efforts were amplified by the growing pressure groups that had formed around the issue as well as by vocal xenophobic MPs who clamored for control to stop the "appalling flood" of immigrants (Foot 1965, 134).

Driven by rumors of an impending ban, nonwhite immigrants started arriving in Britain in ever-increasing numbers, which only boosted the cause of the restrictionist lobby. Whereas net immigration from New Commonwealth countries totaled almost 60,000 in 1960, this number had more than doubled to over 136,000 by 1961 (see Table 5.3a). In light of these developments, the Cabinet decided to introduce control legislation in October 1961. The proposed bill represented a compromise, aimed at appeasing the pro-immigration factions within the party, as it restricted primary immigration by instituting an employment voucher scheme but allowed the unrestricted immigration of dependents. The Labour Party virulently opposed the legislation, and its leader, Hugh Gaitskell, condemned it as a "miserable, shameful, shabby bill" (Messina 1989, 28). To be sure, the Labour Party contained an outspoken anti-immigrant wing of its own. But in contrast to the Conservative Party, its activists had not built up an effective pressure network at the branch level (Deakin 1965, 3–4; Foot 1965, 134; Messina 1989, 24–30).

After months of parliamentary infighting that resulted in numerous amendments, the Commonwealth Immigrants Act passed in 1962 with its central provisions intact.[6] While, on the surface, the act used employment-based measures to curb immigration, many observers denounced it as racially discriminatory—its controls were targeted at nonwhite immigrants and conspicuously excluded Irish citizens. Additionally, the conditions at the time belied any alleged economic rationales of the act. The restrictions came in a period when Britain was experiencing full employment, and economists, both within and outside government, forecast critical labor shortages (Money 1997, 698). As the parliamentary debates testify, the 1962 act was deemed a social, not an economic, necessity. The controls were hoped to alleviate the frictions between the native and the immigrant populations that had arisen as a result of congested schools and housing and insufficient health and welfare services. These tensions were magnified by suspicion of and hostility against cultural, religious, and racial differences. However, given the act's failure to include any kind of dispersal or registration provisions, immigrants would continue to settle in locations of greatest labor scarcity and industrial expansion, which were precisely those industrial areas that suffered from the negative consequences of overcrowding in the first place (Coleman 1994, 39; Patterson 1969, 19–20). Moreover, the decision to allow the continued entry of dependents precipitated even larger inflows of immigrants. In the two years immediately following the act (1963–1965), 57,710 Commonwealth migrants arrived with a labor voucher in hand, but almost twice as many family members entered Britain for permanent settlement during those years (Messina 2001, 264).

5.3.4   Smethwick and the Birth of the Race-Card Thesis

In addition to its failure to stem the flow of immigrants, the 1962 act also failed to curb the growing politicization of immigration and race-related issues. The public's continued rejection of unrestricted immigration and increasing pressure from local constituencies of both parties also led the new Labour leader, Harold Wilson, to concede the need for controls when the act was first due for renewal in November 1963. Having committed to restrictions, the Tory and Labour leaderships hoped to avoid the contentious immigration issue in the 1964 general election. The party manifestos' treatment of the issues was very guarded and neutral, and the Liberal Party did not even mention the subject directly. With the exception of a few marginal seats, the parties also avoided openly courting the immigrant vote, for fear that such a move would alienate the white electorate.[7] Finally, the major parties' central organizations also discouraged local candidates to exploit native resentment against immigrants in their campaigns (Deakin 1965, 10, 160–161).

All these efforts were, however, brought to naught in the constituency of Smethwick (an industrial city in the West Midlands with an immigrant population of 6 percent), whose Conservative candidate, Peter Griffiths, was able to dominate the campaign with his staunchly anti-immigrant platform and whose unexpected victory had a ripple effect that was felt for years to come. The widely publicized election outcome was notable for several reasons. First, Griffiths's xenophobic campaign, associated with the hateful slogan "If you want a nigger neighbour, vote Liberal or Labour," managed to win a seat in a constituency that had been solidly Labour for twenty years. Second, Griffiths's triumph occurred against the national tide. While the overall electorate moved to the left, Smethwick registered the biggest pro-Conservative swing of any seat in the whole country, 10.4 percent against the national average and even 8.8 percent against the average for the West Midlands. Third, and most significant, Smethwick was held up as an example of the electoral advantage that a party could gain by playing the race card in local politics. Gordon Walker, the defeated Labour candidate, was in fact very popular among his constituents,[8] but his focus on national matters during the campaign caused many former supporters who were concerned about the local impact of continued immigration and who had been convinced by his opponent's attacks that Walker would promote a policy of "Let 'em all come," to cast their ballot for Griffiths instead (Hartley-Brewer 1965, 80–103; Saggar 2000, 175–178).

5.3.5   Containment Continues as Controls Are Tightened

Smethwick certainly left its mark on Britain's electoral landscape and on its calculating strategists, but its immediate impact was softened by the still-operating bipartisan consensus of silence on the immigration issue. The major parties' dogged attempts to keep immigration and race relations out of inter-party competition may have failed insofar as the public's interest in these issues rose and hostility against immigration did not abate. However, the Tory and Labour leadership managed to prevent the twin themes of race and immigration from influencing the general elections of 1964 and 1966 on a nationwide scale.

Throughout the 1960s, over 80 percent of the British electorate consistently agreed with the statement that "too many immigrants have been let into this country." Moreover, in the election years of 1964, 1966, and 1970, about 50 percent of those surveyed felt "very strongly" and an additional third felt "fairly strongly" about immigration. To Labour's chagrin, concern over immigration varied by class, with its working-class constituents being most likely to oppose immigration (Butler and Stokes 1974, 303). Given the high salience of the issue in voters' minds and their clear, one-sided preferences, why did immigration fail to make a nationwide impact on the election campaigns of the 1960s?

Indeed, Butler and Stokes considered immigration to be a topic of "high potential" in these elections. But they also showed that voters did not differentiate between the two parties when it came to this contentious issue. Prior to the elections of 1964 and 1966, the majority of those polled (41 and 53 percent, respectively) thought that there was no difference between the parties when it came to "keep[ing] immigrants out" (Butler and Stokes 1974, 306).

Internal divisions within the parties contributed to the electorate's assessment. Additionally, Labour had moved considerably into the restrictionist direction. Wilson's endorsement of the controls instituted by the 1962 act and his government's further, more stringent restrictions imposed on immigration in the White Paper of 1965 blurred any differences the parties may have had on immigration in the electorate's mind.[9] This was quite the intended effect. According to Butler and Stokes, after the Smethwick episode "had revealed the dynamite that lay in the issue, the new Government quickly moved to a position on immigration control that was quite as tough as that of its predecessor" (1974, 304). Labour's narrow majority of three in Parliament and its justified fears that a large share of its electorate harbored deep racial prejudices made the government especially vulnerable on the race and immigration front. It thus gave in to xenophobic mass opinion by imposing harsher controls, but also passed anti-discrimination legislation, the 1965 Race Relations Act, which sought to outlaw racial or religious discrimination in public places. Lacking effective enforcement mechanisms and limited in scope—the act did not cover the realms where offenses were most egregious, employment and housing—the legislation was widely considered a cosmetic way for Labour to "maintain something of its anti-racist credentials" (Layton-Henry 1992, 50). Indeed, Labour's progressive critics contended that by linking antidiscrimination legislation to tighter, race-based immigration restrictions, the act was simply a way for the party "to appear to be slamming the door in a more civilized fashion than the Tories" (Fryer 1984, 383). While such a cynical characterization may be unfair to the intentions of Labour's liberal wing, the fact remains that in the mid-1960s, there was little to distinguish the Conservatives and Labour on matters of immigration and race relations.

The late 1960s confronted the Labour government with further challenges as East African Asians, mostly from Kenya, started migrating en masse to

Britain. Having lived in Kenya for generations, these Asians now suffered discrimination from the newly independent Kenyan government, whose pursuit of "Africanization" policies threatened the Asians' livelihoods and ultimately drove many of them to leave the country.[10] Their status, "Citizens of the United Kingdom and colonies" (CUKC), as created by the 1948 Nationality Act, was not covered by the controls of the 1962 Commonwealth Immigrants Act and thus allowed them free entry into Britain. In 1967, almost 14,000 East Asians arrived from Kenya, presenting the Labour government with a serious dilemma. On the one hand, Britain had a moral and legal obligation to take in these migrants who not only were British passport holders but also faced a hostile government at home.[11] On the other hand, the Wilson government was well aware that the continued admission of thousands of nonwhite migrants—13,000 had arrived in the first two months of 1968 alone—would cause hysteria among its xenophobic electorate. In the end, the government sided with the xenophobes. The 1968 Commonwealth Immigrants Act, hastily prepared and rushed through Parliament, stripped East Asian Africans of their right to enter Britain.[12] The legislation was applauded by the public (72 percent approved of the controls), but loathed by Liberal, Labour, and Conservative politicians alike, who accused the government of strengthening, rather than appeasing, the immigration control movement by pandering to racist opinion (Hansen 2000, 153–164; Layton-Henry 1992, 78–79).

Labour's immigration controls proved to be as harsh as the restrictions sought by its Conservative predecessor. Despite Labour's tough stance in the Kenyan Asian crisis, however, the British electorate soon began to prefer the Tories as their anti-immigrant party of choice. Indeed, by the time the 1970 election season got under way, Tories clearly enjoyed a head start among the restrictionist electorate. The ascent of Enoch Powell, the Conservatives' most notorious racist to this day, the election of Margaret Thatcher as party leader, and the shift of the Labour Party to a less ambiguous, more liberal immigration and integration policy helped to bring down the era of bipartisan consensus politics.

5.4 From Powell to Thatcher: Challenging the Consensus

By the late 1960s, no amount of bipartisan collusion could have kept the issue of immigration out of the national spotlight. It seemed that restrictionist legislation did nothing to diminish the electoral salience of the issue and had instead legitimized a political discourse that catered to racist fear-mongering. The Labour government's promotion of additional antidiscrimination legislation also failed to defuse the politicization of race. Instead, it played into the hands of racist populists, who stirred up the fears and resentment of a multiracial Britain.

5.4.1 The "Powell Effect"

Attempting to reclaim some of its progressive standing, the Wilson government passed the 1968 Race Relations Act, which represented a substantial improvement over existing antidiscrimination legislation. Among other things, the act widened the scope of previous legislation to outlaw racial discrimination in the areas of housing and employment and created an institutional framework at the local level, backed by government funding, to ensure more effective enforcement of its provisions (Ben-Tovim 1986, 29). In addition to tightening the screws on discrimination, the secondary goal of the legislation was to absolve the national leadership from having to tackle problems having to do with race relations at the national level by erecting institutional channels, or "racial buffers," at the level of the local authorities (Katznelson 1973, 179–181; Messina 1989, 44–47). This goal was foiled initially, however, as the announcement of the new Race Relations Act provoked vocal outrage from the Conservative Party's most infamous racist propagandist, Enoch Powell.

Powell had been known for his xenophobic outbursts in the past. A member of the opposition's Shadow Cabinet, he was its most ardent advocate of immigration control and repatriation. Yet the speech that he gave in Birmingham two days before the introduction of the 1968 Race Relations Bill instantaneously catapulted him to nationwide notoriety and made him the personification of the anti-immigrant movement. In his so-called Rivers of Blood speech (see epigraph), Powell turned the logic of the antidiscrimination legislation on its head, arguing that the bill was yet another tool that the immigrant would use to intimidate and dominate the native population.

The media's incessant coverage of the hateful speech helped disseminate the xenophobe's ideas to the public, who extolled Powell with thousands of letters of support and in several opinion polls showed 67 to 82 percent in his favor. Edward Heath, the Conservative leader, was conspicuously less enthusiastic, along with other members of his Shadow Cabinet, some of whom insisted that they would leave the Cabinet unless Powell was sacked. While Heath did end up relieving Powell from his position—amid marches to Parliament by his supporters, chanting "Keep Britain White" and "Don't Knock Enoch"—the Tory leadership felt compelled to acknowledge the massive popularity of Powell's anti-immigrant policies. In 1969 the party came out with a new, far more stringent strategy on immigration control, in time for the upcoming general election (Hansen 2000, 182–190; Layton-Henry 1992, 79–83).[13]

Despite Powell's demotion from the Shadow Cabinet, the 1970 election was fought in his shadow. Even though Heath disassociated himself from Powell, the electorate identified with the latter's xenophobic campaign. In fact, it was when Powell and his ideas came to prominence in the late 1960s that the British voter had begun to draw clear lines between the Conservatives and Labour on matters of immigration. In the summers of 1969 and 1970, majorities of 50 and 57 percent, respectively, believed that the Tories would be tougher on immigration than Labour (the corresponding figures for Labour were only 6 and 4 percent) (Butler and Stokes 1974, 306).

Powell's ascent has widely been credited with bringing about this change in perception, which represented a drastic shift from earlier years, when the majority of the electorate could not distinguish between the two parties on immigration control, and which also occurred at a time when the two parties' stated positions on Commonwealth immigration and integration were essentially the same (Studlar 1978, 53). More controversially, some have attributed the Tories' unexpected victory in the 1970 general election to Powell's anti-immigrant campaign (Miller 1980; Studlar 1978; Wood and Powell 1970). According to Studlar, "the Conservatives gained an estimated increment of 6.7 percent in votes because many people perceived them to be the party more likely to keep immigrants out and voted in accordance with that prescription" (1978, 46).

While others contest the validity of the "Powell effect" (Hansen 2000, 191–192n), it is hard to dispute that the Conservatives had become the anti-immigration party in the public's mind. The 1971 Immigration Act solidified this perception. This legislation essentially extended the notion of an ethnic preference, introduced in Labour's 1968 act, by distinguishing between "patrials," individuals with a parent or grandparent born in the UK, and "non-patrials," Commonwealth or other citizens lacking such a connection. Patrials could enter, settle, and work in the UK without restrictions, while non-patrials were subject to tight immigration controls. The de facto intention and consequence of the act was to discriminate against nonwhite immigrants who, by and large, were classified as non-patrials (Coleman 1994, 59–60; Hussain 2001, 24).

5.4.2 Between Integration and Extremism

The 1971 act showed Heath's restrictionist side; however, the totality of his leadership suggests a more ambiguous record. In what appeared to be a repetition of the Kenyan Asian incident four years earlier, the liberal wing of the Conservative Party scored a rare victory thanks to Heath's handling of the Ugandan Asian crisis. When President Idi Amin announced in August 1972 that he would expel all Asian CUKCs from Uganda, the British government was faced with the prospect of 50,000 British passport holders immigrating to Britain. The crisis received excessive publicity and imparted further momentum to immigration control pressure groups and anti-immigrant MPs, who relentlessly lobbied the government on behalf of their xenophobic constituents. Under considerable pressure, the Heath government—unlike its Labour predecessor—decided to admit the expellees and established the Ugandan Resettlement Board to facilitate their admission, settlement, and integration. The decision was reviled by the Tories' right-wing membership, some of whom decided to join forces with the extremist National Front instead (Layton-Henry 1992, 85–87).

The National Front (NF) was founded in 1966 from an amalgam of several right-wing organizations and extremist splinter groups, with the aim of fighting immigration through constitutional, rather than militant, means. Its program sought a complete and immediate halt to immigration together with repatriation of nonwhite immigrants and their dependents. In the early 1970s the NF's strategy was to appeal to right-wing Conservative voters disgruntled with Heath's performance on the immigration issue and ready to express their disaffection at the polls.[14] Later on, the party scored important electoral successes in run-down inner-city wards—traditional Labour heartlands (Husbands 1983, 7). The success of the National Front was of increasing concern and interest to the Conservative leadership, who feared that the party could split the right-wing vote at the constituency level, but who also hoped that xenophobic working-class voters would opt for the Tories if the party espoused a harder line on immigration control.

Meanwhile, politics at the national level returned to more conventional issues. Inflation, wage controls, industrial relations, housing problems, and membership in the Common Market topped the list of voter concerns in the 1974 elections (Butler and Kavanagh 1975, 273).[15] Yet Labour's narrow victory brought renewed attention to Britain's ethnic minority population, whose residential concentration could translate into pivotal votes.

The Labour Party thus started courting the minority electorate more actively. On the policy side, the Labour government proposed a third Race Relations Bill. Building on previous acts, the legislation extended existing provisions by including direct as well as indirect discrimination. The latter "referred to cases where unjustifiable practices and procedures which apply to everyone have the effect of putting people of a particular racial group at a disadvantage" (Ben-Tovim 1986, 29).[16] The enforcement mechanisms were strengthened considerably; individuals now had the right to take their cases to the County Court or, in employment-related cases, to the Industrial Tribunal.

The Conservative Party reacted by appealing to upper- and middle-class minorities. In response to their strategists' urging, Conservative Party managers set up an ethnic relations unit in their Central Office to convert rich segments of the minority electorate to the Tories' cause and established the Anglo–West Indian Conservative Society and the more successful Anglo-Asian Conservative Society (later called the One Nation Forum; it appealed mostly to Indian professionals, with most of its support base located in London and the South East) (Charlot 1985, 144; Rich 1998, 97). In opposition, the Conservatives also agreed to support the government-sponsored 1976 Race Relations Bill, which passed without concessions to the immigration control lobby.

Notwithstanding these moves, internal splits once again fractured the Conservatives' position on immigration and race-related matters. The Tories' new leader, Margaret Thatcher, had rejected the party's conciliatory stance toward the Race Relations Act and was only prevented from ordering wholesale opposition to the act by a threatened rebellion of more liberal-minded party members (Layton-Henry 1986, 74). In the coming years, Thatcher's leadership would show less restraint. With the election of Thatcher as their party leader, the Conservatives erased any ambiguity in the party's treatment of immigration and minority politics that may have characterized Heath's leadership.

5.5 The Rise of Thatcher and the Breakdown of the Consensus of Silence

Thatcher's rise in the Conservative Party has generally been credited with the decline of the bipartisan era of consensual politics, not only in the area of race and immigration but in the wider realm of British society, economy, and politics (Saggar 2000, 180). In a related development, the British electorate was considered by scholars and strategists to have loosened its partisan identifications by gradually abandoning class-based, ideological voting in favor of more ad hoc, issue-based voting (Studlar 1978, 47). The prospect of luring working-class voters who felt threatened by the influx of nonwhite immigrants to the Conservative cause turned the issue of immigration control into an important element of the Conservatives' electoral strategy.

5.5.1 A Hostile Climate

While both parties had made inroads in appealing to the ethnic minority electorate, a chain of unrelated events put race and racism back in the tabloid press, which was only too eager to sell more papers by tapping into its readers' xenophobia. Enoch Powell had not toned down his hostile rhetoric and continued giving anti-immigrant speeches whose themes were often taken up by right-wing Conservative MPs. The arrival of two Malawi Asian families in Britain in 1976, who, for lack of a better solution, were temporarily housed in four-star accommodations, caused a media panic, warning of an impending flood of Asian immigrants and reinforcing claims that immigrant families were deliberately abusing the state's welfare system. The same year, a series of racist attacks culminated in the murder of a ten-year-old Sikh boy by gangs of white youths in Southall (London), which caused outrage and further escalated an already tense racial climate. The frictions were only exacerbated by John Kingsley Read (leader of the extremist British National Party), who caustically remarked: "One down, a million to go"[17] (Husbands 1983, 11). Amid a climate of racial strife, fear, and resentment, the National Front scored a number of electoral victories that injected the extremist movement with new lifeblood—not only within the NF but also among the anti-immigrant wing in the Tory Party.

Concerned that her party's neglect of immigration-related issues steered voters to the National Front, Thatcher committed the Tories to a rightward course in all matters of policy, including immigration and race relations. While the Conservatives' overall program represented a remarkable shift from previous party manifestos, it took only one event to shore up the Tories' restrictionist credentials. Interviewed on national television in January 1978, Thatcher echoed the Front's credo that "people are really rather afraid that [Britain] might be swamped by people with a different culture," and that this fear would only increase hostility to the country's nonwhite population.[18] Thatcher's remark had the intended large and immediate impact: the British media provided ample coverage of the "swamping interview" and the Conservatives shot ahead in the polls in the week following their leader's statements (Miller 1980, 36). Thatcher's instincts also paid off electorally; in a by-election in Ilford North in March, a poll suggested that the issue of immigration had influenced the vote choice among 29 percent of those surveyed. More portentously, of those who switched from Labour to the Conservatives, fully 48 percent stated that this issue had affected their vote.[19] Although pollsters cautioned not to interpret these figures too literally, the Conservatives' victory in the 1979 general election bolstered their belief in the profitability of acknowledging, if not exploiting, the public's fear of further immigration.

The immigration issue certainly did not, however, dominate the general election. According to a Gallup poll, voters were mostly concerned about bread-and-butter issues, such as inflation, unemployment, strikes, and tax policy,[20] and television coverage concentrated on similar issues (Butler and Kavanagh 1980, 211). However, the Conservatives' manipulation of the issue had the intended effect of co-opting the principal platform of the National Front. Having mobilized all its resources to maximum capacity, the NF nevertheless lost votes across the board. The Conservatives, in contrast, polled well in previous NF strongholds as large pro-Conservative swings were registered in seats where the National Front's losses were particularly steep (Husbands 1983, 15). The 1979 general election has thus been typically held up as a contest in which Tories were able to achieve victory due to "decisive though subtle surges in Conservative electoral support on the basis of popular attitudes towards immigration" (Saggar 2000, 177). Thatcher understood and played on the public's fears that immigrants would claim state resources and undermine the economic position of the working class in particular. As we will see in the following chapter, in 1979 a large share of voters resented the fact that their taxes would pay for benefits that would be enjoyed by "undeserving" immigrants.

In light of the supposed pivotal function of the immigration issue for the party, Thatcher did not want to disappoint her xenophobic support base. As promised in the ambitious party manifesto, the Conservatives were determined to once and for all end immigration via extensive controls and the redefinition of British citizenship laws that had been in existence since 1948.

5.5.2 Thatcher's First Term: Restrictions and Riots

The constraints of office did hamper Thatcher's ambitious reform program somewhat, as liberals within her own party, together with a hostile opposition, balked at some of the harsher proposals contained in the manifesto.[21] Branded as racist by the left while at the same time failing to satisfy the right wing, the Thatcher government "could not find a 'non-racist' formula for stopping New Commonwealth immigration" and thus opted for the only viable solution, linking "the right of entry and permanent abode in the United Kingdom to citizenship" (Layton-Henry 1986, 79). According to one Conservative MP, Timothy Raison, legislation was needed that would "finally . . . dispose of the lingering notion that Britain [was] somehow a haven for all those whose countries [it] once ruled" (quoted in Blake 1982, 182). The 1981 British Nationality Act achieved this goal. It created three classes of British citizenship,[22] only one of which—British citizenship, covering patrials—granted settlement rights. Moreover, and most controversially, the act abandoned a pure ius soli regime, as children born in the UK who did not have at least one parent born or (legally) settled in the country no longer automatically acquired British citizenship.[23] The act thus shed Britain's obligations to its former colonies and brought its citizenship regime more in line with that of its European neighbors. While the act's provisions may not be racially discriminatory when compared with other countries' regimes or even when considered by themselves,[24] they did have the desired effect of restricting the entry of nonwhites into Britain and excluded a whole class of nonwhite immigrant children from British citizenship. Opposition politicians and immigrant groups thus denounced the act as the latest manifestation of institutionalized racism and fought for its repeal (Hansen 2000, 207–208). Conservative right-wingers, meanwhile, bemoaned that the new legislation did not sufficiently rein in immigration—belying the party's stated claim that it was the redefinition of citizenship, rather than immigration control, that had motivated the act (Hussain 2001, 31).

The 1981 Nationality Act was not the only event to stir up racial tensions during Thatcher's first term. Large-scale rioting once again upset the British public in the early 1980s. This time, the riots were initiated not by gangs of white youths but by ethnic minorities responding to what they perceived to be discriminatory police action. Relations between the police and Britain's immigrant population had been strained for decades, going back at least to the 1958 riots. In 1981 these tensions exploded into urban riots in Brixton and Liverpool. When the Brixton police force embarked on operation "Swamp 81"—organized stops and searches to detect and arrest delinquents in the black community that lasted for almost a week, resulting in 118 arrests and 75 charges—Brixton's young black residents took to the streets in violent protest. The rioting caused 226 injuries (150 of them among the police), 200 arrests, 26 burnt buildings and 20 destroyed vehicles. Three months later, violent street disturbances in Liverpool (Toxteth), also inspired by tensions between the police and the minority community, took an even larger toll: they resulted in 700 arrests, 718 injured policemen, and property damage amounting to £15 million. For the first time in Britain, tear gas was used to subdue the insurgents. The Conservative government was quick to condemn the rioters and to express sympathy and support for the police force (Hiro 1991, 88–89; Layton-Henry 1992, 129). In the aftermath of the riots, however, responses grew to be more complex and it soon became evident that the Thatcher administration had to commit to policies that would combat the causes of the riots.

Disentangling the origins of the violence proved to be highly political; explanations abounded. Labour politicians were generally of the view that social exclusion, economic deprivation, unemployment, and urban decay were the main culprits and resisted claims made by some Conservatives that the immigrant community itself was to blame. Several politicians, police officers, and a sensationalist tabloid press even presented a conspiracy theory, suggesting that the violence was not spontaneous in nature, but rather the result of a well-orchestrated plot by black insurgents. Compelled to take positive action, the Home Office commissioned an independent inquiry into the riots, carried out under Lord Scarman. The resulting report came to the conclusion that police action represented the immediate factor triggering the disturbances. However, Scarman emphasized the social context—deprivation, disadvantage, and high unemployment—as the underlying reason that allowed discriminatory police behavior to have such a shocking effect in the first place (Benyon 1986, 227–228; Scarman 1982, 36). Lord Scarman exhorted the government that "urgent action [was] needed if [racial disadvantage was] not to become an endemic, ineradicable disease, threatening the very survival of [British] society" (Scarman 1982, 209). While Thatcher was cutting services in almost every other area of social spending, the report's proposals, along with other high-profile findings and recommendations,[25] forced her government to increase funding for programs fighting racial disadvantage and to commit to spending in order to combat urban decline (Layton-Henry 1986, 90). At the same time, Thatcher dismissed charges that widespread joblessness—in part caused by her administration's stringent economic policies—could justify the riots and rejected calls by the opposition to commit to expansionary policies to cut the highest unemployment levels Britain had seen since the 1930s.[26]

5.5.3 Immigration, Race, and the Neoliberal Project

The public discussion of the riots and their underlying causes also served to put an additional spotlight on the effects of the Thatcher government's sweeping economic program. The Conservative government came to power with an election manifesto that can only be described as a radical departure from previous government practice and ideology. In the economic realm, Thatcher committed her government to a neoliberal reform program that affirmed the primacy of market forces, viewed state intervention in the economy with deep suspicion, and, for the first time, traded in the pledge of full employment for the commitment to reduce inflation. In her government's first term in office, Thatcher acted on almost all of her election promises: her government privatized large sections of the British economy, imposed drastic cuts in public expenditures, severely circumscribed the bargaining power of trade unions, and reduced the income tax, to name but a few achievements. The only areas that were marked for budget increases were traditionally Conservative priorities: defense, law and order, and agriculture. Amid recession—unemployment had shot up from 4.9 percent to 11.6 percent after Thatcher's first two years in office—the government opted for a distributional strategy that placed the burden of economic austerity on the disadvantaged, the jobless, and the poor, while the wealthy and employed saw their economic situations improve (Hall 1986, 100–126; King 1985, 1–15).

Some have argued that the government deliberately employed "divide-and-conquer" tactics (Pierson 1994, 8), "dividing the nation into regional, racial, and age-related enclaves" (Hall 1986, 125).[27] According to Messina (2001) and his review of the relevant literature, this strategy also explains the Conservatives' position on race and immigration policies. While Thatcher's neoliberal reform project delivered few tangible goods to the white working class, the Conservatives purportedly rallied the support of this constituency by distracting it from its economic decline:

> At its most benign, the politics of friends and enemies, expressed transparently in the contentious politics of immigration in Britain during the 1970s and 1980s, distracted native losers of the conservative project from focusing on the primary source of their difficulties. At its most malignant, the politics of friends and enemies exacerbated latent antagonisms among the various races and social classes in the United Kingdom. At every point between these two poles the eventual success of the neoliberal project was facilitated . . . [it] was rational because at no point during its conception or implementation were the central tenets of the neoliberal project intellectually embraced by a majority of the British public. As a result, populist issues, such as immigration control [and law and order], were deliberately added to the neoliberal project mix in order to make it more palatable to the electorate, and especially to the white working class. (Messina 2001, 276–277)

If Messina's interpretation is correct, the Conservatives exploited working-class fears of a multicultural Britain not only to win elections, although this may have been the short-term objective; the manipulation of these sensitive issues also helped the Tories sell economic policies that adversely affected large segments of its xenophobic supporters. The next chapter will provide further evidence that not only class interests but also voter and party positions on race and immigration helped determine party membership.

Over the next decade, the Conservative government focused its attention on issues having to do more with law and order than with immigration specifically. The reform of the Nationality Act and the widely publicized riots of the early 1980s marked the peak that the issues of immigration and race relations would attain during Thatcher's reign. Indeed, observers agree that by the time of the 1983 general election, these matters had virtually dropped from the national political debate (Rich 1998, 98; Saggar 2000, 181). In 1983 and 1985, party members only submitted five and eleven motions on immigration to the party conferences, as concern over social services preoccupied fifty-nine motions (Coleman 1994, 61). Part of the Tory leadership's decision to refrain from politicizing race and immigration in the general elections of the 1980s was due to the fact that going beyond existing legislation, in particular the 1981 Nationality Act, would in fact be so harsh as to violate Britain's obligations under the European Convention on Human Rights (Layton-Henry 1986, 96). In addition, thanks to their early stringency, the Conservatives "removed one of their most attractive issues from the agenda of British electoral politics . . . the traditional immigration issue effectively disappear[ed] from the radar of party competition" (Saggar 2000, 181). Rather than playing the race card, the Tories followed Labour (and the newly formed Alliance Party) in wooing the minority vote.[28]

By the time of the next general election in 1987, only 1 percent of the British electorate thought that race ranked among the most important political issues (Rich 1998, 100). Notwithstanding these developments, observers at the time did not conclude that electorally inspired racism had subsided completely. Large parts of the British population still harbored deep racial prejudices and some thought that "in a political crisis the temptation to exploit them once again might prove irresistible" (Layton-Henry 1986, 97). This crisis would surface in the 1992 election campaign when the Conservatives were in dire need of an electoral lifeline.

5.6 Immigration in the 1990s and Beyond

The 1990s witnessed a transformation of the immigration issue in Britain. Primary mass immigration from the New Commonwealth countries had declined considerably under Thatcher's reign (see Table 5.3c and Figure 5.1), and the British population gradually accepted those immigrants already present, now settled as second- and even third-generation Britons (Saggar 2004, 18). By the late 1980s, however, a new type of immigrant started entering Britain: refugees began applying for asylum in rapidly increasing numbers. While applicants numbered 5,000 in 1988, this number had tripled a year later to 15,000 and to 30,000 in 1990.[29] The following decade saw applications multiply even further (see Table 5.1). The new asylum wave had at least three distinct characteristics: refugees came predominantly from developing countries in Africa and Asia; they did not resemble, in culture or color, previous asylum movements from Soviet-dominated countries and thus also had less in common with British traditions; and their arrival was often facilitated through illegal use of traffickers and false documentation (Hansen and King 2000, 400). The public's suspicion of this new stream of immigrants inspired Conservative Party strategists to play a new type of race card, branding all asylum seekers as illegitimate and "bogus" and exacerbating public hostility further.

5.6.1   The 1992 General Election

The Conservatives' decision to make asylum a campaign theme has to be considered in the wider electoral context. The electoral outlook for the Conservatives in the early 1990s was extremely bleak. Throughout the 1980s, Tories had been successful in labeling Labour as disunited, irresponsible left-wingers who were unfit to govern. However, by the early 1990s, Conservatives had lost their edge on most issues of national concern, and under Neil Kinnock, the Labour Party suddenly appeared to be a true, electable alternative, favored by most voters to tackle the nation's problems.[30] Despite the party's restored credibility, when it came to immigration Labour was still considered by most voters to be "soft" on controls and too minority-friendly for its own good. The 1980s had only reinforced these perceptions as Thatcher's harder line, widespread discrimination, and racism, as well as a more assertive minority electorate, had drawn a clear line between the two major parties, with Labour activists moving the party in a more liberal direction on race issues than perhaps the leadership had desired. As Fitzgerald and Layton-Henry put it bluntly, Labour had "few further racist votes to lose and an increasingly articulate black electorate to satisfy" (1986, 102). While the new Conservative leadership of John Major represented a shift to a more modern and moderate position on issues of race and immigration, the impending defeat at the polls convinced party strategists to exploit this source of Labour's vulnerability.

Less than a year prior to the 1992 general election, Home Secretary Kenneth Baker (dubbed the "Minister for Xenophobia" by *The Independent*)[31] embarked on a campaign to reduce drastically the number of asylum applications—which had increased almost tenfold in three years—in what was to become the most controversial legislative item before the election.[32] The draconian proposals were accompanied by aggressive language by a virulent tabloid press that peaked in the final week of the campaign.[33] They provoked strong criticism from human rights organizations, clergy, the United Nations, and not least Labour, who accused Baker of playing the race card and fear-mongering for electoral purposes. John Major, while disassociating himself from extreme right-wing Tory MPs, nevertheless backed Baker's bill, insisting that good race relations required tough immigration controls. Just weeks before the election, Baker continued to stoke the public's fears in a well-publicized speech and accused the opposition parties of "preparing a deadly political cocktail" by relaxing immigration restrictions.[34] Some have suggested that the Conservative political machine had carefully timed Baker's speech to sway a high number of voters who were still undecided shortly before polling day and thus attribute the Tories' unexpected victory "to a concerted appeal to the lowest political denominator" (Billig and Golding 1992, 163). Others emphasize that the Tories were only able to successfully deploy the race card by linking Labour's opposition to the asylum bill to its perceived lack of credibility and trustworthiness of years past, but still concede the possibility that the row over the asylum bill did play a significant role in the ultimate election outcome (Saggar 1993, 697). Either way, Conservatives drew their own lessons; they figured that the party's manipulation of the asylum issue was a crucial variable in their unlikely election victory and were intent on using it again (Saggar 2001, 762).

5.6.2 The 1990s: More of the Same

The politicization of the asylum question did not abate, but continued throughout the 1990s in ever shriller language. By the mid-1990s, Conservatives were again confronted with prospects of looming electoral downfall. At the same time, at least two developments spurred their anti-immigrant instincts. First, the extremist British National Party had made considerable headway at the local level; second, a strategy paper published in mid-1994 strongly suggested that Conservatives should appear tough on immigration and crime, market research having found that swing voters tended to have very right-wing attitudes on these issues (Kaye 1999, 27). As a result, Conservatives did not refrain from resorting to race-card politics in attempts to siphon votes from the BNP at the local level. The Conservative Party's Central Office, while committed to "good race relations," did not intervene in these local contests (Rich 1998, 110). At the national level, senior politicians devised a strategy on asylum that would even make the National Front proud.

The new anti-asylum campaign, backed by a ferocious tabloid press, focused on refugees' alleged abuse of Britain's welfare benefits. Home Secretary Michael Howard condemned most genuine refugees as "bogus [asylum seekers who in] most cases [were] really economic migrants seeking a better life,"[35] and Social Security Secretary Peter Lilley launched what the *Evening Standard* called "a blitz on benefit fraud" by depriving asylum seekers of their previously held entitlements to public housing and welfare benefits—a "fraud industry [that cost] the taxpayer £10 billion a year."[36] In one of his most aggressive reforms, Lilley offered a £10 reward for post officers "every time they nab[bed] a welfare cheat."[37] Fearful of losing votes on the asylum issue, Tony Blair, Labour's new leader, did not want to oppose the proposals outright and thus tried to return to traditional bipartisan politics by calling for a consensus-building special Commons committee to tackle the contentious issue. Conservative hardliners rejected such a move, for their strategy counted on Blair's opposition to the bill—a strategy that the major papers recognized as a well-orchestrated exercise of agenda setting that aimed to undermine Labour's popularity with the public by exploiting its vulnerability on immigration (Kaye 1999, 30).

In the end, the asylum regulations as well as the wider electoral strategy failed to deliver the desired effect. Lilley's stringent benefits regulations and the contentious restrictions of the 1996 Asylum and Immigration Act were so severe that they encountered several judicial setbacks as attempts to deter asylum seekers by depriving them of welfare entitlements collided with the country's tradition as a modern welfare state. In several court rulings, judges concluded that the harsh measures violated national social welfare legislation, harking back to the two-hundred-year-old Poor Laws and the 1948 National Assistance Act. These defeats were only a prelude to the colossal failure of the Conservative Party at the polls in the 1997 general election. The Conservatives had miscalculated. According to Saggar, "The race card, in essence, was widely thought to amount to a crucial part of a strategy by which electoral survival, possibly victory, might be pulled from the jaws of inevitable electoral defeat" (2000, 175). However, the mainstream media did not take up the asylum issue and instead concentrated on more conventional matters, such as the health system, public expenditure, education, the constitution (that is, devolution), corruption in the Conservative government, and Britain's relationship with the European Union (Butler and Kavanagh 1997, 140). The lack of salience of the immigration and asylum issues corresponded with the public's disengagement. In 1996, these issues did not even make it on the top ten list of the public's main concerns (MORI 2001).

5.6.3 Immigration, Asylum, Race, and New Labour

New Labour's approach to immigration, asylum and race relations has been three-pronged. Prime Minister Blair has made the economic case for managed migration, adopting initiatives to recruit skilled labor to the UK. Additionally, he has followed practices of previous decades, by enacting immigration controls that rival Conservative toughness,[38] while at the same time passing extensive legislation to combat racial discrimination.[39] The appointment of David Blunkett as home secretary in Labour's second term has shifted the balance somewhat. Since Blunkett's arrival, riots involving Asian youths (generally dubbed "race riots") in three northern towns in the summer of 2001, the electoral advances of the extremist BNP in Labour strongholds, as well as the attacks of September 11, 2001, have led the Home Office to replace its emphasis on tolerant multiculturalism with a focus on "core British values" (Randall 2003, 189–190). This emphasis on Britishness may be a poor interpretation of the concept of "community cohesion" developed by a Home Office research report. Following the riots in Bradford, Burnley, and Oldham, these researchers concluded that the pervasive segregation and deep polarization that divided these towns along racial lines had "ensured divisiveness and a perception of unfairness" (Home Office 2001, 11). Government funding programs, for example, fueled "resentment . . . by suggestions that one particular sector of the community was getting a disproportionate share of available monies or . . . that funding was being provided to minority ethnic groups for what some white political leaders saw as being unnecessary or trivial purposes" (Home Office 2001, 18). The report thus called for initiatives that would create more cohesive communities by fostering communication, cooperation, and respect across ethnic lines. The report's recommendations, however, fit uneasily with the public's mood and with Blunkett's leadership.[40]

The Blair government's management of immigration and race relations has occurred in the context of another challenging development: the hardening of public opinion against the country's asylum regime and the incoming refugees. In contrast to its Conservative predecessors, Labour has faced an electorate that has become increasingly aware of—and hostile to—issues surrounding the immigration and settlement of asylum seekers. By the time of the 2001 general election, 19 percent of those surveyed considered race relations and immigration as one of the most important issues facing the country, putting it in fourth place, after law and order (33 percent), health (26 percent), and unemployment (23 percent) (MORI 2001). Moreover, the Conservatives' and the tabloids' repeated mantra that most asylum seekers were bogus started to stick; while in 1997 only 11 percent of Britons thought that economic reasons motivated refugees to seek asylum in another country, this figure had climbed to almost a third by 1999 and to one half by 2002.[41] Despite the Blair government's various measures to curb asylum applications, by 2003, 85 percent of Britons did not think that the government "had immigration under control," 67 percent wanted laws on immigration to be tougher, and 13 percent preferred a complete ban on immigration.[42] Race relations and immigration now competed with the National Health Service and education as the top concern of Britons in 2003 and 2004, with up to 36 percent citing it as one of the most important issues confronting the nation.[43]

The reasons for the return of the immigration issue, now framed in terms of asylum, may be varied, but the MORI polling institute suggests that the negative media coverage has greatly contributed to the public's increased hostility toward immigration and considers the Conservatives' politicization of the issue in the 2001 election a minor factor.[44] Indeed, the Conservatives' stance was ambiguous, reflecting the party's deep divisions. While the party leadership and most MPs signed a pledge months before the election, committing themselves to refrain from exploiting racial prejudices during the campaign, some Tories still hung on to the logic of 1992, stoking anti-immigrant sentiment as an electoral strategy (Saggar 2001, 764–767). As the shadow leader of the House of Commons, Eric Forth, put it bluntly: "All this sucking up to minorities is ridiculous. There are millions of people in this country who are white, Anglo-Saxon and bigoted, and they need to be represented."[45] This view may not represent mainstream Conservatives—but it ensures that, at least in the foreseeable future, the politicization of immigration, asylum, and race will remain in the party's electoral repertoire.

5.7 Conclusion

The political treatment of immigration has taken on many guises since the process of large-scale migration started in Great Britain in the late 1940s. An attitude of laissez-faire and benign neglect characteristic of the early years was soon superseded by consensual appeasement politics. Deep-seated prejudices against ethnically distinct newcomers and rejection of future immigrant inflows led both Labour and Conservative governments to enact successive immigration restrictions in an effort to assuage xenophobic alarmism. At the same time, Labour governments hoped to promote tolerance and integration with the help of several Race Relations acts. Finally, since the 1960s, politicians have discovered that, under the right circumstances, fomenting anti-immigrant sentiment can yield attractive electoral rewards. The most prominent politician associated with playing the race card was Margaret Thatcher. The xenophobic voters who feared that immigrants would usurp public resources and who helped Thatcher gain successive victories also tended to be the losers by virtue of her drastic cuts in public expenditures and overall onslaught on the welfare state.

6

United Kingdom: Quantitative Analysis

6.1   Introduction

This chapter studies the effect that racism and xenophobia among British voters had on redistributive politics and the size of the welfare state in the United Kingdom during the period 1979–1997. The period covers the eighteen years of Conservative government that began with Margaret Thatcher's first victory in 1979 and ended in 1997 with New Labour's landslide victory over John Major's Conservatives. We describe UK politics during this period with a model of political competition between two major parties, Labour (Left) and the Conservatives (Right), where the policy space is two-dimensional: one dimension of competition concerns the size of the welfare state, and the other, race/immigration policy. While class has long been the mainstay of British politics, the previous chapter has shown that issues surrounding race and immigration have become increasingly salient over the last several decades.

Figure 6.1 shows the UK general election results during the 1945–2001 period in terms of both vote share and seat share. In the analysis, we ignore minor parties (the Liberal Party [or the Liberal Democrats], the Scottish National Party, Plaid Cymru, the Green Party, and so on), because national political competition has generally been dominated by the Conservative and the Labour parties.[1]

As in the United States, we employ two approaches (the log utility function approach and the Euclidean utility function approach) in our study of

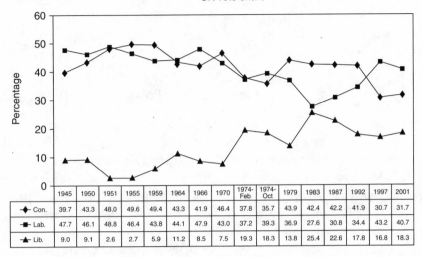

UK vote share

	1945	1950	1951	1955	1959	1964	1966	1970	1974-Feb	1974-Oct	1979	1983	1987	1992	1997	2001
Con.	39.7	43.3	48.0	49.6	49.4	43.3	41.9	46.4	37.8	35.7	43.9	42.4	42.2	41.9	30.7	31.7
Lab.	47.7	46.1	48.8	46.4	43.8	44.1	47.9	43.0	37.2	39.3	36.9	27.6	30.8	34.4	43.2	40.7
Lib.	9.0	9.1	2.6	2.7	5.9	11.2	8.5	7.5	19.3	18.3	13.8	25.4	22.6	17.8	16.8	18.3

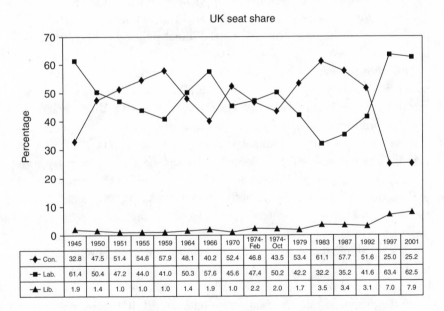

UK seat share

	1945	1950	1951	1955	1959	1964	1966	1970	1974-Feb	1974-Oct	1979	1983	1987	1992	1997	2001
Con.	32.8	47.5	51.4	54.6	57.9	48.1	40.2	52.4	46.8	43.5	53.4	61.1	57.7	51.6	25.0	25.2
Lab.	61.4	50.4	47.2	44.0	41.0	50.3	57.6	45.6	47.4	50.2	42.2	32.2	35.2	41.6	63.4	62.5
Lib.	1.9	1.4	1.0	1.0	1.0	1.4	1.9	1.0	2.2	2.0	1.7	3.5	3.4	3.1	7.0	7.9

Figure 6.1   UK general election results: 1945–2001. Source: BES.

the UK. Our two main sources of data for the UK are the Family Expenditure Survey (FES) and the British General Election Studies (BES). The FES is comparable to the PSID in the United States and the BES is comparable to the American NES.

6.2 Minorities, Race, and Class Politics in the UK

The United Kingdom has long been viewed as one of the most class-based societies in the industrial democratic world, and its politics have been viewed as class politics, with the manual working class generally voting for Labour and the middle class for the Conservatives. In the 1950s and 1960s it was generally agreed that class was preeminent among the factors used to explain party allegiance in Britain. During the Thatcher period (1979–1990), however, many of the postwar class-leveling policies were reversed; this was also a time in which class *de*alignment—the weakening of the class basis of party support—occurred. It is during this period that the phenomenon of working-class Tories and middle-class socialists received much attention among scholars. New lines of division, altering the structure of traditional political competition, have been much discussed.

The basic pattern of changes over time in the relationship between class membership and voting is shown in Table 6.1. We distinguish five social classes according to the Goldthorpe-Heath class classification—(1) the salariat (composed of professionals, managers, and administrators in relatively secure employment); (2) routine nonmanual workers (largely women in office work but with little in the way of promotion or career prospects); (3) the petty bourgeoisie (consisting of employers and the self-employed); (4) the higher levels of the working class (consisting of foremen, technicians, and skilled manual workers); and (5) the lower levels of the working class (covering semi- and unskilled manual workers).

Table 6.1 shows that class has been very important in explaining the voting pattern in the UK. Labour voting is lower both in the salariat and in the petty bourgeoisie, and high in the upper and lower working class, except in 1997, when the proportion of the middle class (classes I, II, III) voting Labour was far higher than at any previous point in the BES series.

Next we turn to the relationship between race/ethnicity and voting, which is summarized in Table 6.2. British minority voters backed the Labour Party in large numbers during the 1979–1997 period: typically four in five minority voters supported Labour, as shown in Table 6.2a, a proportion quite compa-

Table 6.1   Class voting in the UK

Year	I Salariat	II Routine nonmanual	III Petty bourgeoisie	IV Foremen, skilled manual	V Semi- and unskilled manual
Percentage voting Labour					
1964	19	26	15	56	66
1966	24	41	20	67	70
1970	26	40	20	60	61
1974.2	21	29	18	49	61
1974.10	23	32	13	57	65
1979	22	32	13	51	53
1983	12	20	12	38	49
1987	15	26	16	43	48
1992	19	30	17	48	60
1997	39	49	40	64	69
Percentage voting Conservative					
1964	63	59	74	31	26
1966	61	49	67	29	25
1970	63	51	69	36	32
1974.2	55	45	68	31	24
1974.10	52	44	70	28	22
1979	61	52	77	36	34
1983	57	53	71	39	29
1987	53	51	64	35	31
1992	58	54	66	39	28
1997	41	33	43	18	18

Source: BES.

Note: 1974.2 denotes the February election that year; 1974.10, the October election.

rable to the support that U.S. minorities gave to the Democrats during the same period. UK minorities' overwhelming support for Labour appears to be insulated from short-term trends.[2] For instance, neither Labour's defeat in 1983 nor the gradual rise in Labour's fortunes thereafter (including 1997) is reflected among minority voters. Labour's strength among minorities over this period stands in sharp contrast to its poor track record in attracting white voters.

Table 6.2a Voting patterns of UK minorities: Party vote among ethnic minorities in the UK and the United States (percent)

	UK				United States		
Year	Lab.	Cons.	Other	Year	Dem.	Rep.	Other
1974	81	9	10	1976	91	9	0
1979	86	8	6	1980	98	2	0
1983	83	7	10	1984	91	9	0
1987	72	18	10	1988	90	10	0
1992	81	10	9	1992	92	7	1
1997	85	11	4	1996	95	2	3

Source: BES; ANES.

Table 6.2b Voting patterns of UK minorities: UK vote distribution by ethnic groups, 1997 (percent)

Ethnic group	Labour	Conservative	Other
White	47.1	30.9	22
Indian	80.3	17.5	2.2
Pakistani	85.9	7.1	7
Bangladeshi	84.6	5.1	10.3
Black–African	93.2	2.3	4.5
Black–Caribbean	93.9	4.5	1.5
Miscellaneous	72.9	18.6	8.5

Source: BES.

Although minority support for Labour is overwhelming, there is some variation across minority groups. (See Table 6.2b.) In particular, a clear contrast between South Asian and black voters is discernible. Labour voting is four out of five in the case of Asians, but nine out of ten among blacks. Consequently, although the rate of South Asian Tory voting is very low, it is still four times that found among black voters (14 percent versus 4 percent). Among the South Asian voters, Indians are the most likely to be Tory voters (17 percent), a reflection of their better economic position compared with other minorities.

Table 6.2c gives an overview of the relationship among class, race, and voting in 1997. At all levels of social class, minority support for Labour is

Table 6.2c Voting patterns of UK minorities: Race, class, and Labour voting in 1997 (percentage voting Labour)

Class	White	Black/Asian	All
I. Salariat	38	76	39
II. Routine nonmanual	44	86	49
III. Petty bourgeoisie	31	78	40
IV. Foremen and skilled manual	60	93	64
V. Semi- and unskilled manual	63	91	69
All	47	85	58

Source: BES.

markedly higher than that found in the white population. The lowest level of black and South Asian Labour voting is to be found in the salariat, where it is "only" 76 percent, whereas the highest level of white Labour voting is to be found in the lower working class, where it manages to climb to 63 percent. Even the minority petty bourgeoisie support Labour with 78 percent. (The petty bourgeoisie is of particular interest since it is a class that has been disproportionately favorable to the Conservatives, and it is also one where some well-off ethnic minorities, notably Indians and Chinese, have been overrepresented.) Thus Table 6.2 shows that minorities of *all* social class backgrounds back Labour to a degree that would be unthinkable among even those in Labour's traditional white working-class constituency. In this sense, ethnicity clearly dominates class when it comes to party identification in the UK.

However, class seems to divide black and Asian voters in much the same way as it divides whites, with Labour voting being lower both in the salariat and in the petty bourgeoisie, and being more or less equally high in the upper and lower working class. In this sense, the ethnic minority electorate is divided by class in the same *way*, though not necessarily to the same *degree*, as is the white population.

Put differently, it appears that class and race are equally important in British politics. This is in contrast with the U.S. situation, so we claim, where race has been more important in politics than class in the period we studied in Chapter 4.

It is often argued that British politics have gradually moved in a right-wing direction since 1979, reflecting the gradual growing conservatism of UK

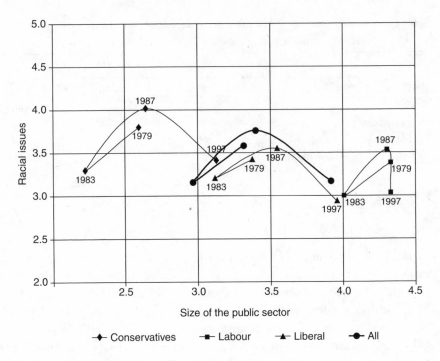

Figure 6.2 Observed average policy positions of party members on a two-dimensional policy space. The larger number in the size of the public-sector dimension represents a more pro-state position on the economic issue, while a larger number in the dimension of race measures, a more conservative position on the race issue. Source: BES.

voters. In terms of seat share, this period is clearly the Conservative period, but vote share is not predominantly in favor of the Conservatives. In particular, when we take into account the vote share taken by the Liberals, it is not clear whether British voters moved in a rightward direction. (See Figure 6.1.)

Some even argue that Labour became the party of the center on traditional economic, as well as social, issues. To check this claim, we examine the average policy positions of party members on a two-dimensional policy space and their evolution over time in Figure 6.2. The definition of the two dimensions, the size of the public sector and the race issue, is given in section 6.3. The larger number in the size of the public-sector dimension represents a more pro-state position on the economic issue, while a larger number in the dimension of race measures a more conservative position on the race issue.

In neither dimension is there evidence that British voters became uniformly more conservative. Voters in 1983 were more conservative on economic issues but less conservative on racial issues than voters in 1979. British voters then recovered the policy positions of 1979 in 1987 by being more liberal on economic issues while being more conservative on racial issues. Finally, in 1997, voters became more left-wing than in 1987 on both issues. Figure 6.2 does not support the claim that New Labour won in 1997 by virtue of being more right-wing than old Labour, although there is evidence that New Labour's manifestos are more rightist that those of old Labour (Evans and Norris 1999).

6.3   Estimation of Parameters

We describe the estimation of model parameters according to the two approaches that we adopted in the U.S. analysis.

6.3.1   Parameters for the Log Utility Function Approach

As in the U.S. analysis, we estimate the two marginal density functions non-parametrically and use them in our numerical computation. In computing the wage distribution of voters, we use the Family Expenditure Survey, while in computing the distribution of racial views, we use the British General Election Studies. The estimated density of wage distribution in 1997 is shown in Figure 6.3. For the sake of comparison, we also present the estimated density function for the United States in 1992.

The observed (effective) tax policies are computed by regressing post-fisc family income against pre-fisc family income. In calculating pre-fisc and post-fisc family incomes from the Family Expenditure Survey, we followed the procedure adopted by the Office for National Statistics. (See appendix 3 of Harris 1999 for details.) This procedure is very close to the procedure that we adopted in Chapter 4 for the United States.

Roughly put, our procedure consists of computing incomes in three stages. We first compute the *pre-fisc income* by adding earned incomes (wages and salaries, imputed employment income, and self-employment income) to other incomes (investment income, occupational pension, and so on). *Disposable income* is then obtained by adding various cash benefits and subtracting income taxes, employee's National Insurance contributions, and council taxes

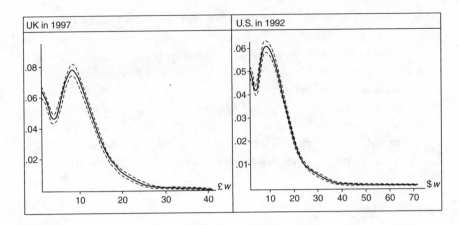

Figure 6.3   Estimated wage distribution. Thick solid lines are density estimates, and thin dashed lines are upper and lower bounds of 95% confidence intervals. Kernel = Gaussian, bandwidth = $h = 0.9 * n^{-1/5} \text{Min}[\text{Var}, (IQR/1.349)]$, where n is the number of samples, Var is the variance, and IQR is the interquartile range. Source: BES and PSID.

from disposable income. In computing cash benefits, we include both contributory cash benefits (retirement pensions, contribution-based job seeker's allowance, incapacity benefits, widow's benefits, maternity pay, and so on) and noncontributory cash benefits (income support, child benefit, housing benefit, income-based job seeker's allowance, invalid care allowance, attendance allowance, war pensions, family credit, and so on). *Post-fisc income* is now obtained by subtracting indirect taxes and adding benefits-in-kind (education, national health service, housing subsidy, travel subsidies, school meals and welfare milk, and so on) to disposable income.

The values of the β's and λ's in the utility function (see equation (2.27)) are estimated using the elasticities of labor supply for males and females, as in the U.S. analysis, using the elasticity estimates of Blundell et al. (1988). They provide the estimates for 1979; we assume that the elasticity of labor supply is not changing rapidly over time.

Figure 6.4 shows the estimated Laffer curve in the UK together with the observed policy pair (t_{obs}, b'_{obs}). As in the United States, the fit of our model is reasonably good; the observed fiscal policy (the large dot) lies very close to the estimated Laffer curve. (Again for the sake of comparison, we also present the estimated Laffer curve for the United States in 1992.)

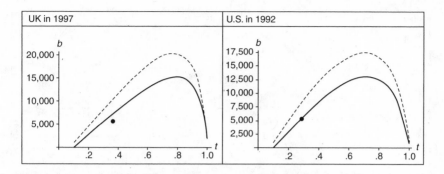

Figure 6.4 Estimation of the Laffer curve according to the log utility function approach. The solid lines represent the estimated Laffer curves when the wage distributions are estimated nonparametrically. The dashed lines represent the estimated Laffer curves when the wage distributions are assumed to be lognormal and the two parameters are estimated by minimizing the L_2-norm of the difference between the lognormal density and the kernel density. The big black dots represent (t_{obs}, b_{obs}), estimated from the data. Source: BES and PSID.

We now turn to the estimation of racism in the UK. To reflect the fact that British racism is a combination of racism (against colored citizens) and xenophobia (against colored foreigners), we construct the racism variable by taking the average of the following two variables from the BES. The scale of this variable is 0 (liberal)–6 (conservative).

1. *Toomanyimmigrants:* Respondent's view on the question "Do you think that too many immigrants have been let into this country or not?," running from 0 (liberal: not many) to 6 (conservative: too many).
2. *Blackequalgtf:* Respondent's view on the question "How do you feel about recent attempts to ensure equality for coloured people? Has equal opportunity for Blacks and Asians gone too far?," running from 0 (liberal: not too far) to 6 (conservative: too far).

The marginal densities of our racism variable are depicted in Figure 6.5.

The log utility function approach is computationally expensive. Because of this we run the models of this approach only for one year (1997). Estimated parameter values are presented in Table 6.3.

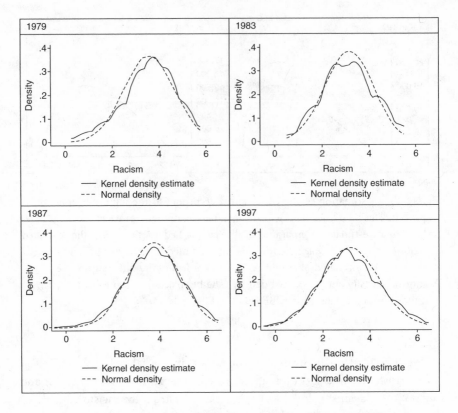

Figure 6.5   The distribution of racism in the UK. Bandwidth = 0.5 for all years. Source: BES.

Before concluding this subsection, we must mention that there are several differences between the U.S. and the UK analyses in spite of our effort to make the two cases as comparable as possible.

First, we did not take into account the possibility that campaign finance might influence the payoff function of the two parties in the UK. In contrast to the United States, campaign finance in the UK is largely public.

Second, we do not try to decompose the four ideological components from various variables using factor analysis. Indeed the lack of a large number of relevant variables in the BES prevents us from doing so.

Third, in the U.S. case, the NES provides information on the public perception about the presidential candidates' position on aid to blacks. There is no analogous information in the BES. Thus although we could identify the

Table 6.3 Estimated parameter values of the models (Summary)

	1979	1983	1987	1997	Source
Parameters in the log utility function model					
w_M: Male hourly wage (£)				7.2066	FES
w_F: Female hourly wage (£)				4.4767	FES
L_M: Male annual working hours				1,976	FES
L_F: Female annual working hours				1,196	FES
Y_M: Male labor income (£)				14240.24	FES
Y_F: Female labor income (£)				5354.13	FES
Y: Earned family income (£)				16595.80	FES
O: Other family income (£)				2654.08	FES
W: Pre-fisc family income (£)				19249.88	FES
X: Post-fisc family income (£)				17499.56	FES
$k_1 = w_F/w_M$				0.6212	FES
$k_3 = O/W$				0.138	FES
Uncompensated elasticity (male)	0.024			0.024	Blundell
Uncompensated elasticity (female)	0.620			0.620	Blundell
t_{obs}: Observed effective tax rate				0.36	FES
b_{obs}: Observed effective per capita transfer (£)				5725.69	FES
C: Per capita public good (£)				3845.8	FES
α				0.52	FES
d				0.20	FES
δ_2				0.092	est.
Parameters in the Euclidean utility function model					
t_{obs} ($=\mu_\theta$: mean of θ)	3.315	2.966	3.394	3.915	BES
r_{obs} ($=\mu_\rho$: mean of ρ)	3.579	3.158	3.758	3.169	BES
t^L_{obs} of militants	4.147	4.004	4.303	4.327	BES
t^R_{obs} of militants	2.597	2.210	2.642	3.128	BES
r^L_{obs} of militants	3.383	2.997	3.534	3.036	BES
r^R_{obs} of militants	3.793	3.299	4.019	3.412	BES
σ_θ (standard deviation of θ)	1.287	1.264	1.193	1.102	BES
σ_ρ (standard deviation of ρ)	1.098	1.043	1.114	1.197	BES
$\rho_{\theta\rho}$ (correlation between θ and ρ)	−0.189	−0.156	−0.184	−0.056	BES
μ_θ in the racism-free environment (option 1)	3.949	3.434	4.009	4.052	BES
σ_θ in the racism-free environment (option 1)	1.278	1.259	1.177	1.102	BES
γ	0.914	0.896		1.000	BES
δ	−0.220	−0.189	−0.198	−0.051	BES
Common parameters					
Observed L vote share (among L-R voters)	0.457	0.394	0.422	0.585	Leeke

Note: FES = Family Expenditure Survey; BES = British General Election Studies; Leeke = Leeke (2003); Blundell = Blundell et al. (1988).

observed tax policies in the log utility model, we were unable to identify the observed race policies of the two parties in the UK.

Finally, again because of lack of information, we were unable to estimate type-distributions separately for whites and minorities.

Thus our estimation in the UK case is cruder than for the United States.

6.3.2 Parameters for the Euclidean Utility Function Approach

On the one hand, our racism variable in the Euclidean utility function approach is the same as the one used in the log utility function approach. A voter's position on the size of the public sector θ is, on the other hand, constructed from the average of the following three variables chosen from the BES. These variables have been scaled differently, and even the same variable is scaled differently across different years. (For example, the variable *Taxation* has 7 levels in 1979, 21 levels in 1983, 11 levels in 1992, and so on.) For all years and all variables, we converted the original levels into the scale of 0 (conservative)–6 (liberal) before taking the average.

1. *Taxation:* Respondent's view on taxation and the health and social services, running from 0 (conservative: cut taxes) to 6 (liberal: increase taxes): "Some people feel that government should put up taxes a lot and spend much more on health and social services. Other people feel that government should cut taxes a lot and spend much less on health and social services. Other people have views in-between. Using the following scale . . . Where would you place your view?"

2. *Nationalization:* Respondent's view on nationalization/privatization, running from 0 (conservative: privatize all industries) to 6 (liberal: nationalize all industries): "Some people feel that government should nationalize many more private companies. Other people feel that government should sell off many more nationalized industries. Other people have views in-between. Using the following scale . . . Where would you place your view?"

3. *Redistributepeople:* Income and wealth must be redistributed to ordinary working people, running from 0 (conservative: do not make incomes equal) to 6 (liberal: equalize incomes): "Some people feel that government should make much greater efforts to make people's incomes more equal. Other people feel that government should be much less concerned about how equal people's incomes are. Other people

have views in-between. Using the following scale . . . Where would you place your view?"

The marginal densities for the ideal size of the public sector and racism-free preferences for the public sector are presented in Figure 6.6.

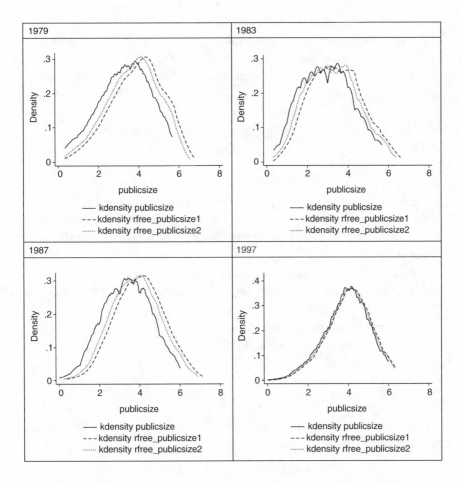

Figure 6.6 The distribution of the preferred size of the public sector and the counterfactual distributions of racism-free preferences. Bandwidth = optimal for all years. Source: BES. kdensity publicsize: the kernel density estimate of the preferred size of the public sector. kdensity rfree_publicsize1: the kernel density estimate of racism-free preferences for the size of the public sector, taking $\rho_{ref} = 1$. kdensity rfree_publicsize2: the kernel density estimate of racism-free preferences for the size of the public sector, taking $\rho_{ref} = 2$.

Overall, the distribution of voter types is similar in 1979 and 1987. Relative to 1979 and 1987, 1983 is the year when both the distribution of ρ and that of θ shift to the left, meaning that voters are less racist and more conservative in the economic dimension than in 1979 and 1987. Thus although all these years are Thatcher years, there are some differences across them. In 1997 (when Labour won), on the other hand, UK voters are less racist and more liberal on economic issues than in 1987.

We approximate the joint distribution by a bivariate normal distribution with estimated parameter values reported in Table 6.3. Marginal densities, shown in Figures 6.5 and 6.6, are quite symmetric; thus the assumption of the normal distribution appears to be reasonable in the UK. Almost all the support of a bivariate normal falls on the square $[0, 7] \times [0, 7]$. We computed the overall means and standard deviations separately for whites and nonwhites, voters and nonvoters, and Left-voters and Right-voters. As in the United States, the difference between voters and nonvoters is not very large. The main differences lie between Left and Right voters and between whites and minorities.

We note that the Liberal Democrats (or the Social Democratic Alliance) are somewhere in the middle between the two major parties, and so describing British national politics as a two-party competition is not unreasonable, for our purposes.

We estimate δ (see equation (2.48)) by running a regression of θ against ρ and a constant. Then we estimate the racism-free demand for two different values of ρ_{ref}: $\rho_{ref} = 1$ (option 1) and $\rho_{ref} = 2$ (option 2).

We run the models according to the Euclidean utility function approach for three election years (1979, 1983, and 1997).

6.4 The PBE and ASE: Computation

We ran the full model and the two counterfactuals according to the two approaches we described in chapter 2.

6.4.1 PUNEs in the Log Utility Function Approach

In the UK, we could not estimate the values of γ, δ_0, and δ_2 empirically (see equation (2.41)); thus we search for γ, δ_0, and δ_2 by adjusting their values by trial and error until the equilibrium vote share is close to the observed vote share.

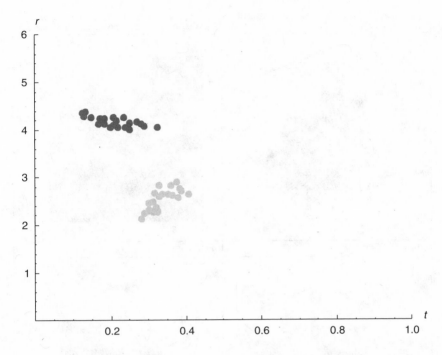

Figure 6.7 UK PUNEs according to the log utility function approach. Light gray dots (in the southeast) are policies for Labour and dark gray dots (in the northwest) are policies for Conservatives.

Figure 6.7 presents the equilibrium values of PUNEs found using this approach. It presents the equilibrium values of (t, r) in the two-dimensional policy space. We see that PUNEs are highly concentrated.

In Figure 6.8, we have drawn the party membership separation hyper-space, together with the observed membership distribution of voter types, for three models: the full model and the two counterfactual models. Figure 6.8 shows that party membership is sensitive to both the economic and the racial positions of voters. We compare the equilibrium separation of citizens into the two parties, determined by the model, with the real party identification estimated from the actual data. Each panel in Figure 6.8 represents the type space, with the wage on the abscissa and the racial view in the ordinate. In the graph we represent different densities of *observed L* party membership across 25 discrete cells with different shades of gray; the darker the cell is, the higher the observed Labour membership. Shown together with the density plots is the party

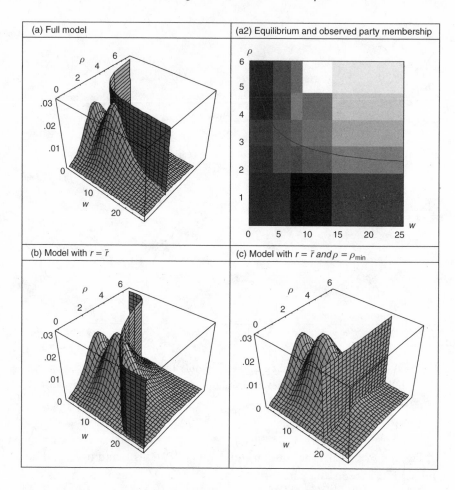

Figure 6.8 Voter separation according to the log utility function approach. Voter separation hyper-planes are drawn at the mean value of equilibrium policy vectors. In the party membership graph (a2), shades of gray represent the density plot of observed L party membership computed from actual data; the darker the cell is, the higher the observed membership. The downward-sloping curves represent the equilibrium party separation graph in the model.

separation graph $\rho = \Psi(w, \tau^L, \tau^R)$, the cutoff hyper-space for party membership in the model. Since there are many PUNEs, there are as many Ψ-graphs as there are PUNEs. The graph of Ψ drawn in Figure 6.8 is based on the mean value of the platform vector (τ^L, τ^R).

Table 6.4 Decomposition of the two effects according to the log utility function approach, 1997 ($\delta_0 = 0.85$; $\delta_2 = 0.092$; $\gamma = 0.1059$)

	Full	$r = $ rbar	$r = $ rbar $\rho = \rho$min	Total effect	PBE	ASE	PBE (%)	ASE (%)
t^L	0.354	0.428	0.533	0.179	0.074	0.105	41%	59%
t^R	0.278	0.333	0.428	0.15	0.055	0.095	37%	63%
r^D	2.538							
r^R	4.181							
t^{exp}	0.327	0.400	0.512	0.186	0.073	0.113	39%	61%
L vote share	0.639	0.702	0.803	0.164	0.063	0.101	38%	62%
No. of PUNEs	22	46	18					

Figure 6.8 shows that racism is salient in the politics of the UK, but in contrast to the United States, class politics are equally important. Indeed the slope of the voter-separating hyper-space is steeper than that for the United States. The empirical party membership also shows many darker cells among the poor voters than in the United States.

We computed PUNEs in the full model and the two counterfactuals, and carried out decomposition analyses. Table 6.4 reports the decomposition of total effects according to the log utility function approach. Again the equilibrium tax rates are differentiated between the two parties. The tax rate proposed by the Labour Party in the full model is about 8 percent higher than that proposed by the Conservative Party.

Our model predicts that the Conservative Party would have proposed an effective marginal tax rate of 42.8 percent in 1997, absent racism. Because of the existence of racism, however, the Conservative Party was able to propose a tax rate of 27.8 percent in this year; thus the effect of racism on the tax rate is about 15 percent for the Conservative Party. The effect of racism on the tax rate proposed by the Labour Party (17.9 percent) is even larger. Absent racism, we predict Labour would have proposed a marginal tax rate of 53.3 percent; due to the existence of racism, it proposed 35.4 percent.

The total effect of racism is large for both parties, and the composition of the total effect is similar across the parties: somewhat more than half of the total effect is due to antisolidarity, but the policy-bundle effect is also of significant size.

6.4.2   PUNEs in the Euclidean Utility Function Approach

We first report graphically those PUNEs in the Euclidean function approach; see Figure 6.9. In each graph, there are five sets of dots; consult the legend of the figure for an explanation of the various dots. Note that the first two sets of dots come from observation; all the others come from the PUNE calculation.

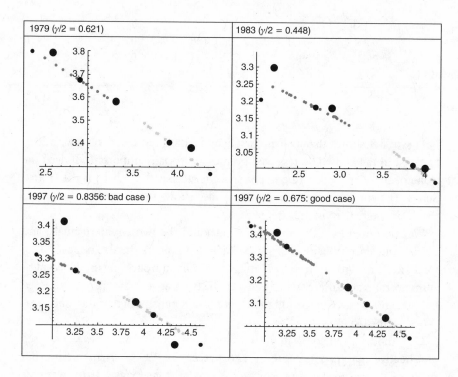

Figure 6.9   PUNEs according to the Euclidean utility function approach. The largest (middle) dot is the *average ideal position of the polity*—this is observed from the survey. The other pair of largest dots are the average *observed* policy positions of those who, in the voter survey, identified with Labour and Conservative. The next largest *pair* of dots constitute the average policies of PUNEs of the two parties, where we take only those PUNEs for which Labour's vote share is within 5 percent of the observed vote share. The next largest pair of dots are the average ideal points of the Militants in the Left and Right parties at PUNEs. Recall that each PUNE comes with a partition of the polity into two party memberships. These dots are the average policy views of those memberships. The very small dots (lighter gray and darker gray) are the policies of the two parties in PUNEs—darker gray is Right, lighter gray is Left.

For the sake of illustration, we present two graphs in 1997 corresponding to different values of γ. If the model were perfect, the second and fourth sets of dots described in the caption would coincide. Thus when the right value of γ is chosen ($\gamma/2 = 0.675$, the last panel in Figure 6.9), then the second pair (number 2 above) of dots should be collinear with the rest. If the "wrong" value of γ is chosen, in contrast, the second pair of dots is not collinear with the rest; the third panel in Figure 6.9 presents the result with a "wrong" value of γ ($\gamma/2 = 0.8356$). Thus we choose the value of γ so that observed polity views are literally "in line" with what PUNE predicts.

Once having chosen γ, our procedure was as follows:

1. Compute many PUNEs for the full model. Select those for which the Left's vote share is within 5 percent of the observed vote share of Labour for the year in question.[3] Compute the average relative bargaining power of the Militants in the two parties at these PUNEs. Denote the values of t in these PUNEs by $\{t_i^L, t_i^R\}$, for Left and Right.

2. Next, run a counterfactual election, as described in Chapter 2, with the same distribution of voter types, but only on the "tax" issue. Here we compute hundreds of PUNEs, which we designate P-PUNEs. We compute the relative bargaining powers of the Militants in each party in each P-PUNE.

3. Select a set of twenty P-PUNEs that minimize the Euclidean distance from the pair of bargaining powers to the average bargaining powers of the Militants in the (full) PUNEs.

4. Finally, replace the true distribution of voter types with the estimated *racism-free* distribution of public-sector-size views, denoted G. (As we have described, we cannot estimate perfectly the racism-free distribution G. We made the computation for two estimates of this distribution, with different means.) Compute hundreds of what we call Q-PUNEs, in the counterfactual election where only the size of the public sector is an issue, and the distribution of voter types is G. Again, select the twenty Q-PUNEs whose pair of bargaining powers is close to the average bargaining powers of step 1.

Thus in the counterfactuals, we attempt to hold the relative bargaining powers of the factions to what they are in the full-model PUNEs. (As in the U.S. analysis, we report the results with unrestricted bargaining power in Appendix Table B.4.)

Table 6.5a Decomposition according to the Euclidean function approach, UK, 1979

	Full	Counter 1	Counter 2i	Counter 2ii
$1-\alpha^L$	0.434599	0.432588	0.423827	0.444072
$1-\alpha^R$	0.369564	0.365889	0.374635	0.375849
t^L	3.91135	3.986	4.54573	4.36037
t^R	2.91539	2.94572	3.51815	3.31542
r^L	3.40507			
r^R	3.67291			
t^{exp}	3.38156	3.4192	4.00596	3.7962
ϕ^L	0.470187	0.455026	0.474497	0.459942

Note: Counter 1 are P-PUNEs; Counters 2i and 2ii are Q-PUNEs under two of the three hypothetical racism-free distributions of voter types. ϕ^L is L vote share.

Table 6.5b The policy-bundle (PB) and antisolidarity (AS) effects, Euclidean function approach, UK, 1979

Party	PBE	ASE$_i$	ASE$_{ii}$	$\dfrac{TOT_i}{std.\ dev.}$	$\dfrac{TOT_{ii}}{std.\ dev.}$
Labour	0.0747	0.5597	0.3744	49.18%	34.81%
Conservative	0.0303	0.5724	0.3697	46.72%	31.01%
Average	0.0376	0.5867	0.3770	48.40%	32.14%

Note: TOT_i is ($PBE + ASE_i$). Std. dev. is the standard deviation of the observed distribution of views on the immigration issue.

Summary statistics for the computed PUNEs and the decomposition of racism effect into the two separate effects in the Euclidean utility function approach are reported in Tables 6.5, 6.6, and 6.7. For each year, we report two tables, one reporting decomposition results and the other reporting PUNEs and the bargaining powers. We report total effect as a percentage of the standard deviation of the (true marginal) distribution of θ. Again we find a substantial policy-bundle effect—both in absolute terms and as a fraction of the total effect, although in one year (for example, 1997), the PBE for the Conservative Party is negative.

Our conclusion is thus that both the policy-bundle and antisolidarity effects are active in British politics. It appears, however, that these effects are substantially smaller in 1997 than they were in 1979 and 1983, despite the fact that the

Table 6.6a Decomposition according to the Euclidean function approach, UK, 1983

	Full	Counter 1	Counter 2i	Counter 2ii
$1-\alpha^L$	0.588988	0.588223	0.605581	0.581059
$1-\alpha^R$	0.37124	0.35893	0.382139	0.364349
t^L	3.85842	3.96622	4.40467	4.19711
t^R	2.70399	2.74274	3.20933	3.04121
r^L	3.01051			
r^R	3.18229			
t^{exp}	3.15074	3.19221	3.66704	3.47935
ϕ^L	0.380858	0.367418	0.382478	0.378788

Note: For explanation of column heads, see note, Table 6.5a.

Table 6.6b The policy-bundle (PB) and antisolidarity (AS) effects, Euclidean function approach, UK, 1983

Party	PBE	ASE$_i$	ASE$_{ii}$	$\frac{TOT_i}{std.\ dev.}$	$\frac{TOT_{ii}}{std.\ dev.}$
Labour	0.1078	0.4385	0.2309	40.77%	25.28%
Conservative	0.0387	0.4666	0.2985	37.71%	25.17%
Average	0.0415	0.4748	0.2871	38.53%	24.52%

Note: For explanation of TOT_i, see note, Table 6.5b.

estimated salience of the race issue is greater in 1997 than in 1979 and 1983. The total effect of racism measured in the Euclidean utility function approach thus ranges between 30 and 50 percent of one standard deviation in 1979, 24–40 percent in 1983, and 11–15 percent in 1997. These results are in fact quite plausible. As we wrote in Chapter 5, by 1997 the British electorate, having lived through eighteen years of Conservative austerity politics, was mainly concerned with the future of Britain's health care system, education, and the size of the public sector. While Tories tried to keep the issues of asylum and immigration alive, voters were preoccupied with traditional class politics.

With each PUNE computation, we have, as well, an endogenous determination of the membership of the two parties, as defined in Chapter 2. Figure 6.10 presents the partition of the space of types for the average PUNE with the correct vote shares.

Table 6.7a   Decomposition according to the Euclidean function approach, UK, 1997

	Full	Counter 1	Counter 2i	Counter 2ii
$1-\alpha^L$	0.361143	0.351087	0.354133	0.378425
$1-\alpha^R$	0.463458	0.47932	0.473069	0.470012
t^L	4.12166	4.1493	4.29099	4.29402
t^R	3.2374	3.18947	3.37563	3.35827
r^L	3.09885			
r^R	3.74812			
t^{exp}	3.74812	3.74849	3.90415	3.88111
ϕ^L	0.580352	0.582771	0.577836	0.559153

Note: For explanation of column heads, see note, Table 6.5a.

Table 6.7b   The policy-bundle (PB) and antisolidarity (AS) effects, UK, Euclidean function approach, 1997

Party	PBE	ASE_i	ASE_{ii}	$\frac{TOT_i}{std.\ dev.}$	$\frac{TOT_{ii}}{std.\ dev.}$
Labour	0.0276	0.1417	0.1447	14.75%	15.01%
Conservative	−0.0479	0.1862	0.1688	12.04%	10.53%
Average	0.0004	0.1557	0.1326	13.59%	11.58%

Note: For explanation of TOT_i, see note, Table 6.5b.

In Figure 6.10, the horizontal axis is θ, the vertical axis is ρ. The figure presents a density plot of the distribution of voter types and the endogenous partition of the polity into Left and Right. (Left types are to the *right* of the line: they have a high value of θ.) Figure 6.10 suggests that the tax issue remains very important in the UK: that is, the race issue is only important in determining party membership for those whose value of θ lies in the interval [3, 4]. This group makes up 31 percent of the polity, according to our estimated bivariate normal distribution for 1997. Thus our model predicts that for 69 percent of the polity, the decisive issue, with regard to party identification, remains the economic issue.

Figure 6.9 offers an interesting comparison. In 1983, note that the average observed position of the polity is very close to the average policy position of the Right party in full PUNEs, and distant from the average policy position of the

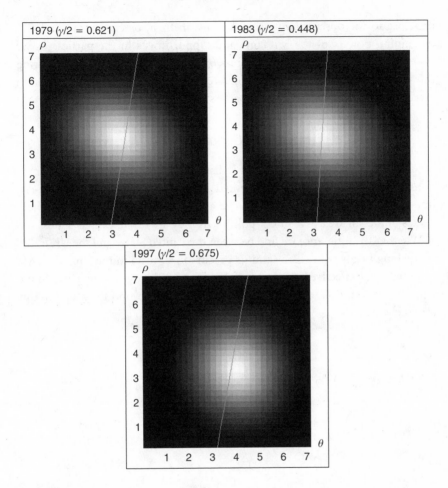

Figure 6.10   UK party partition according to the Euclidean utility function approach.

Left. Thus our model predicts that Labour is "too far left" compared with the average citizen, at least judged by what the Conservatives are proposing. This is reflected in the relatively large bargaining powers of the Militants in the Left. Note, however, that in 1997 the average Labour platform in PUNE is much closer to the average ideal point of the citizenry than is the average platform of Conservatives. This is what the transformation to New Labour under Tony Blair accomplished.

How does the model achieve these historically accurate results? Recall that we fit the model to the data by choosing PUNEs whose party vote shares are close to the observed vote shares. This, in turn, determines the relative bargaining powers of the Militants and Opportunists in the parties. As we have said, we do not offer a theory for *why* Labour moved to the right during this period: such a theory, to be consistent with our model, would have to articulate the *dynamics* of the intraparty struggle between factions.

6.5   Conclusion

We find that the effect of racism on redistribution in the United Kingdom is nonnegligible. In contrast to the United States, however, class politics are as important as race politics. Yet both the antisolidarity and the policy-bundle effects of racism are active in UK politics, as they are in the United States.

Whether the difference we find between the United States and the UK is due to the long history of racism (and its precursor, slavery) in the United States, or to the more effective harnessing of that issue by the right-wing party in the United States (the southern strategy), is a question beyond the scope of this inquiry.

7

Immigration: A Challenge to Tolerant Denmark

7.1   Introduction

Ethnic heterogeneity has come to Denmark only relatively recently. In 1960, the number of foreign nationals was just over 40,000, which at the time constituted less than 1 percent of the population. But even that number vastly overstated the country's diversity. While precise figures are lacking, estimates are that about half of those 40,000 were from other Nordic countries, and over a quarter were from the remaining developed countries of Europe and North America. In total there were thus about 10,000 non-Westerners living in Denmark in 1960 (S. Pedersen 1999, 151–154).

As of 2000, the number of foreign nationals had grown to about 260,000, or 4.9 percent of the total population. This number too needs to be adjusted, although in the opposite direction. By 2000 Denmark also had a fair number of immigrants who had become citizens, and an even larger number of citizens who were the descendants of immigrants, neither of whom are reflected in the 260,000. When one adjusts the number to include these two groups the figure rises to about 375,000, or 7.1 percent of the population (Schultz-Nielsen 2001, 14). And reversing the proportion that existed four decades earlier, only about 20 percent of the 375,000 were from the developed West (S. Pedersen 1999, 154). In sum, the non-Western proportion of Denmark's population had increased over 25-fold in those four decades, from around

---

This chapter was written by Daniel J. Doherty.

0.2 percent to about 5.5 percent. And while more than two-thirds of the immigrants from the developed West are in Denmark for less than five years, the overwhelming majority of non-Western immigrants are making Denmark their home (S. Pedersen 1999, 156). Not surprisingly, it is in the last decade or so that concerns surrounding immigrants and refugees—that some are taking advantage of the generous Danish welfare state, or that their large numbers pose a threat to the Danish way of life—have emerged as significant political issues.

If we look beyond just population figures, 1960 and 2000 provide quite different snapshots. The Denmark of 1960 was characterized by a generous and expanding welfare state and a historical reputation for humanitarianism and tolerance—a reputation most famously earned by the actions of many Danes to save almost all 7,500 Danish Jews from extermination by the Nazis, and freshly enhanced by Denmark's being the first country to sign the 1951 UN Convention Relating to the Status of Refugees. The Denmark of the turn of the millennium has cut back on its provision of social benefits, has tightened its borders, and the leader of its third-largest party has stated that "Denmark is a small homogenous country which must not be disturbed" (Agence France Presse 1997), while the party program proclaims: "Denmark is not an immigrant-country and never has been. Thus we will not accept transformation to a multiethnic society" (Dansk Folkeparti 2004). By looking at demographic trends, political and social developments, polling data, and changes in the law, this chapter will provide a brief chronological exploration of this transition.

7.2   The Early Years: Guest Workers and Their Families

Prior to 1970, Denmark had essentially no restrictions on immigration. It also never had any sizable net influx. From the end of World War II until the mid-1960s, the total number of migrants ranged from 35,000 to 60,000, with net outflows prior to 1959 and small net inflows through the mid-sixties. The nature of these migrants made immigration almost invisible. In a typical year about one-quarter of "immigrants" were Danish citizens returning from abroad. Of the rest, a significant majority were from Norway, Sweden, Great Britain, Germany, and the United States (S. Pedersen 1999, 149).

Then, beginning in the mid-sixties and peaking in 1969 and 1970, Denmark saw an increasing number of "guest workers"—primarily men from

Turkey, Yugoslavia, and Pakistan. With the nation facing a consistently tight labor market, the influx was welcomed and even encouraged by industry and by most government officials. Blue-collar workers and their unions, in contrast, voiced concerns about economic threats (competition for jobs, especially in the winter), crime, and housing shortages. A Gallup survey in late 1970 gave a glimpse of this class divide: of all respondents, 34 percent thought that importing foreign labor benefited the country, while 46 percent believed it did not (20 percent were undecided); the great majority of white-collar workers and businessmen, however, sided with the minority (Jensen 1999, 204–208).

While the proportional increase in non-Western immigrants was dramatic, the overall numbers were relatively low. As of 1972, Denmark still had fewer than 40,000 foreign nationals from countries outside the developed West. Thus despite the concerns of labor, immigration in the late sixties and early seventies remained essentially unrestricted. That is not to say that officials were completely unresponsive to public pressures: a number of restrictive proposals were introduced, and some even became law, most notably a 1970 change in work-permit requirements. In actual impact, though, such changes proved weak and ineffective, and the inflow of guest workers continued unabated (S. Pedersen 1999, 150–153).

In 1973, however, the policy of open borders met the reality of the global oil crisis. Along with the other Western economies, Denmark was thrown into recession and saw a significant increase in unemployment. In response, the Danish government put a freeze on labor-based immigration, which has remained largely in effect ever since. (Because of preexisting agreements, the law did not apply to other Nordic countries or the European Economic Community.) Unlike previous restrictions, this one was generally enforced, and the number of new guest workers fell almost to zero.

The overall impact on immigration, however, was to change the nature, not the number, of non-Westerners entering the country. The guest workers of the prior decade began to receive permanent work and residence permits, and were in turn able to bring their families, including spouses-to-be. This reunification process continued for the next three decades, and along with refugees, accounts for the steady flow of foreigners to Denmark since 1973. Thus while the size of the immigrant community as of the mid-seventies was not especially large, and issues relating to immigrants were relatively minor on the political scene, the seeds of significant future political conflicts had at least partially been sown.

The constitutional structure of any state affects how politics play out, so it will be useful to briefly summarize the structure of Denmark's system. Denmark has a single-chamber parliament called the Folketing, which has 179 seats. Of those, 135 are allocated proportionally in 17 multi-member districts, 40 are allocated proportionally at the national level, and two each come from Greenland and the Faroe Islands.[1] Elections are mandated every four years, but the prime minister, with a minimum notice of three weeks, may call for early elections. Parties must reach a 2 percent threshold for representation. Turnout rates for the national elections have been above 83 percent for every election in the last thirty years.

The current party structure is perhaps best explained by looking at the national election of 1973, an election which ended up having a significant impact on immigration. The 1973 election was arguably the most important election in Denmark since World War II. Polls at the time, asking voters to list the most important problems politicians ought to take care of, showed the top three to be taxes/public expenses, wages versus business income, and general economic conditions; immigration didn't even register (Borre 1975, 212). The importance of the election, however—both broadly for Danish politics and specifically for the issue of immigration—lay in how it restructured the Danish political landscape. Prior to 1973, the five primary parties represented a relatively simple left-right political spectrum. The Left was represented by the Social Democratic Party (SDP)—the dominant party for most of the twentieth century and the primary architect of Denmark's welfare state—and the Socialist People's Party, which had grown out of a split in the Communist Party in 1958. The Liberals (or "Agrarian Liberals") and Conservatives, which both originated in the nineteenth century, represented the Right, with their relative size and relative locations on the ideological spectrum varying over time. In the center were the Radical Liberals, who broke from the Liberals in 1905. (While relatively small, the Radical Liberals were quite influential, as they often tipped the balance of power one way or the other.)

With the election of 1973 a number of other parties entered the picture, and support for the traditional parties fell to 64 percent, a steep drop from the 93–96 percent range for each of the four prior national elections. The three largest of the new parties were the Christian People's Party (4 percent of the popular vote), which campaigned on the issues of abortion, pornography, and sex education; the Center Democrats (7.8 percent), which broke from the right wing of the SDP; and, most significant, the far-right Progress Party (15.9 percent). At the time, the Progress Party's success was built on its opposition to taxes and the welfare state. Toward the end of the seventies, however, as the number of non-Westerners in Denmark continued to rise, some members of the party began to publicly express their anti-immigrant sentiments, and they were not alone—a few Conservative politicians joined the chorus early on, as would, in time, members of other parties. But it was the Progress Party, and in particular its founder, Mogens Glistrup, that took the lead. In the decades to come Progress, and its offspring the Danish People's Party, would build its support around a message that was strongly anti-immigrant and at times blatantly racist. In Glistrup's view, "So long as there are high taxes and Muslims, we've got something to fight for" (*Economist* 1988).

7.3 The Eighties: The Emergence of Refugees

Family reunification ensured a steady inflow of immigrants into Denmark in the eighties. The middle of the decade, however, also saw a dramatic increase in the number of refugees. The Aliens Act of 1983, passed by a center-right government, both clarified and strengthened the rights of asylum seekers. This occurred at a time when the global supply of refugees was on the rise. Thus while all of Europe faced an increasing influx, the upsurge in Denmark was particularly sharp. The number of asylum seekers increased from 332 in 1983 to 4,312 in 1984, 8,698 in 1985, and over 9,000 in 1986, the primary sources being Iran, Iraq, Sri Lanka, and Vietnam (S. Pedersen 1999, 166). Not surprisingly there soon were calls—by politicians from major and minor parties, by leading newspapers, and by the public—to stem the "flood" of refugees attracted to the country by the new law (Jensen 1999, 229).

In September 1986, after three years of the flood, new regulations were adopted. If an asylum seeker arrived from a country where he or she was not considered to be in danger, it was now possible to prevent that person from entering Denmark if he or she did not have a valid passport and visa. To aid in enforcement, airlines and other companies that transported people across the border could now be fined for transporting improperly documented people into the country, and thus they began to police their own passengers. The results were dramatic: about 3,000 asylum seekers entered Denmark in 1987, one-third the number of the previous year (S. Pedersen 1999, 166–167).[2]

While public concerns about immigrants (a term which, from here on, will be shorthand for immigrants and refugees, and at times also for their Danish-born offspring) were present through most of the eighties, and even earlier— and at times, as we have seen, led to government action—the level of that concern, by traditional measures, remained quite low. In a poll taken at the time of the 1987 general election, for example, when asked what they thought was the most important political problem facing the country, only 3 percent of Danes gave immigrants as their top answer, and only 6 percent listed it among their top three (Borre 1987); and these numbers were, if anything, atypically high. In a review of polls from 1970 to 1990, immigration was rarely among the top five concerns of Danes, usually not in the top ten, and often not on the list at all (Borre 1975, 1987; EIU March 1977; Sauerberg 1991). Also telling is the support for the Progress Party. After receiving between 13.6 and 15.9 percent of the popular vote in the three elections from 1973 to 1977—which all occurred *before* the party began adopting an anti-immigrant stance—its numbers declined in subsequent elections: 1979, 11 percent; 1981, 8.9 percent; 1984, 3.6 percent; 1987, 4.8 percent; 1988, 9 percent; 1990, 6.4 percent. Although the low support in the mid-eighties was partially due to the incarceration of the party's founder for tax evasion, the overall decline is evident. Thus while opposition to immigrants was beginning to register on Denmark's radar screen, the public's demand for restrictions on immigrants, or for a xenophobic voice in Danish politics, was still quite limited. This would change in the nineties.

As a further measure of the underlying level of anti-immigrant sentiment, the seventies and eighties also saw few cases of violence directed at foreigners.[3] (This, too, would change in the nineties.) A telling measure of the problem—or the lack thereof—comes from the queen's traditional New Year speech in December 1984, in which she reprimanded Danes for their behavior toward immigrants. It was not anti-immigrant violence, however, that sparked those comments. She was displeased, rather, that Danes were starting to "treat them coldly" (Jensen 1999, 230–231).

One should keep in mind, however, other findings from the same 1987 poll mentioned above. When asked if they agreed with two statements—"Immigration constitutes a serious threat to our national identity" and "If refugees are to live in this country they must conform to Danish culture and way of living"—48 percent and 61 percent of respondents, respectively, said yes (Borre 1987). How, then, does one combine these poll results with the seemingly contradictory numbers mentioned earlier? One possible explanation is that Danes would have liked to have seen tighter restrictions on immigrants, but a host of other issues mattered much more to all but a tiny few. A second possibility is that a strong underlying opposition to foreigners was present, but muted by some other force, such as political momentum, "manners" (of voters and/or politicians), tradition, or the newness of the problem. Whatever caused that muting was about to disappear.

7.4   The Nineties: Xenophobia Emerges, Front and Center

The immediate cause of the emergence of immigration as a major factor in Danish politics was the war in the former Yugoslavia and the thousands of refugees it created. As the discussion thus far should have made clear, the extent to which the Yugoslav refugees were an independent cause as opposed to a catalyst is debatable. Not debatable are the numbers. When voters were asked to list their primary concerns in the national elections of 1994, 1998, and 2001, immigration ranked third, third, and first, respectively, a dramatic change from the elections of prior decades (EIU May 1994; McCarthy 2001; Nielsen 1999). This change in public priorities helped fuel growing support for the political Right, and in particular fueled the emergence of the Danish People's Party, the third-largest party in the legislature.

The calm before this storm began with the 1986 change in refugee regulations, which ushered in a period of stable immigration levels. From 1987 to 1992 the number of residence permits granted to refugees ranged from 3,000 to 4,500; those granted to "family reunification" immigrants ranged from 7,500 to 8,500 (S. Pedersen 1999, 170). While stable, these numbers were still quite sizable, and thus the total number of foreign nationals from non-Western countries doubled over the six years. Nevertheless, public fears about immigration, at least on the surface, did not seem to rise.

Then the war broke out in 1991, quickly creating thousands of refugees. They started arriving in Denmark in 1992 and continued for about three years. The final number was about 22,000, with 18,000 from Bosnia and Herzegovina. (A few thousand refugees also arrived each year from other countries, Somalia and Iraq being the leading contributors.) While most Danes were sympathetic to the Bosnian refugees at first, as the numbers rose and the likelihood of repatriation fell, attitudes changed. Frequent reports of outbreaks of crime near some refugee camps fed the public's anxieties. In a January 1993 opinion poll, 62 percent of Danes wanted the country to adopt stricter immigration laws (EIU March 1993).

The new SDP-led government responded to this situation in a manner that was part progressive and part populist. The progressive actions were the more significant, at least from the perspective of the Bosnians: the government very quickly granted temporary residence permits to the refugees, an action which likely increased the number that chose Denmark as their destination (S. Pedersen 1999, 167). Then, in the spring of 1994, the government announced that more than 16,000 refugees would be allowed to seek asylum (EIU May 1994). Lastly, in January 1995, with the temporary residence permits of thousands of Bosnians about to expire, the government passed a law granting the vast majority of the refugees permanent residence (EIU February 1995). At each step, in particular the last, the government's actions encountered strong opposition from the Conservative, Liberal, and Progress parties, and from the public at large. The commonly stated concerns were the cost of resettlement, the possibility of large numbers of family members coming to join refugees who were given asylum, and crime, although the fact that the refugees were primarily Muslim likely contributed to public unease (EIU May 1994).

The government was not blind to political realities—and thus there were also populist elements in the SDP's response. Beginning in 1993, the government took the lead in the public debate on immigration, floating a number of restrictive proposals.[4] The most significant change actually implemented involved the Aliens Act. The change in law meant that the thousands of asylum seekers appealing their rejected applications were now typically not allowed to remain in Denmark while their appeal was being processed, a reversal of the previous policy, which had come under strong public criticism (S. Pedersen 1999, 167). Not surprisingly, the government called for an election after the 1994 revision of the Aliens Act, but before it passed the January 1995 law that ensured that most of the Bosnian refugees would stay in Denmark. Thus while voters were concerned about immigration, the economy dominated the election, and although the SDP lost seats it was able to stay in power (EIU October 1994). Had it waited until after January, it almost surely would have lost.

In the wake of the rising public concern about immigration emerged the Danish People's Party (Dansk Folkeparti, or DF), which was founded in October 1995 as a breakaway from the Progress Party. The DF was led by a former leader of the Progress Party, Pia Kjærsgaard. Campaigning on a platform built primarily on opposition to immigration and to Danish inclusion in the European Union, the DF quickly achieved levels of popularity the Progress Party hadn't seen in twenty years. On these issues the two parties hardly differed. The DF, however, sought to be politically more pragmatic and substantively more mainstream vis-à-vis the welfare state.[5] This did not mean, though, that the DF's views on immigrants were temperate. After local elections in 1997, Kjærsgaard provided the following explanation for the party's success: "I think people are frightened by the number of immigrants in Denmark. The people who vote for us want to send immigrants back to where they came from" (Reuters 1997). While extreme, she may have been correct. A *Eurobarometer* survey from about the same time found Danes, in questions dealing with immigrants and refugees, to be the most intolerant in the European Union (Bryder 2002, 5).

Most Danish politicians spoke out against the DF for statements such as Kjærsgaard's. The political reality, however, was that if the SDP wanted to remain in power it needed to respond, more strongly than it had before, to people's fears. It did, with a steady stream of restrictions on those seeking to move to Denmark, as well as requirements for those already in the country. Residents seeking to bring family members to Denmark had to substantiate family connections through DNA tests (USCR 1998). Immigrants were now required to attend classes in Danish language and culture in order to obtain certain welfare benefits (EIU November 1997). Noncitizens facing criminal convictions were more likely to be deported (ibid.). More than a dozen new restrictions were added from 1995 through 1997.

These actions were not without cost. The SDP alienated some of its supporters, and many of the measures were passed without the support of the Radical Liberals, one of the three parties in the governing coalition. In the big political picture, though, such costs were minor. Anti-immigrant sentiment among the electorate was a force that could be ignored only at great electoral peril. While the wave of fears stirred up by the Bosnian refugee crisis reached its peak in 1995 and then began to slowly subside, the public's focus on immigrants was kept alive by the steady flow of refugees from other parts of the world. From 1995 to 1997 there were between 5,000 and 6,000 refugees arriving each year. The leading sources were Somalia, averaging about 1,500, and Iraq, with about 800 per year. Most Danes saw little reason to expect these refugees to fit in any better than those who had come before.

By the time of the March 1998 national election, public anxiety about immigrants was as high as ever. Asked what issues had a decisive influence on their vote, 28 percent gave responses related to refugees and immigration. Only eldercare (29 percent) and hospitals/public health (39 percent) scored higher. In addition, 27 percent included "law and order/public safety" in their answer, a response that likely for some euphemistically masked their xenophobia (Nielsen 1999). Not surprisingly, the combined support for the DF (7.4 percent) and the Progress Party (2.4 percent) represented a 50 percent increase in support for the anti-immigrant Right. Catching most analysts by surprise, however, the SDP was able to maintain control of the government.

The years between the elections of 1998 and 2001 showed that immigration was becoming a primary fault line of Danish politics, and even of Danish society. A great deal of national attention was focused on the November 1998 decision of a department store to deny employment to a Muslim female who wore a headscarf. Politicians and newspapers chimed in on both sides. One poll showed that 56 percent of Danes thought shop owners should be allowed to ban headscarves (*Economist* 1999). Similar to developments in France recounted in Chapter 9, the issue, seemingly minor, took on a symbolic importance for those worried about the nature and number of Denmark's immigrants, and for their opponents.

Immigrant-related violence also rose in the late nineties. In November of 1999, riots broke out in Copenhagen after a twenty-three-year-old man of Turkish descent, but born and raised in Denmark, was ordered expelled from the country after he was convicted of a violent theft. The rioters (estimates range from 50 to 150), which included many second-generation immigrants, rampaged through a working-class business district, damaging or destroying almost every shop in the neighborhood and setting several cars on fire. While more severe than most, this was just one of a growing number of cases of immigrant-related violence.

In the meantime the Far Right was solidifying its anti-immigrant reputation, especially vis-à-vis Denmark's Muslim population. "Our entire cultural foundation is crumbling and the government is Islam's willing stooge." That opinion was expressed by the DF's Kjærsgaard in 1999 (*Economist* 1999), who in the same year also proposed that if an immigrant is convicted of a criminal offense, the offender's whole family should be deported from the country— a position she later partially altered, saying that only the offender and his or her parents should be expelled (Barnes 1999). Not to be outdone, Glistrup of the Progress Party said that "foreigners should be interned in camps and 6,000 Muslim girls aged between 12 and 20 should be sold to Paraguay for five million kronor with the profits added to public funds." This comment led to Glistrup's being charged with violating the country's race-hate laws (Agence France Presse 2000), and also led all four of the Progress Party's MPs to quit the party, leaving the party without representation in the Folketing. (The party has been essentially irrelevant since then; it received only 0.6 percent of the vote in 2001, not enough to gain parliamentary representation.)

If the Progress Party was perceived as having gone too far, such was not the case for Kjærsgaard and the DF. The DF was gaining support from low-skilled workers, who previously had been a stronghold of the SDP. According to a poll published in October of 1999, one-third of the members of one of the country's largest trade unions, the General Workers' Union, sympathized with the DF (Barnes 1999). Support for the "New Right" was also found to be strongly negatively correlated with education, as is the case in most countries (Nielsen 1999). In contrast to most right-wing populist parties, however, the DF emerged in a time of economic prosperity and stability: unemployment was below 5 percent and prices were stable. Nevertheless, many Danes saw the growing immigrant population as a threat to their jobs, and even more so as excessively benefiting from state support. This latter concern was not without some foundation: one study found that at the turn of the millennium non-Western immigrants in Denmark were receiving 38 percent of the cash benefits the system paid out (Schultz-Nielsen 2001, 15). While numbers such as these are almost entirely explained by employment and poverty rates, they were easily exploited by immigration's opponents, and helped feed the public's resentment.

The SDP-led government's populist/progressive schizophrenia continued much as it had prior to the 1998 election. One change that received a great deal of attention was the 1998 introduction of a two-tier welfare benefit system, with a three-year "integration period" during which each new refugee would receive only 80 percent of the benefits given to Danish citizens (USCR 1999). Critics appealed to the UN High Commissioner for Refugees on the grounds that the new law violated the 1951 UN refugee convention—the very same convention that Denmark had been the first to sign. After months of tense exchanges between the UNHCR and the Danish government, the government repealed the law in November of 1999. Another law, passed in 2000, barred immigrants under age twenty-five from bringing a foreign spouse to Denmark (Cohen 2000).

While such restrictions appealed to broad anti-immigrant sentiments, the SDP also sought to keep a significant distance from the Far Right. In response to the DF's 1999 proposal to deport whole families if one member committed a crime, the prime minister, Poul Nyrup Rasmussen, went beyond just arguing against the policy. Directing his comments at the DF's leadership, and using language rarely used in public (and usually reserved for unclean pets), he made his opinion of the DF quite clear: "Housetrained you'll never be" (K. Pedersen and Ringsmose 2004). Comments such as these likely appealed to the SDP base, but their impact on the electorate at large is less clear. In the eyes of Erik Carlsen, a political commentator and SDP supporter, the statement was politically suicidal (Polakow-Suransky 2002). Suicidal or not, given the large number of uncommitted voters who were worried about "foreigners" in Denmark, and who thus had some sympathies with the DF, adopting a dismissive tone could not have helped the SDP's reelection effort.

7.5 No Longer Marginal: The Far Right and the Election of 2001

By law, Denmark's next national election was to be held by March of 2002. With the DF a major player on the scene, and with widespread public anxiety about Denmark's "foreign" population, immigration was sure to be one of the leading issues. But when the SDP—hoping to capitalize on security concerns in the wake of the 9/11 attacks in the United States—announced that the election would be held in November 2001, they ensured that immigration, and the position of Muslims in Danish society generally, would be *the* dominant issues. A Gallup poll of early November found that 55 percent considered immigration the most important political issue (McCarthy 2001). A different poll found that over two-thirds of Danes wanted stricter refugee policies, with the proportion being even higher among the highly educated (Agence France Presse 2001). Both the SDP (to some extent) and the Liberals (to a greater extent) adopted anti-immigrant stances, as the DF—and circumstance—largely set the agenda (Polakow-Suransky 2002; Qvortrup 2002). This agenda was probably most memorably captured by a controversial DF election poster of a blond child, accompanied by the warning: "By the time she retires, Denmark will be a majority-Muslim nation" (Karacs 2001). Not to be outdone, a Liberal MP, claiming to speak on behalf of the party, advocated imprisoning between 3,000 and 4,000 of Denmark's Muslims, on the grounds that they could pose a security risk.

The election outcome was almost as shocking as the campaign. For the first time since 1920 the SDP was not the largest party—that prize went to the Liberals. The DF emerged as the third-largest party, with 12 percent of the vote and 22 MPs in the Folketing. And for the first time since 1929 the rightist parties (Liberals, Conservatives, and the DF) had a majority. While the Liberals chose to form a minority government with just the Conservatives, they would inevitably have to rely extensively on the support of the DF in passing legislation, and in turn would have to repay that support.

With the government in new hands, the first parliamentary session was an active one. The DF provided the Liberal-Conservative coalition with the votes necessary for some issues not particularly part of the DF's agenda: a tax freeze; the closing of a number of state-run or state-funded agencies; the privatizing of state-owned enterprises; and a reduction in the number of ministries. Other new policies, as noted by the *Economist*, "might well have been lifted directly from the DF's election manifesto" (EIU April 2002): the tightening of immigration and refugee policy; cuts in foreign aid; the reallocation of funds to the most-needy elderly; and stricter penalties for violence and rape. Even subsequent cuts in cigarette taxes were part of the DF's populist program (EIU January 2003).

Immigration, though, was the DF's clear priority, and it largely got what it wanted. The primary new restrictions, adopted in May 2002, are as follows (Boyes 2002; USCR 2003):

- The definition of a "refugee" is to be limited to those who have a well-founded fear of persecution on grounds of race, religion, nationality, political opinion, or membership in a particular social group. Conscientious objectors or people fleeing war or famine will have no legal right to be deemed refugees.
- If the home country of someone who has been granted refugee status becomes "safe," the refugee will be returned home.
- Permanent-resident permits will be granted after seven years instead of three, and recipients will only get half of the standard welfare benefits during that period. To avoid another battle with the UNHCR, this law applies also to citizens, and technically just requires residence in Denmark for seven of the last eight years—a clever construction.
- In addition to existing age restrictions (passed in 2000) on a resident's seeking to bring a spouse to Denmark, there is a new requirement that the foreign spouse be at least twenty-four.
- Spouses will not be allowed to join their partners in Denmark unless the partner has a sufficiently large apartment and income. An applicant must have at least 7,000 euros in a Danish bank account before he or she can apply to bring his or her spouse into the country.
- Applicants for Danish nationality must pass a test showing linguistic ability equivalent to that of a fourteen-year-old Danish schoolchild.
- Reunification with parents over sixty years old will no longer be allowed.

And with that, the transition was complete. First had come a twenty-year period where fears about foreigners were present, but largely under the surface. Into that mix was stirred a refugee crisis and some political entrepreneurs. Then, in the course of about ten years, Denmark went from having perhaps

Europe's most open borders to having perhaps its most restricted. And those foreign nationals lucky enough to already be on the inside were faced with a new set of hurdles. Denmark's heroic actions during World War II now seem to be those of a different country.

With the political alliance that defines Denmark today, the immigration fault line has had a significant impact on the "welfare spending" fault line. The Liberal-Conservative government may not be as antistate as Goldwater or Thatcher or Gingrich—after all, this is still Denmark. But shrinking the welfare state is one of the government's primary goals, and it is only with the support of the Danish People's Party that it has been able to implement this agenda. Its agenda is thus being aided and abetted by DF voters—largely middle and lower-middle class—who could reasonably be described as victims of that very agenda.

8

Denmark: Quantitative Analysis

8.1 Parties and Issues

The preceding chapter has shown that immigration has turned into a highly salient issue in Danish politics. We will argue that the size of the welfare state and the government's position on immigration are the two most important issues in contemporary Danish politics. Although there are ten political parties active in Denmark, their policies on these two issues are highly correlated. We believe that little is lost by modeling the political contest as one between two parties, one of which is a generic "Left" and the other, a generic "Right." This contrasts with France, where the position of the Extreme Right (Le Pen) on the economic issue is, today, more moderate than the economic position of the center party, and the two-party assumption would not be appropriate.

Our data consist of micro-data from the Danish Election Survey, Year 1998 (2,001 respondents, 327 variables) and Year 2001 (2,026 respondents, 316 variables).[1] Table 8.1 reports the vote shares obtained by the various parties in the 1998 and 2001 elections. In the first column, we report the vote shares obtained from the survey answers (among respondents who answered the question); the second column reports the actual vote shares. Note that reported vote share and actual vote share are generally very close (although respondents in 1998 tend to underreport the vote for the Social Democratic Party).

Table 8.1 Danish political parties: Vote shares (percent)

Party	1998			2001		
	Reported vote share[a]	Actual vote share	Left-Right (11-point scale)	Reported vote share[a]	Actual vote share	Left-Right (11-point scale)
United Left Wing Party	3.2	2.7	1.21	2.7	2.4	1.47
Socialist People's Party	8.8	7.5	2.52	6.4	6.4	2.78
Social Democratic Party	31.5	36.1	4.35	27.6	29.1	4.38
Liberal Democrats	4.5	3.9	4.67	5.5	5.2	4.61
Center Democratic Party	4.4	4.3	5.54	1.2	1.2	Not asked
Christian People's Party	2.2	2.5	5.93	2.1	2.3	5.48
Conservative People's Party	10.7	8.9	7.23	9.0	9.1	6.98
Liberal Party	25.3	24.0	7.55	34.4	31.3	7.32
Danish People's Party	7.2	7.4	8.64	10.9	12.0	8.13
Progress Party	2.2	2.4	8.64	0.3	0.6	Not asked

a. Among voters who answered the question.

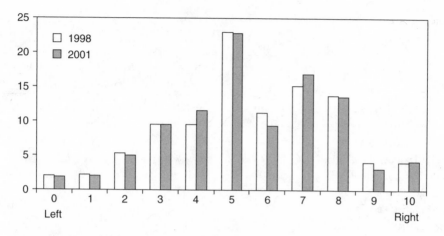

Figure 8.1   Distribution of Left-Right voter identification, Denmark.

Parties are ranked on a Left-Right scale, as perceived by the voters. This scale derives from the answers to the following question: "In politics one often talks about left and right. Where would you place yourself on this scale? Where would you place the various parties on this scale?" (Show a card with 11 possible values, from 0 indicating left to 10 indicating right.) For each party we compute the average answer. Figure 8.1 depicts the distribution of voters' Left/Right identification, that is, answers to the question, "Where would you place yourself?" Although the vote share of the Left parties decreased dramatically between the 1998 and 2001 elections, Left-Right identification among voters remained remarkably stable: the distributions are almost identical. (For 1998, the average answer is 5.6; for 2001, the average answer is 5.5.) Voters' responses on this question may be related to the change in perceived position of parties between 1998 and 2001: while Left parties are perceived to be approximately stable, Right and Extreme Right parties are perceived to move toward the center in 2001.

Table 8.2 presents the average perception among voters of the parties' positions on the economic issue (size of the public sector) and the immigration issue (see the exact definition in section 8.2). Note that on both issues, the ranking of parties is very similar to their ranking on the Left-Right scale. In particular, the two most anti-immigrant parties, the Danish People's Party and the Progress Party, are also the most conservative on the economic issue.[2]

Table 8.2 Danish political parties: Perceived platforms

| | 1998 | | 2001 | |
Party	More public sector	Immigration standpoint	More public sector	Immigration standpoint
United Left Wing Party	1.40	−1.24	1.08	−1.05
Socialist People's Party	1.13	−0.96	0.89	−0.78
Social Democratic Party	0.53	−0.12	0.46	−0.08
Liberal Democrats	0.20	−0.32	0.22	−0.35
Center Democratic Party	−0.07	−0.20	Not asked	Not asked
Christian People's Party	0.00	−0.12	0.07	−0.17
Conservative People's Party	−0.93	0.88	−0.88	1.04
Liberal Party	−1.00	0.88	−1.01	1.07
Danish People's Party	−1.40	1.96	−1.02	1.90
Progress Party	−1.53	1.88	Not asked	Not asked

In order to assess the main political issues in Denmark, we use a question about the problems that respondents perceive as being the most important in Denmark. Table 8.3 reports, for a selection of issues, the number of individuals (in 1998, out of a total of 2,001 respondents) who listed the issue in question as among the four most important problems facing the country (unfortunately we do not have these data for 2001). Problems are ranked according to the number of respondents who reported this specific problem as the single most important in the country (down to a number of 14 respondents).

Clearly the health issue is the single most important problem: over 900 respondents, almost one-half of the sample, name either "Health sector and the hospital sector" or "Nursing homes/domiciliary care" as one of the four most important problems. Immigrant and refugee-related issues appear second (670 respondents), followed by a number of social or economic issues: conditions for the aged (393); families with children/day-care centers (341); employment and unemployment, including labor market policy (303); and social problems including social policy (171). Environmental issues are also considered to be important: environment/environmental issues (377); and pollution (32). These problems are also ranked the highest on the list when individuals are asked which problems were the most important when they decided how to vote.

Table 8.3 The most important problems in Denmark: 1998 election survey

Issues	1	2	3	4	Total
Immigration of refugees and immigrants, including the fight against racism	305	195	123	47	670
Health sector and the hospital sector	305	256	107	38	706
Environment / Environmental issues	168	102	80	27	377
Conditions for the aged	153	161	60	19	393
Employment and unemployment, including labor market policy	147	86	45	25	303
The economy	130	50	26	10	216
Families with children / day-care centers	119	144	62	16	341
Social problems, including social policy	80	58	25	8	171
European Union: in general, and general handling of the Amsterdam treaty	78	52	31	14	175
Nursing homes / domiciliary care	59	88	48	7	202
Balance of payment / foreign debt	34	24	11	6	75
Violence, crime, law and order / justice policy	30	52	45	23	150
Tax reform / tax burden, including deterioration of private pensions	21	20	16	4	61
Unclear answer: everything	20	3	0	0	23
State schools / schools policy	19	42	36	11	108
Distribution of public expenditure	19	13	10	1	43
The pollution problem	16	8	4	4	32
Education / education standards	14	35	27	17	93
Social benefits, including maternity and other such leave	14	9	5	0	28
Welfare state, without further details	14	5	2	0	21
Do not know	28	1	0	0	29
Did not answer	19	362	1,053	1,645	

Question: We have, as you know, just had parliamentary elections, and therefore I would like to ask you what problems you think are the most important ones that politicians should be doing something about today? (Most important problem #1, #2, #3, #4.)

We assume that the issues of hospital/health services, education in state schools, and the unemployment/welfare system are mainly questions about the size of the public sector, and therefore modeling political competition as focusing on the two issues of public-sector size and immigration appears to be an acceptable abstraction.

8.2   Estimation of the Model's Parameters

For Denmark, we use the Euclidean model of preferences, where

$$v(t, r; \theta, \rho) = -(t - \theta)^2 - \frac{\gamma}{2}(r - \rho)^2$$

is the utility function of a voter of type (θ, ρ) on policies (t, r). We must estimate the distribution of voter types, the relative salience of racism/immigration, γ, and the racism-free distribution of voter types.

8.2.1   Distribution of Voter Traits

We next discuss our use of the Danish voter surveys to calibrate the distribution of voter preferences on the size of the public sector and immigration policy. We select two questions that enable us to calibrate both voters' preferences and their views about where the parties stand on the issues in question.

8.2.1.1   The Economic Issue

The economic issue question is

> Among other things, the parties disagree about how big the public sector should be. Some parties say we should cut down on public revenue and expenditure, others say we should expect increasing expenditure and revenue in the future. Here is a scale from 1 to 5, where 1 means the revenue and expenditure should be cut substantially, 2 means that they should be cut a little, 3 means that the public revenue and expenditure are appropriate as they are now, 4 means that they should increase a little and 5 means that they should increase a lot. Where would you place party (name all the parties)? Where would you place yourself?

The distribution of answers to the question "Where would you place yourself?" is presented in Figure 8.2. A very large proportion of respondents are either satisfied with the current size of the public sector or support only a small change in its size. About 37 percent of the respondents think that the current size of the public sector is appropriate, and fewer than 8 percent are in favor of a large change (in either direction). Among the respondents who support a change, a decrease in the size of the public sector receives more support than an increase. Between 1998 and 2001 preferences are quite stable; only a

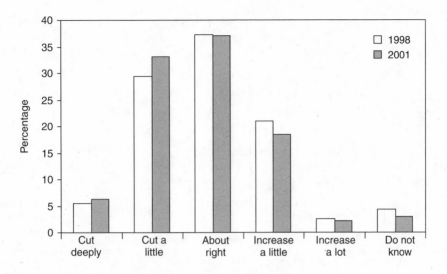

Figure 8.2   Distribution of voter views on public-sector size.

small increase in the number of people who support a smaller public sector is observed.

8.2.1.2   The Immigration Issue

The immigration issue question is

> Among other things, the parties disagree about how many refugees we can take. Some say we take too many. Others say we could easily take more. Here is a scale from 1 to 5, where 1 means that we should take far fewer refugees, 2 means we should take somewhat fewer, 3 means that we should continue to take the same number as now, 4 means that we should take somewhat more and 5 means that we should take a lot more refugees than we do now. Where would you place party X/yourself on this scale?

The distribution of answers to the question "Where would you place yourself?" is given in Figure 8.3. We observe, first, that respondents favor a decrease in the number of refugees accepted. Over 50 percent of the respondents think that the country takes too many refugees, while fewer than 15 percent think that the country should take more. Second, we observe stability of answers in this

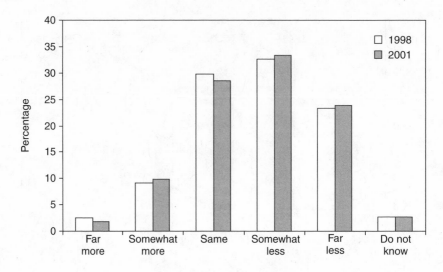

Figure 8.3   Distribution of voter views on the desirable number of refugees.

time period; there is only a slight increase in the number of people wanting fewer refugees.

8.2.1.3   Interpretation of the Variables

The correlation between views on the size of the public sector and the immigrant/refugee issue will play an important part in our analysis of the antisolidarity effect. Figures 8.4a and 8.4b present—respectively for years 1998 and 2001—the distribution of views on the economic issue, by answers to the refugee question. There is globally a strong negative relationship between pro–public-sector and pro–refugee views. In 1998, among people who want far fewer refugees, 18 percent want more public expenditure, and over 50 percent want less public expenditure, versus respectively 1 percent and 20 percent among those who think that the number of refugees is about right. Among people who want far more refugees, over 70 percent want more public expenditure, while only 20 percent of those who think that the number of refugees is about right want a larger public sector. Figures are similar in 2001.

To construct voters' preferences we used only these two questions, although the survey contains many questions regarding individuals' opinions on economic policy and immigration policy. Our choice was constrained by our

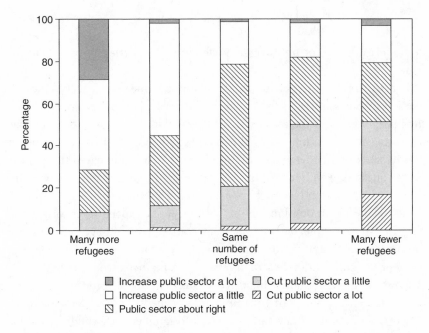

Figure 8.4a   The distribution of economic views by xenophobic type, 1998.

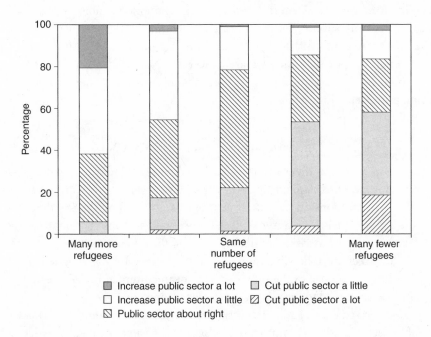

Figure 8.4b   The distribution of economic views by xenophobic type, 2001.

desire to calibrate not only voters' preferences but parties' positions on the issues.

To better understand exactly what these variables mean, we checked the correlation of our selected variables with other related variables. In particular, the interpretation of the economic variable is not obvious: respondents may desire an increase in the size of the public sector because they want a larger police force or more defense or more culture, which would have little bearing on the question we want to study. To gain more information about what respondents had in mind when they answered the question we used, we studied the correlation with opinions about whether public expenditures for specific purposes (for example, defense, the health care system, old-age pensions, environmental problems, cultural purposes, police force, welfare benefits paid to the individual, and aid to refugees) should be increased or not. We find that our economic variable is highly correlated with support for public expenditures targeted to the poor (unemployment benefits, welfare benefits, wage support) and families (day care, subsidies to families with children, education). These are the kind of expenditures that are likely to be influenced by the antisolidarity effect (immigrants are perceived as poorer and as having more children than native Danes). Similarly, our economic variable is negatively correlated with support for an increase of spending on defense or police. We are therefore confident that the variable we use measures the kind of public expenditures with which we are concerned. Note that misinterpretation regarding the immigration variable is less possible, since the scope of the question is in a sense limited.

8.2.1.4   Construction of a Continuous Joint Distribution

Being confident that the two variables selected are good indicators of the preferences we want to estimate, we now construct a joint distribution of voters' traits. The questions on the size of the public sector and on the immigration issue call for qualitative answers. Because we wish to construct quantitative variables, we need to assign numerical values to the different possible answers. We chose to do the following: for both questions, the value 0 is assigned to the status quo (same size of the public sector or same number of refugees). The value $+1$ is assigned to the answer "somewhat more public sector" and "somewhat fewer refugees," and -1 is assigned to the answer "somewhat smaller public sector" and "somewhat more refugees"; the value $+2$ (-2) is assigned to the answer "much larger public sector" and "far fewer refugees" ("much

Table 8.4   Means and standard deviations of voter types

Variable	1998			2001		
	Mean	Std. dev.	Obs.	Mean	Std. dev.	Obs.
θ	−0.15	0.92	1,914	−0.24	0.91	1,967
ρ	+0.67	1.02	1,948	+0.70	1.01	1,972
Correlation	−0.33		1,886	−0.34		1,933

smaller public sector" and "many more refugees"). The quantitative variables thus defined are labeled θ for the economic issue and ρ for the immigration issue.

Descriptive statistics for these two variables are reported in Table 8.4. As noted, individuals are on average favorable to a small decrease in the size of the public sector and to a large decrease in the number of refugees. The correlation coefficient between the two variables is −0.33 in 1998, and −0.34 in 2001. We approximate the joint distribution by a bivariate normal density with mean and standard deviation of the marginal distributions given in Table 8.4 and a correlation coefficient that equals −0.33 in 1998 and −0.34 in 2001.

Remark on the choice of coding. Note that our two variables do not have a direct quantitative interpretation: they do not represent a tax rate or a number of refugees. When choosing the code for the economic variable and the immigration-related variable, we chose to select values that make sense relative to the context of the questionnaire (0 is the value of the status quo for the two options, 1 is the value of the answers "somewhat larger public sector" and "somewhat fewer refugees"). Another option would have been to find numerical values that would have a meaning independent of the survey: for example, to translate answers into desired tax rates or numbers of refugees. This option seemed more hazardous to us in terms of interpretation, given the limited information contained in the survey data, and so we elected not to pursue it.

Note also that a linear transformation of the values scale leaves preferences unchanged, up to a transformation in γ. Since the parameter γ will be estimated from the data, the question of the scale (the multiplicative constant) is unimportant. Given the symmetry in the wording of the question, we chose to assign symmetrical values (relative to the value of the status quo) to the answers "somewhat more" and "somewhat less." The only remaining question is how to compare "a lot more" with "somewhat more." We have chosen to assume that "a lot more" is twice as much as "somewhat more." A different choice would probably have given slightly different results.

8.2.2 Parties' Vote Shares and Platforms

Vote shares obtained by the various parties in the 1998 and 2001 elections, as well as the parties' proposals on the issues we are concerned about, were presented in Tables 8.1 and 8.2. As explained in section 8.1, we model Danish politics in terms of broader coalitions of parties: Left and Right. We define the Left as consisting of the United Left, Socialist People's, Social Democratic, and Liberal Democratic parties. The Right consists of the other six parties (see Table 8.1). We compute the broader parties' vote shares by summing the vote shares of the parties forming the coalition. These are reported in Table 8.5a. We also compute coalitions' positions, defined as the average of the parties' positions on the various issues, weighted by their vote share within the coalition. These are reported in Table 8.5b.

Table 8.5a Parties' vote shares (percent)

	1998 elections		2001 elections	
	Reported vote share	Actual vote share	Reported vote share	Actual vote share
Left	48.0	50.3	42.2	43.1
Right	52.0	49.7	57.8	56.9

Note: See note for Table 8.5b.

Table 8.5b Voters' and parties' positions on size of the public sector and immigration

	1998			2001		
	Pub. sector	Immigration	Vote share (percent)	Pub. sector	Immigration	Vote share (percent)
Left	0.67	−0.37	48.0	0.53	−0.28	42.2
Right	−0.94	0.94	52.0	−0.95[a]	1.18[a]	57.8
Voters	−0.15	0.67		−0.24	0.70	

a. In the 2001 survey there is no question about the perceived position of the Center Democratic Party and of the Progress Party. Since these parties received only a small share of the votes (1.2 and 0.3, respectively), we simply ignore them when computing the average observed policies of the Right coalition.

Table 8.6 Average policy views of Left and Right voter coalitions

Average ideal policy on each issue for—	1998			2001		
	Pub. sector	Immigration	Percentage of voters	Pub. sector	Immigration	Percentage of voters
Voters who vote for a Left party	0.28	0.29	48.0	0.21	0.23	42.2
Voters who vote for a Right party	−0.54	0.97	52.0	−0.59	1.02	57.8
All voters	−0.15	0.67	100.0	−0.24	0.70	100.0

Note that, as far as the immigration issue is concerned, the Right party is closer to the voters' average point of view than is the Left. As to the size of the public sector, the average point of view of voters is equidistant from the Left and Right positions.

If we compare the voters' perceived positions of the parties across time, we see that the Left coalition is viewed as almost stable, with only a very small anti–public-sector, anti-immigrant shift over the three-year period. The Right party, in contrast, is viewed as having made more spectacular changes, becoming much more anti-immigrant over the period.

Another useful indicator of the division of the electorate on these two issues is the average ideal "tax" policy (and the average ideal immigration policy) of respondents who said they voted for a party in the Left coalition, and those of respondents who said they voted for a party in the Right coalition. Results are reported in Table 8.6.

8.2.3 Estimation of the Salience Parameter $\gamma/2$

An individual with ideal public-sector policy θ and ideal immigration policy ρ evaluates the policy platform (t, r) with the utility function $v(t, r; \theta, \rho) = -(t - \theta)^2 - (\gamma/2)(r - \rho)^2$. Therefore, an individual with ideal tax policy θ and ideal immigration policy ρ prefers the policy platform (t, r) to the policy platform (t', r') if and only if

$$(t - t')\left(\theta - \frac{t + t'}{2}\right) + \frac{\gamma}{2}(r - r')\left(\rho - \frac{r + r'}{2}\right) > 0. \tag{8.1}$$

Table 8.7 Party platforms, elicited from voter opinion

	1998			2001		
	Pub. sector	Immigration	Vote share (percent)	Pub. sector	Immigration	Vote share (percent)
Left	0.67	−0.37	48.0	0.53	−0.28	42.2
Right	−0.94	0.94	52.0	−0.95	1.18	57.8

In order to estimate γ, we approximate the choice voters face by a binary choice: they can vote for either the Left coalition or the Right coalition. The platforms and vote shares of these two broad coalitions are given in Table 8.7. In the two-party model, a rational voter with ideal tax policy θ and ideal immigration policy ρ votes for the Right coalition if and only if

$$(t^R - t^L)\left(\theta - \frac{t^R + t^L}{2}\right) + \frac{\gamma}{2}(r^R - r^L)\left(\rho - \frac{r^R + r^L}{2}\right) > 0. \quad (8.2)$$

Using the observed positions of parties reported in Table 8.7, (8.2) yields the following inequalities. For 1998, a voter of type (θ, ρ) should prefer the Right to the Left coalition exactly when

$$\rho > \frac{1.23}{\gamma/2}\theta + \left(0.29 + \frac{0.17}{\gamma/2}\right); \quad (8.3a)$$

for 2001, the analogous inequality is

$$\rho > \frac{1.01}{\gamma/2}\theta + \left(0.45 + \frac{0.21}{\gamma/2}\right). \quad (8.3b)$$

The locus of voter types in type space who are indifferent between the Right and the Left is a straight line containing the type

$$(\theta, \rho) = \left(\frac{t^L + t^R}{2}, \frac{r^L + r^R}{2}\right).$$

In (θ, ρ) space, the indifference curves become flatter as γ increases.

In order to estimate γ, we introduce uncertainty. In the probabilistic model we assume that an individual votes for the Right coalition rather than for the Left if $\alpha\rho_i + \beta\theta_i + k + \varepsilon_i > 0$, where ε_i is a random variable, i.i.d. across individuals, with mean zero. If we assume a standard normal distribution for the disturbances, we can use a probit model to estimate the vote equation. Results are given in Table 8.8, columns (1) and (3).

The empirical estimation of the indifference curves is therefore:

$$\text{Year 1998}: \quad \rho = 1.94\theta + 0.73, \qquad \text{Year 2001}: \quad \rho = 1.45\theta + 0.48,$$

to be compared with the indifference curves from the theory, given above in equations (8.3a) and (8.3b). Note that for each year, we have only one parameter (γ) to adjust two variables (the constant and the slope). The fit of the model will be good if we can fit both the slope $(1.23/(\gamma/2) = 1.94$ for 1998, $1.01/(\gamma/2) = 1.45$ for 2001) and the constant $(0.29 + (0.17/(\gamma/2)) = 0.73$ for 1998, $0.45 + (0.21/(\gamma/2)) = 0.48$ for 2001). In 1998, the former equation yields $\gamma/2 = 0.63$ and the latter, $\gamma/2 = 0.39$; in 2001, the slope equation yields $\gamma/2 = 0.70$, whereas the constant equation gives a very high value for γ.

This result suggests that the relative weight of the race-related issue is quite stable over time, but there is as well a significant party fixed effect that our model does not capture. We can also estimate a constrained empirical indifference curve, where we impose that a voter with ideal policy

$$(\theta, \rho) = \left(\frac{t^L + t^R}{2}, \frac{r^L + r^R}{2} \right)$$

be indifferent (in expectation) between the two parties. In that case, the estimate for $\gamma/2$ is 0.43 in 1998, and 0.66 for 2001. For 1998, a value of $\gamma/2$ between 0.40 and 0.60 seems sensible; in 2001, a value between 0.60 and 0.70 would seem more appropriate. Consistent with the political history presented in the previous chapter, the data appear to reveal an increased importance of the immigration issue in voters' preferences.

Thus far, in the regression of Table 8.8, we have used only the two independent variables *size of the public sector* and *anti-immigration*. Our estimation may be biased if these variables are correlated with other determinants of the vote. To avoid this omitted variable bias we add more controls to the estimation. (See Table 8.8, columns (2) and (4). The definition of the added independent variables is provided in Appendix Table B.5.) Adding controls reduces the size (in absolute values) of the coefficients on *anti-immigration* and *size of the public sector,* but they still remain highly significant. The drop is particularly important in 2001. Yet this does not substantially alter the ratio of these two

Table 8.8 Dependent variable: Vote for the Right coalition (Probit estimation)

	1998		2001	
	(1)	(2)	(3)	(4)
AntiImmigration	0.324**	0.207**	0.409**	0.364**
	(0.035)	(0.044)	(0.036)	(0.043)
ProPublicSector	−0.628**	−0.587**	−0.595**	−0.556**
	(0.040)	(0.048)	(0.041)	(0.046)
Constant	−0.236**	−0.048	−0.195**	0.370
	(0.040)	(0.376)	(0.040)	(0.366)
Law and order		0.212**		0.164**
		(0.044)		(0.041)
Environment		−0.254**		−0.226**
		(0.025)		(0.031)
Household income		0.060**		0.038**
		(0.011)		(0.010)
Female		0.201**		−0.004
		(0.078)		(0.074)
Age		−0.058**		−0.047**
		(0.014)		(0.014)
Age square		0.00065**		0.0004**
		(0.0001)		(0.0001)
City		−0.044[+]		−0.050[+]
		(0.027)		(0.028)
Education		0.122**		0.115**
		(0.045)		(0.043)
Observations	1,739	1,472	1,814	1,644
Log likelihood	−972.98	−754.57	−976.50	−818.20
Pseudo R-squared	0.1916	0.2604	0.2101	0.2715

[+]significant at 10%; *significant at 5%; **significant at 1%.
Note: Standard errors are in parentheses below the value of the coefficients.

coefficients, which is all that matters for our estimation of γ. Indeed, the slope estimation for 1998 yields $\gamma/2 = 0.59$ and for 2001 $\gamma/2 = 0.56$. Thus the value of γ is not very sensitive to the specification.

Conclusion. For 1998, a value of $\gamma/2$ between 0.40 and 0.60 seems sensible; in 2001, a value between 0.60 and 0.70 would seem more appropriate.

8.2.4 Estimation of Counterfactual Preferences

To compute the antisolidarity effect, as we have described in Chapter 2, we need to construct counterfactual "racism-free" demands for the public sector, that is, voter preferences on the size of the public sector that would be observed if hostility toward immigrants and refugees did not reduce the feeling of solidarity. There is no unique way to do this; our results will depend on exactly how we interpret the significant correlation between opinions on the size of the public sector and the immigration issue. We next present several alternative ways of proceeding.

The first option is to consider the distribution of economic preferences by ρ-type. As Figures 8.4a and 8.4b show, there is a strong negative relationship between support for a larger public sector and support for a higher number of immigrants. Table 8.9 presents the mean and standard deviation of desired public-sector sizes conditional upon various values on the immigration issue.

Using $\rho = -2$ as the reference nonracist group is probably too extreme (recall that $\rho = -2$ for an individual who supports admitting many more refugees). The choice of $\rho = -1$ or $\rho = 0$ seems more reasonable. The average value of θ in 1998 (2001) is $+0.44$ ($+0.29$) among respondents with $\rho = -1$ and -0.01 (both years) among the $\rho = 0$ group; it is -0.15 (-0.24) in the whole population.

Another option is to use the question regarding "social rights that should be given to immigrants or refugees":

> Refugees and immigrants should have the same rights to social welfare as Danes, even though they are not Danish citizens.

Figure 8.5 presents the distribution of answers. Note that a large number of Danes oppose giving foreigners the same social rights as the Danes. Some summary statistics on economic preferences by answers to this question are presented in Table 8.10. "Agree" stands for either agree or strongly agree; "don't disagree" stands for the group who neither agrees or disagrees.

Table 8.9 Average desired size of the public sector by degree of xenophobia

	1998			2001		
	Mean	Std. dev.	Obs.	Mean	Std. dev.	Obs.
$\rho = -2$	0.91	0.91	46	0.76	0.85	34
$\rho = -1$	0.44	0.74	181	0.29	0.83	196
$\rho = 0$	−0.01	0.72	581	−0.01	0.72	570
All	−0.15	0.92	1,914	−0.24	0.91	1,967

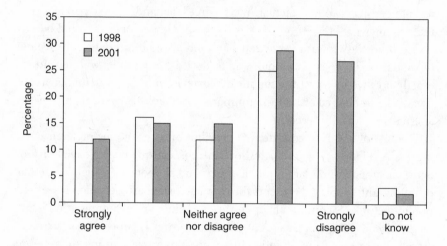

Figure 8.5 Immigrants should be given the same rights as Danes: Distribution of answers.

Table 8.10 Summary statistics on economic preferences by opinion category on immigrants' rights

	1998			2001		
	Mean	Std. dev.	Obs	Mean	Std. dev.	Obs.
Agree	0.17	0.85	529	0.06	0.88	550
Don't disagree	0.08	0.85	765	−0.01	0.86	838
All	−0.15	0.92	1,914	−0.24	0.91	1,967

The conclusion of this preliminary analysis is that a reasonable counterfactual distribution of θ should have a mean between 0.1 and 0.2 and standard deviation about 0.85 for year 1998, and a mean between 0 and 0.1 and standard deviation about 0.85 for year 2001.

A third option is to use regression analysis to explore the empirical relationship between the size of the public sector and views on immigration. We estimate the following model:

$$\theta_i = -\delta\rho_i + X_i'\beta + \varepsilon_i,$$

where X_i is a set of individual characteristics, including social and demographic variables as well as responses to questions about how the respondents feel on a number of justice issues, or about the behavior of people living on welfare. The disturbance term ε_i represents the unobserved characteristics of individual i; it is a zero mean disturbance with standard normal distribution. We estimate the model with OLS. Results are presented in Table 8.11 (the definition of the added independent variables, along with their means and standard deviations, is provided in Appendix Tables B.5 and B.6).

The *anti-immigration* variable is highly significant and has the expected negative sign. Unsurprisingly, people who think that the unemployed are lazy, that too many people take advantage of the system, or who think that a higher level of justice is not desirable tend to favor lower tax rates. The young, female respondents tend to support a larger public sector.

There is no canonical way to decide upon the exact list of the variables that should be included on the right-hand side of the regression in Table 8.11. The following example will show why this is the case. If we regress θ on ρ alone with 1998 data, the coefficient on ρ is -0.30 (column 1). Now consider adding the variable *TakeAdvantage* to this regression, which measures whether the respondent thinks that too many people take advantage of the public system and receive benefits although they do not need them (see Appendix Table B.5 for the exact definition). The correlation between *AntiImmigration* and *TakeAdvantage* is very large: 0.40. If we add the variable *TakeAdvantage* to the regression, the coefficient on *AntiImmigration* drops to -0.20 (*TakeAdvantage* is the variable that induces the biggest drop in the absolute value of the coefficient when added to the regression). Whether we should add this variable to the right-hand side of the regression depends on how we interpret the correlation between *AntiImmigration* and *TakeAdvantage*. If we believe that both

Table 8.11 Dependent variable: ProPublicSector (Estimation with OLS)

	1998		2001	
	(1)	(2)	(3)	(4)
AntiImmigration	−0.295**	−0.0173**	−0.308**	−0.226**
	(0.020)	(0.023)	(0.019)	(0.023)
Constant	0.043⁺	0.105	−0.028	0.051
	(0.024)	(0.203)	(0.023)	(0.191)
Unemployed Lazy		−0.103**		−0.044**
		(0.018)		(0.017)
TakeAdvantage		−0.104**		−0.125**
		(0.020)		(0.018)
Same econ. conditions for all		0.088**		0.104**
		(0.016)		(0.015)
Household income		−0.017**		−0.021**
		(0.006)		(0.006)
Female		0.313**		0.203**
		(0.043)		(0.041)
Age		0.014⁺		0.013⁺
		(0.008)		(0.007)
Age squared		−0.0002*		−0.0002*
		(8.10)		(7.10)
City		−0.018		0.015
		(0.015)		(0.015)
Education		−0.036		−0.061**
		(0.025)		(0.023)
Observations	1,886	1,483	1,933	1,645
R-squared	0.1066	0.2411	0.1166	0.2156

⁺significant at 10%; *significant at 5%; **significant at 1%.
Note: Standard errors are in parentheses below the value of the coefficients.

hostility toward immigrants and a negative opinion of people who live on welfare are determined by the same psychological or social traits—for example, some intrinsic general distrust—then the *TakeAdvantage* variable should be added. On the other hand, it might be argued that people who have a low opinion of welfare recipients do so because ethnic minorities are overrepresented among them. In this case, including the *TakeAdvantage* variable on the right-hand side of the equation will induce an underestimate of the direct influence of *AntiImmigration* on support for a larger public sector.[3] The question is hard to settle. We chose here to add all possible variables to the right-hand side of the regression.

The numbers in Table 8.11 above suggest that an increase of 1 point (on the $[-2, 2]$ scale) in the level of xenophobia reduces the *ProPublicSector* by $\hat{\delta} = 0.17$ in 1998 and by $\hat{\delta} = 0.23$ in 2001. We use this estimator to construct what we will define as racism-free demands for the public sector. We proceed as follows.

1. We select a critical level of *AntiImmigration* ρ_{ref} that we take to be the nonxenophobic threshold.
2. We define all individuals with $\rho \leq \rho_{ref}$ to be free of racism, and take their observed preferences for the public sector to be their racism-free economic preferences.
3. For all individuals with $\rho > \rho_{ref}$, we assume that there is some racism at play, and define their racism-free economic preferences to be those they would have if $\rho = \rho_{ref}$.

More specifically, consider an individual with observed ideal policy θ and ρ. We define a racism-free demand for public sector by:

$$\theta \text{ if } \rho \leq \rho_{ref}, \text{ and } \theta + \delta(\rho - \rho_{ref}) \text{ if } \rho \geq \rho_{ref}.$$

We will consider three different values for ρ_{ref}: $\rho_{ref} = -2$ (option 1), $\rho_{ref} = -1$ (option 2), $\rho_{ref} = 0$ (option 3). Table 8.12 presents the mean and standard deviation of the racism-free economic preferences for the three options and the two years under study. The last line also presents the figures for observed preferences. Note that the obtained values are almost identical in 1998 and 2001. In 2001, there is a slight decrease in the observed demand for public sector compared with 1998, but an increase in the coefficient δ balances this effect, so that racism-free demands are practically the same. It should also be

Table 8.12   Racism-free economic preferences: Various options

	1998		2001	
	Mean	Std. dev.	Mean	Std. dev.
Racism free, option 1	0.33	0.87	0.37	0.86
Racism free, option 2	0.15	0.87	0.15	0.86
Racism free, option 3	−0.01	0.88	−0.05	0.87
Observed preferences	−0.15	0.91	−0.24	0.91

noted that these values are very similar to those obtained with the simpler methods presented above.

We conclude that a reasonable set of racism-free distributions of public-sector preferences for both years are normal distributions with mean = 0, mean = 0.15, mean = 0.3, and standard deviation 0.85.

8.3   Political Equilibrium: Observation and Prediction

We chose the distribution of types (θ, ρ) to be a bivariate normal distribution whose parameters are given in Table 8.4. Almost the entire support of the distribution lies in the square $[-2, 2] \times [-2, 2]$.

We describe the computation of equilibrium PUNEs. We perform these computations for various values of γ; our choice of the one to report here will be explained below. We find that the best-fitting value of γ indeed lies in the interval, for each year, that was estimated in section 8.2. For each value of γ, we computed many (approximately one hundred) PUNEs. We then selected those for which the Left vote share is within 5 percent of the observed vote share for Left in that election.[4]

In Figure 8.6a we graph the selected PUNEs for 1998 for the value of salience $\gamma/2 = 0.5$. The space of the figure is (t, r). The three rectangular shapes in the figure are, reading from left to right, the average policy position (that is, ideal point) of those who, in the voter survey, identified themselves with one of the Right parties, the average ideal point of all respondents, and the average ideal point of those identified with Left parties. The pair of larger circular dots are the average values of the PUNEs;[5] the pair of smaller circular dots are the average ideal points of the Militants in the PUNEs calculated. (Of course, it is to be expected that the average PUNE values are more moderate than the

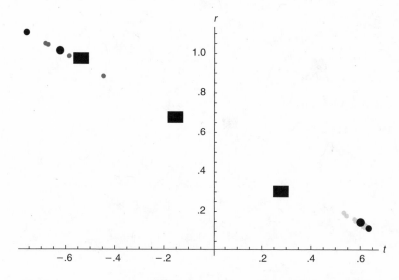

Figure 8.6a PUNEs, 1998, $\gamma/2 = 0.5$. Abscissa is t, ordinate is r. The three rectangular dots are the average observed ideal points of all voters (middle), of Right voters (upper left), and of Left voters (lower right). The two larger circular discs are the average PUNE policies of R and L. The smallest pair of black dots are the average policy views of the Militants in R and L at the PUNEs. The cluster of dark gray dots at the upper left are PUNE policies of the Right; the cluster of light gray dots at the lower right are PUNE policies of the Left.

average values of the Militants in the two parties.) The very small dots are the PUNE policies of the two parties.

Note that the Right party average PUNE is quite close to the average policy ideal of voters who identify with Right. In contrast, the Left party average PUNE is considerably more extreme than the average policy value of Left voters—it is more left on the size of the public sector, and less xenophobic than are Left voters.

We can now describe why we choose to report the results for $\gamma/2 = 0.5$: note that the three rectangular dots, which report *observed values*, are (virtually) collinear with the PUNE values. This characterizes the value $\gamma/2 = 0.5$. For larger and smaller values of γ, that collinearity fails to hold. In this sense, the value $\gamma/2 = 0.5$ gives the best fit of the model to the data. (Recall that we also used this method when calibrating the Euclidean model for the UK.)

The model's fit, however, is deficient with respect to vote share. We ended up selecting only PUNEs for which the Left share was greater than 40 percent:

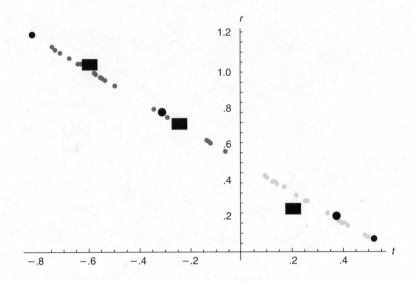

Figure 8.6b   PUNEs, 2001, $\gamma/2 = 0.6$. See caption for Figure 8.6a.

indeed, among these PUNEs, the Left share was on average 43.7 percent. The observed Left share, however, was higher: 48 percent. Therefore our model predicts that the Left should not have received as many votes as it did in 1998.

If the model were perfect, then we would expect that the average ideal point of the Militants in Left and Right would coincide with the average observed policy preferences of voters who identify with Left and Right. We do not achieve this coincidence of model and data: the Militants are considerably more extreme than the party members who identify with parties in Figure 8.6a. The PUNE analysis predicts that the Left and Right parties are more extreme than are the voters who identify with them.

In Figure 8.6b we graph the PUNEs for 2001: this time, the choice of $\gamma/2$ (to achieve the desired collinearity of observation with data) is 0.6. Notice that the average Right policy in PUNEs is very close to the average policy view of voters in 2001: it is not surprising that Right won 58 percent of the vote in that election. Left, on the other hand, has not compromised as much as Right. For this year, the average vote share of Left among selected PUNEs is 43.6 percent; the observed Left vote share is 42.2 percent.

Indeed, this contrast between the Right policies in PUNEs in 1998 and 2001 leads us to conjecture that the major explanation for the growth in Right's vote share between 1998 and 2001 was not the change in the distribution of voter

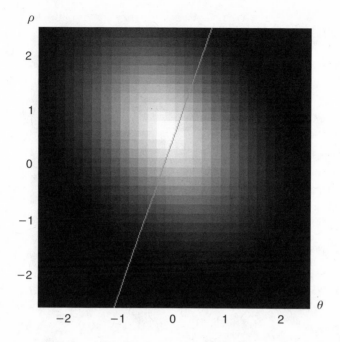

Figure 8.7a Density plot of voter types and partition of type space into two party constituencies, 1998, $\gamma/2 = 0.5$.

preferences, but rather a strengthening of the Opportunist faction in Right over this period, while a comparable strengthening did not occur for Left's Opportunists. In both elections, it appears that the Left party is considerably more radical on both issues than its observed constituency.

It must be emphasized that our utility function has only one degree of freedom, γ; had we a more complex utility function, we would be able to calibrate the model to better fit the data. In particular, it might be desirable to characterize each voter with a personal value of the salience parameter. That, however, would make our type space three-dimensional, which would make the numerical computation of equilibria considerably more complex.

We next display the predicted partition of the space of voter types into the two party memberships at the average of the PUNEs in the figures. Note from equations (8.3a) and (8.3b) that the set of types that prefer one policy to another is the set of types below or above a straight line in (θ, ρ) space. In Figures 8.7a and 8.7b we present the partition of voter types into the party memberships for the average of the PUNEs in 1998 and 2001. The space is

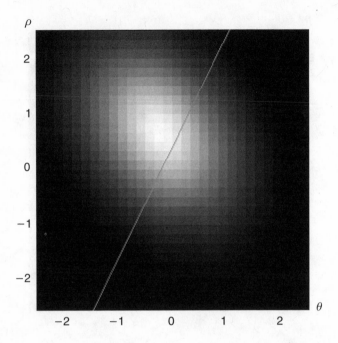

Figure 8.7b Density plot of voter types and partition of type space into two party constituencies, 2001, $\gamma/2 = 0.6$.

(θ, ρ). The Left comprises all types below the line; the Right comprises all types above the line.

By examining equation (8.2), we see that, at a PUNE, the slope of the line separating the Left and Right constituencies is $(t^L - t^R)/(r^R - r^L)$. Note that this ratio is just the negative reciprocal of the slope of the line segment joining the policy pair (τ^L, τ^R). We see, by comparing Figures 8.7a and 8.7b, that the salience of the immigration issue increased during this period. This, of course, is reflected in the increase in the estimated value of γ.

8.4   The Policy-Bundle and Antisolidarity Effects: Computation

Our procedure for computing the PBE and the ASE for each of the two years studied is as follows.

1.   In a given year, we compute, for each PUNE, the "expected tax rate," which is the share-weighted tax rates of the two parties.

2. We also have calculated the bargaining strengths of the Militants in L and R at each PUNE (recall formula (2.18)). We view these bargaining strengths as the "missing data" of our problem. We estimate a kernel density function for the distribution of bargaining strengths, in the selected PUNEs, for each party.[6] Using this density, we assign predicted frequencies to each PUNE. We then average the PUNEs using these frequencies. In this way, our relatively small set of selected PUNEs acts as a statistical proxy for what we would get were we to compute thousands of PUNEs. In particular, we derive from this procedure an *average expected tax rate* from the observed PUNEs. Denote this tax rate by t^{exp}. Denote the average bargaining strength in these PUNEs of the Opportunists in Right (Left) as $\alpha^R(\alpha^L)$.

3. The first counterfactual experiment, as we described in Chapter 2, contemplates an election in which only the policy t is an issue. The relevant distribution of voter types is simply the marginal distribution on the first component θ of types. We now compute PUNEs for this unidimensional election: call these P-PUNEs. For each P-PUNE, there is a pair of Opportunist bargaining strengths in L and R. We then choose a small selection of those P-PUNEs, for which the pair of Opportunist bargaining strengths is close to the ordered pair (α^L, α^R)—to be precise, we select P-PUNEs for which the relative bargaining strengths of the Opportunists in Left and Right are within .05 of the α^L and α^R, respectively. We denote the average expected tax rates in this selection of P-PUNEs by t_I^{exp}. We take this to be the tax rate equilibrium, purged of the policy-bundle effect. Among these P-PUNEs, the estimate of the policies is quite tight.

4. For the second counterfactual, which computes the antisolidarity effect, we change the distribution of voter types to the estimated racism-free distribution, G, described in section 8.2. We take the racism-free distribution to be a normal distribution on θ with standard deviation 0.85 and mean in the set $\mu^* \in \{0, 0.15, 0.3\}$. Thus for our chosen value of γ, we compute three versions of the second counterfactual, according to the hypothesized value of μ^*.

5. For the second counterfactual, we again compute many PUNEs—call them Q-PUNEs. We then take a selection of those whose bargaining powers are close to (α^L, α^R), as described above. Again the estimate is quite tight. Denote the average value of the expected tax rate in these Q-PUNEs by $t_{II}^{exp}(\gamma, \mu^*)$.

Table 8.13a Summary of PUNEs in the three models, Euclidean function approach, Denmark, 1998 ($\gamma / 2 = 0.5$)

	Full	Counter 1	Counter 2i	Counter 2ii	Counter 2iii
$1-\alpha^L$	0.731055	0.718366	0.733613	0.732541	0.736997
$1-\alpha^R$	0.914898	0.924348	0.887179	0.91434	0.919532
t^L	0.597959	0.258282	0.479073	0.616917	0.769767
t^R	-0.624704	-1.01873	-0.70043	-0.575166	-0.42721
r^L	0.138909				
r^R	1.00706				
t^{exp}	-0.0887433	-0.252758	-0.0497369	0.0927246	0.243317
ϕ^L	0.438355	0.599853	0.55177	0.560356	0.560182

Note: Counter 1 are P-PUNEs; Counters 2i, 2ii, and 2iii are Q-PUNEs under the three hypothetical racism-free distributions of voter types.

6. The PBE and the ASE, which are functions of (γ, μ^*), are then given by:

$$PBE(\gamma) = t_I^{exp}(\gamma) - t^{exp}(\gamma)$$

$$ASE(\gamma, \mu^*) = t_{II}^{exp}(\gamma, \mu^*) - t_I^{exp}(\gamma).$$

Clearly the total effect of xenophobia on the size of the public sector is:

$$TOT(\gamma, \mu^*) = PBE(\gamma) + ASE(\gamma, \mu^*) = t_{II}^{exp}(\gamma, \mu^*) - t^{exp}(\gamma).$$

7. Finally, we indeed also decompose these effects by party, so there is a Left and Right PBE and ASE as well as the averages described here.

Table 8.13a summarizes the equilibrium values of the PUNEs, P-PUNEs, and Q-PUNEs for 1998. Table 8.13b presents a summary of the PBE and ASE, decomposed by party, and on average, for 1998. Tables 8.14a and 8.14b do the same thing for 2001.

The appropriate way to think of the size of these effects is in comparison to the standard deviation of the distribution of ideal public-sector values (θ), which is 0.92 in 1998 and 0.91 in 2001. By definition, the PBE is invariant with respect to changes in μ^*. We list the total effects, under the two or three ways of specifying parameters for the racism-free distribution of voter ideal points on the size of the public sector, as fractions of that standard deviation.

Table 8.13b The policy-bundle (PB) and antisolidarity (AS) effects, Euclidean function approach, Denmark, 1998 PUNEs ($\gamma / 2 = 0.5$)

Party	PBE	ASE_i	ASE_{ii}	ASE_{iii}	$\frac{TOT_i}{std.\ dev.}$	$\frac{TOT_{ii}}{std.\ dev.}$	$\frac{TOT_{iii}}{std.\ dev.}$
Left	$-.340$	.221	.359	.511	-12.9%	2.05%	18.7%
Right	$-.394$	.318	.444	.592	-8.26%	5.43%	21.5%
Average	$-.164$	.203	.345	.496	4.24%	19.7%	20.2%

Note: TOT_i is ($PBE + ASE$). Std. dev. is the standard deviation of the observed distribution of views on the immigration issue.

Table 8.14a Summary of PUNEs in the three models, Euclidean function approach, Denmark, 2001 ($\gamma / 2 = 0.6$)

	Full	Counter 1	Counter 2i	Counter 2ii	Counter 2iii
$1-\alpha^L$	0.56	0.558061	0.562401	0.549585	0.562779
$1-\alpha^R$	0.3554	0.362347	0.345634	0.346406	0.356011
t^L	0.3733	0.432718	0.651918	0.784376	0.941452
t^R	-0.3083	-0.392884	-0.11009	0.0297519	0.171746
r^L	0.1862				
r^R	0.7573				
t^{exp}	-0.0107816	-0.0721156	-0.175818	0.317618	0.465924
ϕ^L	0.4365	0.387788	0.375048	0.381223	0.381522

Note: For explanation of column heads, see note, Table 8.13a.

Table 8.14b The policy-bundle (PB) and antisolidarity (AS) effects, Euclidean function approach, Denmark, 2001 PUNEs ($\gamma / 2 = 0.6$)

Party	PBE	ASE_i	ASE_{ii}	$\frac{TOT_i}{std.\ dev.}$	$\frac{TOT_{ii}}{std.\ dev.}$
Left	.059	.219	.352	30.6%	45.2%
Right	$-.085$	.283	.423	21.8%	37.1%
Average	$-.061$	.248	.390	20.6%	36.2%

Note: For explanation of TOT_i, see note, Table 8.13b.

Let us examine first the results for 2001. Here, the PBE for the Left party is positive; it is slightly negative for the Right, and slightly negative for the average value. We have already observed in the United States and the UK that the policies of Left and Right, in the Euclidean model, tend to diverge in the first counterfactual from what they are in the full-model PUNEs, and this occurs here as well. The ASE is large and positive, so that we estimate that the *total effect* of Danish xenophobia is to decrease the size of the public sector by between 21 and 36 percent of one standard deviation on the observed distribution of views of what that size should be. This is substantial. The big political shock of 2001—recall from the previous chapter that for the first time since 1920 the SDP was not the largest party—was accompanied by a big fiscal shock.

For 1998, we have a peculiar result: the PBE for the *Left* party is negative. This is hard to believe: it would suggest that many antiracist but fiscally conservative voters voted Left in 1998, because they preferred the Left's policy on the immigration issue to the Right's. In any case, on average, we estimate that the total effect of xenophobia is to reduce the size of the public sector by between 4 and 20 percent.

What seems clear is that the effect of xenophobia has increased significantly between the 1998 and 2001 elections, a conclusion that is consistent with popular observation.

Although the data do not exist, at this writing, to perform our analysis for the Danish parliamentary elections that took place on February 8, 2005, it is nevertheless worthwhile reporting the results, which we do in Table 8.15. The anti-immigrant Danish People's Party came in third, increasing its parliamentary representation by 15 seats, and its vote share from 12 percent (2001) to 13.2 percent. The Social Democrats' vote share fell from 27.6 percent in 2001

Table 8.15 Danish 2005 elections: February 8, 2005, Folketing election provisional results

Party	Vote share (percent)
Liberal Party (Venstre)	29.0
Social Democratic Party	25.9
Danish People's Party	13.2
Conservative People's Party	10.3
Danish Social-Liberal Party	9.2
Socialist People's Party	6.0
Unity List—Red-Green	3.4
Christian Democrats	1.7
Center Democrats	1.0
Minority party	0.3

to 25.9 percent. The Venstre (Liberal) Party prime minister Anders Fogh Rasmussen was reelected; the Reuters news release about the election began by stating that "Rasmussen began a second term on Wednesday under pressure to cut welfare spending and take the heat off taxpayers after a popular crackdown on immigrants over the past three years," adding further that the prime minister had "surpassed his 2001 campaign promise to cap taxes by reducing them fractionally."[7]

8.5 Conclusion

Like all equilibrium models, ours is best viewed as one that describes a political system in which preferences of voters are stable. In periods when voter preferences are in flux, we cannot expect the PUNE model to give perfect predictions. With stable constituencies, party entrepreneurs will come to know their constituencies' interests well, and we can expect that those entrepreneurs who wish to represent constituents will do so with more precision than when voter preferences are unstable and constituencies are shifting. The mechanism by which this occurs may well be that those Militants who rise within the party structure *are* the ones who best represent the constituents' interests. Once ensconced, however, a particular Militant will have a career within the party that may last for years or decades. Thus in periods of voter-preference flux, the established Militants in a party may cease to represent its evolving constituency.

Our policy space is only two-dimensional. In reality, the policy space has many more dimensions. In particular, it is possible, in reality, to differentiate public-sector policy toward immigrants from policy toward natives: for example, immigrants may receive less favorable treatment with regard to transfer payments than natives, as is currently the case in Denmark. To represent this possibility in our model would require a third policy dimension. With such a third dimension, the antisolidarity effect should decrease, because presumably parties could then propose to retain high public-sector benefits for natives, while reducing them for immigrants. We cannot, therefore, predict that the *total* size of the welfare state will radically fall in Denmark despite our estimates of the total effects.[8] Indeed, the Danish People's Party, with its native working-class base, advocates cutting welfare-state benefits only for immigrants, not for natives.

This point illustrates the necessity for political economists to model political competition as occurring over multidimensional policy spaces. Our work begins this task, although, as we have just noted, it still falls short of what is ultimately desirable. The binding constraints, at this point, are two: first, the availability of reliable data on voter preferences over multidimensional policy spaces and, second, the difficulty of computing equilibria (PUNEs) in real time, when the dimension of the type space and/or policy space is larger than two.

A technical remark: the dimension of the equilibrium manifold, in a two-party PUNE model, will be two, regardless of the dimension of the policy space or the type space. That dimension is related only to the number of parties and the number of independent factions within parties. If there are k independent factions in each party and n parties, then in the fully endogenous PUNE model, the dimension of the equilibrium manifold will be $n(k - 1)$. For this chapter, we have $n = 2$ and $k = 2$.

9

Immigration and the Political Institutionalization of Xenophobia in France

9.1   Introduction

Like most Western industrialized nations, France has taken in large numbers of immigrants over the last several decades. The influx of these foreign populations has left an indelible mark on various facets of French life. One of immigration's most visible impacts has been its transformation of the country's ethnic and religious character. Once predominantly white and Catholic, France has turned into a multicultural nation whose second religion is Islam. This demographic shift has not only transformed French society and culture; it has also reconfigured French politics.

A sizable portion of France's voters, fearing that immigration erodes their national identity, social status, and safety, has abandoned the traditional parties of the moderate Left and Right and turned to anti-immigrant, xenophobic political movements that promise to return France back to the French. The Front National (FN), headed by its notorious leader, Jean-Marie Le Pen, has been most successful in stoking and collecting the anti-immigrant vote. Parties of the Left and Right have oscillated in their approach to the FN and its far-right platform, flirting with the Front's xenophobic slogans during some campaigns, only to marginalize the extremist movement when distance to its

This chapter was written by Rafaela Dancygier.

237

themes appeared to be more expedient politically. Regardless of the main-stream's behavior, after two decades of solid performances at the polls, the FN and its platform have secured a structural position in France's electoral space.

This chapter charts the ascendancy of immigration as a salient issue in France's political landscape and traces the concomitant rise of the FN, whose xenophobic rhetoric tapped into and further fueled the growing racism of the French electorate. The chapter begins by briefly outlining France's long history with immigration and then turns to the political implications of immigrant settlement in France. While immigration policy of the first decades after World War II was a largely bureaucratic endeavor designed to meet the economic and demographic demands of the country, the establishment of immigrant com-munities in France gave rise to social and economic tensions that politicians at both the local and the national level soon seized upon for political pur-poses. This chapter maps out the prominent controversies and debates that helped politicize the issue of immigration, promoted the rise of Le Pen and his nationalistic party in the 1980s, and contributed to the FN's electoral en-durance into the twenty-first century. As immigration started losing some of its political salience in the mid-1990s, the Front successfully transformed itself from a one-issue movement focused on closing French borders into a party that links a host of concerns—unemployment, law and order, cultural iden-tity, national sovereignty, inter alia—to immigration and the multiculturalism it engenders. The following pages also trace the evolution of the FN voter. The Front's electorate defies the traditional Left-Right categorization and best fits the "ethnocentrist" label: a constituency that is more xenophobic, insecure, and prejudiced than the average French voter.

This chapter is not meant to give a comprehensive overview of France's political history with immigration. Instead, it focuses on the important po-litical events, elections, and turning points that have propelled the issue of immigration into the political limelight and shows how the major parties have shaped—and been shaped by—the politicization of immigration. The chapter thus presents a rather stylized account of France's political treatment of immi-gration, and the reader is encouraged to turn to the reference texts for a more complete presentation of this topic.

9.2 Immigration in France: A Brief Sketch

France has a long and varied history of immigration. Beginning in earnest in the second half of the nineteenth century, immigration has since influenced the demographic, economic, and sociopolitical development of the French nation-state. Although the impact of immigration has been profound and wide-ranging, it has never quite occurred as planned. Instead, the inflow and settlement of foreign migrants, controlled and guided by ambitious state planners, has strayed from the envisioned course. Thus immigrants sometimes arrived in fewer numbers than expected, while overstaying their official welcome at other times (Verbunt 1985, 127). Official suspensions of immigration were routinely circumvented as immigrant families reunited in the host country. Waves of illegal immigration also seemed to escape the control of the French state.

In the late nineteenth century, the French government, prompted by employers, began official recruitment of immigrants to ease acute domestic labor shortages that were brought about by sharp declines in the country's birthrate. Until World War I, the immigrant population consisted mainly of European migrants, with the majority originating from Belgium and Italy and smaller numbers hailing from Germany, Switzerland, and Spain. Most of these foreign workers were employed in industries that required few or no skills, such as mining, construction, and textiles, as well as the agricultural sector (Tapinos 1975, 2; Verbunt 1985, 128). World War I initiated a new wave of immigration, as many previous economic migrants had returned to their homelands while a great number of young Frenchmen left for the battlefields. Large-scale labor recruitment from France's colonies in North Africa and Indochina as well as from southern Europe and Poland filled wartime labor market needs for the duration of the hostilities (Lequin 1992, 334–335). While most of these foreigners were repatriated once the war ended, the French economy again confronted a severe scarcity of domestic labor in 1919, triggering renewed labor migration from neighboring countries as well as from Poland and North Africa.[1] Between 1914 and the onset of the Depression, France saw a dramatic increase of its foreign population, which more than doubled, rising from 1.2 million to 2.66 million (corresponding to an increase of 3 to 6.59 percent of the population) during those years. In light of the deteriorating economy and rising unemployment levels of the early 1930s, France introduced its first laws restricting immigration in 1932, to be followed by further curbs in 1938 and 1940 (DeLey 1983, 198).

Following World War II, the confluence of high casualties, low birthrates, and economic reconstruction reversed previous trends and gave rise to a resumption of immigration. France embarked on an immigration project that would not end until 1974. During those thirty years, the so-called Trente

Glorieuses, France imported over two million foreign workers. A 1945 law created the Office National d'Immigration (ONI), which was put in charge of recruiting foreign labor to fill vacancies in the expanding sectors (mostly construction, public works, and heavy industry), to avoid the occupational and regional dislocation of French workers (especially in the traditional agricultural sector), and to stave off upward wage pressures and stimulate investment (DeLey 1983, 199; Hollifield 1992, 54). While the importation of migrant labor was no new undertaking, compared with previous periods of growth-motivated immigration there was "one major difference—the state was leading the effort to recruit foreign labor and modernize the economy, rather than following the lead of the private business sector" (Hollifield 1992, 54). Immigration thus became an integral component of France's *étatiste* policy of economic recovery and industrial expansion. It is important to note that not only economic imperatives dictated the French immigration project. The organized inflow of foreigners was also part of a deliberate strategy to restore the country to its great power status through aggressive repopulation (Freeman 1979, 69). Populationnistes—a group consisting of academics and policymakers—pushed for higher birthrates but also influenced the nation's immigration agenda. They motivated the government's decision to promote the permanent settlement of European Catholics—immigrants who would be "culturally and ethnically compatible" with the French nation (ibid., 55).

In the first two decades following the war, migrant labor from Spain, Italy, and Portugal, but also from North Africa, arrived in France, to be followed by a smaller influx of immigrants from sub-Saharan Africa.[2] Colonial obligations often interfered with the Populationnistes' ethnic preferences. Up until Algeria's independence in 1962, Algerians could travel and settle in the metropole without restrictions. After 1962, close to one million so-called *pieds-noirs* (Algerian-born Frenchmen) came to France, disproportionately locating in southern France, especially Marseilles. In addition, about one hundred thousand Algerian Muslims whose loyalty lay with the French government (so-called *harkis*) moved to the mother country. By 1970, 19.75 percent of France's immigrant population hailed from Algeria (Fetzer 2000, 56; Freeman 1979, 23, 75; Tapinos 1975, 47–67).

In addition to the more organized migration flows that were channeled through ONI, large numbers of immigrants entered France illegally every year. Initially clandestine immigration took place with the tacit encouragement of the state, as most illegal immigrants soon became eligible for work permits *(régularisation);* by 1968, over 80 percent of France's foreign workers had crossed the French border illegally, leading some to the conclusion that "the government had lost control over immigration" (DeLey 1983, 199). By the early 1970s, this lax official attitude toward immigration policy came to an end. The oil crisis, ensuing economic recession, and rising unemployment fueled the public's growing discontent with immigration. As did other Western European countries at the time, the French government responded to the economic downturn by severely restricting legalizations in 1973 and by putting an abrupt stop to legal worker migration in 1974. In spite of successive governments' efforts to reduce the number of foreigners living in France and to prevent further waves of immigrants entering the country since then, France's immigrant population has increased ever since (see Table 9.1). Indeed, one unintended consequence of the categorical immigration ban was to encourage those migrant workers already living in France to settle permanently and to reunite with their families who, by and large, were allowed to immigrate. After the official suspension of immigration in 1974, over half a million spouses and children of immigrant workers entered the country (Fetzer 2000, 57). While the government attempted to discourage family reunifications through tight regulations, human and civil rights groups contested restrictive policies on the basis of humanitarian as well as constitutional grounds. Their lobbying efforts enabled many foreign families to reunite (Hollifield 1992, 84). Family reunification changed the immigration process from guest-worker immigration to settlement immigration, which significantly altered public perceptions of immigration. Moreover, since the early 1980s, the number of refugees seeking asylum in Western Europe has risen dramatically.[3]

From the immediate postwar period until the mid-1970s, France's immigration regime can thus be characterized as very heterogeneous, both in the type of policies pursued and in the type of labor it attracted. Colonial obligations, bilateral accords, employer-based recruitment through ONI, illegal immigration, and claims for asylum combined to increase France's immigrant population from 1.99 million in 1946 to 3.89 million in 1975. While earlier migration waves attracted familiar, white-skinned Europeans, the new immigrants also consisted of darker-skinned Africans. Questions of immigration thus became intertwined with questions of race. One steady undercurrent pervading French politics of immigration has been the concern—both among the public and among elites—that immigration would indelibly alter the racial makeup of the nation. While the Populationnistes' plan to repopulate France succeeded insofar as the country received large shares of immigrants that showed higher fertility rates than the native population, it failed to

Table 9.1 French population by country of birth and nationality, 1911–1999 (thousands)

Year	Total population	Born in France			Born abroad				
		French by birth	French by acquisition	Non-French nationals	French by birth	French by acquisition (a)	Non-French nationals (b)	Immigrant population (a)+(b)	Immigrant population (percent)
1911	39,192	37,652	85	218	127	168	942	1,100	2.92
1921	38,798	36,847	80	277	164	174	1,255	1,429	3.88
1926	40,228	37,384	45	325	187	204	2,084	2,288	6.12
1931	41,228	37,937	55	291	216	306	2,423	2,729	7.19
1936	41,183	38,220	100	288	248	416	1,910	2,326	6.09
1946	39,848	36,908	301	310	343	552	1,434	1,986	5.38
1954	42,781	39,571	295	245	377	773	1,520	2,293	5.79
1962	46,456	42,133	336	220	905	931	1,931	2,861	6.79
1968	49,756	44,009	297	402	1,766	1,019	2,262	3,281	7.46
1975	52,599	45,907	280	667	1,858	1,112	2,775	3,887	8.47
1982	54,296	47,169	254	845	1,991	1,167	2,870	4,037	8.56
1990	56,652	49,556	472	739	1,719	1,308	2,858	4,166	8.41
1999	58,518	51,342	800	509	1,559	1,555	2,754	4,309	7.36

Source: INSEE 1996; data for 1999 taken from http://www.recensement.insee.fr.

Note: This table follows the French classification, whereby children born to immigrant parents in France are not considered immigrants. Persons who were born abroad but who acquired French citizenship always remain immigrants according to this classification. Persons coming from Algeria, even though juridically French and born in French territory before Algerian independence in 1962, are counted among Non-French nationals born abroad. From 1954 to 1968, they are counted as Algerian Muslims. In contrast, repatriates from Algeria, French by birth, are not considered immigrants.

attract the desired type of immigrant—white European Catholics who would be easily and invisibly absorbed into French culture and society. While in 1968 over 70 percent of foreigners living in France were of European origin, this share had plunged to 48 percent by 1982.[4] Because of steady inflows and family expansion, by the early 1990s Muslim migrants from Algeria, Morocco, and Tunisia (so-called Maghribins) constituted almost two-thirds of France's four-million-strong foreign population, not counting their one million children who were entitled to French citizenship if born in France.[5] In light of these demographic developments, the reform of France's nationality laws soon moved to the forefront of the national political debate. Thus while 1974 marked the end of state-sponsored immigration into France, the mid-1970s also witnessed the increasing politicization of immigration and integration policy.

9.3   The Politicization of Immigration

Parliamentary debates about immigration control polarized the country's political elites. Parties of the Right were anxious to tighten France's immigration laws, while leftist opposition leaders often saw themselves as defenders of immigrant interests. Led by President Giscard d'Estaing and neo-Gaullist prime minister Jacques Chirac, the center-right government introduced measures that would decrease the number of foreigners living in France, limit family reunification, and encourage repatriation (aide au retour), often through financial incentives tied to return migration. The Socialist and Communist opposition blocked the Conservatives' immigration bill, outraged in particular by their plan to facilitate the forcible expulsion of migrants, and condemned it as "immoral, unjust and racist."[6] While the Left's opposition softened some of the bill's more stringent provisions, the government did manage to pass legislation that would considerably tighten residency regulations and impose tougher entry restrictions. In addition to official policy, political leaders put indirect pressure on immigrants residing in France to leave the country by deliberately stoking an already hostile political climate. Politicians "made sure that people understood that there was a connection between the presence of two million immigrant workers and the unemployment of one million French workers" and also insinuated a link "between the presence of immigrants (i.e., young African males) and the insecurity in the cities" (Verbunt 1985, 154).[7]

In the early 1980s, with the election of Socialist president François Mitterrand and a left-wing majority in parliament, official policy toward foreigners already residing in France softened. The right to family reunification was re-instituted and amnesty initiatives for undocumented migrant workers were reintroduced. One of Mitterrand's first acts in office was to grant legal residence status to 130,000 Algerian immigrants who had entered the country illegally. Consistent with the Socialists' campaign promises to respect ethnic pluralism in all spheres of public life, the Socialist government also passed a set of laws extending the right of free association to foreigners. Moreover, the Mitterrand administration undertook a series of reforms aiming at the social integration and economic advancement of France's foreign population (DeLey 1983, 202–209; Safran 1985, 54). Among the Socialists' more controversial campaign promises was the proposal to introduce local voting rights for foreigners who had been living in France for five years or longer. These generous proposals did not, however, coincide with the public's mood. While the Socialist government tried to integrate foreigners through national laws and initiatives, the accommodationist spirit of Mitterrand's policies fell on deaf ears at the local level, where years of mismanaged immigration policy and misguided integration policy had helped create a noxious social climate.

9.3.1   The Politics of Exclusion

Several factors contributed to the deterioration of social relations between the native French population and the local immigrant communities in the late 1970s, when intergroup relations grew increasingly hostile. Successive housing policies adopted by the French government contributed to the growing ghettoization and segregation of France's immigrant population. In the 1950s, faced with a critical housing shortage, the French state constructed provisional housing for immigrants that resembled the shantytowns and slums *(bidonvilles)* that many of these immigrants had escaped in the first place. Those foreign workers who did not live in *bidonvilles* tended to concentrate in poor, inner-city districts, occupying dilapidated dwellings that had been deserted by French tenants. By the late 1960s, as migrant families reunited and settled in France, the government recognized the need for additional, improved housing, destroyed the *bidonvilles,* and initiated several new housing policies, which generally exacerbated rather than remedied the problems they sought to solve. Judging African families as generally "unadjusted" to French society and customs, the government built housing complexes *(cités de transits)* where intensive education aimed at social integration would prepare these foreigners for life in French towns, among French neighbors. Transitional in theory, these shabbily built *cités* instead became long-term homes and deteriorated into the very ghettos that they were meant to eliminate. In a similar development, native residents began abandoning neighborhoods containing *foyers* (hostels originally built for Algerians during the war of independence), which came to be predominantly occupied by single male migrants in the 1970s and 1980s, causing further segregation. Finally, many immigrant families who had previously lived in *bidonvilles* or who could no longer afford inner-city housing moved to cheap public housing projects in the suburbs (called Habitats à Loyer Modéré, or HLMs), which were funded by the state and partly subsidized by employers (Hargreaves 1995, 69–70; Verbunt 1985, 147–149).

Certain projects, suburbs, and neighborhoods soon became dominated by immigrants, whose heavy concentration gave rise to strong resentment by the native French, many of whom perceived immigrants as illegitimate competitors for social welfare and scarce public services (Verbunt 1985, 155).[8] These sentiments were confirmed in several opinion polls. In 1984, 53 percent of those polled thought that immigrants illegitimately benefited from social assistance; in the following year, the great majority (71 percent) were convinced that immigrants collected more money being unemployed in France than working in their country of origin (Gastaut 2000, 301). Politicians, in particular those of the Communist Party (PCF), were eager to exploit these resentments and prejudices for political gain. The poor neighborhoods where immigrants tended to concentrate were often located in districts that had traditionally been strongholds of the PCF. Despite their ideological commitment to international working-class solidarity, a number of Communist mayors chose to portray migrant workers as competitors that divided the laboring classes by keeping down wages and weakening the labor movement as a whole. As early as 1969, Communist mayors in the Paris region called for a more balanced distribution of immigrants among all Paris communes, since immigrant populations (who were disproportionately poorer) consumed more public services than their French neighbors. By the early 1980s, several local administrations had instituted official quota systems that limited the number of immigrants and their children in state institutions such as schools, summer camps, and, most notably, public housing (Schain 1985, 174–179). Local election campaigns often centered on the question of which candidate would be toughest on immigration and immigrant demands.

These developments were exemplified and thrust into the national spotlight by one particular incident: *l'affaire du bulldozer* in the Paris suburb of Vitry.

The town's Communist mayor refused to accept three hundred Africans from Mali who were relocated from a neighboring suburb and housed in a *foyer* in Vitry. To forcefully underscore his position, on Christmas Eve of 1980, the mayor evicted the African migrants and sent bulldozers to demolish the hostel.[9] The bulldozer affair was only the latest and most blatantly brutal in a series of politically motivated offensives against immigrants at the local level. Heavily publicized, it ignited a national discussion about the so-called *seuil de tolérance* (threshold of tolerance), according to which intergroup conflict would be inevitable once the immigrant population reached some (pseudoscientifically specified) share of the population. Following the example of Vitry, local politicians of both the Left and the Right used this concept to justify their refusal to accommodate more immigrants in their communities (Gastaut 2000, 466–477). In the 1983 municipal elections, right-wing politicians made electoral gains as playing the anti-immigrant card had turned out to be a vote winner. In several cities, center-right politicians portrayed immigrant families as welfare scroungers, criminals, and as generally responsible for unemployment as well as for violence and unrest.[10] It was in this heated climate of resentment and xenophobia that the racist Front National scored its first electoral victory and emerged as a viable political actor.

9.4   The Rise of Le Pen

Founded in 1972, the Front National operated in relative obscurity during its first decade of existence. It generally appealed to less than 1 percent of the French electorate in national elections, and Jean-Marie Le Pen, its founder and charismatic leader, failed to collect the five hundred signatures necessary to run in France's presidential election of 1981 (Davies 1999, 3).[11] In the party's early years, its extremist platform pushed it to the fringes of France's political space. Campaigning on fiercely nationalistic, anti-immigrant programs, the FN called for the forcible repatriation of all non-European immigrants, for a ban on all further immigration, and for a wholesale reform of France's nationality laws. It warned of immigration's role in eroding French values, identity, and unity, and championed French sovereignty in all areas of national policy, which it considered under threat by globalization, in particular by international migration and European integration. The FN also campaigned on a law-and-order platform, calling for the restoration of the death penalty, among other harsh law enforcement measures. In the early 1980s, the FN's electoral fortunes began to turn when the extreme right-wing party scored 17 percent in parliamentary by-elections in Dreux. Foreshadowing later successes, the Front registered its highest vote shares in working-class neighborhoods that had defected from the Left or abstained. The town also shared many of the characteristics of future FN strongholds: it was an industrial town fifty miles west of Paris, severely hit by the economic crisis and home to a sizable share of immigrants, many of whom occupied the publicly subsidized HLMs. The FN blamed the town's high unemployment and crime rates on the immigrant population and claimed that a restoration of the local economy and of public order could only be achieved once all immigrants were sent back to their home countries (Bréchon and Mitra 1992, 71–73). Following its first local victory, the FN experienced its first nationwide breakthrough in the 1984 European elections, where it attained over 11 percent of the vote and managed to elect ten representatives to the European Parliament. This was only the first in a series of electoral performances that would give the FN notoriety as well as long-sought prominence in France's electoral arena.

9.5   The Mainstreaming of Xenophobia

By the mid-1980s, immigration had established itself as a major issue on the nation's political agenda. Previously treated as a technical and bureaucratic policy domain, immigration policy had become heavily politicized and assumed a "political and mythical dimension" (Withol de Wenden 1991, 322) that it still has not shed.

9.5.1   "Will the French Ever Be French Again?"

The French media played its part in hyping the issue, publishing alarmist reports of immigrant-inspired crime and conveying an image of France being invaded and overrun by immigrants. In 1985, the conservative newspaper *Le Figaro* featured a cover provocatively asking, "Will the French ever be French again?" Below the headline, it showed Marianne, the symbol of the French Republic, wearing a chador (Simmons 1996, 159). In light of this sensationalist coverage, the Socialist government realized that its integrationist, immigrant-friendly policies could soon prove to be an electoral liability in the legislative elections of 1986. It thus backtracked on some of the more generous measures (notably extending local voting rights to immigrants), reintroduced repatriation assistance (renamed *aide à la réinsertion,* to denote the Socialists' recognition of integration—albeit not in France), restricted family reunification by making it conditional on rigid housing requirements, which many immigrants could not meet, and emphasized its crackdown on illegal immigration and tough border controls (Hargreaves 1995, 191; Simmons 1996, 158; Withol de Wenden 1991, 323–324). In spite of these efforts, in the public's image, the Socialists would remain the party that was at best ambiguous and at worst "soft" on immigration.

The center-right forces, well aware of the Socialists' relative weakness in this issue area, developed a platform for the upcoming parliamentary elections that would push immigration, in particular nationality laws, front and center. In its platform *(Une Stratégie de Gouvernement)*, the neo-Gaullist party Rassemblement pour la République (RPR) included an entire chapter entitled "Bringing immigration under control" *(Maîtriser l'immigration)*. The language and policies developed in this chapter seemed to be taken right out of Le Pen's playbook. The party questioned the value of a multicultural society in which most foreigners did not respect but rather undermined France's culture and identity. It accused immigrants of abusing the welfare state, living on the dole, and creating a climate of fear and crime. The survival of the French nation was at stake and the best way to protect France's economy, society, and cultural heritage would be through stringent immigration controls, large-scale repatriations, and a reform of the country's nationality laws, which were deemed too permissive. In short, in the mid-1980s, the Right unabashedly sought to appeal to FN voters (Gastaut 2000, 210–211).

The proposal that attracted the most national attention was the reform of France's nationality laws. For over a century, France had granted citizenship to children born in France to immigrant parents. This emphasis on jus soli came under sharp attack from the Extreme Right, who insisted that the growing population of Franco-Maghribins threatened French security and identity and showed no loyalty to French ideals and values. In short, French citizenship needed to be earned and deserved (summarized in the FN's slogan and book: *Être Français, Cela se Mérite*). France's nationality laws were said to grant the privilege of French citizenship too easily, creating a whole generation who were French on paper, but not in spirit (that is, creating *Français de papier* rather than *Français de cœur*). In their joint 1986 platform, the center-right parties co-opted Le Pen's rhetoric and called for a repeal of the automatic acquisition of citizenship (Brubaker 1992, 138–143). While the debate surrounding France's citizenship regime featured several intellectual currents,[12] it was the nativist argument that was heard the loudest. The Right decried the Socialists' policy on multicultural *insertion* and pleaded for a return to assimilation.[13]

Since the Right's nationalistic arguments insisted that North African Muslim immigrants were inherently unassimilable, exhibiting behavior and values that were intrinsically incompatible with those espoused by French society, the natural conclusion would be to strip today's immigrants of their entitlement to French citizenship (Brubaker 1992, 149; Feldblum 1999, 69–70). The public seemed to be more persuaded by the right-wing rhetoric of exclusion than by the Left's recognition of multiculturalism. Center-right parties narrowly regained parliament in the 1986 legislative elections and the Front National, polling close to 10 percent nationwide, sent thirty-five representatives to parliament.[14]

The center-right government, however, found out that it was considerably easier to spout anti-immigrant slogans as an opposition strategy than to in fact pass and implement policies consistent with such rhetoric once in office. The Chirac government not only was confronted with strong opposition in parliament, but also faced splits among its own. Some centrist coalition politicians had become increasingly uncomfortable with the radicalization of the Nationality Code debate and, fearing to be associated with the exclusionist Extreme Right, withdrew their support from the initiative. At the same time, grassroots antiracism campaigns, which had increasingly gained organizational strength and nationwide prominence, opposed the reforms vigorously.[15] To make matters worse for the government, the proposed reforms stalled due to unanticipated legal and technical implications of the proposals.[16] The government, unable to work out these difficulties, appointed a special commission to examine France's Nationality Code as the public, unable to follow the legal complexities, lost interest in the issue. When the commission returned with the recommendation to leave the Nationality Code intact, the government retreated from its initial position that citizenship could not be conferred automatically and indeed endorsed the principle of jus soli (Brubaker 1992, 156–158; Withol de Wenden 1991, 327). As the center-right coalition retreated from its attack on jus soli, the FN capitalized on the center-right's apparent inconsistency and made sure the issue retained its salience. According to one observer, the government's backtracking

> induced Le Pen to give increasing play to the issue. It offered him the chance to contrast the distinctiveness and consistency of his own position with the government's waffling retreat toward a position only marginally different from that of the Socialists . . . As the proposal's positional coordinates changed—as it drifted toward the right and toward the extreme

regions of French political space—so too did the way the mainstream right parties and the government positioned themselves on the issue. (Brubaker 1992, 159–160)

While its performance on the Nationality Code reforms was unsatisfactory to most right-wing voters, the Chirac government attempted to please its more extremist electorate by enacting a series of restrictive immigration laws. The 1986 Pasqua laws severely restricted entry and residence requirements, facilitated deportations of illegal immigrants, and substantially increased police powers by excluding the judicial branch from expulsions—1,700 non–European Community immigrants were instantly deported because they were deemed to present a threat to public order. Trying to prevent desertions to the FN in the upcoming presidential elections, the Chirac government made sure that these deportations received heavy publicity and media coverage.[17]

9.6   The 1988 Presidential Election

In the run-up to the 1988 presidential elections, the mainstream parties thus tried to portray themselves as being tough on immigration. The two right-wing candidates, Raymond Barre and Jacques Chirac, appropriated Le Pen's nationalistic and anti-immigrant language to appeal to their fringe constituencies. Chirac's interior minister, hardliner Charles Pasqua, underlined his party's proximity to many of the FN's themes, claiming that "the Front National has the same preoccupations, the same values as the majority. It merely expresses them in a more brutal and noisy way" (as quoted in Simmons 1996, 91). At the same time, Barre and Chirac—aware that extremist positions on immigration risked alienating crucial centrist voters—made sure to emphasize economic policies. They ran on traditional conservative economic platforms, such as cutting taxes, reducing employers' social security contributions,[18] and offering low levels of income support for the poor and long-term unemployed.[19] Economic issues were, however, generally overshadowed by a focus on law and order and immigration, since the stock market crash of 1987 did not allow the government to tout its economic achievements (Goldey and Johnson 1988, 198). President Mitterrand capitalized on the Right's positional dilemma. No longer constrained by the weakened Communists, Mitterrand moved to the center in the economic domain (campaigning for a "capitalism with a human face")[20] while sticking to his previous election promise that immigrants would be granted local voting rights—once the public was prepared to accept such a move. Given that public opinion as well as Mitterrand's own party was at the time clearly not ready to extend the local franchise to immigrant residents,[21] this tactical move served to galvanize the Front National and put pressure on Chirac to side with the extremists (Goldey and Johnson 1988, 201). Mitterrand further outmaneuvered his right-wing opponents by giving Le Pen access to the media, ensuring that the xenophobe's views got sufficient airtime to exacerbate the position of the Right (Thränhardt 1995, 330).

The election results proved the effectiveness of Mitterrand's strategy. In the first ballot, the Right split its vote, almost evenly, among Chirac (19.8 percent), Barre (16.5), and Le Pen (14.6). Not only did this represent the worst showing of the orthodox Right since 1945, it was also the highest score ever received by a candidate of the Extreme Right (Goldey and Johnson 1988, 201). Over four million voters had turned out to support Le Pen, a result which the extremists rightly called an "earthquake" (Simmons 1996, 92). The majority of Le Pen voters (65 percent) gave Chirac their support in the second round, but this did not prove to be sufficient. Mitterrand, who obtained 33.9 percent of the votes in the first round, won the second ballot with 54 percent of the vote and his Socialist Party regained control of the legislature in the ensuing parliamentary elections. Despite the Right's efforts to present itself as tough on immigration, to the potential FN voter, it was probably the moderate Right's failure to stand firm on the Nationality Code reform that came to mind, tipping the balance in favor of Le Pen and his followers at the ballot box. The mainstream Right parties' flirtation with the Extreme Right thus appears to have been a gamble that did not pay off. It undermined their credibility both among centrist voters, who were alienated by their racist rhetoric, and among more extremist elements, who were dissatisfied with the parties' wavering on the Nationality Code reform and who, in any event, had the option of voting for a genuine xenophobe. Crucially, the Right's irresponsible manipulation of xenophobia helped Le Pen and his extremist themes secure a permanent position in France's political landscape.

After the shock of the 1988 election, pundits and academics alike were eager to explain the *effet Le Pen*—who were the four million voters who cast their ballot for the extremist leader? At first glance, the Le Pen electorate appears eclectic: Le Pen was more popular among males (18 percent) than among females (11 percent), and drew support among small businessmen, shopkeepers, and craftsmen (23 percent), manual workers (18 percent), the self-employed (21 percent), and those with vocational training (18 percent) (Perrineau 1997, 102).[22] Some observers dismissed the Le Pen vote as a protest vote that lacked political coherence. According to Mayer and Perrineau (1992, 130), the Lepeniste electorate in 1988 had a "hybrid character." Le Pen voters generally had no consistent partisan attachment, crossed all age and occupational groups, and, judging from previous elections, were likely to switch to other candidates in the future as different issues motivated their vote choice in different elections (Mayer and Perrineau 1992). However, viewed from another perspective—one that does not focus on voters' socioeconomic profiles—a different conclusion emerges.

The fact that Le Pen supporters did not fall neatly along the orthodox Left-Right continuum indeed disguised the coherence of the Le Pen electorate. Introducing an additional dimension, Mayer (1993) finds that the more ethnocentrist voters are, the more likely they are to support Le Pen at the polls.[23] Ethnocentrist voters are concentrated among the poorer, less educated, economically insecure sections of the electorate and tend to be more prejudiced and authoritarian in their social and political outlook. As sociocultural and class characteristics interact among Le Pen's constituency, ethnocentrism goes a long way in explaining the absence of the traditionally class-based partisan identification patterns seen in the Le Pen vote (N. Mayer 1993, 31). Thus the xenophobic candidate "succeeded in mobilizing in every social group most of those with an obsession about immigrants and foreigners, an attitudinal characteristic obviously in large measure independent of conventional social-structural situations" (Husbands 1991, 410). Well aware of the heterogeneous, cross-class character of his constituency, Le Pen embarked on an electoral strategy in the 1990s that capitalized on the wide-ranging nature of his party's appeal. In the meantime, the politics of racism and xenophobia remained popular.

9.7 Xenophobia Remains in the Headlines

Before the political mainstream could recuperate from the 1988 shock, several contentious events involving the country's immigrant community helped to keep xenophobia in the national headlines and consciousness. One of the most notorious incidences stoking anti-immigrant sentiments was the so-called headscarf affair *(affaire du foulard)*. When, in the fall of 1989, three Muslim girls from the Paris suburb of Creil insisted on wearing their headscarves to school against the principal's objection that such a display of religiosity was an affront to the separation of church and state, a national debate on the compatibility between France's professed secularism on the one hand and multiculturalism's religious claims on the other ensued. The media jumped on this local dispute and forced the national leadership to take a stand. The French Left was split, divided between defenders of secular education (as well as feminists), who demanded banning the headscarf from the classroom, and those who argued that such a decision would violate personal liberties and undermine tolerance and respect for diverse value systems. The Right cautiously endorsed the ban, but was generally careful to prevent this issue from turning into a divisive national controversy (Bréchon and Mitra 1992, 66–68). The Front National did not harbor such reservations. The party, helped by the mainstream parties' ambiguity and by the torrent of media coverage, was able to exploit the incident for its own political purposes. The affair, rich in symbols and rhetoric, once again put the spotlight on the FN's major campaign themes and allowed Le Pen, who vigorously supported the ban, to present himself as the sole guardian of French identity and culture. As the debate wore on, the public's opinion on the matter became increasingly hostile, and previously latent xenophobia became more overt (Bréchon and Mitra 1992, 68).[24] Invigorated by these developments, the FN scored significant successes in parliamentary by-elections in Dreux and Marseilles (Perrineau 1997, 63).

The *affaire du foulard* came to a (provisional) conclusion when the Conseil d'État (the highest administrative court) decided to allow the wearing of religious insignia in public schools, provided they did not represent religious propaganda or interfere with educational aims. Other confrontations between the Islamic minority and members of France's white population were not always solved through bureaucratic means. The early 1990s were marked by an outbreak of racist violence. A series of racially inspired clashes occurred in France's impoverished, heavily immigrant suburbs.[25] Delinquent immigrants were generally portrayed to be the culprits in these heavily publicized incidents; the youths were perceived to cause particular violent disturbances as well as being responsible for a climate of insecurity and fear more generally. The 1991 Gulf War also served to fuel xenophobia when the conservative media seized the opportunity to question Franco-Maghribins' loyalty to the French state.[26] Several violent outbreaks were linked to the war, as recurrent alarmist newspaper editorials warned that Arab immigrants had been turned into "a pro-Iraq Fifth Column," and would soon unleash a war of their own on French soil (Gastaut 2000, 438). In this hostile climate, 71 percent of French believed that there were "too many Arabs" in their country and 42 percent confessed that they disliked Maghribins.[27]

Xenophobic press coverage certainly exacerbated these tensions, but the political mainstream did not try to alleviate them. While Mitterrand had been working to implement the Socialists' integrationist agenda (repealing the restrictive Pasqua laws, creating the Haut Conseil à l'Intégration, and allocating additional funding for poor neighborhoods), some Socialist politicians, most notably Prime Minister Edith Cresson, did not shy away from playing the anti-immigrant card. Cresson's suggestion to forcibly expel illegal immigrants by the planeload touched off a media firestorm and earned her criticism both from her own party and from Le Pen, who dismissed the prime minister's statement as a vacuous media stunt, designed to distract from the Socialists' lax record on immigration.[28] The center-right parties seemed to agree with Le Pen's assessment and continually criticized the Socialist government's immigration record as dangerously permissive. Chirac went further and, despite the lesson of 1988, once again courted extremist voters by lamenting the "overdose of immigrants" whose "noise and smell" were a great burden on French society.[29] As Bréchon and Mitra put it, "the availability of the National Front and the cooptation of parts of its language by its adversaries help[ed] create a 'normal' issue out of racism, which has to compete with the more established issues of class, material welfare, and partisanship" (1992, 80). In short, racism had become mainstream.

9.8 Conventional Politics Return as a New Cleavage Is Born

The late 1980s and early 1990s were thus a time when immigration and the integration of France's large Maghribi minority had turned into traditional campaign issues, albeit treated in a more populist and less technocratic fashion than the more orthodox topics. In the years that followed, however, immigration lost some of its electoral cachet. Moreover, an altered political environment seemed to undermine the FN's electoral viability. Notwithstanding these challenges, the FN and its leader were able to fortify their position in the French political system.

By the mid-1990s, France's flagging economy had become the country's number one concern. Unemployment hovered around the 12 percent mark, putting over three million Frenchmen out of work. In the run-up to the 1993 legislative elections, the French voter, increasingly frustrated with the country's gloomy economic outlook, was no longer persuaded by the Front's simplistic equation between immigration and unemployment.[30] The economic slowdown and high and rising unemployment levels thus caused the electorate to shift its attention back to the more traditional political dimension, prompting some to conclude that Le Pen's days as an influential wildcard had been numbered.[31] To be sure, anti-immigrant sentiment did not abate. In 1995, fully 73 percent agreed with the statement that too many immigrants were living in France (Mayer and Roux 2004, 106). But in an effort to woo the FN's electorate, the moderate Right had taken an increasingly tough line on immigration policy. The RPR promised that, if elected, it would put a stop to family reunifications, tighten the laws governing asylum-based immigration, and restrict immigrants' access to social welfare entitlements. It even took up the contentious issue of Nationality Code reforms, which had proved so politically costly in the 1980s. The center-right coalition did indeed win the 1993 parliamentary elections (the FN obtained 12.4 percent of the vote but did not manage to win any seats in parliament) and, headed by Prime Minister Édouard Balladur of the center-right Union pour la Démocratie Française (UDF), pursued its ambitious reform project rapidly.[32] One of its first acts in office was to tighten the requirements regulating access to French citizenship; the Pasqua-Méhaignerie law for the first time annulled the automatic acquisition of French nationality and instead required most children born in France to immigrant parents to request French citizenship.[33] In light of the government's tough record on immigration, the 1995 presidential campaign did not feature the usual calls for harsher reforms in this area and candidates generally shied away from the issue altogether.[34]

9.8.1 From Protest to Pariah to Programmatic Party

In addition to the moderate Right's hard line on immigration, the FN had to fight its growing isolation. Mainstream parties, including Chirac's RPR, had come to the conclusion that their own electoral fortunes were best served by marginalizing, rather than courting, Lepeniste ideas and by ending the practice of expedient alliances with the FN at the local level. The growing salience of economic issues and the concomitant decline (and cooptation) of the immigration issue perhaps decreased the political dividends Le Pen could reap by capitalizing on his standing as the nation's prime xenophobe. But together with FN strategists, Le Pen still managed to broaden his appeal by developing a more comprehensive—but no less xenophobic—program. In solidifying its base while reaching out to new constituencies, the FN turned immigration into "an 'omnibus issue', a matrix through which most other issues could be channeled: unemployment, education, law and order, the economy, culture, social expenditure, housing policy and so on" (Hainsworth and Mitchell 2000, 444). The party thus consciously sought to cast off its image as a protest party. Proclaiming "a new cleavage is born" *(un nouveau clivage est né),* the FN recognized that a new cleavage structure had been emerging and molded itself accordingly (Perrineau 1997, 81).[35] In addition, the center-right parties' refusal to enter into alliances with the FN, as well as recurrent revelations of government scandals, prompted Le Pen to sharpen his attacks against the corrupt political ruling class and allowed him to run as an antiestablishment candidate.

The Front's 1993 manifesto, *300 mesures pour la renaissance de la France,* testifies to the party's expanded scope. Five broad headings—*l'identité, la prospérité, la fraternité, la sécurité, la souveraineté*—laid out the FN's policy proposals, which ranged from protecting the socially excluded, cutting taxes and public expenditures, improving the health system, supporting small domestic businesses, restoring law and order, and ending immigration, to containing globalization through protectionism and unilateralism. While the party took moderate positions on the size of the public sector more generally, one of its most prominent economic policy proposals, the idea of "national preference" for state services, was rather radical. Developed in the 1980s by FN member Jean-Yves Le Gallou, this concept envisions a profound transformation of the country's administrative, judicial, and social procedures based on a distinction between French nationals and foreigners. This distinction would serve as the guiding principle in the distribution of state services (Le Gallou 1985, 13, 61). The FN bemoaned the bureaucratic, anonymous, and dehumanized allocation of state benefits and insisted that the distribution of these services should instead reflect the communal brotherhood and solidarity of the French people. It thus urged the abolishment of the RMI (the state's main welfare program), which had in any case been "invalidated" by the Socialists, who the FN claimed had allowed and promoted its rampant abuse by immigrants, and called for the creation of "an allocation of national solidarity . . . based on national preference" (Front National 1993, 223–225). In other words, in all areas of public services, French nationals would receive priority over their immigrant neighbors.

9.8.2   The 1995 Presidential Election

This platform served as the FN's programmatic basis for the 1995 presidential campaign. In an attempt to link up its policy of "national preference" to the election's major themes, the FN portrayed this scheme as not only morally superior to the current system but also more fiscally responsible: excluding immigrants from most state services would cut public expenditures drastically. The other candidates also emphasized economic and social themes. The campaigns of Jacques Chirac and his rival Prime Minister Balladur recognized unemployment as the nation's main concern and proposed measures to assist the long-term unemployed. Both demanded a reduction in employers' social security contributions and vowed to cut back France's ballooning public-sector deficits.[36] Chirac, with little room to differentiate himself from Balladur, recast himself as a "compassionate conservative," focusing on the importance of family values and offering "salaries" for mothers.[37] The campaign of the Socialist candidate, Lionel Jospin, echoed similar economic and social themes, but offered slightly different proposals. Jospin also endorsed cuts in employers' contributions, but added a call for a reduced workweek to help create jobs. Like the other candidates, he reached out to the poor and the long-term unemployed, albeit in more concrete terms, promising additional resources for poor suburbs, the creation of social housing, and increased support for the elderly, infirm, and disabled.[38]

After a somewhat sluggish campaign, those who voted for the moderate Right split their vote in the first round, with 20.8 and 18.6 percent voting for Chirac and Balladur, respectively. Jospin was the surprise winner in the first round, obtaining 23.3 percent of the vote, but was later beaten by Chirac in a 52.6–47.4 runoff. Le Pen received a respectable 15 percent of the vote in the first round. The 1995 presidential campaign was thus a rather conventional one. It responded to the public's concern over bread-and-butter issues and put the divisive issues related to immigration temporarily on hold. While the campaign's focus on traditional mainstream issues, together with the media's weariness of covering the extremist leader, did not provide Le Pen with the massive exposure of earlier years, he nevertheless succeeded in mobilizing a considerable 15 percent of the electorate to come out and vote for him on election day. This result is especially impressive given that some of the votes obtained by Philippe de Villiers (4.7 percent), a far-right, fiercely anti–European Community candidate, may have originally been destined to go to Le Pen's cause.

Le Pen's strategy of broadening his appeal to reach new and hold on to old constituencies seemed to have worked. His base stayed remarkably loyal—fully 91 percent of voters sympathizing with Le Pen supported him in the first round, far outstripping partisan loyalty among other candidates.[39] Moreover, Le Pen's success among the French working class stands out as a particular achievement of the 1995 election. While estimates vary somewhat, members of the working class turned out in greater numbers than ever before to support a candidate of the Far Right.[40] In contrast, the Socialists hemorrhaged votes among this bloc; the first-round working-class vote share in the presidential elections dropped from 42 percent in 1988 to only 25 percent in 1995.[41] Perrineau aptly calls this phenomenon "the Left–Le Pen dynamic" (1997, 80) and considers it one of the most important aspects of the FN's development. Among the unemployed and those who considered themselves underprivileged (*défavorisés*), Le Pen turned out to be the most popular candidate (Marcus 1996, 308). These electors also tend to be the ones who were most disaffected, generally displaying an apathetic, undifferentiated attitude toward politics. N. Mayer (2002) reports that 23 percent of those who considered themselves to be "neither left nor right" voted for Le Pen in 1995, leading her to conclude that the Lepeniste electorate absorbs two contrasting camps: those of the ideologically committed Extreme Right and those of the politically apathetic "*ninisme*" (N. Mayer 2002, 46).

Le Pen also succeeded in transforming himself from a one-issue candidate into a genuine alternative to the mainstream, at least as far as his electorate was concerned. Immigration certainly motivated many of Le Pen's supporters, but according to poll results, almost half of his constituents did not consider immigration among the top two issues deciding their vote (Shields 1995, 30). According to Shields,

> The overriding impression is of a vote which channels fears and frustrations on a whole range of issues, from immigration and criminality to unemployment, social deprivation, and the effects of economic recession, within a wider constellation of anxieties over European integration, Islamic fundamentalism, political corruption, national identity, and 'traditional values,' *inter alia.* While the FN continues to prosper in and around areas . . . with large immigrant communities . . . the Le Pen vote in 1995 extends far beyond these parameters. (Ibid.)[42]

In geographic terms, Le Pen's electoral forays were also extensive. Le Pen had his best results in traditional strongholds (northern France, the greater Paris region, Lyons, the east and the Mediterranean littoral), and on a nationwide basis, his vote showed an upward trend. Over two-thirds of France's *départements* showed a net increase in the Lepeniste vote, and Le Pen supporters numbered over 20 percent in eleven *départements*, up from eight in the previous election (Marcus 1996, 308; Shields 1995, 28). Given this solid performance, the Front leader felt cheated by Villiers—Le Pen was convinced that without the latter's interference, he would have qualified for the second round runoff.[43] The 2002 presidential elections would provide a more opportune environment.

9.8.3 On the Road to 2002

In many ways, the run-up to the 2002 presidential election appeared to be a repeat of the period leading up to the 1995 election. The FN proved its endurance at both the national and the local level. It scored important victories in the 1995 and 2001 municipal elections and also performed well in the 1997 legislative elections, where it polled over 15 percent. Similar to the early 1990s, however, several developments conspired to make the FN appear less of an electoral threat to the political mainstream than it in fact was. The crucial difference was that this time around, Le Pen's strong performance in the presidential election was hard to ignore.

The most significant development concerned the Front National itself. Over the years, two factions had developed and coexisted within the party, but by the late 1990s, their visions about the FN's future role in French politics had become too incompatible to be contained in one party. The internal battle was one over strategy, not ideology. Frustrated with the Front's increasing marginalization by the country's political establishment, Bruno Mégret, intellectual father of many FN programs and strategies, spearheaded a faction that wanted to take the FN out of political isolation and into a governing alliance with the country's moderate Right. Le Pen and his followers, however, stood firm in their rejection of the country's ruling political class and insisted on presenting the FN as a genuine alternative to the political status quo. As Mégret's strategic vision gained popularity among growing sections of the FN's rank and file, he and his followers broke away to found a splinter party (Mouvement National Républicain, or MNR) in January 1999, in time for the year's European Parliament election (Adler 2001, 38). This first electoral test came as a major setback for Le Pen—the split had fragmented the Lepeniste vote. His Front National only received 5.8 percent of the votes as the MNR managed to siphon off 3.3 percent.[44] But even the combined vote share of just over 9 percent came as a disappointment; in all previous elections of the 1990s, the FN had scored in the double digits. In light of this electoral performance, the notion that the FN was finally facing its "inexorable decline" took hold among the media as well as among the French political establishment.[45]

The absence of immigration as a prominent political issue in the years lead-ing up to the 2002 presidential election further buttressed this view. According to some, "to the degree that the saliency of immigration was associated with the ascendancy and implantation of the FN from 1984 to 1998, so too is the decline of immigration as an issue associated with the precipitous decline, iso-lation and marginalization of the parties of the far right" (Adler 2001, 33). Indeed, immigration was not an overt issue in the upcoming campaigns. How-ever, the major themes dominating political life in 2001–2002 were insecurity, unemployment, and law and order—issues that were at least implicitly linked to immigration in the public's mind. In the 2001 municipal elections, fought in the shadow of rising crime rates and numerous reports of urban unrest, fear of crime and violence had replaced fear of unemployment as the num-ber one issue concerning the French electorate.[46] The presidential candidates took their cues from their nervous constituents. President Chirac and Social-ist prime minister Jospin, the two frontrunners, each tried to convince the French voter that they would be the more aggressive in enforcing law and order. Chirac adopted the New York slogan of "zero tolerance" while Jospin insisted he would be "tough on crime, and tough on the causes of crime."[47] Both also stressed the importance of the French community in restoring public order. Chirac countered Jospin's catchphrase, "Life together," with his motto "Together, a great France" (Ysmal 2003, 944). All other issues—the economy, reform of the welfare state, European integration, to name but a few—took a backseat in the 2002 campaign, and were either evaded or equivocated on by Jospin and Chirac (Bell and Criddle 2002, 650). Consequently, polls showed that the majority of the French electorate discerned no difference between the two candidates and grew increasingly dissatisfied and uninterested in the cam-paign. In January 2002, a poll revealed that only 29 percent of French in fact wanted them to be candidates; 59 percent wished for new personalities (Ysmal 2003, 944–951).

9.8.4   The 2002 Presidential Election

With the benefit of hindsight, it appears that the political configuration was a very opportune one for Le Pen to make a historic impact. While immi-gration was not explicitly mentioned by the mainstream, the ascendancy of insecurity and fear as central campaign themes fit well with Le Pen's ethnocentrist electorate, who generally exhibit high levels of subjective and objective insecurities—conditions that the Front leader had already been able to tap into in the previous presidential election. It is also important to note that the appeal of Le Pen's position on security and justice extended beyond his supporters: in the wake of the first round of the 2002 presidential election, 40 percent of those polled approved of Le Pen's views on these matters.[48] Moreover, the apparent interchangeability of the two mainstream candidates played into Le Pen's critique of the political establishment, which he had long accused of representing the same misguided ideas.[49] In 2002, 26 percent of French agreed with this critique, up from 19 percent five years earlier.[50]

Le Pen's xenophobic ideas also echoed the mood in the country, notwithstanding their lack of coverage. Immigration's absence belied the electorate's continued dislike of foreigners and increasing racism. According to a 2000 report published by the Commission Nationale Consultative des Droits de l'Homme (CNCDH), 63 percent of those polled thought that too many Arabs were living in France, compared with 43 and 21 percent who felt that France had too many blacks and Asians, respectively. The study found that rejection of immigrants was most often justified on economic and social grounds, because immigrants were believed to be a burden on the social security system and the main culprit behind unemployment. An overwhelming 73 percent thought that large shares of immigrants came to France to profit from the country's social benefits. This trend is consistent with the analysis in the next chapter, which shows that by 2002 anti-immigrant attitudes were closely linked to preferences for a smaller public sector. Despite these linkages to economic problems, the report noted that this increase in racism, not only confined to public opinion but also to be found in a rise in violent acts, occurred as the economy was recovering and unemployment was on the decline. Over half of those surveyed believed that immigration was the principal cause behind the nation's growing crime rate and insecurity.[51]

While growing segments of the French electorate seemed amenable to Lepeniste ideas, the configuration of candidates proved equally advantageous for the extremist candidate. A total of sixteen candidates had managed to qualify and ended up fragmenting the vote among them. What was most remarkable about the 2002 lineup was the division of the Left, which fielded an eclectic group of candidates, including three anti-establishment Trotskyites (who gained over 10 percent of the vote), Europhobe Chevènement (5.3 percent), Guyanese deputy Taubira (2.3 percent), Communist Hue (3.4 percent), and the Green candidate Mamère (5.3 percent). Faced with such competition, Jospin was only able to mobilize 16.2 percent of the voters. On the Right, there was no credible challenger to Chirac, whose vote share was thus not threatened to be split in half as had been the case previously. Nevertheless, his result—19.9 percent—was disappointing; it made him the president reelected with the lowest vote share in the Fifth Republic (Bell and Criddle 2002, 646–652). On the extreme right, things looked favorable for Le Pen. Pasqua and Villiers did not make the cut, which probably freed up some votes for the Front's leader. Le Pen's major rival, Mégret, however, did manage to collect the necessary five hundred signatures and ran on a platform very similar to that of Le Pen. But in 2002, Mégret did not turn out to be a threat to the former, winning only 2.3 percent of the vote. The division of the Left and the weakness of the Right thus contributed to Le Pen's electoral fortunes: winning 16.9 percent of the first presidential ballot, Le Pen came in second, beating Jospin by 0.7 points, and entering the second-round runoff. Chirac won the second ballot with 82 percent of the vote—but the shock of the first ballot lingered.

As Le Pen's triumphant performance sent shock waves throughout the country and the rest of the world, a period of soul-searching began.[52] In an attempt to explain Le Pen's electoral upset, commentators offered various answers, ranging from a generalized culture of indifference[53] to a working class that was not treated with the dignity it deserved.[54] An analysis of Le Pen's supporters, however, simply reaffirms previous trends. In 2002, Le Pen's electorate drew primarily on males (21 percent of males compared with 13 percent of females voted for Le Pen) and again represented all age groups. The Front leader scored his best results among the unemployed (fully 38 percent of whom supported Le Pen), manual workers (30 percent), those employed in agriculture (20 percent), and small businessmen, shopkeepers, and craftsmen (20 percent).[55] With regard to issues, insecurity was the highest priority among Le Pen voters; 68 percent mentioned that this major campaign theme motivated their decision to vote for Le Pen (immigration and employment were mentioned by 57 and 27 percent, respectively) (Martin 2003, 16).

As in earlier years, Le Pen was able to appeal to a diverse, cross-class electorate that can best be subsumed under the ethnocentrist label. According to N. Mayer's analysis, in the 2002 election, a voter's attitudes toward immigrants proved to exert an equal influence on his vote choice as on his position on economic issues. This result, which had been in the making for the past two decades, leads Mayer to conclude that "ethnocentrism is on its way to becoming a structural issue in France's electoral scene" (Mayer and Roux 2004, 117; author's translation). Some generational trends may, however, work against the Front. Surveys have shown that a large and growing generational gap cuts through the French electorate, with young voters exhibiting much lower levels of intolerance and ethnocentrism than their older counterparts (Mayer and Roux 2004, 108–109). Marine Le Pen, daughter of the party boss, will certainly attempt to rally the young French electorate to the Front's cause. While an aging Jean-Marie Le Pen may soon step down from political life, the xenophobic Front leader has helped give rise to a transformation of the French political field which may be here to stay—at least until a new generation of French citizens becomes of voting age.

9.9   Conclusion

The politics of immigration and integration in France have occupied an important place in France's political landscape for over two decades. Although the salience of these issues has varied from election to election, they and the related concerns and anxieties they trigger among the French electorate will most likely not disappear in the near future. Indeed, the rise of international Islamic terrorism has focused renewed attention on France's Muslim population.

Today, debates about immigration and immigrant integration into French society do not only conjure up fears about unemployment and urban unrest. Rather, fear of an Islamic fundamentalism flourishing within French borders pervades these discussions, providing the Front's major theme of insecurity with an additional, more terrifying quality. A more recent debate surrounding the wearing of the Islamic headscarf illustrates how this added dimension of fear has permeated public thinking and discussion about the presence of immigrants in France. In this controversy, which began in the fall of 2003, it was not only the assertion of French secular identity that was at stake. The debate, and the ultimate banning of the Islamic headscarf from public schools in March 2004, invoked the potential horrors of Islamic terrorism. Some proponents of the ban viewed the headscarf as a dangerous form of religious expression, if not a symbol of allegiance to Islamic fundamentalism; they consequently understood its banning as an attempt to curb the radicalization of French Islam.

In sharp contrast with the resolution of the *affaire du foulard* fifteen years earlier, the proposed ban was passed with an overwhelming parliamentary majority that crossed party lines. If nothing else, this rare show of partisan unity is a sign that politicians are taking their electorate's uneasiness with immigration and multiculturalism seriously. Thirty years after the "official" end of immigration, French politics and society are still walking the tightrope between exclusion and integration. Until a lasting, national consensus on immigrant integration has been found, xenophobic political leaders will try their best to pull the country in the exclusionary direction.

10

France: Quantitative Analysis

10.1 Parties and Voter Opinion

In this chapter we study how the existence of racism and xenophobia in the French electorate has affected redistributive politics since roughly the mid-1980s. As we saw in the previous chapter, the Extreme Right has become a crucial player in French politics during this time. Before turning to a description of our data and of the major political issues in the campaigns, we briefly present below the various political parties competing in the presidential elections, together with their vote shares. Appendix Tables B.7, B.8, and B.9 present a full description of the results of the French presidential elections for the years 1988, 1995, and 2002. We will describe French politics in terms of broader coalitions: Left, Right, and Extreme Right. The composition of the coalitions is also given in the Appendix B tables just mentioned. We compute the broader parties' vote shares by summing the vote shares of the parties forming the coalition; see Table 10.1. The Extreme Right movement, led by Jean-Marie Le Pen, increased its vote share by almost 6 percentage points between 1988 and 2002, whereas the Left coalition lost about 6 percentage points.

Our data consist of micro-data from the Post-Electoral Survey 1988, the Post-Electoral Survey 1995, and the French Electoral Panel 2002.[1] These surveys include questions about demographic characteristics (for example, age, gender), social and financial position (for example, marital status, income, labor status), voting behavior (for example, party preferences, determinants of

Table 10.1 French coalitions' vote shares (percent)

	1988	1995	2002
Left	49.0	40.6	42.9
Right	36.5	44.2	37.9
Extreme Right	14.4	15.3	19.2

the vote), and preferences over economic and social issues (for example, taxation, economic policies, law and order, immigration).

In order to assess the relative importance of the various issues in explaining voters' party choices on election day, we first present a brief overview of the 1995 and 2002 electoral campaigns, focusing on the issues perceived as the most important by the voters.[2] For the year 1995, we rely on the following question.

> Here are a number of problems that France has to face nowadays. On a scale from 0 to 10, could you assign a score to each of these problems, according to the importance it had in deciding your vote in the first round of the presidential election? The place of France in the world, security of persons, social protection, immigration, purchasing power and wages, education of the youth, unemployment, sharing of working time, European construction, environment, AIDS, corruption, exclusion.

Table 10.2 reports the answers. The first column reports the percentage of respondents who give each mentioned issue one of the two highest values on the 0–10 scale; the second column reports the percentage of respondents who give one of the lowest three values. The third column gives the average score, and the fourth, the standard deviation. Problems are ranked by average score.

As we saw in the foregoing chapter, economic issues preoccupied the French electorate in 1995. Unemployment appears to be the most important issue, with an average score of 8.9; almost three-quarters of the respondents give it a score of 9 or 10. Education of youth, social protection, and exclusion come next. Immigration appears only toward the bottom of the table.

For the year 2002, we use the following question.

> Among the following problems, which will be the most important when you decide how to vote? Pollution, unemployment, immigration, so-

Table 10.2 France's most important problems, 1995

Issue	Score 9–10	Score 0–2	Mean	Std. dev.	Obs.
Unemployment	72.9	2.5	8.9	2.0	3,897
Education of the youth	56.8	2.9	8.3	2.2	3,881
Social protection	49.1	3.0	8.0	2.2	3,892
Exclusion	49.3	4.2	7.9	2.4	3,853
Purchasing power and wages	46.1	3.8	7.8	2.3	3,883
AIDS	48.3	9.1	7.5	2.9	3,848
Corruption	46.1	7.5	7.5	2.7	3,843
Security of persons	37.3	7.3	7.2	2.7	3,885
Environment	26.9	6.2	6.8	2.5	3,865
Sharing of working time	29.1	9.2	6.7	2.7	3,829
Immigration	30.6	13.0	6.5	3.0	3,864
Place of France in the world	21.5	9.7	6.4	2.7	3,860
European construction	20.1	11.5	6.2	2.7	3,827

cial inequalities, political scandals, delinquency, conditions in schools, pensions, European construction, fight against terrorism, sovereignty of France, tax cuts. Which is the second most important problem, third most important problem?

Table 10.3 shows that the single most important problem is unemployment: one-third of the respondents rank it as the most important problem, and almost two-thirds of the respondents rank it as one of the three most important problems. The second most often cited problem is delinquency, the third is social inequalities. Immigration appears fourth; it is mentioned by 18 percent of the respondents as one of the three most important problems. Thus, as in 1995, unemployment is still the most important issue; however, law and order and immigration issues have become more salient to voters over the period.

We assume that unemployment, education, and social inequalities are mainly questions about the size of the public sector, and therefore modeling political competition as focusing upon the two issues of public-sector size and immigration/law and order appears to be an acceptable abstraction. Since many French voters link problems related to crime and law and order to the presence of immigrants (see previous chapter), it is reasonable to model immigration/law and order as making up one policy dimension.

Table 10.3 France's most important problems, 2002 (percent)

Issue	1	2	3	All
Unemployment	33.4	16.8	10.8	61.0
Delinquency	19.6	22.3	14.8	56.7
Social inequalities	14.0	14.7	9.9	38.6
Immigration	6.5	6.2	5.7	18.4
Pensions	5.5	8.8	12.7	27.0
Pollution	5.4	5.5	7.1	18.0
Schools	3.4	6.0	6.6	16.0
Tax cuts	3.1	5.6	9.5	18.2
Fight against terrorism	2.8	4.6	7.5	14.9
Political scandals	2.1	3.3	4.4	9.8
European construction	2.0	3.0	5.1	10.1
Sovereignty of France	1.1	1.2	2.0	4.3
Did not answer	1.3	2.0	3.9	7.2

Note: Problems are ranked by the number of people who rank this specific problem as the single most important problem. Total number of observations: 4,107.

10.2   Political Equilibrium with Three Parties

We propose that the spectrum of political parties can be captured, for our purposes, with a model that postulates three parties: a Left, a Right, and an Extreme Right. The Left party of the model will correspond to the union of four or six parties; the Right will correspond to the union of three parties; the Extreme Right will correspond to either one or two parties (see Appendix Tables B.7, B.8, and B.9). We propose in this section a model of political equilibrium in which three parties compete on a two-dimensional policy space, which, in our application, will be the *size of the public sector* and the *policy toward immigrants*. This model is a simple extension of the two-party model we have worked with thus far. To be absolutely clear, we develop the model from the beginning.

The data of the model consist of the information $(H, \mathbf{F}, T, v, n)$, where:

- H is a space of *voter types* equipped with a probability distribution $\mathbf{F}$;
- $v(\cdot, h)$ is the utility function of a voter type defined on the policy space T, and
- n is the number of parties.

The equilibrium will consist in: a tuple $(L, R, ER, \tau^L, \tau^R, \tau^{ER})$, where:

- (L, R, ER) is a partition of the set of voter types into *party member-ships* or *constituencies:* $L \cup R \cup ER = H$, $\quad L \cap R = \varnothing$, $\quad L \cap ER = \varnothing$, $R \cap ER = \varnothing$
- $\tau^J \in T$ is the equilibrium platform of party J, for $J = L, R, ER$.

There will be no confusion if we refer to a *party* and its *constituency* by the same variable: for example, *ER* for Extreme Right.

For our application, a voter's type will be an ordered pair (θ, ρ), where θ is the voter's ideal public-sector size (which we sometimes call, for short, her "tax rate") and ρ is her position on the immigration issue. The policy space T is a set of ordered pairs (t, r), which we may take to be the real plane, where t is a party's policy on the size of the public sector and r is its policy on immigration. The utility function of the polity is a function $v : T \times H \to \mathbb{R}$ given by

$$v(t, r; \theta, \rho) = -(t - \theta)^2 - \frac{\gamma}{2}(r - \rho)^2. \tag{10.1}$$

We refer to $\gamma/2$ as the *relative salience of the immigration issue,* and assume it is the same for all voters.

Given three policies $(\tau^L, \tau^R, \tau^{ER})$ proposed by the parties, we define $\varphi^J(\tau^L, \tau^R, \tau^{ER})$, for $J = L, R, ER$, as the fraction of the polity who prefer the policy of party J to the other two policies. In our model, if the policies are distinct, then the set of voters indifferent between two policies will always have **F**-measure zero, and so, in the case of distinct policies, these three fractions sum to unity.

We will assume that the Extreme Right party is a passive member of the party-competition game: it proposes a fixed policy, which could be viewed as the ideal policy of its organizers. Modeling the Extreme Right in this way is less than ideal: we would have preferred to model it as a party with factions that behave in the manner of the other two parties. Doing so, however, immensely complicates the computation of equilibrium—already a time-consuming task—and so we have elected to treat the policy it proposes as exogenously given.[3] Its *membership,* however, will be endogenous.

Suppose the members of a party consist in all citizens whose types lie in the set $J \subset H$. We define the *average welfare function* for this party as a function mapping T into the real numbers defined by:

$$V^J(\tau) = \int_{h \in J} v(\tau; h) d\mathbf{F}(h). \tag{10.2}$$

That is, $V^J(\tau)$ is just (a constant multiplied by) the average utility of the coalition J at the policy τ.

Definition A *party-unanimity Nash equilibrium* (PUNE) *for the model* $(H, \mathbf{F}, T, v, 3)$ *at the exogenous ER policy* τ^{ER} is:

1. a partition of the set of types $H = L \cup R \cup ER$, possibly ignoring a set of measure zero;
2. a pair of policies (τ^L, τ^R) such that:

    2a. Given (τ^L, τ^{ER}) there is no policy $\tau \in T$ such that:

    $$V^R(\tau) \geq V^R(\tau^R) \text{ and } \varphi^R(\tau^L, \tau, \tau^{ER}) \geq \varphi^R(\tau^L, \tau^R, \tau^{ER})$$

    with at least one of these inequalities strict;

    2b. Given (τ^R, τ^{ER}) there is no policy $\tau \in T$ such that:

    $$V^L(\tau) \geq V^L(\tau^L) \text{ and } \varphi^L(\tau, \tau^R, \tau^{ER}) \geq \varphi^L(\tau^L, \tau^R, \tau^{ER})$$

    with at least one of these inequalities strict;

3. for $J = L, R, ER$, every member of coalition J prefers policy τ^J to the other two policies, that is $h \in J \Rightarrow v(\tau^J, h) > v(\tau^{J'}, h)$ for $J' \neq J$.

There are, as usual, two "free" parameters in this equilibrium concept, corresponding to the relative bargaining powers of the factions in the L and R parties. Thus we can expect that, if there is an equilibrium, there will be a two-parameter manifold of equilibria, where the elements in this manifold are associated with different pairs of relative bargaining strengths of the pairs of factions in L and R. This indeed turns out to be the case, as we will see below.

With differentiability, we can characterize a PUNE as the solution of a system of simultaneous equations. Denote by $\nabla_J \varphi^J(\tau^L, \tau^R, \tau^{ER})$ the gradient of the function φ^J with respect to the policy τ^J. Denote by ∇V^J the gradient of V^J. Then we can write the necessary conditions for a PUNE where τ^L and τ^R are interior points in T as:

$$(FOC) \begin{cases} \text{(1a) there is a nonnegative number } x \text{ such that} \\ \quad -\nabla_L \varphi^L(\tau^L, \tau^R, \tau^{ER}) = x\nabla V^L(\tau^L) \\ \text{(1b) there is a nonnegative number } y \text{ such that} \\ \quad -\nabla_R \varphi^R(\tau^L, \tau^R, \tau^{ER}) = y\nabla V^R(\tau^R). \end{cases}$$

Condition (1a) says that the gradients of the vote share function and the average welfare function for party L point in opposite directions at the solution, and so, assuming local convexity, there is no direction in which the policy of the party can be altered so as to increase both the party's vote share and the average welfare of the party's constituents. Thus conditions (1a) and (1b) correspond exactly to the conditions (1a) and (1b) in the definition of PUNE. (All policies are interior in our application, since T is an open set.)

Our next task is to characterize PUNE as a system of equations, which requires us to formulate precisely the party constituencies. Denote the set of types who prefer a policy $\tau^a = (t^a, r^a)$ to policy $\tau^b = (t^b, r^b)$ by $\Omega(\tau^a, \tau^b)$, and compute that

$$\Omega(\tau^a, \tau^b) = \begin{cases} \{(\theta, \rho) \mid \rho < \psi(\tau^a, \tau^b, \theta)\} & \text{if } r^a < r^b \\ \{(\theta, \rho) \mid \rho > \psi(\tau^a, \tau^b, \theta)\} & \text{if } r^a > r^b \end{cases} \tag{10.3}$$

where

$$\psi(\tau^a, \tau^b, \theta) = \frac{(t^b)^2 - (t^a)^2 + 2\theta(t^a - t^b) + (\gamma/2)((r^b)^2 - (r^a)^2)}{2(r^b - r^a)}. \tag{10.4}$$

We will specify the value of the policy r so that larger r means more xenophobic (anti-immigrant). Thus, at equilibrium, we will expect that $r^L < r^R < r^{ER}$. For an equilibrium with this characteristic, it follows from (10.3) that the constituency L will be precisely:

$$L = \{(\theta, \rho) \in H \mid \rho < \min[\psi(\tau^L, \tau^R, \theta), \psi(\tau^L, \tau^{ER}, \theta)]\},$$

for these are the types who will prefer policy τ^L to both other policies. In like manner, we have:

$$ER = \{(\theta, \rho) \mid \rho > \max[\psi(\tau^{ER}, \tau^R, \theta), \psi(\tau^{ER}, \tau^L, \theta)]\}$$

and R, of course, comprises the remaining types (except for a set of measure zero). In shorthand, if we define:

$$m(\tau^L, \tau^R, \tau^{ER}, \theta) = \min[\psi(\tau^L, \tau^R, \theta), \psi(\tau^L, \tau^{ER}, \theta)]$$

$$M(\tau^L, \tau^R, \tau^{ER}, \theta) = \max[\psi(\tau^{ER}, \tau^R, \theta), \psi(\tau^{ER}, \tau^L, \theta)]$$

and we denote the vector consisting of all three policies as $\boldsymbol{\tau}$, then we have:

$$L = \{(\theta, \rho) \mid \rho < m(\boldsymbol{\tau}, \theta)\}, \quad R = \{(\theta, \rho) \mid m(\boldsymbol{\tau}, \theta) < \rho < M(\boldsymbol{\tau}, \theta)\},$$

$$ER = \{(\theta, \rho) \mid \rho > M(\boldsymbol{\tau}, \theta)\}.$$
(10.4a)

Assuming the support of the distribution $\mathbf{F}$ is the real plane, we can therefore write:

$$\varphi^L(\tau) = \int_{-\infty}^{\infty} \int_{-\infty}^{m(\tau,\theta)} d\mathbf{F}(\theta, \rho),$$
(10.5a)

where the inside integral is over ρ and the outside integral is over θ, and in like manner:

$$\varphi^R(\tau) = \int_{-\infty}^{\infty} \int_{m(\tau,\theta)}^{M(\tau,\theta)} d\mathbf{F}(\theta, \rho), \quad \varphi^{ER}(\tau) = \int_{-\infty}^{\infty} \int_{M(\tau,\theta)}^{\infty} d\mathbf{F}(\theta, \tau).$$
(10.5b)

Similarly, we can write:

$$V^L(\tau^L) = \int_{-\infty}^{\infty} \int_{-\infty}^{m(\tau,\theta)} v(\tau^L; \theta, \rho) d\mathbf{F}(\theta, \rho),$$

$$V^R(\tau^R) = \int_{-\infty}^{\infty} \int_{m(\tau,\theta)}^{M(\tau,\theta)} v(\tau^R; \theta, \rho) d\mathbf{F}(\theta, \rho).$$
(10.6)

The corresponding average welfare function for the ER is irrelevant, because the ER plays a fixed policy.

Now we substitute these expressions into the first-order conditions (FOC), and we have fully modeled PUNE—that is, condition (2) of the definition of PUNE holds by construction.

The first-order conditions now comprise four equations in six unknowns—the four policy unknowns of the Left and Right parties, and the two Lagrangian multipliers x and y. If there is a solution, there will (generically) be, therefore, a two-parameter family of solutions. As we described earlier, the points in this family or manifold can be viewed as corresponding to equilibria associated with different relative bargaining strengths of the pairs of factions in the parties L and R.

10.3   Estimation of Model Parameters

10.3.1   Distribution of Voter Traits

10.3.1.1   Description of the Questions and Distribution of Answers

In the equilibrium model, parties propose platforms consisting of an economic issue (amount of social expenditures) and an immigration policy. We must select some questions that allow us to estimate voters' preferences on these two types of issue. Ideally, we would like to use identical questions for all three years to see how voters' opinions on these issues have evolved. Unfortunately, very few questions are asked all three years.

The *economic issue* is

Can you tell me if the word "privatization" has a rather positive or negative connotation for you?

Figure 10.1 presents the distribution of answers. Respondents are quite evenly split into two groups: those with a (quite or very) positive opinion about privatization, and those with a negative opinion, the former being slightly more numerous. The distribution is quite stable through time, with only a small shift toward more negative feelings.

This question is an indicator of general economic liberalism. Now, to construct an index of voters' preferences on the economic issue, we also want to integrate some more specific questions about welfare programs and social security. Unfortunately, the surveys are designed in such a way that no such questions are available for all three years.

For 1988, we use the following question:

Do you agree with the following statement? The State should guarantee a minimum income to all households.

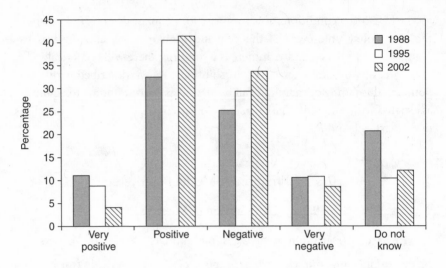

Figure 10.1   Connotation of the word "privatization": Distribution of answers.

For 1995 and 2002, we use the following question:

> Can you tell me if the word Solidarity has a rather positive connotation for you?

The distribution of answers is displayed in Figure 10.2. In all three years, the distribution of answers is very similar. One might be concerned that the questions used for the year 1988 on the one hand (support for a minimum income for all) and 1995 and 2002 on the other hand (connotation of the word "solidarity") describe quite different feelings. In particular, the scope of the latter question seems much broader, since solidarity need not mean economic solidarity. Yet it turns out that we probably do not err when we take the answers to these two questions as describing the same kind of opinions, as we will argue below. For the time being, we assume that the answers to these questions are a satisfactory proxy for support for state welfare programs.

We define voters' preferences on the economic issue as being some aggregate of general economic antiliberalism and support for welfare programs, as characterized by the questions mentioned above. More precisely, we choose to give each answer a score on a 0–3 scale (on the antiprivatization scale, the value 0 means a very positive connotation of the word "privatization," and the value 3 means a very negative connotation; on the pro-welfare scale, 0 means the lowest possible support, and 3 means the highest possible support). Then we take the economic view as being the sum of these two scores. Neglecting re-

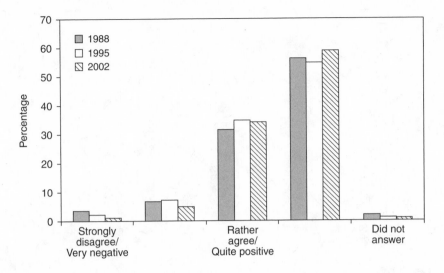

Figure 10.2   The state should provide minimum income for all (1988) / Connotation of the word "solidarity" (1995, 2002): Distribution of answers.

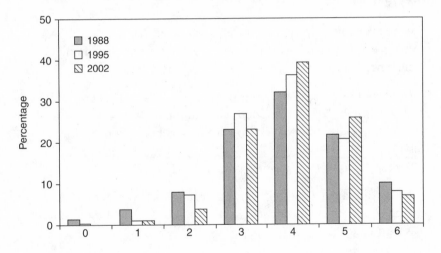

Figure 10.3   Distribution of economic views.

spondents who do not answer either question used to construct the index, we summarize the results in Figure 10.3. The distribution of views is quite stable through time, with a slight shift in favor of a bigger public sector. See Appendix Tables B.10–B.13 for all statistics on the economic variables.

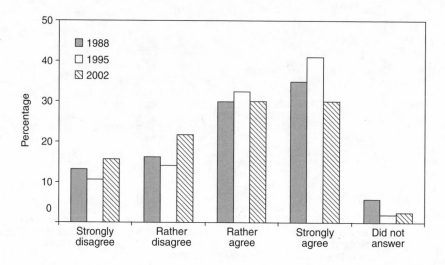

Figure 10.4   There are too many immigrants in France: Distribution of answers.

The *immigration issue* is investigated through responses to two questions. The first is

> Would you say that you fully agree, rather agree, rather disagree or fully disagree with the following statement? There are too many immigrants in France.

The distribution of answers is shown in Figure 10.4. A large majority of respondents think that there are too many immigrants in France. The distribution of views is quite stable through time, with a peak of anti-immigrant feeling in 1995.

The second immigration issue question is

> Would you say that you fully agree, rather agree, rather disagree or fully disagree with the following statement? Nowadays we do not feel at home as we used to.

The distribution of answers is shown in Figure 10.5.

We use these two questions to define voters' preferences on the immigration issue. More precisely, here again we give each answer a score on the 0–3 scale (on both the "Too many immigrants" scale and the "Do not feel at home" scale, the value 0 means that the respondent strongly disagrees with the statement, and the value 3 means that he or she strongly agrees). We take the immigration view as being the sum of these two scores.

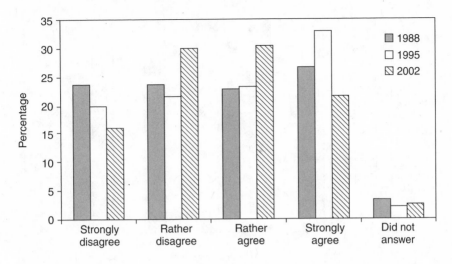

Figure 10.5   We do not feel at home as we used to: Distribution of answers.

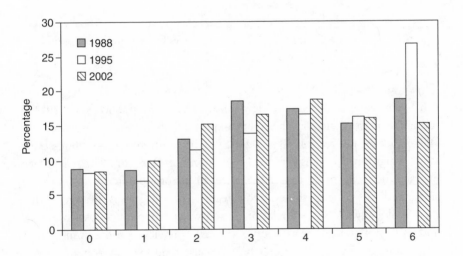

Figure 10.6   Distribution of anti-immigration views.

Neglecting respondents who do not answer either question, the distribution of this index is given in Figure 10.6. The distribution of views is quite stable through time, with a peak of anti-immigration feeling in 1995. See Appendix Tables B.14–B.17 for all statistics on the anti-immigrant variables.

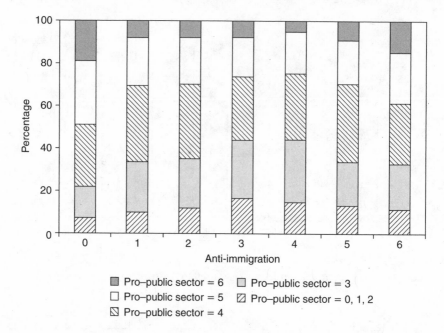

Figure 10.7   Distribution of pro–public-sector views by anti-immigration views, 1988.

The correlation between the views on the size of the public sector and the immigration issue will play an important part in our analysis. Figures 10.7 and 10.8 depict for the years 1988 and 2002 the distribution of pro–public-sector views, partitioned by answers to the immigration question. The percentage of respondents in the first three categories of the pro–public-sector index are small, and so we merge these three categories on the graphs. It appears that there is globally a U-shaped relationship between pro–public-sector opinions and anti-immigration views. People with extreme views on the immigration issue (either very negative or very positive) also tend to support higher levels of public spending. When we consider the first five types of immigration view (from 0 to 4), we observe a negative relationship between anti-immigrant feelings and pro–public-sector views. Then the relationship goes the other way. Yet some striking differences are to be noted between 1988 and 2002. In 2002 the negative relationship appears to be much more important than in 1988. This is confirmed by the observation of average economic view by immigration type for both years. See Figure 10.9.

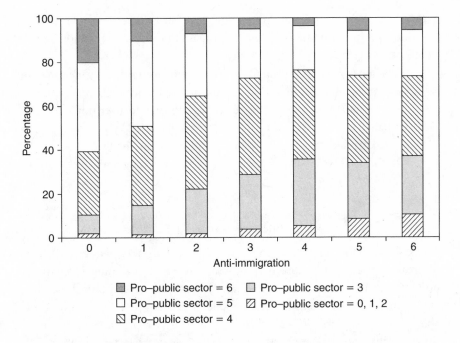

Figure 10.8   Distribution of pro–public-sector views by anti-immigration views, 2002.

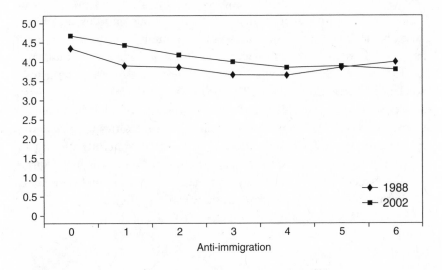

Figure 10.9   Average pro–public-sector view by anti-immigration view.

When we consider the evolution of the joint distribution of economic opinions and immigration related feelings, the main findings are the following:

1. The marginal distributions are quite stable through time. One can note a peak in anti-immigration feeling in 1995, and a slight increase in the support for more public sector, yet these shifts over time are quite small.
2. The correlation between these two opinions has changed a great deal. In 2002, the globally negative relationship is much stronger than in 1988.

10.3.1.2   Interpretation of the Variables

To construct voters' preferences, we rely on a small number of questions only, whereas in the survey more questions are available regarding individuals' opinions on economic policy or immigration policy (recall our choice was constrained, because, to the extent possible, we tried to select questions available for all three years). To understand better exactly what the distribution of these variables means, we check the correlation of our selected variables with other related variables.

In particular, one might be concerned about the changes reported between 1988 and 2002 in the correlation between the economic views and the immigration views. One could argue that this relationship is spurious, and mainly caused by the change in the definition of the economic index. Indeed, recall that in 1988, we used a question about minimum income for all households, and in 1995 and 2002 we used a question about the connotation of the word "solidarity." As we said earlier, it is possible that the word solidarity has a broader sense than just economic solidarity, and that people who resent the presence of too many immigrants will tend to have negative feelings toward the word solidarity if it is understood as a feeling of fraternity for all people living in France. Yet, as we shall now show, other questions in the survey provide further evidence for the strong negative correlation in 2002 between anti-immigration feelings and support for welfare programs.

In the 2002 survey, the following question about welfare programs is available:

As far as the "Revenu Minimum d'Insertion" is concerned [the RMI is the main welfare program in France], would you rather say that

1. People may tend to be happy with it and not look for work.
2. It helps people get through hard times.

Fifty-seven percent of the respondents (who answered the question) selected the first answer. A majority of people tend to think that welfare programs create strong disincentives to work, and that people living on welfare do not try hard to reenter the labor market. The correlation between answers to this question and opinions on the immigration issue is very large, as shown in Figure 10.10. Among people with the most negative feelings toward immigrants, about 75 percent tend to have a low opinion of people living on welfare, whereas this percentage drops to less than 45 percent in the three most immigrant-friendly groups. This is to be compared with the distribution in 1988, as shown in Figure 10.11. In 1988 on the contrary, there is rather a positive—though weak—relationship between anti-immigrant feelings and support for welfare programs.

Appendix Tables B.18 and B.19 present the correlations between the *ProPublicSector* and *AntiImmigration* variables and several other opinions on economic, social, or cultural issues. The numbers reported in these tables add

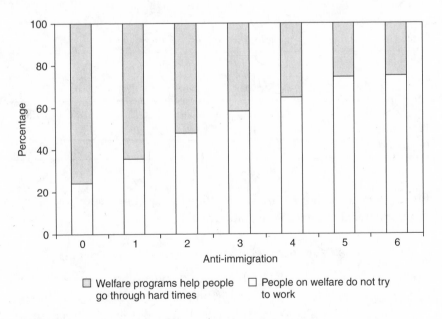

Figure 10.10 Opinions on welfare programs by anti-immigration type, 2002.

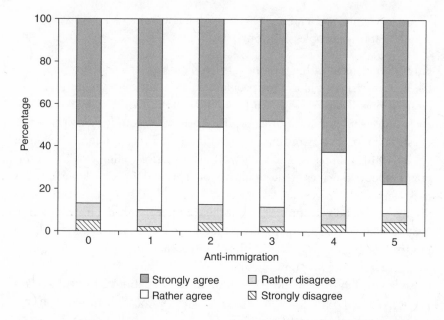

Figure 10.11 The state should provide income for all: Distribution of answers by anti-immigration type, 1988.

Table 10.4 Parameters of the joint distribution of voters' views

	1988		1995		2002	
	Mean	Std. dev.	Mean	Std. dev.	Mean	Std. dev.
AntiImmigration	3.48	1.87	3.79	1.93	3.36	1.84
ProPublicSector	3.86	1.31	3.91	1.10	4.06	1.01
Correlation	−0.05		−0.25		−0.25	

further evidence to the increasing correlation through time between economic views and opinions on the immigration issue.

10.3.1.3 Construction of a Continuous Joint Distribution

Confident that the two variables selected in the first subsection are good indicators of the preferences we want to estimate, we now construct a joint distribution of voters' traits. We approximate the joint distribution by a bivariate normal density with parameters reported in Table 10.4. Figures 10.3 and 10.6

Table 10.5   Voters' average views by constituency

	Left voters	Right voters	Extreme Right voters	All
1988				
Mean ProPublicSector	4.30	3.16	3.62	3.86
Mean AntiImmigration	2.93	3.75	4.99	3.48
2002				
Mean ProPublicSector	4.48	3.66	3.84	4.06
Mean AntiImmigration	2.25	3.28	5.04	3.36

suggest that a normal approximation is adequate for the distribution of economic views; for the distribution of immigration views, the normal fit is not so good for 1995.

10.3.2   Average Position by Constituency

In the survey, respondents were also asked which party they voted for in the various elections. This allows us to compute the average views on both issues by constituency, as defined by the broad coalitions presented above. These average values, which can be interpreted as the equilibrium ideal position of the Militants in each party, are reported in Table 10.5 for years 1988 and 2002. The Extreme Right voters are the most extreme on the immigration issue, but they have moderate views on the economic issue (although they are closer to Right voters than to Left voters on that issue). The main differences between 2002 and 1988 are that in 2002, the *L* and *R* electorates tend to be closer to each other on the economic issue, and the *ER* and the *L* electorates tend to be further apart on the immigration issue.

10.3.3   Estimation of Counterfactual Preferences

As in earlier chapters, we want to construct counterfactual xenophobia-free economic preferences, that is, viewpoints on the size of the public sector that would be observed if the hostility toward immigrants and refugees did not reduce the feeling of solidarity. There is no obvious procedure for constructing these preferences. Our approach depends upon how we interpret the large correlation between opinions on the size of the public sector and opinions on

Table 10.6   Parameters of the distribution of economic views for different levels of xenophobia

| | 1988 | | | 2002 | | |
ProPublicSector	Mean	Std. dev.	Obs.	Mean	Std. dev.	Obs.
AntiImmigration=0	4.35	1.25	291	4.68	0.96	308
AntiImmigration=1	3.90	1.26	267	4.43	0.90	360
AntiImmigration=2	3.86	1.22	395	4.18	0.91	541
AntiImmigration=0,1,2	4.02	1.26	953	4.38	0.93	1,209
All	3.86	1.31	3,156	4.06	1.01	3,602

the immigration issue, on which evidence has been provided (see Figures 10.7 and 10.8).

We cannot expect, given the available data, to provide definitive evidence that the correlation is indeed a causality—that is, that xenophobia indeed *causes* a decrease in the support for the public sector—or to give any final answer as to the exact size of this effect. Our goal in this section is less ambitious: it is to provide some weak evidence that this correlation remains even when we control for demographic factors, and to provide a range of values for the effect.

As a first approach to computing the potential magnitude of this effect, we begin with the most obvious analysis, which is to consider the distribution of economic preferences by *AntiImmigration* view. Table 10.6 presents the mean and standard deviation for various distributions among those whom we class as not xenophobic. Using *AntiImmigration* = 0 as the reference nonracist group is probably too extreme. The choice of *AntiImmigration* = 1 or *AntiImmigration* ≤ 2 seems more reasonable.

Table 10.6 only reports cross-tabulations. It might be argued that the correlation is the indirect result of the existence of common determinants of immigration views and economic views. For example, in 2002, age is negatively correlated with anti-immigrant feelings and (slightly) positively correlated with support for a larger public sector; see Figure 10.12. It might be argued that young people tend to be more educated and more open-minded, hence less subject to negative stereotypes, which would explain the strong positive relationship between age and xenophobia. As to economic views, young people—who are severely hurt by unemployment—support a slightly higher level of public-sector services than older people. On the other

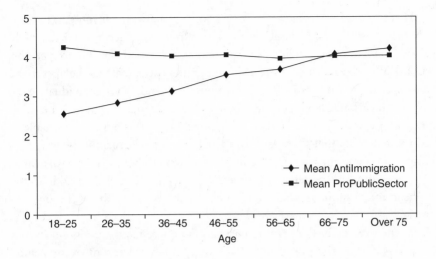

Figure 10.12   Average economic and immigration views by age groups, 2002.

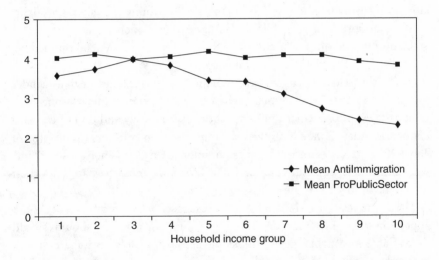

Figure 10.13   Average economic and immigration views by income groups, 2002.

hand, some other variables are negatively (or positively) correlated with both anti-immigrant views and pro–public-sector views—for example, household income. See Figure 10.13.

There is a very strong negative relationship between income and xeno-phobia. Several explanations have been put forward to account for this rela-tionship. First, poor individuals potentially suffer more from the competition on the job market with low-skilled immigrants (or at least so they perceive) and live in the same urban neighborhoods. Second, poor individuals have lower education, and higher levels of education tend to diminish negative stereotypes about foreigners or immigrants. As far as the income variable is concerned, note that there is only a small negative correlation between in-come and economic views: richer individuals tend to be less in favor of a large public sector, but the relation is weak. Views on the size of the public sector depend much more on values and opinions about justice than on economic variables.

To check whether the negative correlation between anti-immigrant feeling and support for the public sector still obtains when we control for demo-graphics variables, we run multivariate regression analysis. See Table 10.7, columns (2) and (4). In columns (2) and (5), the *AntiImmigration* variable is significant and carries the expected negative sign. The coefficient is much larger (in absolute value) in 2002 than in 1988. Young, female respondents tend to support a larger public sector. Note that, somewhat surprisingly, in 2002, opinions about the size of the public sector do not depend on income, once all other variables are taken into account.

So far, we have only controlled for demographic variables, such as gender and age. But subjective opinions might also be important in determining eco-nomic views, in particular opinions that people are lazy and do not try hard enough, or that money incentives are important. In columns (3) and (6) of Table 10.7, we also control for these opinions. Unsurprisingly, respondents who think that people are lazy and that monetary incentives are important tend to favor lower tax rates.

There is no clear-cut decision as to the exact set of the variables that should appear on the right-hand side of the regression. For instance, should we add the variable measuring views on "people are lazy / people on welfare do not try hard enough," which is highly correlated with anti-immigrant views? The answer depends on how we interpret the correlation between *AntiImmigration* and this variable. If we believe that hostility toward immigrants and a nega-tive opinion of people who live on welfare are both determined by the same psychological or social traits (for example, some intrinsic general distrust), then the variable should be added. On the other hand, it might be argued that people who have a rather low opinion of those who live on welfare do so

Table 10.7 Dependent variable: ProPublicSector, OLS estimation

	1988			2002		
	(1)	(2)	(3)	(4)	(5)	(6)
AntiImmigration	−0.032*	−0.079**	−0.034**	−0.138**	−0.151**	−0.103**
	(0.013)	(0.014)	(0.014)	(0.009)	(0.010)	(0.012)
Household income		−0.142**	−0.123**		−0.010	−0.010
		(0.016)	(0.016)		(0.009)	(0.009)
Female		0.112*	0.101*		0.060$^+$	0.051
		(0.049)	(0.049)		(0.033)	(0.035)
Education		−0.060**	−0.057**		−0.019**	−0.017*
		(0.011)	(0.011)		(0.007)	(0.008)
Age		−0.005**	−0.004**		−0.010$^+$	−0.013*
		(0.0015)	(0.001)		(0.006)	(0.006)
Age squared					0.00010$^+$	0.00013*
					(0.00006)	(0.00006)
French people are lazy (1988) / People on welfare do not try to work (2002)			−0.273**			−0.259**
			(0.025)			(0.038)
Money incentives are important to make people work (1988) / Financial help should be withdrawn from families where children are delinquent (2002)			−0.137**			−0.0891**
			(0.023)			(0.018)
Constant	3.970**	5.150**	5.941**	4.514**	4.839**	4.763**
	(0.049)	(0.151)	(0.161)	(0.034)	(0.146)	(0.156)
Observations	2,971	2,715	2,569	3,475	3,475	3,182
R-squared	0.0022	0.0661	0.1271	0.0621	0.0674	0.0889

$^+$significant at 10%; *significant at 5%; **significant at 1%.

precisely because ethnic minorities are overrepresented among the unemployed and the poor. In that case, including this variable on the right-hand side of the equation is likely to induce some underestimation of the direct influence of *AntiImmigration* on support for a larger public sector. The question does not have any straightforward answer.

The numbers in Table 10.7 suggest that an increase of 1 point (on the 0 to 6 scale) in the level of xenophobia reduces the *ProPublicSector* by a constant between 0.03 and 0.08 in 1988 and by a constant between 0.10 and 0.15 in 2002. We use this estimator to construct what we will define as "racism-free demand for public sector." We next describe our procedure.

1. We select a reference level of *AntiImmigration* ρ_{ref} that will be considered as the nonxenophobic threshold.
2. For all individuals with *AntiImmigration* less than or equal to ρ_{ref}, we assume that there is no antisolidarity effect in play, and consider that their observed preferences for the public sector are also the ASE-free economic preferences.
3. For all individuals with *AntiImmigration* greater than ρ_{ref}, we assume that there is some ASE in play, and define their ASE-free economic preferences as those that they would have, were their *AntiImmigration* preferences the reference value specified.

More specifically, consider an individual with observed ideal policy θ_i and ρ_i. We define his racism-free demand for public sector by:

$$\theta_i \quad \text{if } \rho_i \leq \rho_{ref},$$

$$\theta_i + \delta(\rho_i - \rho_{ref}) \quad \text{if } \rho_i \geq \rho_{ref},$$

where δ is the decrease in the support for public sector generated by an increase of 1 point on the xenophobia scale.

We will consider two different values for ρ_{ref}: $\rho_{ref} = 1$ (option 1), $\rho_{ref} = 2$ (option 2). For each option we present the estimate for two values of δ. Table 10.8 presents the mean and standard deviation of the racism-free economic preferences for the two options defined above, and the two years under study. The last row also presents the figures for observed preferences. As observed earlier, the ASE effect is much stronger in 2002 than in 1988. Note that the values obtained are similar to those obtained with the simpler analysis summarized in Table 10.6.

Table 10.8   Parameters of the distributions of counterfactual xenophobia-free economic preferences, based on multivariate regression analysis

	1988		2002	
	Mean	Std. dev.	Mean	Std. dev.
Option 1, $\delta = 0.03$ in 1988 / $\delta = 0.10$ in 2002	3.91	1.30	4.22	1.00
Option 1, $\delta = 0.08$ in 1988 / $\delta = 0.15$ in 2002	3.99	1.31	4.30	0.99
Option 2, $\delta = 0.03$ in 1988 / $\delta = 0.10$ in 2002	3.93	1.30	4.25	0.99
Option 2, $\delta = 0.08$ in 1988 / $\delta = 0.15$ in 2002	4.06	1.30	4.42	0.98
Observed preferences	3.86	1.31	4.06	1.01

Table 10.9   Parameters of the distributions of counterfactual xenophobia-free economic preferences

ProPubSector	1988		2002	
	Mean	Std. dev.	Mean	Std. dev.
Observed	3.86	1.31	4.06	1.01
Counterfactual$_i$	3.90	1.25	4.15	0.90
Counterfactual$_{ii}$	4.00	1.25	4.30	0.90
Counterfactual$_{iii}$	4.10	1.25	4.45	0.90

The conclusion of this section is that a reasonable set of distributions of the "racism-free demand for the size of the public sector" for both years are the three normal distributions with characteristics presented in Table 10.9.[4]

10.4   Political Equilibrium: Observation and Prediction

We computed PUNEs for both 1988 and 2002 for many values of $\gamma/2$. We report the results for $\gamma/2 = 0.35$ in 1988, and $\gamma/2 = 0.40$ in 2002: these values gave us a very good fit of the model to the data. We chose the distribution of types (θ, ρ) to be a bivariate normal distribution whose parameters are given in section 10.3. Almost the entire support (.998) of the distribution lies in the square $[-2, 10] \times [-2, 10]$.

We describe the computation of equilibrium PUNEs. We set the ER policy at the average value, for each dimension, of voters who identified with the

ER party. For each value of γ, we computed many (approximately twenty) PUNEs.[5] Recall that to compute a PUNE, we must solve four simultaneous equations in six unknowns, such that two of the unknowns, the Lagrangian multipliers, are nonnegative. We indeed find many PUNEs, as predicted by the theory.

In Figures 10.14 and 10.15, we graph these PUNEs for 1988 and 2002. The space of the figure is (t, r); consult the caption of Figure 10.14. Recall that we fix the *ER* PUNE policy at its observed value. Note that the figures display the *weighted average PUNE* for Right and Left, as well as the average ideal policy of the constituencies of the three parties. (We describe the weights below.)

We note that the weighted average PUNEs of the L and R parties are quite close in the policy space to the observed ideal policies of the constituencies of those parties. This suggests that the model is fitting the data well. If the Militants had all the bargaining power in their expected parties, then we would predict that the L and R parties propose in equilibrium exactly the average ideal policies of their constituencies.

Nevertheless, the fits are imperfect. In 1988, note that in PUNEs, Left is more extreme on public sector policy than its membership—this cannot be accounted for by the influence of Opportunists, who would push the party toward a less extreme view than its membership's. On the immigration issue, the Left in the average PUNE has the same policy as its membership. Right is less extreme on the immigration issue than its membership (which could be accounted for by Opportunists in Right trying to take votes away from Left); it plays the same policy on the economic issue as its membership's.

In 2002, the observed average policy positions of the L and R memberships are so close to the weighted average PUNE values that we hesitate to attribute any significance to the differences. The parties seem to be very close to their members' views in this year.

We remind the reader that our utility function has only one degree of freedom, γ; thus, it seems quite remarkable that the model appears to fit the data as well as Figures 10.14 and 10.15 show.

The set of PUNEs computed for these values of γ are presented in Tables 10.10 and 10.11. The second and third columns, labeled "$1 - \alpha$" and "$1 - \beta$," present the relative bargaining power of the Militants at the PUNE, in the L and R parties, respectively. A relative bargaining power of 0.5 means the

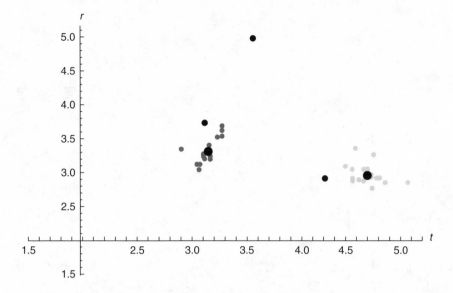

Figure 10.14 1988 PUNEs. The dark gray dots are Right, the light gray dots are Left, the three small black dots are the average policies of the observed party constituencies, and the two larger black dots are the weighted average values of the PUNEs of Right and Left.

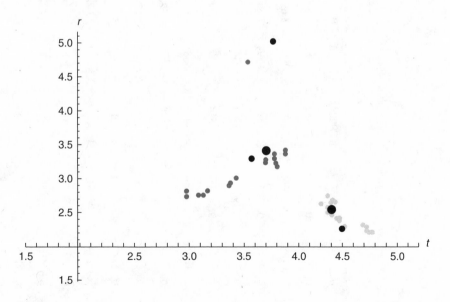

Figure 10.15 2002 PUNEs. See the caption for Figure 10.14 for interpretation.

Table 10.10 PUNEs computed for 1988, France

$\gamma/2$	$1-\alpha$	$1-\beta$	t^L	t^R	t^{ER}	r^L	r^R	r^{ER}	ϕ^L	ϕ^R	ϕ^{ER}
0.35	0.626846	0.387777	4.79084	3.15463	3.62	2.91875	3.28249	4.99	0.37652	0.358075	0.265405
0.35	0.371024	0.254882	4.48383	3.22086	3.62	3.0907	3.21553	4.99	0.399552	0.338762	0.261686
0.35	0.462882	0.0314609	4.54797	3.32994	3.62	2.88078	3.6334	4.99	0.406229	0.34345	0.250321
0.35	0.495333	0.13208	4.61195	3.28994	3.62	2.90314	3.52743	4.99	0.396421	0.349836	0.253744
0.35	0.577923	0.394746	4.72764	3.16847	3.62	2.97413	3.22861	4.99	0.380607	0.35374	0.265653
0.35	0.554547	0.263442	4.69514	3.20867	3.62	2.91469	3.41683	4.99	0.388134	0.354522	0.257344
0.35	0.316018	0.731984	4.08449	3.88681	3.62	2.67988	3.7995	4.99	0.438383	0.243015	0.318603
0.35	0.681671	0.38232	4.85378	3.2085	3.62	2.85134	3.34515	4.99	0.366993	0.366802	0.266205
0.35	0.652836	0.622694	4.74963	2.93558	3.62	3.27459	3.35596	4.99	0.40628	0.352203	0.241517
0.35	0.529179	0.162548	4.65119	3.28817	3.62	2.88577	3.53458	4.99	0.392618	0.353702	0.25368
0.35	0.451543	0.0638124	4.5537	3.32204	3.62	2.90356	3.55191	4.99	0.401345	0.344381	0.254274
0.35	0.639991	0.398798	4.80648	3.14636	3.62	2.91288	3.27565	4.99	0.37516	0.358619	0.266221
0.35	0.624887	0.127152	4.7356	3.32733	3.62	2.77768	3.68933	4.99	0.387395	0.362839	0.249765
0.35	0.42736	0.259017	4.55347	3.21439	3.62	3.04315	3.2742	4.99	0.396726	0.343428	0.259846

0.35	0.857579	0.603632	5.073	3.11373	3.62	2.8647	3.04136	4.99	0.340254	0.370726	0.28902
0.35	0.552794	0.443253	4.69564	3.10865	3.62	3.02188	3.1251	4.99	0.385243	0.346722	0.268034
0.35	0.507579	0.427087	4.65179	3.09531	3.62	3.04635	3.11021	4.99	0.390095	0.343031	0.266874
0.35	0.40574	0.289254	4.04959	3.94274	3.62	2.25181	3.51338	4.99	0.369129	0.284688	0.346183
0.35	0.571692	0.324584	4.72248	3.19126	3.62	2.93525	3.33452	4.99	0.383193	0.355509	0.261299
0.35	0.806905	0.268395	4.97488	3.32449	3.62	2.70871	3.60777	4.99	0.354579	0.38634	0.259081

Table 10.11 PUNEs computed for 2002, France

$\gamma/2$	$1-\alpha$	$1-\beta$	t^L	t^R	t^{ER}	r^L	r^R	r^{ER}	ϕ^L	ϕ^R	ϕ^{ER}
0.4	0.679803	0.65597	4.74045	3.42673	3.84	2.21941	2.95304	5.04	0.370829	0.289801	0.33937
0.4	0.283534	0.0764118	4.37288	3.85196	3.84	2.50409	3.24671	5.04	0.405383	0.268469	0.326148
0.4	0.345788	0.633118	4.3749	3.21688	3.84	2.64825	2.8353	5.04	0.43918	0.232558	0.328262
0.4	0.704447	0.892428	4.70381	3.17947	3.84	2.30018	2.7821	5.04	0.394564	0.257269	0.348167
0.4	0.548245	0.000891854	4.27677	3.59661	3.84	2.65213	4.7433	5.04	0.562005	0.238308	0.199686
0.4	0.678406	0.912822	4.67544	3.13383	3.84	2.32696	2.77771	5.04	0.402875	0.249547	0.347578
0.4	0.362391	0.152243	4.44802	3.75736	3.84	2.42069	3.25981	5.04	0.400812	0.278084	0.321105
0.4	0.375953	0.141278	4.4505	3.84514	3.84	2.40169	3.36443	5.04	0.40084	0.282705	0.316456
0.4	0.700826	0.676349	4.75946	3.42004	3.84	2.20439	2.93263	5.04	0.367829	0.290817	0.341354
0.4	0.316936	0.0936083	4.39559	3.84471	3.84	2.48107	3.31508	5.04	0.407281	0.272604	0.320115
0.4	0.399608	0.866907	4.34291	3.01149	3.84	2.7413	2.82303	5.04	0.46428	0.213092	0.322628
0.4	0.277229	0.0838577	4.34981	3.95084	3.84	2.56771	3.40132	5.04	0.417505	0.264603	0.317892
0.4	0.418626	0.886693	4.40941	3.02194	3.84	2.65717	2.75062	5.04	0.451834	0.217391	0.330775

0.4	0.292731	0.08979	4.36396	3.95251	3.84	2.54918	3.41617	5.04	0.415957	0.267488	0.316555
0.4	0.435106	0.188009	4.49715	3.94635	3.84	2.29341	3.44459	5.04	0.386729	0.299435	0.313836
0.4	0.261411	0.0623887	4.35563	3.86613	3.84	2.52177	3.21243	5.04	0.404499	0.265784	0.329717
0.4	0.646508	0.581963	4.71846	3.48323	3.84	2.22346	3.02089	5.04	0.371642	0.294191	0.34167
0.4	0.369003	0.1612	4.45282	3.7645	3.84	2.41829	3.2805	5.04	0.401303	0.278951	0.319746
0.4	0.0728585	0.664841	4.24668	3.05439	3.84	2.46226	2.46732	5.04	0.444384	0.192958	0.362658

factions are equally strong in the bargaining game. When the relative bargaining power is greater (less) than 0.5, then the Militants (Opportunists) are more powerful in the party in question.

The observed vote shares in the 1988 election were (0.49, 0.365, 0.144), respectively, for L, R, ER. The average shares of the parties in the PUNEs in the above table are (0.39, 0.35, 0.26). Thus we predict that the Left should receive fewer votes, and the Extreme Right more votes, than they did in reality.

In 2002, the observed vote shares for L, R, and ER were (0.429, 0.379, 0.192). Compared with 1998, the Left lost substantially and the Extreme Right gained substantially. The average shares in the PUNEs reported in Table 10.11 for L, R, and ER are (0.42, 0.27, 0.31). This time, we correctly predict Left's share, but we predict that ER should have more, and R fewer, votes than they did in reality. The common factor of these two election years is that we predict the ER should have had a larger vote share than it did, and the two major parties in total should have a smaller vote share.

We now describe how we computed the average PUNE policies of the parties L and R from the computed part of the PUNE manifold. We did not simply average the observed PUNEs. Rather, we view the PUNE manifold as being parameterized by the ordered pairs $(1 - \alpha, 1 - \beta)$, that is, the relative bargaining powers of the Militants in L and R at the PUNE. This parameterization corresponds to our view that the *missing data,* which, if we knew it, would fix a particular PUNE, are these relative bargaining powers.

Thus our first step was to estimate a density function of the two relative bargaining powers from the computed bargaining powers that we found. We used kernel density estimation. Figure 10.16 shows the kernel density function derived from the observed bargaining powers of the Militants in Left in the 1988 PUNEs, and Figure 10.17 shows the analogous kernel density for Right. The modes of these density functions are 0.56 and 0.34 for Left and Right, respectively, indicating that the Militants are "usually" more powerful in Left than in Right. (We do not know whether this corresponds to real perceptions.) We next weighted each PUNE tax rate (for Left and Right) by a factor proportional to the estimated frequency of that PUNE, as measured by the kernel density of its bargaining power. It is the weighted average of the tax rates, so computed, that determines what we call the *weighted average PUNE,* and the corresponding large black points plotted in Figures 10.14 and 10.15. The average vote shares for the three parties are also computed using this weighting technique.[6]

We present these weighted average policies in Table 10.12.

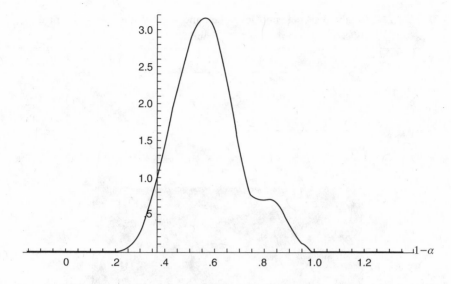

Figure 10.16 Kernel density function of the value $1 - \alpha$ for Left in 1988 PUNEs.

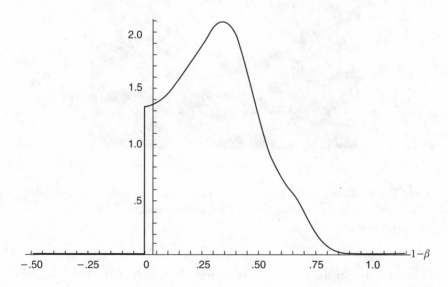

Figure 10.17 Kernel density function of the value $1 - \beta$ for Right in 1988 PUNEs.

Table 10.12 Weighted average policies of Left and Right, and observed average
policies of Extreme Right, 1988 and 2002

(t,r)	1988	2002
Left	(4.69, 2.95)	(4.40, 2.53)
Right	(3.20, 3.32)	(3.78, 3.39)
Extreme Right	(3.62, 4.99)	(3.84, 5.04)

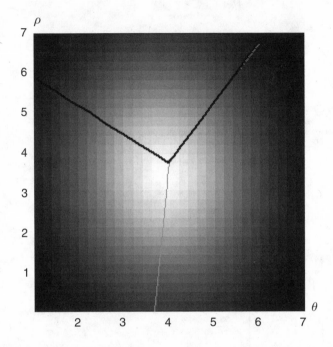

Figure 10.18 Partition of the type space into party memberships, average PUNE,
1988. The three regions, reading from the left and proceeding counterclockwise, are
Right, Left, and Extreme Right.

We next display the predicted partition of the space of voter types into the
three party memberships at the average of the PUNEs in Tables 10.10 and
10.11. Note from equations (10.3) and (10.4) that the set of types that prefer
one policy to another is the set of types below or above a piece-wise linear
graph in (θ, ρ) space. In Figures 10.18 and 10.19 we present the partition of

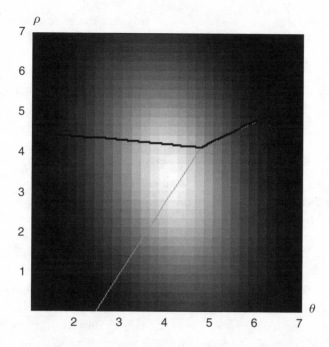

Figure 10.19 Party partition, 2002 PUNEs. See caption for Figure 10.18.

voter types into the three party memberships for the average of the PUNEs of Tables 10.10 and 10.11. The figures present three regions drawn over a density plot of the distribution of voter types: in the density plot, light color means high density. The space is (θ, ρ). Types to the right of the light line constitute Left; types to the left of the light line constitute Right; types in the upper region of the figures constitute Extreme Right.

We remark upon these two figures. In 1988, for voters whose value of ρ is less than 3.5, we observe *class politics:* these voters choose between the L and R parties, and their choice is determined very sharply by their position on the size of the public sector (those for whom $\theta < 4$ choose Right and those for whom $\theta > 4$ choose Left). On the other hand, those who are xenophobic ($\rho > 3.5$) choose either between Right and Extreme Right or between Left and Extreme Right, depending on their view on the economic issue. Interestingly, the most xenophobically moderate voters who belong to Extreme Right are those whose positions on the size of the public sector are *moderate:* this is because Le Pen proposes a moderate position on the size of the public sector. Thus, as a voter's position becomes more extreme on public-sector size (either more Right or more Left), he has to have more incentive to vote for ER. That incentive must be an increasingly radical xenophobic position.

In 2002, however, we observe a quite different equilibrium structure of party constituencies. First, we no longer have such clear class politics for those who are moderate on the immigration issue. For voters for whom $2.5 < \theta < 5$, we must know their position both on immigration and on the public sector to predict whether they identify with Left or Right, where the Right attracts the more xenophobic voters. (That is, the light line has a significantly positive slope in Figure 10.19.) Second, we observe *immigration politics* in the sense that whether a voter chooses ER, on the one hand, or one of the moderate parties, on the other, is quite precisely predicted by his view on immigration: if and only if $\rho > 4$, the voter chooses Extreme Right.

Thus the important change that we observe, between 1988 and 2002, is the increasing salience of the noneconomic issue in French politics, and in particular of the immigration issue. Our model probably captures a broader change in concern about noneconomic issues such as security or law and order, as well as immigration. Indeed, voters' views on the immigration issue and on the law-and-order issue are strongly correlated. Recall that the law-and-order and immigration issues became prominent in the 2002 election campaign; compare the ranking of the "security" and "immigration" issues in Table 10.2 (for 1995) and Table 10.3 (for 2002). In the previous chapter we saw that over the years, Le Pen has tried to link immigration to a host of problems afflicting French society, including crime and insecurity—these figures seem to indicate that this strategy has been largely successful.

Next, we decompose the vote share going to the three parties, as a function of the voters' view on the economic question, from the observed data and from the model. In 1988, Figure 10.20 decomposes the share of the vote going to L, R, and ER for five values of the public-sector question: $\theta \in \{0, 1, 2\}, \theta = 3, \theta = 4, \theta = 5,$ and $\theta = 6$. Table 10.13 shows the predicted vote shares computed from the average PUNE according to the same partition of public-sector views. The predicted and observed shares show a decrease in the R share and an increase in the L share as θ increases, although predicted changes are more extreme than they are in the data. The table of predicted vote shares also shows

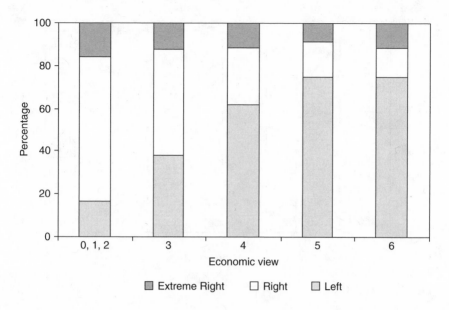

Figure 10.20   Distribution of vote share according to public-sector view, observed.

Table 10.13   Distribution of vote share according to public-sector view, predicted from PUNE, 1988

Ideal t	Left	Right	Extreme Right
0+1+2	0.	0.811742	0.189562
3	0.	0.682287	0.319129
4	0.392168	0.219349	0.388483
5	0.819256	0.	0.180744
6	0.955244	0.	0.0447565

a decrease in the share of the ER as θ increases, something that is not perfectly true in the observed data.

Figure 10.21 and Table 10.14 present the same information for 2002. In 2002, we predict an increase in the Left vote and a decrease in the Right and Extreme Right vote as θ increases, patterns which also appear in the observed data.

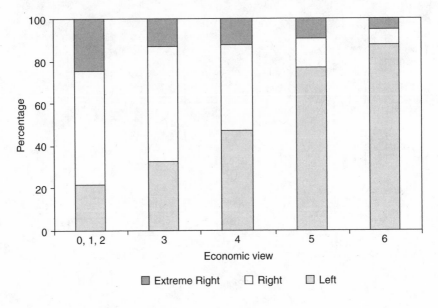

Figure 10.21   Party vote shares by economic view, observed.

Table 10.14   Party vote shares by economic view, predicted from PUNE, 2002

Ideal t	Left	Right	Extreme Right
0+1+2	0.00468154	0.522186	0.473133
3	0.0796293	0.527036	0.393335
4	0.381704	0.293586	0.32471
5	0.749344	0.0138493	0.236806
6	0.889189	0.	0.110811

Overall we believe the model performs well, especially given the fact that there is only one parameter, γ, which we can choose to achieve a good fit. The main error the model makes is its prediction of too large a vote share for the *ER* party. This, however, is not surprising, for two reasons. First, many voters are strategic,[7] and hence voters who actually prefer the policy of *ER* may vote for either *R* or *L* so that their vote will count (in the sense that *ER* will surely be the third party). Second, many voters follow family tradition in their party identification, and the Le Pen party is a relatively new phenomenon. On this count, our predicted vote shares may be closer to what vote shares will be as time passes, and family traditions change.

It should also be pointed out that our choice of a two-dimensional space of types, H, is a limitation. Ideally we would like to differentiate voters according to the salience they assign to the immigration issue; this would require a three-dimensional type space, where a voter's type would be (θ, ρ, γ). While the theory of PUNEs on such a type space is no more complex than on the two-dimensional type space, the computational problems become forbidding, because the equation solving required for computing PUNEs would involve computing three-dimensional numerical integrals instead of two-dimensional integrals. Given the existing *Mathematica* software, this is, for all practical purposes, not feasible. We estimate that computing solutions with this specification would increase our computation time by an order of magnitude. In addition we would need reliable data to estimate voters' saliences, which we do not at this time possess.

10.5   The Policy-Bundle and Antisolidarity Effects: Computation

As we described earlier, to compute the antisolidarity effect and the policy-bundle effect, we perform two counterfactual computations.

In the first counterfactual, we compute PUNEs for a model with *two parties,* in which the policy space is unidimensional. We consider PUNEs in the counterfactual for which the distance from the ordered pair of bargaining powers in the counterfactual PUNEs is close to the average ordered pair of bargaining powers in the PUNEs of the full model.

We chose a two-party model for the counterfactual, because, first, it would be computationally difficult to find equilibria for three *endogenous parties* (in the counterfactual model, we have no way to set the policy of the *ER* party exogenously). Second, were politics indeed unidimensional, it is questionable whether an *ER* party would receive an appreciable vote share, so a two-party model is a reasonable counterfactual.

Recall that, in the first counterfactual, we use the *actual distribution* of voter types, **F**. This counterfactual is equivalent to holding an election where the government's position on the immigration issue is fixed, and all voters take it to be so. We call these P-PUNEs. We again take as the summary statistic the average of weighted tax policies found in all P-PUNEs for which the ordered pair of bargaining powers of the Opportunists in the two parties lies within a circle of radius 0.05 about the ordered pair of bargaining powers of the PUNEs, on average, of the full model. Denote this value by t_I^{exp}.

For the second counterfactual, which computes the antisolidarity effect, we changed the distribution of voter types to the estimated racism-free distribution, described in section 10.3. For 1988 we took the racism-free distribution to be a normal distribution on θ with standard deviation 1.25 and mean in the set $\mu^* \in \{3.90, 4.0, 4.10\}$. For 2002 we took the standard deviation to be .90, and the mean to lie in the set $\mu^* \in \{4.15, 4.30, 4.45\}$. (See Table 10.9.) Thus we ran three versions of the second counterfactual for each year. Call the equilibria of this model Q-PUNEs.

For each counterfactual, we again compute the summary statistic for expected policy on the size of the public sector as the average over all Q-PUNEs whose bargaining-power distances are close to the bargaining powers of the PUNEs in the full model. Denote this value by $t_{II}^{exp}(\mu^*)$.

In the unidimensional models, it remains the case that there is a two-manifold of PUNEs. The policy equilibria live, now, in a two-dimensional space (one dimension for each party), and so the PUNEs pave a region in the plane. We computed approximately two hundred PUNEs for each version of the counterfactual models.

We now define the PBE and the ASE:

$$PBE = t_I^{exp} - t^{exp}$$

$$ASE(\mu^*) = t_{II}^{exp}(\mu^*) - t_I^{exp}.$$

Clearly the total effect of xenophobia on the size of the public sector is:

$$TOT(\mu^*) = PBE + ASE(\mu^*) = t_{II}^{exp}(\mu^*) - t^{exp}.$$

As for other countries, we also report the PBE and ASE for each party. Tables 10.15 and 10.16 report the results. The "a" tables report average PUNEs and bargaining powers for the three models (full and two counterfactuals), and the "b" tables report the PBE and ASE.

As we have previously said, the appropriate way to think of the size of these effects is in comparison to the standard deviation of the distribution of ideal public-sector values, which is 1.31 in 1988 and 1.01 in 2002. By definition, the PBE is invariant with respect to changes in μ^*. In 1988, it appears to be

Table 10.15a   Policies and bargaining powers in the full model and the
counterfactuals, Euclidean function approach, France, 1988

	Full	Counter 1	Counter 2i	Counter 2ii	Counter 2iii
$1-\alpha^L$	0.538	0.539178	0.535575	0.527455	0.562463
$1-\alpha^R$	0.278	0.295237	0.308694	0.307125	0.303448
t^L	4.626	4.91747	4.87538	4.96183	5.1376
t^R	3.326	3.82404	3.82087	3.91661	4.06393
r^L	2.896				
r^R	3.417				
t^{exp}	3.9054	4.20471	4.20059	4.29563	4.43359
ϕ^L	0.38618	0.348334	0.360044	0.362708	0.344431

Note: Counter 1 are P-PUNEs; Counters 2i, 2ii, and 2iii are Q-PUNEs under the three
hypothetical racism-free distributions of voter types.

Table 10.15b   The policy-bundle (PB) and antisolidarity (AS) effects, Euclidean
function approach, France, 1988

Party	PBE	ASE_i	ASE_{ii}	$\dfrac{TOT_i}{std.\ dev.}$	$\dfrac{TOT_{ii}}{std.\ dev.}$
Left	.291	−.042	.044	19.0%	25.6%
Right	.498	−.0032	.093	37.8%	45.1%
Average	.299	−.004	.091	22.5%	29.8%

Note: TOT_i is $(PBE + ASE_i)$. Std. dev. is the standard deviation of the observed distribution of
views on the immigration issue.

large, about one-fourth of the above standard deviation for the average policy.
The ASE is insignificant in 1988. In 2002, however, the PBE is insignificant,
but the ASE is strongly positive. Evidently the antisolidarity effect has increased substantially in this period and the policy-bundle effect has decreased
significantly.

We believe these results are intuitively sensible. In 1988, redistribution was
viewed by most French citizens as helping the poor, who were not perceived
as being very different from the rest of the population: hence the small antisolidarity effect. By 2002, however, many viewed the poor as primarily immigrant, and the antisolidarity effect is significant. Recall from the previous
chapter that in 2001, 73 percent thought that the majority of immigrants came

Table 10.16a Policies and bargaining powers in the full model and counterfactuals, Euclidean function approach, France, 2002

	Full	Counter 1	Counter 2i	Counter 2ii	Counter 2iii
$1-\alpha^L$	0.431	0.418765	0.432912	0.429829	0.425752
$1-\alpha^R$	0.455	0.465856	0.454574	0.437726	0.446092
t^L	4.396	4.4348	4.66542	4.82857	4.95977
t^R	3.776	3.54138	3.55682	3.74001	3.86676
r^L	2.533				
r^R	3.395				
t^{exp}	4.05738	4.0132	4.12522	4.28952	4.42651
ϕ^L	0.421869	0.528327	0.512391	0.505015	0.511694

Note: For explanation of column heads, see note, Table 10.15a.

Table 10.16b The policy-bundle (PB) and antisolidarity (AS) effects, Euclidean function approach, France, 2002

Party	PBE	ASE_i	ASE_{ii}	$\dfrac{TOT_i}{std.\ dev.}$	$\dfrac{TOT_{ii}}{std.\ dev.}$
Left	.039	.231	.394	26.7%	27.5%
Right	−.235	.015	.199	−21.7%	−3.6%
Average	−.044	.112	.276	6.7%	23.0%

Note: For explanation of TOT_i, see note, Table 10.15b.

to France to take advantage of the country's social benefits. Le Pen's accusation that immigrants deliberately abused France's welfare state had thus started to stick, and his party's "national preference" proposals to exclude immigrants from most public services have most likely contributed to the increasing antisolidarity effect.

11

Conclusion

11.1 The Rise of the New Right Movement

In earlier eras, socialists of all persuasions considered the extension of the franchise an important and irreversible step that would lead to massive income redistribution. The syllogism was simple. Since most people suffered from poverty inherent in the market organization of society, and since elections are decided by numbers, full expropriation of asset holders would become the electoral expression of an immense majority.

But twentieth-century universal suffrage has neither engendered full expropriation of the rich by the poor nor ensured the universal victory of left-wing parties. One common explanation has been that polities have come to understand or believe that such expropriation would have catastrophic effects on the formation of wealth, due to the role of private incentives for entrepreneurial activity and skill formation. We have not evaluated that view here, but rather have focused upon the existence of important secondary issues that have divided citizens—in particular, those who benefit from income redistribution. We chose the issue of ethnic minorities/immigration as the most important secondary issue for the countries and period that we studied; we argued that these issues realigned voters in complex ways.

As we documented in Chapters 3 and 4, racism toward blacks has been a prominent secondary issue in the United States since the nation's founding. The salience of the race issue in U.S. politics, leading to the departure of the Dixiecrats from the Democratic Party after the civil rights movement and the

307

Republicans' exploitation of the southern strategy, enabled the Republicans to remain viable without compromising their position on the economic issue. Although we did not study these earlier years in this book, we conjecture that the departure of the Dixiecrats moved redistributive politics significantly to the right, through the policy-bundle effect. We believe that the significant conservatization of American politics for the period we studied, 1972–1992, is in large part due to the realignment of voters on the race issue.

We observe a similar phenomenon in Western Europe, where many countries have experienced a rapid rise of "New Right" parties. Some of these parties formed in the 1970s; most came into their own during the 1980s and early 1990s. These parties run in elections under such diverse labels as the National Front in Britain and France, the Progress Party in Denmark and Norway, the Republicans in Germany, and the Freedom Party in Austria. They represent a racist and xenophobic backlash against the multiculturalization of Western European societies, caused by the influx of immigrants from non-Western countries, particularly from the Islamic, African, and Far Eastern regions. High unemployment rates have exacerbated this backlash.

In some countries, such as France and Denmark, the New Right movement has reached an alarming level. In other countries (such as the UK), the New Right parties do not have a significant parliamentary representation, but infect traditional conservative parties with xenophobia.

That politics are multidimensional is not a new discovery. Analytical political economists, however, have not paid serious attention to multidimensionality, because they have lacked a tool for analyzing that kind of political competition. The traditional Downsian model cannot be successfully extended to a multidimensional environment. Our solution has been to employ the concept of party-unanimity Nash equilibrium (PUNE), which possesses equilibria when policy spaces are multidimensional. We hope that we have shown that the PUNE model is tractable and can be fit to data.

In the following sections we briefly review the strategies we have used, and then summarize our results. Finally we will discuss some limitations of our approach.

11.2   Recapitulation

The central idea of our study has been that the views of voters on the issues of racism and immigration affect the observed political equilibrium on the size of the public sector. This occurs for two reasons: (1) racist voters may wish to reduce the size of the welfare state if they view its benefits as going in large part to "undeserving" minorities or immigrants, and (2) conservative parties can "bundle" together racist or xenophobic platforms with conservative economic platforms, thus attracting votes from poor and working-class natives who are racist or xenophobic, and who would otherwise not vote for them. We called the effect on the size of government expenditures from the first cause the antisolidarity effect (ASE), and the effect of the second cause the policy-bundle effect (PBE).

To estimate these effects, we argued that a model of political equilibrium is required in which parties compete on a two-dimensional policy space. A policy (t, r) presents a party's position on the size of the public sector or the tax rate, t, and on the race or immigration question, r. Voters are characterized as being of a variety of types, where type is also drawn from a two-dimensional space. In our "log utility" model, a voter's type is an ordered pair (w, ρ), where w is the voter's (representative) wage rate and ρ is her position on the race/immigration issue; in the "Euclidean utility" model, the type is denoted (θ, ρ), where θ is the voter's position on the size of the public sector, and ρ is her position, again, on the race issue. A voter's type, in either model, characterizes her utility function over the policy space, once various parameters that are universal to all voters are estimated.

Denote, generically, the policy space by T and the type space by H. Denote the probability distribution of types in a population by $\mathbf{F}$. Let the number of parties, which we take to be exogenous, be n. Denote the utility function of a voter by $v : T \times H \to \mathbb{R}$. The data of our model of political equilibrium constitute the set $\{T, H, \mathbf{F}, v, n\}$. We modeled political equilibrium as a contest between the n parties, where both the membership/constituency of the parties and their policies emerge endogenously from the model, given the data.

Let $n = 2$, which was our choice for all countries except France. In brief, the equilibrium is a (static) Nash equilibrium between parties, where each party plays a best response to the policy proposal of the other party. "Best-response," however, is nontraditional. We view parties as composed of factions—Opportunist, Reformist, and Militant—each of which has a distinct payoff function. Opportunists care only about maximizing vote share, or the probability of victory; Militants care only about remaining principled regarding the wants of the party's constituency; Reformists care only about maximizing constituents' expected utility. These factions bargain with one another in the face of the opposing party's proposal. A best response by party A to a policy proposal τ^B of party B is a solution to A's interfaction bargaining problem, when facing τ^B. We pointed out that, mathematically, the Reformists are gratuitous; we could in fact represent all equilibria of this game as the consequence of bargaining between Opportunists and Militants in the parties.

As we said, this model possesses equilibria when the policy space is multidimensional. Moreover, party policies are differentiated, unlike in the Downsian model. The drawback of the model is that it possesses many equilibria—indeed, a two-dimensional set (or manifold) of equilibria in the space $T \times T$. Nevertheless, a two-dimensional manifold in a four-dimensional space is still "small." We argued that the multiplicity of equilibria was due to "missing data": if we knew the relative bargaining powers of the factions (Opportunists relative to Militants) in each party (supplying two numbers), then we could determine equilibrium uniquely.[1] We did not, however, attempt to estimate such numbers in our study *directly*; rather, we deduced what these bargaining powers must be by fitting the model to the observed data.

Indeed, we do not claim that actual parties have factions that sit down at a bargaining table. Rather, our model attempts to represent the two pulls on a party in a democracy—to win votes and to represent its constituency. The conceptual innovation of the PUNE model is that it represents these two pulls by endowing the actors (parties) in the game with *several payoff functions,* rather than trying to summarize their behavior as the maximization of one payoff function. Indeed, it is this "trick" that gives us equilibria in a political game with multidimensional policy spaces.

We estimated the distribution of types **F** from election-study and panel data sets for each of our countries. We estimated universal parameters of the utility function where possible.

In estimating the distribution of types, we used two different methods. In the case of the log utility function model, we estimated that distribution nonparametrically, while assuming that the wage rate and the racial view were independently distributed. (Of course, we checked that independence was empirically reasonable.) In the case of the Euclidean utility model, we estimated the distribution parametrically, without assuming that the voter's position on the size of the public sector and her position on the race issue were independent. A bivariate normal distribution performed quite well.

Using a nonparametrically estimated distribution function is computationally expensive. It generates a smaller number of PUNEs than with a parametric distribution function because the nonparametrically estimated distribution function is less smooth, and the root-finding procedure of the computer program is more likely to miss solutions of the system of simultaneous equations.

Conclusion

We computed equilibria (PUNEs) of our model, and, as predicted, we find a two-dimensional set of them. To narrow down this set, we chose equilibria by imposing the requirement that the computed equilibria match, at least approximately, the vote shares of the empirical counterparts of the parties in the elections that we modeled. This procedure usually sufficed to determine quite sharp predictions of equilibrium policy. We then computed the bargaining powers of the factions in the two parties at these equilibria.

We then simulated two counterfactual elections. In the first counterfactual, we ran an election where, by hypothesis, the only policy is t. No issue of race or immigration appears on the political agenda (or, alternatively, the government's position on the race issue is fixed). Voters, however, are still equipped with their actual preferences, which include their attitudes toward minorities and/or immigrants. In this election, there will be no policy-bundle effect, but the antisolidarity effect will still hold sway. (That is, a racist voter might still vote for a small public sector because he dislikes financing transfers to minorities.) Thus the difference between equilibrium policies in this counterfactual election, on the t issue, and in the election of the full model, is a measure of the PBE.

Again, there is a two-dimensional manifold of equilibria in this counterfactual election. In the Euclidean model it is easy to compute hundreds, or even thousands, of them. How did we choose among them? We cannot refine the set of equilibria by looking at vote shares, because this is a counterfactual election, so there are no observed vote shares. For any PUNE, we can compute the imputed relative bargaining powers of the party factions. We chose equilibria from the first counterfactual election to *match the bargaining powers* of the chosen equilibria in the full model. Thus in our estimate of the PBE, we attempt to control for the bargaining powers of factions, so that our measure of the PBE does not *also* include an effect from a change in relative bargaining powers of the factions. This procedure is applied only to the Euclidean utility function approach, in which we find many PUNEs. We did not apply it in the log utility function approach, because we did not find many PUNEs, and there were very few overlapping bargaining powers among those we obtained.

We then ran a second counterfactual election: this time, we altered the preferences of voters, making them nonracist. Again, this second counterfactual election is over only the dimension of public-sector size (or the tax rate). Again we chose equilibria to match the bargaining powers of the factions in the full model when we took the Euclidean utility function approach. The difference between the equilibrium values of t in this counterfactual election and in the

Conclusion

election of the full model is now capturing both the PBE and the ASE—in other words, the total effect of racism on the size of the public sector. Finally, we estimate the ASE by subtracting the PBE from the total effect. We proceed to summarize our results.

11.3   The Log Utility Function Approach

The log utility function approach takes into account labor-supply responses of voters with respect to changes in the (effective) income tax rate; we applied it to two countries, the United States and the United Kingdom.

We were able to estimate a reasonably complex and highly articulated utility function for the United States, with a somewhat less articulated utility function for the UK. (This is largely due to the nonavailability of detailed information in the UK data sets.) We thus have more confidence in our model of the United States than in our one of the UK.

The utility function contained ten parameters, as well as the voter's type. Many of these parameters were estimated independently from data; some were chosen "structurally," that is, to produce equilibria of the model that gave a good fit to the observed political equilibria. The type-distribution is estimated nonparametrically, and those nonparametrically estimated distributions are used in our numerical computation.

Direct comparison of the UK and U.S. results is problematic, because the survey questions in the data sets are different. Moreover, we modeled the "intraparty" influence of types differently: for the United States, we gave more weight to wealthy voters than to poor voters in formulating the party's utility function, while we gave equal weight to all voters in the UK parties. We have empirical evidence justifying this move for the United States; we have no comparable evidence for the UK.

For the United States, we ran the model for four (pooled) periods: 1976–1980, 1980–1984, 1984–1988, and 1988–1992. In all these periods, we computed empirically the affine fiscal policies and compared them with the equilibrium policies. We found that the affine fiscal policy is a good approximation of U.S. fiscal policy, and our model produces surprisingly accurate predictions of the observed fiscal policy: observed fiscal policies are very close to the Laffer curve estimated from the model.

The equilibrium tax rates are differentiated between the two parties; the tax rate proposed by the Democratic Party is usually 12 to 16 percent higher than that proposed by the Republican Party.

Conclusion

The estimated effect of racism on redistribution in the United States is large, although the precise effect varies across time, reflecting changes in the distribution of voter traits. In 1984–1988, for instance, the effect of racism on the tax rate is about 16.5 percentage points for the Republican Party and about 13 percentage points for the Democratic Party. In other words, voter racism pushes both parties in the United States significantly to the right on the economic issue.

We examined the equilibrium party membership, and our model predicts an alignment of political parties in the United States primarily along the racial issue, in the sense that party membership is best characterized by a partition of the space of voter types that differentiates citizens primarily according to their racial views, not their incomes. If, somehow, the race issue were to disappear from U.S. politics, we predict that there would be realignment so that party membership would be defined primarily by differentiation of voters along the economic dimension. Thus we claim that in this period, the race issue transformed what *would have otherwise been class politics* into *race politics*.

We predict that, absent race as an issue in American politics, fiscal policy in the United States would look quite similar to fiscal policy in northern Europe. See Table 11.1 for the most aggregated summary.

For the UK, we ran the log utility model for only one year, 1997.

In the UK, party membership was sensitive to both economic and racial positions of voters. Racism is clearly salient in UK politics, but in contrast to the United States, class politics are equally important. The slope of the voter-separating hyper-space (in the space of voter types) is steeper than that for the United States.

Again, the equilibrium tax rates are differentiated between the two parties in the UK; the tax rate proposed by the Labour Party in the full model is about 8 percent higher than that proposed by the Conservative Party.

The log utility function model predicts that the Conservative Party would have proposed an effective marginal tax rate of 42.8 percent in 1997, absent

Table 11.1 Reduction in income tax marginal rate, due to racism, log utility model (percentage of income)

	1976–80	1980–84	1984–88	1988–92	1997
U.S.	18	11	16	14	
UK					19

racism. Because of the existence of racism, however, it was able to propose a tax rate of 27.8 percent in that year; thus the effect of racism on the tax rate is about 15 percentage points for the Conservative Party. The effect of racism on the tax rate of the Labour Party is also large. Absent racism, we predict it would have proposed a marginal tax rate of 53.3 percent; due to the existence of racism, it proposed 35.4 percent.

We also find that, as in the U.S. case, both the policy-bundle effect and the antisolidarity effect are important in the UK.

11.4   The Euclidean Utility Function Approach

In addition to the log utility function model, we also ran the Euclidean model for the United States and the UK, in hopes of being able to make some comparisons among all four countries with the same model. For Denmark and France, the Euclidean utility model is the only approach we took: we assumed a Euclidean utility function on the two issues of t and r, where a voter is characterized as having an ideal policy on these issues of θ and ρ, respectively. We decided not to use the log utility function approach for these countries in part because the income tax is relatively less important there, not only because of the value-added tax but because we felt that the tax issue, as such, is not as salient in these countries as it is in the United States and the UK.

As we discussed, the Euclidean model is in general simpler than the log utility model; it possesses some practical advantages. First, it allows us to use a bivariate normal distribution of types with dependence between the two characteristics. Second, equilibria for a three-party model can be obtained without significant computational cost. On the negative side, we have only one free parameter in the Euclidean utility function, the relative salience of one issue to the other. This simplicity makes it more difficult to fit the model to the observed data. We assumed that the relative salience was constant across the polity. In the quantitative analysis chapters, we described how we estimated from the election-study data the interval in which the relative salience parameter, γ, lies. We chose the precise value of γ to give the best fit of the equilibrium model results to the data: we used a "collinearity" test that we described in those chapters. This method gave us values that were consistent with our econometric estimates of the relative salience.

For France, we felt that the two-party model was inadequate, because the Extreme Right party of Le Pen, the Front National, takes a position on the economic issue that lies between the policies of the socialists and the conser-

Table 11.2 Reduction in size of public sector due to racism/xenophobia, Euclidean utility model. Two estimates for each experiment.

	1979	1983	1984–88* 1988	1988–92	1997* 1998	2001* 2002
U.S.			.35*/.25* **13.8%**	.50/.38 **17.9%**		
UK	.48/.32 **18.8%**	.39/.25 **17.6%**			.14*/.12* **5.6%**	
Denmark					.04/.20 **5.6%**	.21*/.36* **9.9%**
France			.23/.30 **15%**			.067/.23 **9%**

Note: Units: Fraction of standard deviation of the distribution of ideal points on public-sector size. Boldface units: For example, for France 1988, the *larger* figure (.30 s.d.) is equivalent to 15 percentage points of that cumulative distribution at its mean. Asterisks in the body of the table refer to elections in the asterisked year in the column heading.

vatives, but a policy on immigration that lies to the right of those two blocs. We did not, however, estimate a fully endogenous three-party model for France.[2] We fixed the policy of the Extreme Right party in France at the average value of the ideal points of those who were observed to have voted for it, as recorded in the election-study data. The policies of the other two parties, and the memberships of all three parties, were fully endogenous. Again, we chose equilibria from the two-dimensional equilibrium manifold in order to replicate the observed vote shares of the three parties.

In brief, our results from the Euclidean utility model were as follows. See Table 11.2 for the aggregate summary.

For the United States, we ran the model for two periods: one with pooled data from 1984 and 1988, and the second with pooled data from 1988 and 1992. For the earlier period, we found a negligible PBE (we refer now to the average effect, not the single-party effects), and a substantial ASE, which was between 25 and 34 percent of one standard deviation on the estimated distribution of ideal points of American voters concerning the size of the public sector. Given the nature of the survey question upon which we based the voters' types, we cannot translate this directly into desired tax rates. In the later period, we again found a negligible PBE, and a substantial ASE—between 40 and 52 percent of one standard deviation of the above distribution. Our qualitative result is that the PBE is negligible in this model, and that the total effect is substantial and increasing over this period.

When we disaggregate the average effect into two single-party effects, we get a puzzling result. The ASE is indeed positive for both parties. But the PBE is positive for the Left (Democratic) party and *negative* for the Right (Republican) party. Thus the negligible average PBE that we report is in fact an average of a positive and a negative number, each of which is not so small in absolute value. We cannot explain why this occurs. Evidently, the parties tend to *diverge* in policy in the first counterfactual election, compared with their positions on the tax rate in the full model. All we can say is that this is an artifact of the Euclidean model, and it reduces our confidence in disaggregating the total effect (ASE plus PBE) into its two components when using the Euclidean model.

For the UK, we ran the Euclidean model for three years: 1979, 1983, and 1997. Again the average PBE is positive but quite small: this time, for 1979 and 1983, both single-party effects are small, although in 1997, the Conservative single-party effect is again negative. The ASE is large for 1979 and 1983: in both years it is at least 20 percent of one standard deviation (on the distribution of ideal public-sector views) and sometimes as much as 47 percent. In 1997 it is much smaller—between 11 and 13 percent of one standard deviation. Thus we see what appears to be a clear pattern of reduced ASE as the Labour Party has become stronger.

Denmark has eleven parties. Nevertheless, because the election-study data tell us that voters perceive parties to be more conservative on the public-sector issue as they become more xenophobic, we decided that a two-party model was adequate for our purposes. We ran the model for two years, 1998 and 2002. The social democrats formed the government in 1998, and the conservatives did in 2001. For 1998, we found a *negative* PBE of 17.8 percent of one standard deviation, and a positive ASE of between 22 and 38 percent for our first two estimates of the racism-free distribution of voter preferences: thus under our various counterfactuals, the total effect in Denmark is positive, and perhaps significantly so. For 2001, the PBE is again negative, but much smaller in size (6.7 percent of one standard deviation); the ASE is larger than in 1998, between 27 and 43 percent of one standard deviation. Thus according to all indications, the effect of xenophobia on the size of the public sector has increased over this short period, which is consistent with popular perceptions of the power switch to the conservatives.

For France, we ran the Euclidean model for 1988 and 2002. The pattern here is quite different. In 1988 the PBE is positive and significant—at 22.8 percent of one standard deviation. The ASE, however, is insignificant in this year. In 2002, the year of the Le Pen surprise in the general election, the PBE is insignificant, but the ASE has become significant, at between 11 and 27 percent of one standard deviation. It is possible to tell a story that rationalizes these results. We are hesitant, however, to put too much credence in the estimates of the French effects, for the following reason. As we have said, we specified the position of the Extreme Right (Le Pen) in the PUNE model exogenously, and we computed the equilibrium value of the public-sector size in the full model for France as the share-weighted average of the positions of the *three* parties in the PUNEs. The counterfactual elections, however, had two endogenous parties. Therefore the ASE and PBE for France include, as well as the effects we are interested in, the effect of moving from three parties to two. For this reason, we have less confidence in the results than we have with the countries in which we specified the full model as one with two parties.

Note that in Table 11.2, we have presented the aggregate effects of racism/xenophobia in two ways: as fractions of the standard deviation of the distribution of ideal points on public-sector size, and also (indicated in boldface) as the equivalent fraction of the cumulative distribution, computed from the mean of the distribution. The table indicates that racism shifts the equilibrium on public-sector size between 5 and 20 percentage points to the right on that cumulative distribution.

We note that a superior "Euclidean" approach might be to use a utility function which is a full quadratic form on two variables, that is,

$$v(t, r; \theta, \rho) = -(t - \theta)^2 - \beta(t - \theta)(r - \rho) - \gamma(r - \rho)^2.$$

Doing so would give us one more parameter to fit the data, and might eliminate the negative PBEs. This will be an exercise for future work.

Finally, we offer a brief comparison of the Euclidean model results and the log utility model results for the United States and the UK.

In both countries, the two models generate a large average effect of racism, but effects on individual parties and the two decomposition effects are different across the two models.

For the United States, the two models generate similar results in that the PBE is smaller than the ASE. When we disaggregate the average effect into two single-party effects, however, we get different results. Both the ASE and the PBE are positive for both parties in the log utility model, but this is not the case in the Euclidean model. The ASE is indeed positive for both parties, but the PBE is positive for the Left (Democratic) party and negative for the Right (Republican) party. We do not know why this occurs. All we can say is that it is somewhat difficult to compare the two models directly. Although they are conceptually similar, there is no reason to believe that empirically the two models will result in identical results. Also, although we incorporated the disproportionately large influence of the rich in determining the payoff functions of political parties in the log utility model, there is no obvious way of incorporating the same idea in the Euclidean utility model, because the voter's wage is not a dimension of her type in the Euclidean model.

For the UK, we used the two models in 1997. As in the U.S. case, the two models generate similar results in the following sense, in that the PBE is much smaller than the ASE. When we disaggregate the average effect into two single-party effects, however, we get different results. Both the ASE and the PBE are positive for both parties in the log utility model, but this is not the case in the Euclidean utility model.

One result appears to be consistent. In both the United States and the UK, the ASE is larger than the PBE on average. But how these two effects affect Left and Right differs across the models.

11.5   Limitations

We believe that the main limitations of the model are of three kinds: the small dimension of the space of voter types (two), the small dimension of the policy space (two), and the small number of parameters in the Euclidean utility function (one). We discuss these in turn.

With regard to the space of voter types, it would clearly be better to be able to distinguish voters not only with regard to their income or public-sector view and their position on the race/immigration issue, but also with regard to the *relative salience* that the race/immigration issue has for them. For doubtless this salience does vary across the polity, and that variation could be just as important as the variation in their ideal positions, upon which we have focused. To add salience differentiation to the model would give us a three-dimensional space of voter types. Conceptually, there is no complication in the notion of PUNE, but computationally, the problem becomes more difficult. The partition of the polity into the two party memberships now becomes a problem involving triple, instead of double, numerical integration. This entails a large increase in computation time. We opted, for this project, not to attempt this.

Conclusion

Concerning the dimension of the policy space: we have tried to argue that, for the time period in question, the issues of public-sector size and race/immigration were the two most salient issues for the countries in question. This argument could be questioned: adding a third issue might be advisable. Moreover, as we have pointed out, it would be useful, at least in France and Denmark, to separate out the all-encompassing "public-sector size" issue into "public-sector size" and "benefits for immigrants." For when immigrants are not citizens, it is possible to differentiate their treatment from the treatment of citizens. In the United States, with respect to black citizens, this cannot be done—at least it cannot be done legally in the post–civil rights era. (Prior to the civil rights movement, government aid in the South went almost entirely to whites; see Katznelson 2005.) Therefore our estimates of the effects of xenophobia on the size of the public sector for these countries are probably only upper bounds for the true effects.

We have already remarked upon the costs of using a Euclidean utility function with only one parameter other than voter type. Indeed one parameter did not give us enough flexibility; overfitting, underfitting, and puzzling results are all the consequences of working with such a restricted utility function. We have suggested that using the full quadratic form for the two-dimensional Euclidean model would probably improve the analysis.

Other limitations should also be mentioned. We have modeled only national elections, not parliamentary or congressional politics. We have assumed that voters are sincere, not a good assumption in multiparty elections. Our model treats the engine of politics as the distribution of voter preferences; to some extent, these preferences are endogenous, and reflect what elite opinion-makers propagate. Modeling that phenomenon would take us a good deal further away from a classical equilibrium approach.

Despite all these limitations, we believe that there is significant value added to our understanding in the extension of the standard single-policy-dimension, single-type-dimension (1×1) Downsian analysis to a 2×2 analysis. Not only do we answer questions that were unposable in the Downsian framework, but we present a more compelling theory of political competition.

We look forward to the work of other researchers, who will be able to extend our analysis to higher dimensions (say, 3×3) in the future, with faster computer speeds, more highly articulated political data sets, and tractable models of political competition for multiparty parliamentary democracy. Our project only begins a rigorous study of the multifaceted relationships among racism, xenophobia, and distribution.

11.6   Final Remark

We have written of the surprise to many, especially to those in the socialist camp, that universal suffrage did not swiftly usher in socialist regimes. In some countries, of course, perhaps it did: whether the Nordic social democracies qualify as "socialist" is a question we cannot pursue here, but they may well do so. Our conjecture is that conservative political parties, which represent the *economic* interests of only a small fraction of the polity, maintain a foothold in the democratic arena when and if they succeed in appealing to a much larger fraction of the polity on noneconomic issues. We have argued that in the late twentieth century, in several advanced democracies, the most successful such issue to exploit was race and ethnicity. Indeed, the Nordic social democracies may well have achieved their degree of economic solidarity precisely because of the homogeneity of their working classes during the period of consolidation of the welfare state: see Alesina and Glaeser (2004) and Desmet, Ortuño-Ortin, and Weber (2005) for evidence on the effect of heterogeneity, from a much larger sample of countries than we have studied here. Desmet and colleagues define a measure of linguistic diversity, for a country; linguistic diversity, so measured, is strongly inversely correlated with the fraction of GNP dispensed in social transfers.

In the United States, it appears that the conservative strategy to maintain mass appeal is changing from a reliance on racial issues to a reliance on religious-moral ones. Whether the religious gambit will prove as effective as race has been in enabling the Republicans to maintain their extreme economic position is an open question. In Europe, at least in a number of countries, Islamic fundamentalism has become a burning issue. The success with which European polities deal with this problem will likely have important consequences for the welfare states of those countries. We believe the responsibility for developing an effective policy lies with the Left, for recent history indicates that the Right will exploit xenophobia to protect the economic interests of the wealthy class.

Appendix A: Statistical Methods

Appendix B: Additional Tables

Notes

References

Index

A

Statistical Methods

A.1   Kernel Density Estimator and Asymptotic Statistics

(1) The kernel density estimate for variable x with a sample $\{x_i\}$, which is independently and identically drawn from an unknown density f, is given by

$$\hat{f}(x) = \frac{1}{N_x} \sum_{i=1}^{N_x} \left(\frac{1}{h_x} K \left(\frac{x - x_i}{h_x} \right) \right),$$

where x_i is the ith sample point for variable x, N_x is the number of observations for variable x, h_x is a bandwidth (or a smoothing parameter), and $K(.)$ is a kernel function.

The kernel estimator clearly depends on the choice of a kernel and a bandwidth, but it is well known that the choice of a kernel is a minor issue. Indeed the difference between the values of the Mean Integrated Square Error attained by most kernels and the optimal kernel, often called the Bartlett-Epanechnikov kernel, is small (Silverman 1986, 43). We chose the Gaussian kernel.

In contrast, the selection of a bandwidth is crucial. Several methods for estimating an optimal bandwidth have been suggested in the literature (for example, cross-validation methods, plug-in methods), but these methods are computationally expensive and the rate of convergence is extremely slow, being of the order of $N_x^{-1/10}$. In addition, when the criterion function used in estimating the optimal bandwidth has several local minima, quite different values of estimated bandwidths may be derived for data sets coming from the same distribution. Therefore, in setting the optimal bandwidth, we follow Silverman's rule of thumb:

$$h_x^{opt} = 0.9 * N_x^{1/5} \text{Min} \left[\text{Var}_x, \frac{\text{IQR}_x}{1.349} \right],$$

where N is the number of samples, Var is the variance, and IQR is the interquartile range.

One minor issue is that the above estimates are based on the assumption that the support of the density is the entire real line. This assumption may generate a somewhat inaccurate estimate if the support is bounded. We find that the estimate of the wage distribution is somewhat inaccurate around the origin, because there are many nonworking individuals. So we adjust the density estimate by using the reflection method described in Silverman (1986, 30). More precisely, we estimate the wage density by the formula:

$$\hat{f}(x) = \frac{1}{N_x} \sum_{i=1}^{N_x} \left(\frac{1}{h_x} K \left(\frac{x - x_i}{h_x} \right) + \frac{1}{h_x} K \left(\frac{x + x_i}{h_x} \right) \right).$$

(2) The bias of the kernel estimator is:

$$\text{Bias} \hat{f} \equiv E\hat{f} - f = \int K(\psi)[f(h_x \psi + x) - f(x)]d\psi \approx \frac{h_x^2}{2} \mu_2 f''(x),$$

where $\psi = \frac{x - x_i}{h_x}$, and its variance is given by

$$\text{Var} \hat{f} = \frac{1}{N_x h_x} \int K^2(\psi) f(h_x \psi + x) d\psi - \frac{1}{N_x} \left[\int K(\psi) f(h_x \psi + x) d\psi \right]^2$$

$$\approx \frac{1}{N_x h_x} f(x) \int K^2(\psi) d\psi.$$

(See Pagan and Ullah 1999, 22.)

It is well known that under some regularity conditions, the kernel estimator is asymptotically unbiased ($\lim E\hat{f} = f$), consistent weakly ($\hat{f} \xrightarrow{p} f$) and strongly ($\hat{f} \xrightarrow{a.s} f$), and asymptotically normal ($\sqrt{N_x h_x}(\hat{f} - f) \xrightarrow{d}$ Normal$(0, f \int K^2(\psi) d\psi)$). Hence a pointwise 95% confidence interval for the density estimate is:

Appendix A

$$\hat{f}(x) \pm 1.96 \frac{1}{\sqrt{N_x h_x}} [f(x) \int K^2(\psi) d\psi]^{1/2}.$$

By replacing f with its consistent estimator (i.e., $\hat{f}$) and computing $\int K^2(\psi) d\psi$ (which is approximately 0.2821 if the kernel is Gaussian), we obtain the asymptotic confidence interval for $\hat{f}$.

(3) The bivariate density estimate $\hat{h}(\mathbf{z})$ for a sample $\{\mathbf{z_i}\} = \{(x_i, y_i)\}$ is given by the formula

$$\hat{h}(x, y) = \frac{1}{Nh^2} \sum_{i=1}^{N} \left(\frac{1}{h} K \left(\frac{x - x_i}{h}, \frac{y - y_i}{h} \right) \right)$$

$$= \frac{1}{Nh^2 \sqrt{\mathbf{V}}} \sum_{i=1}^{N} \left(\tilde{K} \left(\frac{(\mathbf{z} - \mathbf{z}_i)' \mathbf{V}^{-1} (\mathbf{z} - \mathbf{z}_i)}{h^2} \right) \right),$$

where N is the number of observations for $\{\mathbf{z_i}\}$, $\mathbf{V}$ is the sample covariance matrix of the data, $K(., .)$ is the standard bivariate normal distribution, and $\tilde{K}(.)$ is the function such that $\tilde{K}(\mathbf{z}'\mathbf{z}) = K(\mathbf{z})$; if $K(., .)$ is the standard bivariate normal, $\tilde{K}(u)$ is equal to $\frac{\exp(-\frac{1}{2}u)}{2\pi}$ (Silverman 1986, 78).

The independence assumption requires testing $H_0 : h(x, y) = f(x)g(y)$. Ahmad and Li show (Pagan and Ullah 1999, 71) that under H_0 and as $h \to 0$ and $Nh^2 \to \infty$, $T_1 = \frac{Nh\bar{I}_1}{\hat{\sigma}_3} \xrightarrow{d} \text{Normal}(0, 1)$, where

$$\hat{\sigma}_3 = \frac{1}{N^2} \sum_{i=1}^{N} \hat{f}(x_i) \sum_{i=1}^{N} \hat{g}(y_i) \int [K_x(\psi)]^2 d\psi \int [K_y(\psi)]^2 d\psi,$$

and

$$\bar{I}_1 = \frac{1}{(Nh)^2} \sum_{i \neq j} \sum_j K_x \left(\frac{x_i - x_j}{h} \right) K_y \left(\frac{y_i - y_j}{h} \right)$$

$$+ \frac{1}{(N^2 h)^2} \sum_{i \neq j} \sum_j K_x \left(\frac{x_i - x_j}{h} \right) \sum_{i \neq j} \sum_j K_y \left(\frac{y_i - y_j}{h} \right)$$

$$- 2 \frac{1}{N^3 h^2} \sum_{i \neq j} \sum_{j \neq k} \sum_k K_x \left(\frac{x_i - x_j}{h} \right) K_y \left(\frac{y_j - y_k}{h} \right),$$

where $K_x(.)$ is the kernel for $\hat{f}(.)$ and $K_y(.)$ is the kernel for $\hat{g}(.)$.

Appendix A

A.2   The Kolmogorov-Smirnov Statistic

The Kolmogorov-Smirnov statistic is intended to evaluate the goodness of fit of two empirical distribution functions in terms of the sup norm. Suppose $\hat{F}_{N_1}(x)$ and $\hat{F}_{N_2}(x)$ are the empirical distribution functions of two (independent) samples $(X_1, \ldots, X_{N_1})$ and $(Y_1, \ldots, Y_{N_2})$. The KS statistic is $KS = \sup \left| F_{N_1}(x) - F_{N_2}(x) \right|$. Smirnov derives the limiting distribution of $\sqrt{\frac{N_1 N_2}{N_1 + N_2}} KS$: $\lim_{N_1, N_2 \to \infty} \Pr(\sqrt{\frac{N_1 N_2}{N_1 + N_2}} KS \leq z) = 1 - 2 \sum_{i=1}^{\infty} (-1)^{i-1} \exp(-2i^2 z^2)$. The p-value for the KS statistic is obtained by evaluating the limiting distribution of the KS statistic. Exact p-values can be computed, but we use the first 5 terms to form the approximate p-values.

A.3   Local Regression Scatter Plot Smoother

A local regression scatter plot smoother known as lowess fits a line to a scatter plot by estimating the relationship between y and x at a number of target points over the range of the observed x values. It first identifies the q nearest neighbors of a target point x_0, denoted by $N(x_0)$, and then calculates weights w_i for each point in $N(x_0)$ using a weight function

$$W \left(\frac{|x_0 - x_i|}{\max_{N(x_0)} |x_0 - x_i|} \right).$$

Then it regresses y on $(1, x)$ for local linear fitting, using weighted least squares. Repeating this procedure for each target point traces out a function, the smoothed fit of y against x. As in the case of density estimation, the calculated smoother clearly depends on the choice of a weight function and a bandwidth. The choice of a weight function is a minor issue; we chose the tricube weight function: $W(z) = (1 - z^3)^3 \mathbf{I}_{[0,1]}(z)$. Bandwidths could be estimated using cross-validation or plug-in methods as in the case of density estimates.

326

B

Additional Tables

Tables B.1–B.19 follow on pages 328 to 358.

Table B.1 PUNEs and the decomposition of U.S. racism effect ($\delta_0 = 0.9$)

	Full	$r =$ rbar	$r =$ rbar, $\rho = \rho$min	Total effect	PBE	ASE	PBE (%)	ASE (%)
1976–1980								
α^D (mode)	0.6042							
α^R (mode)	0.2493							
t^D	0.3371	0.3619	0.4716	0.1345	0.0248	0.1097	18.44%	81.56%
t^R	0.2027	0.3321	0.4157	0.2130	0.1294	0.0836	60.75%	39.25%
r^D	3.2162							
r^R	4.2044							
t^{exp}	**0.2872**	**0.3537**	**0.4605**	**0.1733**	0.0665	0.1068	38.37%	61.63%
D vote share	0.4966	0.7251	0.8017	0.3051	0.2285	0.0766	74.89%	25.11%
No. of PUNEs	6	30	15					
1980–1984								
α^D (mode)	0.5026							
α^R (mode)	0.2742							
t^D	0.3985	0.4072	0.4433	0.0448	0.0087	0.0361	19.42%	80.58%
t^R	0.2094	0.3638	0.4109	0.2015	0.1544	0.0471	76.63%	23.37%
r^D	3.1437							
r^R	3.9426							
t^{exp}	**0.3301**	**0.3920**	**0.4336**	**0.1035**	0.0619	0.0417	59.75%	40.25%
D vote share	0.5204	0.6487	0.7013	0.1809	0.1283	0.0526	70.92%	29.08%
No. of PUNEs	13	43	18					
1984–1988								
α^D (mode)	0.4993							
α^R (mode)	0.3204							
t^D	0.3573	0.3801	0.4731	0.1158	0.0228	0.0930	19.69%	80.31%
t^R	0.2309	0.2842	0.3824	0.1515	0.0533	0.0982	35.18%	64.82%
r^D	2.9184							
r^R	3.8346							
t^{exp}	**0.3072**	**0.3504**	**0.4550**	**0.1478**	0.0432	0.1046	29.23%	70.77%
D vote share	0.4496	0.6903	0.8002	0.3506	0.2407	0.1099	68.65%	31.35%
No. of PUNEs	18	48	13					
1988–1992								
α^D (mode)	0.6393							
α^R (mode)	0.1759							
t^D	0.3044	0.3237	0.4097	0.1053	0.0193	0.0860	18.33%	81.67%
t^R	0.1642	0.2987	0.3999	0.2357	0.1345	0.1012	57.06%	42.94%
r^D	2.9781							
r^R	4.0335							
t^{exp}	**0.2642**	**0.3162**	**0.4067**	**0.1425**	0.0520	0.0905	36.52%	63.48%
D vote share	0.5476	0.7012	0.6924	0.1448	0.1536	−0.0088	106.08%	−6.08%
No. of PUNEs	12	30	13					

Table B.2a PUNEs and the decomposition of U.S. racism effect, Euclidean function approach (when bargaining powers are not restricted), 1984–1988

	Full	Counter 1	Counter 2i	Counter 2ii
$1-\alpha^D$	0.245104	0.486597	0.511553	0.52448
$1-\alpha^R$	0.26025	0.504362	0.526168	0.48243
t^D	3.02084	3.37193	3.8187	3.73251
t^R	2.5324	2.19913	2.57882	2.54923
r^D	2.8905			
r^R	3.83879			
t^{exp}	2.78408	2.79703	3.20799	3.11578
D vote share	0.515018	0.507677	0.506355	0.484496

Note: Counter 1 are P-PUNEs; Counters 2i and 2ii are Q-PUNEs under two of the three hypothetical racism-free distributions of voter types.

Table B.2b Policy-bundle (PB) and antisolidarity (AS) effects, Euclidean function approach (when bargaining powers are not restricted), 1984–1988

Party	PBE	ASE_i	ASE_{ii}	$\dfrac{TOT_i}{std.\ dev.}$	$\dfrac{TOT_{ii}}{std\ dev.}$
Democratic	0.3511	0.4468	0.3606	63.3%	56.5%
Republican	−0.3333	0.3797	0.3501	3.7%	1.3%
Average	0.0219	0.4110	0.3188	33.6%	26.3%

Note: TOT_i is $(PBE + ASE_i)$. Std. dev. is the standard deviation of the observed distribution of views on the racism issue.

Table B.2c PUNEs and the decomposition of U.S. racism effect, Euclidean function approach (when bargaining powers are not restricted), 1988–1992

	Full	Counter 1	Counter 2i	Counter 2ii
$1-\alpha^D$	0.439624	0.514357	0.482832	0.487626
$1-\alpha^R$	0.416716	0.519976	0.499244	0.478727
t^D	3.3263	3.43721	4.06049	3.88275
t^R	2.4131	2.22649	2.9176	2.77078
r^D	3.1669			
r^R	4.45699			
t^{exp}	2.85792	2.83509	3.49919	3.32199
D vote share	0.492704	0.505642	0.50658	0.497789

Note: For explanation of column heads, see note, Table B.2a.

Table B.2d Policy-bundle (PB) and antisolidarity (AS) effects, Euclidean function approach (when bargaining powers are not restricted), 1988–1992

	PBE	ASE_i	ASE_{ii}	$\dfrac{TOT_i}{\text{std. dev.}}$	$\dfrac{TOT_{ii}}{\text{std. dev.}}$
Democratic	0.1109	0.6233	0.4455	58.7%	44.5%
Republican	−0.1866	0.6911	0.5443	40.4%	28.6%
Average	−0.0228	0.6641	0.4869	51.3%	37.1%

Note: For explanation of TOT_i, see note, Table B.2b.

Table B.3 Variables from the National Election Studies

Variable name	Definition and coding
Abortion law	There has been some discussion about abortion during recent years. Which one of the opinions on this page best agrees with your view? 1. By law, abortion should never be permitted. 2. The law should permit abortion only in case of rape, incest, or when the woman's life is in danger. 3. The law should permit abortion for reasons other than rape, incest, or danger to the woman's life, but only after the need for the abortion has been clearly established. 4. By law, a woman should always be able to obtain an abortion as a matter of personal choice.
Aid to blacks	Some people feel that the government in Washington should make every possible effort to improve the social and economic position of blacks (1970: Negroes) and other minority groups. Others feel that the government should not make any special effort to help minorities because they should help themselves. 1. Government should help minority groups/blacks 2 . . . 6 7. Minority groups/blacks should help themselves
Bible authority	Here are four statements about the Bible and I'd like you to tell me which is closest to your own view. 1. The Bible is God's word and all it says is true. 2. The Bible was written by men inspired by God but it contains some human errors. 3. The Bible is a good book because it was written by wise men, but God had nothing to do with it. 4. The Bible was written by men who lived so long ago that it is worth very little today.
Black deserve	Over the past few years blacks have gotten less than they deserve. 1. Agree strongly; 2. Agree somewhat; 3. Neither agree nor disagree; 4. Disagree somewhat; 5. Disagree strongly.
Black difficult	Generations of slavery and discrimination have created conditions that make it difficult for blacks to work their way out of the lower class. 1. Agree strongly; 2. Agree somewhat; 3. Neither agree nor disagree; 4. Disagree somewhat; 5. Disagree strongly.

Variable name	Definition and coding
Black effort	It's really a matter of some people not trying hard enough; if blacks would only try harder they could be just as well off as whites. 1. Agree strongly; 2. Agree somewhat; 3. Neither agree nor disagree; 4. Disagree somewhat; 5. Disagree strongly.
Black favor	Irish, Italians, Jewish and many other minorities overcame prejudice and worked their way up. Blacks should do the same without any special favors. 1. Agree strongly; 2. Agree somewhat; 3. Neither agree nor disagree; 4. Disagree somewhat; 5. Disagree strongly.
Civil rights too fast	Some say that the civil rights people have been trying to push too fast. Others feel they haven't pushed fast enough. 1. Too slowly; 2. About right; 3. Too fast.
Feeling (affect) thermometer ratings	We would like to get your feelings toward some of these groups (Blacks, Whites, Poor People, Women's Liberation, Labor Union) . . . We call it a "feeling thermometer" because it measures your feelings towards groups. . . . If you don't know too much about a group or don't feel particularly warm or cold toward them, then you should place them in the middle, at the 50 degree mark. If you have a warm feeling toward a group or feel favorably toward it, you would give it a score somewhere between 50 degrees and 100 degrees, depending on how warm your feeling is toward the group. On the other hand, if you don't feel very favorably toward some of these groups—if there are some you don't care for too much—then you would place them somewhere between 0 degrees and 50 degrees.

Govt spending	Some people think the government should provide fewer services, even in areas such as health and education, in order to reduce spending. Other people feel that it is important for the government to provide many more services even if it means an increase in spending. Where would you place yourself on this scale, or haven't you thought much about this?
	    1. Government should provide many fewer services: reduce spending a lot.
	    2 . . . 6
	    7. Government should provide many more services: increase spending a lot.

Table B.3 (continued)

Variable name	Definition and coding
Govt defense spending	Some people believe that we should spend much less money for defense. Others feel that defense spending should be greatly increased. Where would you place yourself on this scale or haven't you thought much about this? 1. Greatly decrease defense spending. 2 . . . 6 7. Greatly increase defense spending.
Govt environmental spending	Should federal spending on <item> be increased, decreased or kept about the same? 1. Increased; 2. Same; 3. Decreased or cut out entirely.
Govt food stamp spending	Should federal spending on <item> be increased, decreased or kept about the same? 1. Increased; 2. Same; 3. Decreased or cut out entirely.
Govt health insurance	There is much concern about the rapid rise in medical and hospital costs. Some feel there should be a government insurance plan which would cover all medical and hospital expenses. Others feel that medical expenses should be paid by individuals, and through private insurance. Where would you place yourself on this scale, or haven't you thought much about this? 1. Government insurance plan. 2 . . . 6 7. Private insurance plan.
Govt public school spending	Should federal spending on <item> be increased, decreased or kept about the same? 1. Increased; 2. Same; 3. Decreased or cut out entirely.
Govt social security spending	Should federal spending on <item> be increased, decreased or kept about the same? 1. Increased; 2. Same; 3. Decreased or cut out entirely.
Helpful	Would you say that most of the time people try to be helpful, or that they are mostly just looking out for themselves? 1. Just look out for themselves; 2. Try to be helpful.

Variable name	Definition and coding
Job guarantee	Some people feel that the government in Washington should see to it that every person has a job and a good standard of living. Others think the government should just let each person get ahead on his/their own. And, of course, some other people have opinions somewhere in between. Where would you place yourself on this scale, or haven't you thought much about this? 1. Government see to job and good standard of living. 2 . . . 6 7. Government let each person get ahead on his own.
Less equality	The country would be better off if we worried less about how equal people are. 1. Agree strongly; 2. Agree somewhat; 3. Neither agree nor disagree; 4. Disagree somewhat; 5. Disagree strongly.
Party of presidential vote	Whom did you vote for, for President? 1. Democrat; 2. Republican; 3. Major third-party candidate.
Political ideology: Liberal-conservative scale	We hear a lot of talk these days about liberals and conservatives. Here is a 7-point scale on which the political views that people might hold are arranged from extremely liberal to extremely conservative. Where would you place yourself on this scale? 1. Extremely liberal; 2. Liberal; 3. Slightly liberal; 4. Moderate; 5. Slightly conservative; 6. Conservative; 7. Extremely conservative.
Political party affect	This is the number of Democratic (Republican) party 'likes' minus the number of Democratic (Republican) party 'dislikes' (VCF0314–VCF0315). −5 Maximum negative . . . +5 Maximum positive
School prayer	Some people think it is all right for the public schools to start each day with a prayer. Others feel that religion does not belong in the public schools but should be taken care of by the family and the church. Have you been interested enough in this to favor one side over the other? (IF YES) Which do you think— schools should be allowed to start each day with a prayer or religion does not belong in the schools? 1. Schools should be allowed to start with prayer; 3. Other; depends; both (1964–1968); DK; no interest; 5. Religion does not belong in the school.

Table B.3   (continued)

Variable name	Definition and coding

Strong govt	Some people are afraid the government in Washington is getting too powerful for the good of the country and the individual person. Others feel that the government in Washington is not getting too strong. Do you have an opinion on this or not?
	   1. Opinion: the government has not gotten too strong.
	   2. DK; depends; other; pro-con; no interest; no opinion.
	   3. Opinion: the government is getting too powerful.

Take advantage	Do you think most people would try to take advantage of you if they got a chance, or would they try to be fair? 0. Would try to be fair; 1. Would take advantage.

Trust govt	People have different ideas about the government in Washington. These ideas don't refer to Democrats or Republicans in particular, but just to government in general. We want to see how you feel about these ideas. How much of the time do you think you can trust the government in Washington to do what is right—just about always, most of the time or only some of the time?
	   1. None of the time; 2. Some of the time; 3. Most of the time;
	      4. Just about always.

Urban unrest	There is much discussion about the best way to deal with the problem of urban unrest and rioting. Some say it is more important to use all available force to maintain law and order—no matter what results. Others say it is more important to correct the problems of poverty and unemployment that give rise to the disturbances. Where would you place yourself on this scale, or haven't you thought much about this?
	   1. Solve problems of poverty and unemployment.
	   2 . . . 6
	   7. Use all available force.

Waste tax money	Do you think that people in the government waste a lot of money we pay in taxes, waste some of it, or don't waste very much of it? 1. A lot; 2. Some; 3. Not very much.

335

Variable name	Definition and coding
Women equal role	Recently there has been a lot of talk about women's rights. Some people feel that women should have an equal role with men in running business, industry and government. Others feel that a women's place is in the home. Where would you place yourself on this scale or haven't you thought much about this? 1. Women and men should have an equal role. 2 . . . 6 7. Women's place is in the home.

AGE: Age of respondents (VCF 0101).

COHORTS: To see the cohort effect, we construct cohort dummies from AGE. Our baseline cohort is the civil rights movement cohort, that is, people born in 1935–1947.

    PRE-CRM-COHORT: pre-civil rights movement cohort (1 for people born before 1935; 0 otherwise).

    POST-CRM-COHORT: post–civil rights movement cohort (1 for people born after 1948; 0 otherwise).

EDUCATION: 1 = Grade school or less (0–8 grades); 2 = High school (12 grades or fewer, incl. noncollege training if applicable); 3 = Some college (13 grades or more but no degree); 4 = College or advanced degree.

FEMALE: 1 = female; 0 = male.

INCOME: Only income brackets are provided in the NES. We chose a midpoint in each income bracket and converted it to the unit of $10,000.

MARRIED: Respondent's marital status: 1 = married; 0 = otherwise.

MOBILITY: There are two questions asking about how people are getting along financially these days. One question asks whether the respondent is better off than (1), the same as (2), or the worse off than (3) he/she was a year ago (personal financial situation in past yr). The other question asks about personal financial situation in next yr. From these two questions, we constructed two dummy variables measuring upward mobility and downward mobility.

UPMOBILE = 1 if the respondent is financially better off now than in last year and his/her personal financial situation is expected to be better next year; 0 otherwise.

DOWNMOBILE = 1 if the respondent is financially worse off now than in last year and his/her personal financial situation is expected to be worse next year; 0 otherwise.

PROTESTANTISM: 2 = Protestant and attend church more than twice in a month; 1 = Protestant but do not attend church regularly (less than twice in a month); 0 = otherwise.

PASTECONOMY: Would you say that over the past year the nation's economy has gotten better, stayed about the same or gotten worse? 1. Better. 3. Stayed same. 5. Worse.

REGION: 1. Northeast (CT, ME, MA, NH, NJ, NY, PA, RI, VT); 2. North Central (IL, IN, IA, KS, MI, MN, MO, NE, ND, OH, SD, WI); 3. South (AL, AR, DE, D.C., FL, GA, KY, LA, MD, MS, NC, OK, SC, TN, TX, VA, WV); 4. West (AK, AZ, CA, CO, HI, ID, MT, NV, NM, OR, UT, WA, WY).

UNEMPLOYED: Unemployment dummy constructed from VCF0116 (Respondent's WORK STATUS): 1 = Temporarily laid off or unemployed; 2 = Otherwise.

UNIONMEM: Union membership dummy constructed from VCF0127 (HOUSEHOLD UNION MEMBERSHIP): 1 = Someone in household belongs to a labor union; 2 = No one in household belongs to a labor union.

URBANISM: This variable represents respondent's sampling address. 1 = Central cities; 2 = Suburban area; 3 = Rural areas and small towns.

Table B.4a Decomposition with unrestricted bargaining powers, Euclidean function approach, UK, 1979

	Full	Counter 1	Counter 2i	Counter 2ii
$1-\alpha^L$	0.434599	0.510198	0.475027	0.524333
$1-\alpha^R$	0.369564	0.498685	0.452144	0.512589
t^L	3.91135	3.94786	4.50841	4.32633
t^R	2.991539	2.74204	3.40508	3.11746
r^L	3.40507			
r^R	3.67291			
t^{exp}	3.38156	3.33289	3.95378	3.71944
L vote share	0.470187	0.492588	0.498036	0.496414

Note: For explanation of column heads, see note, Table B.2a.

Table B.4b Policy-bundle (PB) and antisolidarity (AS) effects with unrestricted bargaining powers, Euclidean function approach, UK, 1979

Party	PBE	ASE_i	ASE_{ii}	$\frac{TOT_i}{std.\ dev.}$	$\frac{TOT_{ii}}{std.\ dev.}$
Labour	0.0365	0.5606	0.3785	46.28%	32.17%
Conservative	−0.1733	0.6630	0.3754	37.96%	15.66%
Average	−0.0487	0.6209	0.3866	44.36%	26.19%

Note: For explanation of TOT_i, see note, Table B.2b.

Table B.4c Decomposition with unrestricted bargaining powers, Euclidean function approach, UK, 1983

	Full	Counter 1	Counter 2i	Counter 2ii
$1-\alpha^L$	0.588988	0.441276	0.490011	0.506824
$1-\alpha^R$	0.37124	0.501893	0.481495	0.498353
t^L	3.85842	3.41695	4.02693	3.83914
t^R	2.70399	2.27385	2.88117	2.66953
r^L	3.01051			
r^R	3.18229			
t^{exp}	3.15074	2.86263	3.44678	3.24362
L vote share	0.380858	0.515706	0.492547	0.492304

Note: For explanation of column heads, see note, Table B.2a.

Table B.4d Policy-bundle (PB) and antisolidarity (AS) effects with unrestricted bargaining powers, Euclidean function approach, UK, 1983

Party	PBE	ASE_i	ASE_{ii}	$\dfrac{TOT_i}{std.\ dev.}$	$\dfrac{TOT_{ii}}{std.\ dev.}$
Labour	−0.4415	0.6099	0.4222	12.58%	−1.44%
Conservative	−0.4301	0.6073	0.3957	13.22%	−2.57%
Average	−0.2881	0.5842	0.3810	22.09%	6.93%

Note: For explanation of TOT_i, see note, Table B.2b.

Table B.4e Decomposition with unrestricted bargaining powers, Euclidean function approach, UK, 1997

	Full	Counter 1	Counter 2i	Counter 2ii
$1-\alpha^L$	0.361143	0.532481	0.479189	0.510451
$1-\alpha^R$	0.463458	0.469944	0.487817	0.479677
t^L	4.12166	4.51229	4.5195	4.53527
t^R	3.2374	3.44299	3.52946	3.51836
r^L	3.09885			
r^R	3.34731			
t^{exp}	3.74812	3.94917	4.03417	4.01453
L vote share	0.580352	0.477101	0.509114	0.486828

Note: For explanation of column heads, see note, Table B.2a.

Table B.4f Policy-bundle (PB) and antisolidarity (AS) effects with unrestricted bargaining powers, Euclidean function approach, UK, 1997

Party	PBE	ASE_i	ASE_{ii}	$\dfrac{TOT_i}{std.\ dev.}$	$\dfrac{TOT_{ii}}{std.\ dev.}$
Labour	0.3906	0.0072	0.0230	34.09%	36.03%
Conservative	0.2056	0.0865	0.0754	25.44%	24.47%
Average	0.2010	0.0850	0.0654	24.92%	23.21%

Note: For explanation of TOT_i, see note, Table B.2b.

Table B.5 Definition of the independent variables in Tables 8.8 and 8.10

Variable name, definition, and coding

ProPublicSector

Among other things, the parties disagree about how big the public sector should be. Some parties say we should cut down on public revenue and expenditure, others say we should expect increasing expenditure and revenue in the future. Where would you place yourself?

Public revenue and expenditure should be cut down a lot (−2)

Public revenue and expenditure should be cut down a little (−1)

Public revenue and expenditure are appropriate as they are now (0)

Public revenue and expenditure should increase a little (+1)

Public revenue and expenditure should increase a lot (+2)

AntiImmigration

Among other things, the parties disagree about how many refugees we can take. Some say we take too many. Others say we could easily take more. Where would you place yourself?

We should take a lot more refugees than we do now (−2)

We should take somewhat more refugees than we do now (−1)

We should keep on taking the same number as we do now (0)

We should take somewhat fewer refugees than we do now (+2)

We should take far fewer refugees than we do now (+2)

Law and Order

I am now going to mention some viewpoints from the political debate that one can agree with or disagree with. Violent offenses should be punished more severely than they are today.

Strongly disagree (−2)

Slightly disagree (−1)

Neither agree or disagree (0)

Agree (+1)

Strongly agree (+2)

Environment

I am now going to mention some viewpoints from the political debate that one can agree with or disagree with. The economic growth should be ensured through the building up of industry, even if it conflicts with environmental interests.

Strongly agree (−2)

Agree (−1)

Neither agree or disagree (0)

Slightly disagree (+1)

Strongly disagree (+2)

Variable name, definition, and coding

Same Econ Conditions
I am now going to mention some viewpoints from the political debate that one
can agree with or disagree with. In politics one should aim to provide the
same economic conditions for everyone, regardless of education or
occupation.
Strongly disagree (−2)
Slightly disagree (−1)
Neither agree or disagree (0)
Agree (+1)
Strongly agree (+2)

Unemployed Lazy
I am now going to mention some viewpoints from the political debate that one
can agree with or disagree with. In reality, many of the unemployed don't
want to take a job.
Strongly disagree (−2)
Slightly disagree (−1)
Neither agree or disagree (0)
Agree (+1)
Strongly agree (+2)

Take Advantage
I am now going to mention some viewpoints from the political debate that one
can agree with or disagree with. There are too many getting social security
benefits, who don't need it.
Strongly disagree (−2)
Slightly disagree (−1)
Neither agree or disagree (0)
Agree (+1)
Strongly agree (+2)

Household income
What is your household's total annual gross income—that is, before taxes?
Under 75,000 kr (1)
Between 75,000 and 99,999 kr (2)
Between 100,000 and 124,999 kr (3)
Between 125,000 and 149,999 kr (4)
Between 150,000 and 174,999 kr (5)
Between 175,000 and 199,999 kr (6)

Variable name, definition, and coding

> Between 200,000 and 249,999 kr (7)
> Between 250,000 and 299,999 kr (8)
> Between 300,000 and 349,999 kr (9)
> Between 350,000 and 399,999 kr (10)
> Between 400,000 and 449,999 kr (11)
> Between 450,000 and 499,999 kr (12)
> Between 500,000 and 599,999 kr (13)
> Between 600,000 and 699,999 kr (14)
> Between 700,000 and 799,999 kr (15)
> 800,000 kr and over (16)

City
  What type of town do you live in?
    Rural district (1)
    Town with less than 10,000 inhabitants (2)
    Town with 10,001–50,000 inhabitants (3)
    Town with 50,001–500,000 inhabitants (4)
    Capital city area (5)

Education
  What level of schooling did you complete?
    Primary schools, 7 years or less (1)
    Primary and lower secondary school, 8/9 years (2)
    10 years schooling/School-leaving exam (3)
    Matriculation/Senior high school exam (4)

Table B.6 Means and standard deviations for the independent variables in Tables 8.8 and 8.10.

| | 1997 | | | 2001 | | |
	Mean	Std. dev.	Obs.	Mean	Std. dev.	Obs.
AntiImmigration	0.67	1.02	1,948	0.70	1.01	1,972
ProPublicSector	−0.15	0.92	1,914	−0.24	0.91	1,967
Law and Order	1.38	1.01	1,976	1.43	0.99	2,008
Environment	0.54	1.29	1,933	0.49	1.28	1,944
Unemployed Lazy	0.09	1.40	1,935	0.02	1.39	1,977
Take Advantage	0.64	1.23	1,844	0.54	1.27	1,886
Same Econ Cond.	−0.42	1.39	1,933	−0.29	1.41	1,968
Household income	8.59	3.91	1,746	9.58	4.15	1,857
Female	0.46	0.50	2,001	0.48	0.50	2,026
Age	46.00	16.63	2,000	47.41	19.95	2,026
City	2.89	1.44	1,998	2.73	1.34	2,023
Education	2.72	1.09	1,992	2.76	1.08	2,025

Table B.7a Results of the 1988 presidential election, France

	First round April 24	Second round May 8
Number of registered voters	38,179,118	38,168,869
Total number of ballots	31,059,300	32,085,071
Number of valid ballots	30,436,744	30,923,249
Abstention (in percent)	18.6%	15.9%

Table B.7b Results of the 1988 presidential election, France, by candidate

Candidate	First round		Second round		Coalition
	No. of voters	Percentage of total	No. of voters	Percentage of total	
F. Mitterrand (Parti Socialiste)	10,381,332	34.1	16,704,279	54.0	L
J. Chirac (Rassemblement pour la République)	6,075,160	20.0	14,218,970	46.0	R
R. Barre (Union pour la Démocratie Française)	5,035,144	16.5			R
J.-M. Le Pen (Front National)	4,376,742	14.4			ER
A. Lajoinie (Parti Communiste)	2,056,261	6.7			L
A. Waechter (Verts)	1,149,897	3.8			L
P. Juquin (Parti Communiste Diss.)	639,133	2.1			L
A. Laguiller (Lutte Ouvrière)	606,201	2.0			L
P. Boussel (Parti des Travailleurs)	116,874	0.4			L

Table B.8a Results of the 1995 presidential election, France

	First round April 23	Second round May 7
Number of registered voters	39,993,954	39,976,944
Total number of ballots	31,346,960	31,845,819
Number of valid ballots	30,464,552	29,943,671
Abstention (in percent)	21.62%	20.34%

Table B.8b Results of the 1995 presidential election, France, by candidate

Candidate	First round		Second round		
	No. of voters	Percentage of total	No. of voters	Percentage of total	Coalition
L. Jospin (Parti Socialiste)	7,098,191	23.30	14,180,644	47.4	L
J. Chirac (Rassemblement pour la République)	6,348,696	20.84	15,763,027	52.6	R
E. Balladur (Union pour la Démocratie Française)	5,658,996	18.58			R
J.-M. Le Pen (Front National)	4,571,138	15.00			ER
R. Hue (Parti Communiste)	2,632,936	8.64			L
A. Laguiller (Lutte Ouvrière)	1,615,653	5.30			L
P. de Villiers (Mouvement pour la France)	1,443,235	4.74			R
D. Voynet (Verts)	1,010,738	3.32			L
J. Cheminade (Solidarité et progrès)	84,969	0.28			ER

Table B.9a Results of the 2002 presidential election, France

	First round April 22	Second round May 5
Number of registered voters	41,194,689	41,191,151
Total number of ballots	29,495,733	32,831,501
Number of valid ballots	28,498,471	31,066,781
Abstention (in percent)	28.40%	20.29%

Table B.9b Results of the 2002 presidential election, France, by candidate

Candidate	First round		Second round		Coalition
	No. of voters	Percentage of total	No. of voters	Percentage of total	
J. Chirac (Rassemblement pour la République)	5,665,855	19.88	25,540,874	82.21	R
J.-M. Le Pen (Front National)	4,804,713	16.86	5,525,907	17.79	ER
L. Jospin (Parti Socialiste)	4,610,113	16.18			L
F. Bayrou (Union pour la Démocratie Française)	1,949,170	6.84			R
A. Laguiller (Lutte Ouvrière)	1,630,045	5.72			L
J.-P. Chevènement (Mouvement des Citoyens)	1,518,528	5.33			L
N. Mamère (Verts)	1,495,724	5.25			L
O. Besancenot (Ligue Communiste Rév.)	1,210,562	4.25			L

J. Saint-Josse (Chasse Pêche Nature et Tradition)	1,204,689	4.23	R
A. Madelin (Démocratie Libérale)	1,113,484	3.91	R
R. Hue (Parti Communiste)	960,480	3.37	L
B. Mégret (Mouvement National Républicain)	667,026	2.34	ER
C. Taubira (Parti Radical de Gauche)	660,447	2.32	L
C. Lepage (CAP 21)	535,837	1.88	R
C. Boutin (Union pour la Démocratie Française)	339,112	1.19	R
D. Glückstein (Parti des Travailleurs)	132,686	0.47	L

Table B.10 Distribution of economic antiliberalism (percent)

Question: Does the word "privatization" have a positive or negative connotation for you?

Answer	1988		1995		2002	
	Includes "no answer"	Excludes "no answer"	Includes "no answer"	Excludes "no answer"	Includes "no answer"	Excludes "no answer"
Very positive	11.1	13.9	8.8	9.8	4.1	4.7
Positive	32.5	40.9	40.5	45.2	41.4	47.1
Negative	25.2	31.8	29.4	32.9	33.7	38.4
Very negative	10.6	13.4	10.8	12.1	8.6	9.1
No answer	20.7		10.4		12.1	
Obs.	4,032	3,199	4,078	3,652	4,107	3,609
Mean (scale 0–3)	1.45		1.47		1.53	
Std. dev. (scale 0–3)	0.89		0.83		0.73	

348

Table B.11 Distribution of support for welfare programs (percent)

Question: The state should guarantee a minimum revenue to all households. (1988)
Does the word "solidarity" have a positive or a negative connotation for you? (1995, 2002)

Answer	1988		1995		2002	
	Includes "no answer"	Excludes "no answer"	Includes "no answer"	Excludes "no answer"	Includes "no answer"	Excludes "no answer"
Strongly disagree / Very negative	3.6	3.7	2.2	2.2	1.1	1.1
Rather disagree / negative	6.7	6.8	7.2	7.3	4.9	4.9
Rather agree / positive	31.5	32.1	34.8	54.2	34.2	34.5
Strongly agree / Very positive	56.2	57.4	54.7	55.3	58.9	59.4
No answer	2.0		1.1		0.9	
Obs.	4,032	3,952	4,078	4,031	4,107	4,069
Mean (scale 0–3)		2.43		2.43		2.52
Std. dev. (scale 0–3)		0.78		0.72		0.65

Table B.12 Correlation between Antiliberalism and Support for welfare

	1988	1995	2002
Correlation Antiliberalism / Pro-welfare	0.19	−0.01	0.06
Obs.	3,156	3,633	3,602

Table B.13 Distribution of economic views (percent)

	1988		1995		2002	
	Includes "no answer"	Excludes "no answer"	Includes "no answer"	Excludes "no answer"	Includes "no answer"	Excludes "no answer"
0	1.0	1.3	0.2	0.3	0.1	0.1
1	3.1	3.9	1.1	1.2	0.8	0.9
2	6.3	8.1	6.3	7.1	3.5	3.9
3	18.0	22.9	23.9	26.8	20.2	23.1
4	25.0	31.9	32.2	36.2	34.4	39.3
5	17.1	21.9	18.3	20.6	22.5	25.7
6	7.8	10.0	7.0	7.9	6.2	7.0
No answer	21.7		10.9		12.3	
Obs.	4,032	3,156	4,078	3,633	4,107	3,602
Mean		3.86		3.91		4.06
Std. dev.		1.31		1.10		1.01

Table B.14 Distribution of views about the number of immigrants (percent)

Question: There are too many immigrants in France.

Answer	1988		1995		2002	
	Includes "no answer"	Excludes "no answer"	Includes "no answer"	Excludes "no answer"	Includes "no answer"	Excludes "no answer"
Strongly disagree	13.2	14.0	10.6	10.8	15.7	16.1
Disagree	16.2	17.2	14.1	14.3	21.7	22.3
Agree	29.9	31.7	32.4	33.0	30.0	30.8
Strongly agree	34.9	37.1	41.0	41.8	30.0	30.0
No answer	5.8		1.9		2.5	
Obs.	4,032	3,796	4,078	4,000	4,107	4,003
Mean (scale 0–3)		1.92		2.06		1.76
Std. dev. (scale 0–3)		1.05		1.00		1.06

Table B.15 Distribution of feelings on whether one feels at home (percent)

Question: Nowadays, we do not feel at home as we used to.

	1988		1995		2002	
	Includes "no answer"	Excludes "no answer"	Includes "no answer"	Excludes "no answer"	Includes "no answer"	Excludes "no answer"
Strongly disagree	23.5	24.4	19.9	20.4	16.0	16.4
Disagree	23.8	24.6	21.5	22.0	29.8	30.6
Agree	22.6	23.4	23.3	23.8	30.4	31.3
Strongly agree	26.7	27.6	33.0	33.8	21.3	21.9
No answer	3.4		2.3		2.4	
Obs.	4,032	3,893	4,078	3,984	4,107	4,007
Mean (scale 0–3)		1.54		1.71		1.58
Std. dev. (scale 0–3)		1.13		1.14		1.00

Table B.16 Correlation between Too many immigrants / Do not feel at home
anymore

	1988	1995	2002
Correlation Too many immigrants / Do not feel at home	0.46	0.64	0.58
Obs.	3,689	3,919	3,919

Table B.17 Distribution of anti-immigration views (percent)

	1988		1995		2002	
	Includes "no answer"	Excludes "no answer"	Includes "no answer"	Excludes "no answer"	Includes "no answer"	Excludes "no answer"
0	8.0	8.7	7.8	8.1	8.0	8.4
1	7.8	8.5	6.8	7.1	9.5	10.0
2	11.9	13.0	11.0	11.5	14.5	15.2
3	17.0	18.5	13.4	13.9	15.8	16.5
4	15.9	17.3	15.9	16.6	17.8	18.7
5	13.9	15.2	15.6	16.2	15.2	16.0
6	17.1	18.7	25.5	26.6	14.5	15.2
No answer	8.5		3.9		4.6	
Obs.	4,032	3,689	4,078	3,919	4,107	3,919
Mean		3.48		3.79		3.36
Std. dev.		1.87		1.93		1.84

Table B.18 Correlation of opinion variables with ProPublicSector and AntiImmigration, 1988

	ProPublicSector	AntiImmigration
Economic issues		
The French do not work hard enough.	−0.19	0.20
If everybody earned the same amount of money, they would have no incentive to work.	−0.14	0.13
Whether children perform well at school or not depends more on their social background than on their own skills.	0.05	0.05
When speaking about someone who made a fortune in a few years, do you rather feel admiration or distrust?	−0.13	−0.04
To face economic hardships, do you think that the state should trust private firms and give them more freedom or rather impose more controls and regulation on them?	0.60	−0.02
Can you tell me if the word "profit" has rather a positive connotation for you?	−0.18	0.03
Can you tell me if the word "stock exchange" has rather a positive connotation for you?	−0.19	0.00
Can you tell me if the word "nationalizations" has rather a positive connotation for you?	0.28	−0.19
Can you tell me if the word "firm" has rather a positive connotation for you?	−0.15	−0.03
The "Impôt sur les grandes fortunes" (a tax paid only by very wealthy households) should be reenacted.	0.40	−0.09
If the social security system were suppressed, would you say that it would be very terrible, quite terrible, somewhat terrible or not a problem at all?	0.18	−0.02
Immigration issues		
Jews have too much power in France.	0.08	0.48
Muslims living in France ought to have mosques to practice their religion.	0.02	0.44
Law and order / Society issues		
Death penalty should be reenacted.	0.00	0.56
In a society, one needs hierarchy and chiefs.	−0.09	0.28
Homosexuality is morally condemnable.	−0.02	0.28
The role of women is before anything else to have children and raise them.	0.03	0.32

Table B.18 (continued)

Note: When the wording of the variable appears as a statement (e.g., "The French do not work hard enough"), the variable is coded as a binary variable which takes value 1 if the respondent agrees with the statement and value 0 otherwise. When the wording of the variable appears as a yes-or-no question (e.g., "Can you tell me if the word 'profit' has rather a positive connotation for you?"), the variable is coded as a binary variable which takes value 1 if the respondent answers yes and value 0 otherwise. For the question "When speaking about someone who made a fortune . . . ," the coding is 1 if the answer is "admiration" and 0 if the answer is "distrust." For the question "To face economic hardship . . . ," the coding is 0 if the answer is "the state should trust private firms . . ." and 1 otherwise. For the question "If the social security system were suppressed . . . ," the coding is 0 if the answer is "not a problem at all" and 1 otherwise.

357

Table B.19 Correlation of opinion variables with ProPublicSector and AntiImmigration, 2002

	ProPublicSector	AntiImmigration
Economic issues		
(1) Firms should have the right to hire or fire depending on the situation. (2) Firms should undergo control by the state before being allowed to fire. Do you agree most with (2)?	0.22	−0.02
(1) People may tend to be happy with the "Revenu Minimum d'Insertion" (a welfare benefit) and not look for work. (2) It helps people go through hard times. Do you agree most with (2)?	0.20	−0.33
The number of civil servants should be reduced. Do you agree?	−0.26	0.16
The word "profit" has rather a positive connotation for you.	−0.30	0.10
The SNCF (national railway company) would work better if it were privatized. Do you agree with this statement?	−0.31	0.25
Immigration issues		
The presence of immigrants in France is an opportunity of cultural enrichment.	0.19	−0.59
Some races are less gifted than others.	−0.17	0.49
Jews have too much power in France.	−0.14	0.42
Can you tell me if the word "Islam" has rather a positive connotation for you?	0.12	−0.45
Can you tell me if the word "United States" has rather a positive connotation for you?	−0.18	0.17
In France, the blacks and Maghribi are too often treated as second-order citizens.	0.19	−0.34
Law and order / Society issues		
Death penalty should be reenacted.	−0.24	0.54
In a society, one needs hierarchy and chiefs.	−0.14	0.28
To fight against delinquency, family benefits should be withdrawn from families with juvenile delinquents.	−0.20	0.44
Can you tell me if the word "authority" has rather a positive or negative connotation for you?	−0.07	0.22
Same-sex couples should have the right to adopt children.	0.13	−0.26
Homosexuality is an acceptable way of living one's sexuality.	0.12	−0.29

Note: See note, Table B.18.

Notes

1. Introduction

1. Karl Marx, "Free trade and the Chartists," *New York Daily Tribune,* August 25, 1852.

2. See McWilliams (1939) for a classical study of how growers used racism to prevent farm labor from organizing. See Roemer (1979) for a model of "divide and conquer" in the workplace.

3. Of course, the opposite case is theoretically possible. If the economic issue is more salient than the race issue, the (1, 1) voter will vote Democratic, although that party does not represent his views on the race issue, and the (0, 0) voter will vote Republican despite the Republican party's stance on race issues, which he dislikes. In this case, the voter separation curve should be steeper. This is, however, not the empirical case in the United States, although it has typically been the case in the UK. See Chapters 4 and 6 for details.

4. The Dixiecrats are described in Chapter 3 below.

5. This statement is not precise. There are singular cases when Downsian equilibrium exists with multi-dimensional policy spaces; see Roemer (2001, chap. 1).

6. Harold Hotelling (1929) first proposed what we now denote as the Downs model.

7. Indeed, both uncertainty and ideological parties are necessary to produce an equilibrium with policy differentiation. With certainty, the equilibrium of the Wittman model has both parties playing the median voter's ideal policy. For details, consult Roemer (2001, §3.6).

8. Our research was completed before the fall of 2005, when two important events transpired: the riots in French cities by North African residents, and the publication of cartoons in the Danish newspaper *Jyllands Posten* that enflamed the Islamic

world. These events are, however, consistent with our decision to study France and Denmark.

9. It is also worth remarking that both racism and nationalism were created in Europe at the beginning of the nineteenth century, reaching a historical climax in the fascist period of 1930s Europe, a period noted for the intensity of racism.

10. Jean-Marie Le Pen also once denounced his former deputy, Bruno Mégret, who had formed a rival "nationalist" party, as "racist." We note that *Action Française*, a right-wing nationalist journal, has argued since 1927 for an equivalence of the concepts of "racism," "xenophobia," "nationalism," and "being truly French" (Miles and Brown 2003).

2. Political Equilibrium: Theory and Application

1. The precise statement is that these two goals are equivalent as long as it is not feasible to achieve a vote share of unity. This will be the case at the equilibria in our applications.

2. We are here representing the Opportunists as having the vNM utility function $\pi(\tau, \tau^2)$; recall that in section 2.4.1, we represented them as having the vNM utility function $\mathbf{F}(\Omega(\tau, \tau^2))$ and we discussed these two alternatives.

3. There is a housewife whose actual *labor income* is zero while her husband's labor income is quite large. This is not inconsistent with our assumption that a wife's imputed *wage rate* is proportional to her husband's wage rate (and therefore positive), because the wife may rationally opt for not participating in the labor market. As we will see below, a wife may provide no labor supply if her husband's labor income is sufficiently high.

4. Since O is the asset income accumulated from the past labor income, not *current* labor income, voters take O as given when they choose labor supply, and so we did not use the relationship between O and W when we derived the labor supply functions.

5. Our approach is justified if an allocation of *individual* time between work and leisure for singles is similar to the allocation of *family* time between work and leisure for married couples, and the total endowment of time available for singles (λ_S) is similar to the total endowment of time available at the family level for married couples ($\lambda_M + k_1\lambda_F$). Note that λ is the time that can be allocated between work and leisure after housekeeping (including child rearing) is finished. Each individual of a married couple generally spends more time than a single in housekeeping and child rearing, so λ_M and λ_F will be much smaller than λ_S. We do not think that a model with separate subutility functions for singles and married couples would produce very different results. Attitudes of singles toward redis-

tribution may be different from those of married couples, not because they have different utility functions, but rather because singles have lower wage rates, on average, than married couples.

6. Equivalently, both parties are constrained to propose $r = \bar{r}$.

7. It is well known that the order of decomposition is not unique, and so researchers usually compute each effect by taking the average of the effects obtained from all possible orders of the decomposition. We do not do this because the computation is quite intensive and the difference due to different orders of decomposition is usually not large.

3. History of Racial Politics in the United States

1. Lott quoted in Edsall (2002, sec. A, p. 6).

2. Sullivan quoted in Rutenberg and Barringer (2002, sec. A, p. 31).

3. Dean quoted in "Dean Makes Racial-Political History," *Black Commentator*, December 11, 2003.

4. Carmines and Stimson (1989) suggest that it is a fruitless academic endeavor to trace the origin of racial issues in American politics simply because some event or issue cluster always seems to predate what might be identified as the critical moment. For example, the election of 1964 was certainly critical, but this event was preceded by the court-enforced school desegregation in Little Rock following *Brown v. Board of Education*, which in turn was preceded by desegregation of the armed forces, which was preceded by the passage of the Thirteenth, Fourteenth, and Fifteenth amendments, which was preceded by the Civil War, which was preceded by the "slave as three-fifths of a person" compromise, and so on. Ultimately Carmines and Stimson conclude, "we ought not look for the origin of racial issues in American politics because racial issues predate American politics" (62).

5. The exact phrasing of the three-fifths clause of the Constitution is found in section 2 of Article I: "Representatives and direct Taxes shall be apportioned among the several States which may be included within this Union, according to their respective Numbers, which shall be determined by adding to the whole Number of free Persons, including those bound to Service for a Term of Years, and excluding Indians not taxed, three fifths of all other Persons." It was altered by section 2 of the Fourteenth Amendment.

6. It is interesting that states' rights were utilized as a rationale for the defense of the two racial scourges in U.S. history, namely slavery and later segregation.

7. The authors' analysis indicates that realignments in the standard meaning of the term occurred only in the 1850s.

8. As norms shifted toward equality, appeals to race could no longer be made explicit. As will be discussed further below, such appeals were made through code words, and indeed, it is increasingly difficult to identify racist rhetoric as it is masked with legitimately conservative ideology.

9. This circumstance perhaps supports the contention of Poole and Rosenthal's model that the economic cleavage once again reemerged as the primary one.

10. For a more detailed analysis of electoral capture, see Frymer (1999). The concept of electoral capture refers to "those circumstances when the group has no choice but to remain in the party. The opposing party does not want the group's vote, so the group cannot threaten its own party's leaders with defection. The party leadership, then, can take the group for granted because it recognizes that, short of abstention or an independent (and usually electorally suicidal) third party, the group has no where else to go. Placed in this position by the party system, a captured group will often find its interests neglected by their own party leaders" (8). Frymer claims that African Americans were electorally captured by the Republicans between 1866 and 1932 (see pages 49–86) and by the Democrats from 1964 to the present (87–119).

11. Thurmond's earlier career as a legislator and lawyer reveal support for the abolition of the poll tax, the provision of secret balloting, and the prosecution of lynchings of African Americans. This record leads Kari Frederickson (2001) to claim, "Thurmond's racism drew from a well-worn paternalism that stressed responsibility for black southerners. However, victory demanded that Thurmond maintain the support of the more radical elements within the movement" (171).

12. Thurmond quoted in Frederickson (2001, 140).

13. Various political scientists have offered theories, including racial threat, that might account for the white flight from the southern wing of the Democratic Party as African Americans began to flock to it. See Giles and Hertz (1994), Huckfeldt and Kohfeld (1989), Bobo (1988), and Oliver and Mendelberg (2000), among others.

14. While most analysis of the realignment genre refer to the election of 1932 as the last electoral realignment, Kinder and Sanders (1996, 218) make a convincing argument that 1964 constitutes a full realignment. They highlight that the election was precipitated by a divisive and intense crisis on racial matters, that it offered voters a clear choice in Johnson versus Goldwater on both sides of the issue, and that the election witnessed a record increase in voter turnout. Poole and Rosenthal's analysis also perceives something akin to a realignment occurring in 1964, although they refer to it as a mere "perturbation" (Poole and Rosenthal 1997, 109–111).

15. Himelstein (quoted in Kinder and Sanders 1996, 223) defines a racial code as "a word or phrase which communicates a well-understood but implicit meaning to part of a public audience while preserving for the speaker deniability of that

meaning by reference to its denotative meaning . . . Code words are intended as rhetorical winks, and if they are too easily detected they lose their deniability and thus their effectiveness." This definition is similar to Mendelberg's notion of implicit racial appeals.

16. Nixon quoted in Carter (1996, 30).

17. Wallace quoted in J. Mayer (2002, 86).

18. McGovern quoted in J. Mayer (2002, 113).

19. It is interesting to note that the electoral success attributed to the exploitation of the Horton story and the racial politics that it involved led to increasing use of similar tactics in other elections, especially in the South. We quote Dan Carter's findings at length: "For thirty years, most respectable candidates preferred to leave the explicit manipulation of racial fears to politicians like George Wallace who operated on the periphery of American politics. But that line has been eroding since the Ailes ads of the 1988 campaign. In several high-profile races at the beginning of the 1990s, candidates reached down into the grab bag of racial fears to drum up votes. In Louisiana, former Ku Klux Klan leader David Duke, a state representative who had gained the gubernatorial nomination of the Louisiana Republican Party, finished second to Edwin Edwards in Louisiana's open primary, edging out incumbent governor Buddy Roemer . . . In Alabama, Republican Guy Hunt won reelection to the governorship after repeatedly linking his Democratic opponent with black leaders through television advertisements. And North Carolina senator Jesse Helms showed how devastating racial fears could be in his campaign against Harvey Gantt, a black former mayor of Charlotte who had drawn strong support from white voters. Against the surprisingly popular Gantt, Helms used the race issue at every turn, most powerfully in a television ad in which a white worker crumpled a job rejection letter to the accompaniment of a sober voice: 'You were qualified for the job, but it had to go to a minority because of quotas'" (Carter 1996, 82–83).

20. Clinton condemned as racist Sista Soulja's comment in reference to the L.A. riots, "I mean if black people kill black people every day, why not have a week and kill white people" (quoted in J. Mayer 2002, 242).

21. For a more detailed analysis of the theory of electoral capture, see Frymer (1999).

22. For more on the theory of the long realignment of the South toward the Republican party as it was solidified during Reagan's presidency, see Black and Black (2002).

23. The last portion of the passage—"these women are inner-city substance-abusing blacks spawning a criminal class"—is quoted by Carter from the *New York Times*, November 16, 1994.

4. United States: Quantitative Analysis

1. Higher-income blacks are not more likely to vote Republican, as are their white counterparts. In the 1992 NES survey, for instance, every black earning $75,000 ($N = 23$) voted for Clinton.

2. See Kinder and Sanders (1996), Sniderman and Piazza (1993), and contributions in the volume edited by Sears, Sidanius, and Bobo (2000).

3. Researchers often use political ideology as a controlling variable in their regressions, and frequently find that political ideology is a strong predictor of voting pattern and attitude toward social policies. But to the extent that political ideology is a *mixture* of various political attitudes, it is not clear what can be inferred from a statistically significant coefficient on "political ideology." A similar point was made by Best (1999) about Stimson's (1999) "policy mood" variable. By extracting four core components from the survey materials, we are decomposing the ambiguous concept of political ideology into orthogonal dimensions.

4. Precise wordings for these variables are reported in Appendix Table B.3. We chose an approximately equal number of variables (two or three) for each factor. Some better variables, in particular regarding libertarianism, are available in some years, but we are constrained to choose the variables that are available for all coverage years; otherwise our measurement will be inconsistent across years. Our choice of covered years is also, by and large, driven by the availability of these ten variables.

5. We do not wish to call compassion *egalitarianism,* for compassion is neither sufficient nor necessary for egalitarianism. For instance, feminism can also be based on an egalitarian view. Conversely a person can be compassionate even if she rejects the egalitarian principle, perhaps, due to the disincentive effect of equality (for example, "compassionate conservatives"). Finally, egalitarianism is a complex view, which spans views from outcome egalitarianism to opportunity egalitarianism to an equal treatment principle.

6. It is interesting to note that this factor loads negatively on the welfare thermometer, although its loading is almost nil for the poor thermometer. This result is consistent with Gilens's (1999) observation that "welfare," "AFDC," or "food stamps" in the United States are "code words" for blacks. Our factor analytic solution is robust. Factor scores obtained from an oblique solution (using promax rotation, not reported here) are nearly identical to those from the orthogonal solution (using varimax rotation).

7. Because we computed factor scores year by year, they have mean zero and standard deviation 1 for all years. Average scores cannot be directly compared across years.

8. Obviously bivariate correlations may not reveal the true correlation. Our multivariate regressions of four political factors on demographic factors, however, exhibit similar patterns.

9. When dependent variables take more than three different values, we run OLS regressions rather than ordered probit regressions, because ordered probit regressions are less robust than OLS when (unknown) error terms are not normally distributed. When dependent variables take more than three values, the choice between OLS and ordered probit regressions is usually arbitrary. Although we do not report the details here, ordered probit regressions do not change our results.

10. Kinder and Mendelberg (2000) push this issue further and establish two important points. First, the racially oriented individualism index, such as "blacks should try harder," is a potent component of opposition to racial policy while it has *no* effect on race-neutral policies focusing on general social class or gender. Second, in contrast, measures of race-neutral individualism *do not* influence attitudes on racial policy issues, although they *do* have effects on the role of government and general (that is, race-neutral) social policies. Thus they call the view "blacks should try harder" *racialized individualism*. In other words, this kind of measure mixes convictions about individual responsibility with resentment directed toward blacks. Schuman et al. (1997) point out that white acceptance of any role in having created black disadvantage appears to occur most clearly when responsibility is treated as shared by both races, rather than as focused entirely on whites themselves.

11. We checked a possible nonlinear effect of income by adding a quadratic term of the income variable. There is no evidence that income exercises a nonlinear effect. We also checked whether entering the log of income improves the result. We found no difference. Indeed all the four components of political ideology are very weakly correlated with incomes.

12. A similar finding, that authoritarianism is strongly correlated with racism in some European countries, is reported by Pettigrew (2000).

13. In 1980, for instance, the "born-again" white Christians gave Reagan 61 percent of their vote. Comparatively speaking, they tend to be rural, southern, and less educated than the rest of the population.

14. We also note that the level of trust is much lower in evangelical groups than among average white Americans.

15. We point out that Abramowitz's racism variables mainly measure Jim Crow racism.

16. One may argue that ordered probit regressions may allow one to estimate the cut-off points as well as regression coefficients for categorical dependent variables, but it is well known that estimates obtained from the maximum likelihood estimation method are not robust if the error term is not normally distributed. This problem is serious for the estimates of the cutoff points. We do not attempt to estimate these cutoff points. We used the OLS estimation method, which is more robust to possible misspecifications, after taking the logistic transformation of the dependent variable.

17. When we estimate the distribution of voter types, however, we avoid the problem of censoring by assuming that blacks are distributed on the support of [0.5, 1.5] according to a normal distribution with mean 1 and a small variance. See section 4.3. In econometric estimation, censoring is not a problem as long as the racism variable appears as an explanatory variable or when the regressions are undertaken for whites and blacks separately. Also no whites have racism-induced aid-to-blacks scores less than 1.5.

18. Indeed estimating a fully bivariate density when the correlation between the two variables is very weak does more harm than good, because kernel estimates of joint densities are in general inaccurate unless the sample size is large. Silverman (1986, 92–93) describes the "empty-space phenomenon," where very few points are around the origin when the dimension is greater than 1.

19. Positive taxable income at the family level does not necessarily mean that the wage rate earned by the male in the family is positive.

20. Is the distribution of incomes among respondents in the NES close to the distribution of incomes among respondents in the PSID? We compared percentile incomes in the NES with the corresponding percentile incomes in the PSID; we find that they are very similar.

21. Another way of constructing the joint density for the entire population is to form bivariate densities separately for whites and blacks and then add these two densities with weights according to their population weights. In drawing pictures, we used this method; in numerical computations, however, we use the first method because it saves on computation time.

22. There may be some bias in our estimated post-fisc incomes. First, taxes reported in the PSID are calculated after taking out exemptions but not deductions. Also the post-fisc income does not include tax credits (such as child credit, or Earned Income Credit [EIC]). These two facts will generate a downward bias in the estimated post-fisc incomes. Second, we are unable to include the housing rent subsidy and the monetary value of public education or public health (such as Medicaid), because there is no information about their value. This will also generate downward bias in the estimated transfer amounts and hence in post-fisc incomes.

23. Two factors explain the gradual increase. First, female participation in the labor force has increased, which has increased the fraction of females who earn positive wages, and many female workers moved from part-time to full-time. Second, the wage rates for female employees relative to those of male employees have improved. The ratio k_1 is somewhat higher if we confine the calculation to samples of working individuals. It was about 0.51 in 1984 for samples with working individuals, but the general tendency is the same.

24. They estimate elasticities by several methods; we chose those elasticities recommended in Blundell et al. (1988).

25. The tax rate that maximizes government revenue, according to the Laffer curve, is about 0.71–0.74, substantially higher than Laffer conjectured.

26. This constraint is not tautological, because we are imposing the condition that the vote share our model predicts at the *observed* platform be equal to the observed vote share. We will compute the equilibrium platforms and the predicted vote share at the *equilibrium* value, and compare this with the observed vote share.

27. Thus there may be some bias in our estimated coefficients in this period.

28. But this is not true in general. The bargaining powers vary over years. We find that in party D, the bargaining power of the Opportunists is usually around 0.55. But in the Republican Party, Militants are much stronger. The mean bargaining power of the Opportunists in the Republican Party is 0.1940 in 1976–1980, 0.2214 in 1980–1984, 0.4909 in 1984–1988, and 0.0705 in 1988–1992.

29. $I_{[0,1]}(z)$ is an indicator function which takes the value of 1 if z is in the interval $[0, 1]$ and 0 otherwise.

30. This does not mean that there have been no attempts at explaining the disparity between the theoretical prediction of the Downsian models and the historical observation. Bénabou and Tirole (2002) show that beliefs in a just world may affect redistribution politics in a significant way. Bénabou and Ok (2001) and Piketty (1995) show how perceptions about social mobility can affect the equilibrium outcome. Although there have been some attempts to examine the effect of social mobility and/or beliefs in a just world on political outcomes with cross-country regressions, whether Americans changed their beliefs significantly during the period in a way consistent with the prediction of these models is a question for future research.

5. History of Racism and Xenophobia in the United Kingdom

1. See "Domestic issues back under spotlight," http://www.mori.com/polls/2003/mpm030428.shtml, accessed August 2004.

2. "Last-chance election for Britain, Hague says," *The Times*, March 5, 2001.

3. In Great Britain, the term "ethnic minority," as used by the census, refers to Asian or Asian British (Indian, Pakistani, Bangladeshi, Other Asian), Black or Black British (Black Caribbean, Black African, Black Other), Chinese, and Other. Individuals who belong to one of these groups are generally first- and second-generation immigrants. The remainder of this chapter will use the terms "immigrants" and "minorities" interchangeably.

4. According to the 1961 census, over three quarters of immigrants originating from the "British Caribbean, India, Pakistan, British Africa (excluding . . . South Africa), Cyprus and Malta were resident in the Greater London area" (Patterson 1969, 195).

5. According to the government-sponsored 1968 PEP (Political and Economic Planning) Report investigating discrimination in England, "those coloured people actually housed [in council housing] might be housed discreetly and inconspicuously to avoid hostility from white residents, directed against both the coloured people themselves and the local council. Such discretion might also take the form of housing them in old properties acquired by the council in localities scheduled for redevelopment, rather than council estates where the fact that they were council tenants would be obvious" (Daniel 1968, 177). Daniel goes on to note that these actions, often based on complex, bureaucratic rules, presented particular dilemmas for local authorities: "As one [bureaucrat] put it: 'Whatever you do the liberals cry racialist and the racialists cry nigger lover' " (183).

6. The Ministry of Labour issued three types of labor vouchers. Employers who offered specific employment to specific Commonwealth citizens applied for Category A; Commonwealth citizens with specific skills (particularly health care professionals) applied for Category B vouchers; and Category C vouchers covered all remaining applicants, whose origin countries received no more than a quarter of the vouchers (Gish 1968, 25).

7. One Conservative politician expounded on the dilemma: "I think personally it's awfully dangerous to do anything specifically designed to attract the immigrant vote . . . because this would involve alienating, if one did it in the wrong manner . . . the affections of the white electorate who feel in an area like this, very strongly, that the area has been deteriorating rapidly by virtue of the sudden influx of coloured people from overseas" (Deakin 1965, 161).

8. Hartley-Brewer reports that a "survey conducted . . . in the spring of 1964 showed that of a small sample of the electorate questioned in Smethwick a clear majority thought Mr Gordon Walker well-balanced, sincere and up-to-date in his thinking, and no less than 92 per cent considered him to be 'aware of the nation's problems'. This was at a time when 88 per cent of the sample strongly favoured the restriction of immigration, compared with 57 per cent of those questioned in a number of other marginal constituencies" (1965, 102–103).

9. The 1965 White Paper drastically reduced the number of employment vouchers to Commonwealth citizens from 20,000 to 8,500 (with 1,000 allocated to Malta) and abolished category C vouchers (used by those who lacked specific qualifications or job offers). The basic premise behind the controls was the Labour government's belief that racism was a problem of numbers; reducing the number of nonwhite immigrants, it was argued, would help improve race relations (Katznelson 1973, 142).

10. Large parts of the African community resented the Kenyan Asians' economic success and also questioned their allegiance to the newly independent African nation. These suspicions deepened when the majority of Asians decided to retain their British passports, granted to them by the 1948 Nationality Act, for adop-

tion of Kenyan nationality would have meant forfeiting them. At the same time, those Asians who did apply for naturalization were often prevented from obtaining Kenyan citizenship, as Kenyans claimed that naturalization was simply a strategic tool that allowed Asians to continue exploiting Africans. Most Asians concluded that Kenya's new leadership would deny them their political rights and economic opportunities and thus left for Britain (Hansen 1999, 816–817).

11. At the time, Iain Macleod, the colonial secretary from 1959–1961 who promoted the African decolonization movement, claimed that during his tenure, the Conservative government had assured the Asian community in Africa that their rights to enter Britain would be upheld if the new African governments proved to take hostile actions against them. Hansen (1999) presents archival evidence to prove the existence of this pledge.

12. The act stipulated that British passport holders must also have a "qualifying connection" to the UK if they wanted to escape entry restrictions; that is, citizens "of the UK and colonies would come under immigration control unless they could show that they themselves or at least one parent or grandparent had been born in the UK, or had acquired citizenship by adoption, registration or naturalisation in the United Kingdom or by registration in a Commonwealth country" (Hussain 2001, 23).

13. There were four main planks to this new strategy: (1) Commonwealth citizens would no longer be entitled to permanent settlement and would only be permitted if they were accepted for a particular job in a specific location, (2) work permits of Commonwealth citizens would be subject to annual renewal and would not be sufficient to grant permanent settlement rights, (3) the immigration of dependents would be made discretionary, and (4) an immigrant's right to enter should be decided upon in the originating country, preceding arrival in the UK (Hansen 2000, 188).

14. Members of the Conservative Party themselves sympathized with the NF, going so far as to canvass with the Front's candidates in the 1973 parliamentary by-election at Uxbridge (resulting in a sizable 8.2 percent of the vote) (Husbands 1983, 8).

15. There were two general elections in 1974. Labour was only able to govern with a minority after the February election and thus called for elections in October when it was returned with 319 out of 635 seats.

16. For example, indirect discrimination would be said to exist if a company were to rule out hiring applicants from the inner city, and if the outcome of such a rule would be to hire from an almost exclusively white applicant pool at the expense of the black inner-city population (Layton-Henry 1992, 60).

17. "McKinnon's law; Incitement of racial hatred should still be treated in Britain as a criminal offence," *The Economist*, January 5, 1978.

18. "A quiver of innuendo; Mrs Margaret Thatcher should say, not hint," *The Economist*, February 4, 1978.

19. "How many votes swung by race?" *The Economist*, March 11, 1978.

20. "Election attitudes; Who swung Tory?" *The Economist*, May 12, 1979.

21. In the election manifesto, the Conservatives controversially proposed to establish a "Register of those Commonwealth wives and children entitled to entry for settlement under the 1971 Immigration Act" and also promised to "introduce a quota system, covering everyone outside the European Community, to control all entry for settlement" (Layton-Henry 1986, 76–77). Intraparty revolts and opposition resistance led the Thatcher government to drop these two well-publicized commitments (ibid., 77–79).

22. The first category, British citizenship, would cover those with close personal ties to the United Kingdom; the second class, British Dependent Territories citizenship, created for individuals with a personal connection to an existing dependent territory (that is, colonies that had not gained independence, most obviously Hong Kong); and British Overseas citizenship, which applied to those CUKCs who had no personal connections with either (for example, British Asians in East Africa) (Hussain 2001, 27).

23. There are two ways for these children to obtain British citizenship. First, one of their parents acquires British citizenship or right of abode in the UK; second, one of their parents has been resident in the UK for at least ten years without having left the country for more than ninety days in any year (Hansen 2000, 214).

24. According to Hansen (2000), existing scholarship has exaggerated the racial motives behind Britain's immigration and nationality policies of the postwar period (see pp. 212–221 for Hansen's discussion of the 1981 British Nationality Law).

25. Shortly before the publication of the Scarman report, the Parliamentary Select Committee on Home Affairs issued its report on "Racial Disadvantage," which had selected Liverpool as one of the areas for detailed study. The report found that discrimination and disadvantage in housing, employment, and education continued to afflict the city's minority population as patterns of deprivation were perpetuated and passed on to the next generation. The report advised the government to take immediate action to combat racial disadvantage; most of its policy recommendations were, however, rejected by the government. Additionally, Michael Heseltine, environment secretary, prepared a confidential report ("It Took a Riot") in which he called for large-scale government initiatives to tackle the economic and social problems distressing the inner cities (Layton-Henry 1986, 88–89).

26. "Violence spreads to third English city, Thatcher to speak," *Associated Press*, July 8, 1981.

27. Hall elaborates on the uneven cost of recession: "For instance, the average unemployment rate in Britain was 13 percent during 1984–85; but it reached 20 percent

among those below 20 years of age and 50 percent among black youth in many inner-city areas. Similarly, the unemployment rate in southern England was 8–9 percent versus 15 percent in Scotland, Wales, and the North" (Hall 1986, 125).

28. This was most conspicuously done with its campaign advertisement featuring a well-dressed, professional-looking West Indian or Asian man, with the caption reading: "Labour says he's black. Tories say he's British." While Conservative strategists intended to present themselves as a true alternative to what they considered to be a minority community captive to Labour, the ad backfired, as its target group was deeply insulted (Charlot 1985, 145–147).

29. "Plans to halt 'racket' on immigration anger Labour," The Times, November 1, 1991.

30. Before the 1992 general election, Labour led on the three issues that concerned the country the most: the National Health Service, unemployment, and education were respectively identified by 41, 39, and 23 percent of voters as the most important issues, and Labour enjoyed an advantage in all three over the Conservatives. Inflation and taxation, the Tories' stock issues, only concerned 11 and 10 percent of respondents, respectively (Sanders 1993, 194–195).

31. "Commentary: Mr Baker's bogus bogy," The Independent, July 5, 1991.

32. "Plans to halt 'racket' on immigration anger Labour," The Times, November 1, 1991.

33. Baker proposed several measures to restrict the possibility of asylum: by greatly expanding the number of origin countries and regions that were deemed "safe," a substantial number of refugees could be turned away without a hearing; asylum applications would not be considered if applicants had not applied at the time of arrival to Britain, even if they came from "unsafe" countries; appeals procedures would be restricted; and, to encourage tighter passenger controls, fines on airlines who carried illegal refugees would be doubled from £1,000 to £2,000 (these fines go back to the 1987 Carrier Liability Act, enacted by the Thatcher government). See "Refugees face loss of sanctuary; The Asylum Bill is far tougher than expected," The Independent, November 2, 1991.

34. "Election 1992: Major supports Baker and fuels immigration row," Financial Times, April 8, 1992. Baker also argued that another ingredient of this "deadly political cocktail" was the opposition's electoral reform proposals (introducing some form of proportional representation), which would allow extremist parties to gain prominence.

35. "Howard hits at 'bogus' migrants," The Guardian, February 18, 1995.

36. "Lilley goes to war on welfare cheats," Evening Standard, October 11, 1995.

37. "A safe haven but not a soft touch; Lilley strips bogus asylum-seekers of right to handouts," Daily Mail, October 12, 1995.

371

38. The 1999 Immigration and Asylum Act withdrew cash benefits from asylum applicants and instead instituted a food voucher scheme (generally opposed by human rights organizations for its stigmatizing effect and later rescinded); set up a dispersal system to spread asylum seekers more evenly throughout the country; and reduced the opportunities for appeal of an application's rejection to one, with illegal migrants having no right of appeal at all (Hansen and King 2000, 401).

39. The 2000 Race Relations (Amendment) Act extended the scope of the 1976 act to cover the police and public authorities. It was passed after the well-publicized Macpherson inquiry's findings that problems of institutional racism pervaded the British police force.

40. Blunkett took up the report's call for greater community cohesion in multi-ethnic towns in a rather one-sided manner. Favoring assimilation over "unbridled multiculturalism," he urged all ethnic minority members to speak English at home and included an English-language requirement for the naturalization of spouses of British citizens and a prerequisite that all aspiring citizens have "sufficient knowledge about life in the UK" in the 2002 Nationality, Asylum and Immigration Act (Randall 2003, 189).

41. See "Race Relations—21 June 2002," http://www.mori.com/mrr/2002/c020621.shtml, accessed August 2004.

42. See "British Views on Immigration," http://www.mori.com/polls/2003/migration.shtml, accessed August 2004.

43. See "MORI Political Monitor: Recent Trends," http://www.mori.com/polls/trends/issues12.shtml, accessed August 2004.

44. See "Race Relations—21 June 2002," http://www.mori.com/mrr/2002/c020621.shtml, accessed August 2004.

45. "Il Duce's heirs; The Tory leaders make centrist noises, but he and his supporters betray some frightening right-wing tendencies," *New Statesman*, December 10, 2001.

6. United Kingdom: Quantitative Analysis

1. One might argue that the Liberal Party is no longer a negligible party, at least since 1979, and thus Britain has been becoming a "multiparty system." Although the Liberals have garnered about 15–20 percent of votes since 1979, their seat share has been negligible (see Figure 6.1). The Liberal Party has always taken up the center ground between the two major parties except in 1997, when it was slightly to the left of Labour on some issues.

2. One notable exception to this trend, however, is the desertion of Labour by many Muslim voters in protest against the party's participation in the Iraq war.

3. When there was a substantial third-party vote in the UK election, we looked at Labour's share as a fraction of the total Labour-Conservative vote share. That is, we ignored the third party.

7. Immigration: A Challenge to Tolerant Denmark

1. These latter four representatives, by unwritten agreement, generally do not vote on issues affecting the mainland, and usually are not members of any of the mainland parties.

2. Perhaps the most important direct political ramification of the refugee flow of the mid-eighties was not fully felt until 1993. Beginning in 1982, Conservative prime minister Poul Schlüter led a center-right government coalition. In 1989 evidence emerged that the government's minister of justice had for two years unlawfully delayed the reuniting of Tamil refugees from Sri Lanka with their families. When the scandal came to light, the minister of justice promptly resigned. That was not the end, however, of the "Tamil affair." The prime minister claimed to know nothing about the actions of his minister, and promised to resign if an official inquiry found otherwise. Four years later, in January 1993, a judicial inquiry did find otherwise, and Schlüter resigned, allowing the SDP to return to power.

3. A major exception to the lack of violence took place in the summer of 1985, when three bombs were set off in Copenhagen, one at an airline office and the other two at a synagogue, killing one person and wounding twenty-six. The Islamic Jihad claimed responsibility, saying the attacks were in response to an Israeli attack on a south Lebanese village. This triggered violent attacks on immigrants in a number of places throughout the country. The most significant attacks occurred in the city of Kalundborg, where for two nights in late July hundreds of young Danes, many of them unemployed, gathered outside a small hotel that housed refugees (mostly from Iran and the Middle East), throwing home-made bombs at the buildings and physically attacking some individuals. A number of refugees and two police officers were injured.

4. Ironically, a number of these proposals ultimately formed a major part of the 2001 immigration reforms discussed below, which were passed by a Liberal-Conservative coalition government with the support of the Far Right.

5. A 1996 policy statement of the Progress Party stated that "[t]he main task of the Progress Party is the dismantling of the Welfare State and the Public Trustee State" (Fremskridtspartiet 1996).

8. Denmark: Quantitative Analysis

1. Our sources are the "Danish Election Survey 1998," which was originally collected by AC Nielsen AIM for Jørgen Goul Andersen, Johannes Andersen, Ole Borre, and Hans Jørgen Nielsen and the "Danish Election Survey 2001," originally collected by Jørgen Goul Andersen, Ole Borre, Hans Jørgen Nielsen, Johannes Andersen, Søren Risbjerg Thomsen, and Jørgen Elklit. These surveys, along with the related documentation, have been placed, for future access, in the Danish Data Archive (archive numbers DDA-4189 and DDA-12516). The results and interpretation in the current chapter are the sole responsibility of the authors.

2. This contrasts with the French situation, where the main xenophobic party, the Front National, tends to adopt intermediary positions on economic issues, trying to attract an electorate of both self-employed conservative individuals and blue-collar workers supportive of more public-sector expenditure.

3. It is straightforward to deduce the direction of the bias in the simple starting case here where *AntiImmigration* is the single included variable, because it only depends on the sign of the correlation between *AntiImmigration* and *TakeAdvantage*. When more than one variable is included, what is required to deduce the direction of the bias is the correlation between *AntiImmigration* and *TakeAdvantage* net of the effect of other right-hand-side variables. Here the partial correlation between *AntiImmigration* and *TakeAdvantage* remains positive, though smaller (0.27).

4. For 1998, we took all PUNEs with a Left vote share of over 40 percent. We did not find PUNEs with a vote share of 48 percent, which was our target for that year.

5. That is, the average value of the share-weighted average of the parties' policies, over selected PUNEs. A sophisticated form of averaging was used. We computed kernel densities of the bargaining powers in the PUNEs, and then weighted each PUNE with its predicted "frequency," so computed. This procedure reflects our view that the "missing data" in the analysis are the bargaining powers of the factions.

6. A superior procedure would be to compute a kernel density for the two-dimensional distribution of bargaining-power pairs. But we would need many more PUNEs for such a density to be statistically significant.

7. February 9, 2005. http://www.reuters.com/newsArticle.jhtml?type=worldNews&storyID=7578459.

8. We contrast this with the United States, where voter racism is directed primarily toward African Americans, who, as citizens, cannot be legally discriminated against, as can aliens. Thus we would expect the size of the welfare state to be more affected by voter racism in the United States than by voter xenophobia in Denmark.

9. Immigration and the Political Institutionalization of Xenophobia in France

1. In addition to economically motivated migration, during the interwar years France received a large share of Jewish immigrants from Germany as well as Spaniards who fled the Franco regime.

2. Over two decades, the French government signed bilateral labor recruitment treaties with a number of countries: Italy (1946 and 1951), Greece (1954), Spain (1961), Morocco, Mali, Mauritania, Tunisia and Portugal (1963), Senegal (1964), Yugoslavia and Turkey (1965) (Freeman 1979, 74).

3. In France alone, the number of migrants applying for asylum increased from less than 20,000 in 1981 to over 60,000 in 1989. The rate of acceptance of these claims dwindled over the same period (from 78 to 28 percent), reflecting the public's concern that refugees were in fact motivated by economic gain rather than by religious or political persecution. However, many of those denied asylum remained in the country illegally (Hargreaves 1995, 21).

4. "Le Pen Is Mightier," Survey, France, *The Economist*, November 23, 1991, 7.

5. "France; In Bad Odour," *The Economist*, June 29, 1991, 43.

6. "France; You'll have to go," *The Economist*, June 2, 1979, 44.

7. In 1976, then prime minister Jacques Chirac expressed this sentiment on television: "A country in which there are 900,000 unemployed, but where there are two million immigrants, is not a country in which the problem of employment is unsolvable." See Gastaut (2000, 252).

8. The share of immigrants living in HLMs increased rapidly. Fifteen percent of households headed by a foreign national occupied these dwellings in 1975, 24 percent in 1982, and by 1990, this share had risen to 28 percent; in the same year, only 14 percent of households headed by a French national lived in HLMs (Hargreaves 1995, 70).

9. "France; Keep France white for reds," *The Economist*, February 21, 1981, 64.

10. "A whiff of racism in France," *The Economist*, September 17, 1983, 45.

11. In order to qualify as a candidate in France's presidential election, candidates must be at least twenty-three years old and must be endorsed by five hundred elected officials from at least thirty different *départements*.

12. For a summary of nativist, communitarian, and voluntarist arguments of both the Left and the Right in the Nationality Code debate, see Feldblum (1999, 60–71).

13. From the mid-1970s to the mid-1980s, France's left-wing parties—recognizing the ethnic and cultural diversity of the last immigration wave compared with earlier periods—rejected the concept of assimilation, which it associated with notions of ethnic superiority and fascism, and instead called for *insertion*. This concept

was "used . . . to designate the right to refuse assimilation, to defend and preserve collective identity, and to refuse to adapt to the dominant French culture" (Weil and Crowley 1994, 114–115).

14. The 1986 legislative elections were the only ones to use proportional representation, allowing the FN to translate its 10 percent vote share into a comparable seat share. Later elections again adopted a first-past-the-post, second-round runoff system.

15. In a parallel development, the government's plans to reform parts of higher education came under sharp attack by students who mobilized massive protests against the reforms. The opposition became increasingly radicalized and violent and resulted in the death of an Algerian student, leading the government to scrap the education reforms. As the student movement made attempts to link their protests to campaigns against racism and the citizenship reform, the latter became increasingly politically costly (Brubaker 1992, 154).

16. The government encountered legal difficulties in its proposal to alter Article 23 of France's Nationality Code, which attributes French citizenship to a child that is born in France when at least one of the two parents was also born on French territory. According to Brubaker, "To exclude second-generation Algerian immigrants would have required legislators to specify that 'France' meant France in its present boundaries, so that the parents of the second-generation immigrants, themselves born in pre-independence Algeria, would not count as having been born 'in France.' But this would have amounted to a denial of the French colonial past, in particular the long-standing claim that Algeria was an integral part of France" (1992, 152).

17. "France set to liberalise immigration laws," *The Guardian,* May 30, 1989.

18. "French economy; A taxing debate," *The Economist,* March 5, 1988, 67.

19. "The fable of the tortoise, the sphinx and the racehorse," *The Economist,* April 9, 1988, 43.

20. "Mitterrand redivivus," *The Economist,* May 14, 1988, 14.

21. In the mid-1980s, polls repeatedly showed that more than 60 percent opposed allowing immigrants to vote in local elections (Simmons 1996, 159).

22. For an electoral breakdown by demographic groups, see http://www.tns-sofres.com/etudes/dossiers/presi2002/histo1988.htm#2, accessed July 2004.

23. Mayer (1993) conceptualizes ethnocentrism as a combination of positions taken on matters such as immigration, patriotism, tolerance, and security. More specifically, the author uses answers to the following questions to construct an ethnocentrism scale: (1) Jews have too much power in France; (2) It is only fair for Muslims in France to have mosques to practice their religion; (3) Nowadays we do not feel as at home as we used to; (4) There are too many immigrants in France; (5) I am proud to be French (N. Mayer 1993, 24).

24. For a discussion of the evolution of the public's stance on the headscarf issue in 1989, see Gastaut (2000, 570–578).

25. Hargreaves (1995, 73) describes these confrontations as follows: "Most of these recent disturbances have been characterized by a very similar pattern: an unarmed youth of immigrant origin involved or suspected of involvement in petty crime (most commonly, the theft a motor vehicle) has been shot dead by a police officer, and this has been followed by an outbreak of street violence by other youths."

26. "Les immigrés dans le miroir du Golfe," *Le Monde*, March 14, 1991.

27. "France; in bad odour," *The Economist*, June 29, 1991, 49.

28. "Mme Cresson évoque les 'charters' pour les clandestins," *Le Monde*, July 9, 1991; "Le dispositif gouvernemental sur l'immigration pâtit de la polémique sur les propos de Mme Cresson," *Le Monde*, July 11, 1991.

29. "Trop," *Le Monde*, June 21, 1991.

30. "France; Enough of Le Pen," *The Economist*, January 30, 1993, 48.

31. Ibid.

32. "Code de la nationalité, procédure pénale, contrôles d'identité et Constitution— Le garde des sceaux annonce cinq réformes," *Le Monde*, May 7, 1993.

33. "Saisi par les parlementaires socialistes et communistes Le Conseil constitutionnel valide la réforme du code de la nationalité," *Le Monde*, July 22, 1993. This law was later repealed by a Socialist-led government.

34. "L'immigration n'est plus au centre du débat présidentiel; Hormis MM. de Villiers et Le Pen, les principaux candidats sont d'une rare discrétion sur les conséquences des lois du ministre de l'intérieur," *Le Monde*, April 19, 1995.

35. Perrineau cites the president of the FNJ (the FN's youth branch) Samuel Maréchal (also Le Pen's son-in-law) in a piece that appeared in the FN's publication, *Présent*, on September 17, 1994.

36. "France, unpredictable after all," *The Economist*, March 11, 1995, 49.

37. "The rise, again, of Jacques Chirac," *The Economist*, March 25, 1995, 53.

38. "Économie: le nécessaire et le possible," *Le Monde*, March 8, 1995.

39. See election results at http://www.tns-sofres.com/etudes/dossiers/presi2002/histo1995.htm#0, accessed July 2004. The only party that comes close to these levels of loyalty is the Communist Party: 76 percent of PC supporters voted for the party in the first round.

40. Perrineau (1997, 102) reports that 30 percent of workers *(ouvriers)* voted for Le Pen; Shields (1995, 28) provides a figure of 27 percent.

41. For 1988 and 1995 election results see http://www.tns-sofres.com/etudes/dossiers/presi2002/histo1988.htm and http://www.tns-sofres.com/etudes/dossiers/presi2002/histo1995.htm#0, accessed July 2004.

42. Shields also notes that it is not Le Pen's charismatic personality that draws his supporters to the polls. In a 1995 poll, only 10 percent of Le Pen's electorate voted on the basis of his personality, compared with 86 percent who voted on the basis of his program. In contrast, 45 percent of Chirac voters were attracted to the latter's personality, compared with 51 percent who voted for his program (1995, 33).

43. "M. de Villiers juge burlesque l'appel de M. Le Pen à se retirer," *Le Monde*, April 18, 1995.

44. Another of Le Pen's foes, Villiers, teamed up with former interior minister Pasqua and probably drew on some of the Front's supporters. The ardently nationalistic, anti–European Union Villiers-Pasqua ticket received just over 13 percent of the vote.

45. "La droite plurielle à l'épreuve," *Le Figaro*, June 23, 1999.

46. "Le débat sur l'insécurité a dominé les élections municipales," *Les Echos*, April 3, 2001.

47. "Two splendid programmes, spot the difference," *The Economist*, March 23, 2002, 47.

48. See SOFRES survey results, http://www.tns-sofres.com/etudes/pol/280502_frontnational_r.htm, accessed July 2004.

49. Le Pen generally accused Chirac of being worse than Jospin, for while he fundamentally disagreed with the leftist ideas of the latter, he detested the betrayal of conservative ideas by the former. In a 2002 interview, Le Pen stated: "When Jospin, man of the left, displays left politics, it is detestable but not immoral. When Chirac, man of the right, displays left politics, it is detestable and immoral. This is why I say he is worse than Jospin." Quoted in "Le président du Front national affirme que la droite sera 'écrasée', à la présidentielle et aux législatives, si jamais il ne peut pas être candidat," *Le Figaro*, March 29, 2002.

50. See http://www.tns-sofres.com/etudes/pol/280502_frontnational_r.htm, accessed July 2004.

51. "Le rapport de la Commission des droits de l'homme s'alarme de la progression du racisme en France," *Le Monde*, March 22, 2001.

52. "L'examen de conscience a commencé dans les cités où prospèrent les incivilités et sévit la violence; Le vote Le Pen vu des banlieues," *Le Figaro*, April 25, 2002.

53. "Au royaume des aveugles; En l'excluant, le systéme de représentation politique ne fait que renforcer Le Pen," *Libération*, May 13, 2002, 5.

54. "Pourquoi Le Pen?" *Les Echos*, May 22, 2002, 56.

55. "Études politiques, enquêtes et reportages aprés le séisme du premier tour; Qui a voté Le Pen?" *Le Figaro,* April 23, 2002.

10. France: Quantitative Analysis

1. The CEVIPOF Post-Electoral Survey 1988 was produced by the CEVIPOF and carried out by SOFRES. It took place just after the 1988 presidential election, between May 9 and May 20, and includes 4,032 respondents representative of the French population above age eighteen (nonregistered voters were excluded). The CEVIPOF Post-Electoral Survey 1995 was also produced by the CEVIPOF and carried out by SOFRES. It took place just after the 1995 presidential election, between May 8 and May 23, and includes 4,078 respondents representative of the French population above age eighteen and registered on electoral lists. The data of the French Electoral Panel 2002 (PEF2002) were produced by the CEVIPOF, the CIDSP, the CECOP with the support of the Ministry of Interior, the FNSP, and the University of Montreal. This electoral study took place in three waves between April and June 2002, carried out by TN-SOFRES. It includes 10,138 interviews, 4,107 in the first wave, carried out before the first round of the presidential election between April 8 and April 20; 4,017 interviews after the second round, between May 15 and May 31; and 2,013 after the legislative elections between June 20 and 28. All these data are available at the Socio-Political Data Archive (CIDSP). The results and interpretation in the current chapter are the sole responsibility of the authors.

2. Unfortunately, no such questions are available in the 1988 survey.

3. We believe, though, that modeling the Extreme Right in such a way conforms with reality, in that its leader, Le Pen, has had the most say in determining his party's policies. As discussed in the previous chapter, factions that have been displeased with the direction of the FN have tended to leave the party.

4. We chose the standard deviations in Table 10.9 to be slightly smaller than observed values because we are suppressing some heterogeneity in immigration views by combining the three lowest categories.

5. We do not compute more PUNEs because even this computation requires about twelve hours of computer time for each value of γ. And we tried many more variations of the model than we report here.

6. We note that our technique is imperfect. Ideally, we should compute a kernel density function over the two-dimension manifold of ordered pairs of bargaining powers (α, β). This would have required computing many more PUNEs. Our technique computes the unidimensional kernel density function for each bargaining power separately, which is conceptually incorrect. Nevertheless, we believe that this method of weighting is superior to taking a simple numerical average of PUNE values.

7. Our PUNE analysis assumes voters are sincere. We chose not to try to model strategic voting.

11. Conclusion

1. However, there may be an existence problem: for some pairs of bargaining strengths, there will be no PUNE. In particular, if the Opportunists have all the power in both parties, then the associated PUNE is the Downsian equilibrium, which, we know, does not in general exist.

2. Actually, we tried to estimate a fully endogenous three-party model, but did not find equilibria. Either they do not exist, or they occupy such a small region in the policy space that it is difficult to find them by randomization methods. We suspect the latter.

References

Abramowitz, A. 1994. "Issue evolution reconsidered: Racial attitudes and partisanship in the U.S. electorate." *American Journal of Political Science* 38 (1): 1–24.

Adler, F. 2001. "Immigration, insecurity and the French far right." *Telos* 20: 31–48.

Alesina, A., and E. Glaeser. 2004. *Fighting poverty in the US and Europe.* New York: Oxford University Press.

Alesina, A., E. Glaeser, and B. Sacerdote. 2001. "Why doesn't the US have a European-style welfare state?" *Brookings Papers on Economic Activity* 2: 187–254.

Alvarez, M., and J. Brehm. 1997. "Are Americans ambivalent toward racial policies?" *American Journal of Political Science* 41: 345–374.

Agence France Presse. 1997. "Polls open in Danish local elections amid race debate." November 18.

——— 2000. "Extreme-right Danish party leader charged with race hate crime." January 21.

——— 2001. "Danish xenophobia rising, center-right gaining ahead of vote." November 18.

Barnes, H. 1999. "Muted debate where the consensus rules." *Financial Times* (December 17).

Bartels, L. 2002. "Economic inequality and political representation." Mimeo, Princeton University.

Bell, B. 1997. "The performance of immigrants in the United Kingdom: Evidence from the General Household Survey." *Economic Journal* 107 (2): 333–344.

Bell, D., and B. Criddle. 2002. "Presidentialism restored: The French elections of April–May and June 2002." *Parliamentary Affairs* 55 (4): 643–663.

References

Bénabou, R., and E. Ok. 2001. "Social mobility and the demand for redistribution: The POUM hypothesis." *Quarterly Journal of Economics* 116 (2): 447–487.

Bénabou, R., and J. Tirole. 2002. "Belief in a just world and redistributive politics." Mimeo, Princeton University.

Ben-Tovim, G. 1986. *The local politics of race, public policy, and politics.* Basingstoke: Macmillan.

Benyon, J. 1986. "Spiral of decline: Race and policing." In Z. Layton-Henry and P. B. Rich, eds., *Race, government, and politics in Britain.* Basingstoke: Macmillan.

Best, S. 1999. "The sampling problem in measuring policy mood: An alternative solution." *Journal of Politics* 61 (3): 721–740.

Billig, M., and P. Golding. 1992. "Did race tip the balance?" *New Community* 19 (1): 161–163.

Black, E. 1976. *Southern governors and civil rights: Racial segregation as a campaign issue in the second reconstruction.* Cambridge, MA: Harvard University Press.

Black, E., and M. Black. 1987. *Politics and society in the south.* Cambridge, MA: Harvard University Press.

——— 1992. *The vital South.* Cambridge, MA: Harvard University Press.

——— 2002. *The rise of southern Republicans.* Cambridge, MA: The Belknap Press of Harvard University Press.

Black Commentator. 2003. "Dean makes racial-political history." December 11.

Blake, C. 1982. "Citizenship, law and the state: The British Nationality Act 1981." *Modern Law Review* 45 (2):179–197.

Blundell, R., and T. MaCurdy. 1999. "Labor supply: A review of alternative approaches." In O. Ashenfelter and D. Card, eds., *Handbook of Labor Economics.* Vol. 3. Amsterdam: Elsevier Science.

Blundell, R., C. Meghir, E. Symons, and I. Walker. 1988. "Labour supply specification and the evaluation of tax reforms." *Journal of Public Economics* 36: 23–52.

Bobo, L. 1988. "Group conflict, prejudice, and the paradox of contemporary racial attitudes." In P. Katz and D. Taylor, eds., *Eliminating racism: Profiles in controversy.* New York: Plenum Press.

Borre, O. 1975. "The general election in Denmark, January 1975: Toward a new structure of the party system." *Scandinavian Political Studies* 10/75: 211–216.

——— 1987. "Some results from the Danish 1987 election." *Scandinavian Political Studies* 10 (4): 345–355.

Bowles, S., C. Fong, and H. Gintis. 2001. "Reciprocity and welfare state." Mimeo, University of Massachusetts at Amherst.

Boyes, R. 2002. "Denmark ready to adopt strictest asylum law in EU." *The Times* (May 30).

References

Bréchon, P., and S. K. Mitra. 1992. "The National Front in France—The emergence of an extreme right protest movement." *Comparative Politics* 25 (1): 63–82.

Brubaker, R. 1992. *Citizenship and nationhood in France and Germany.* Cambridge, MA: Harvard University Press.

Bryder, T. 2002. "The xenophobic theme in the Danish election campaign 2001." Paper presented at the annual meeting of the Swedish Political Science Association, October 6–8.

Butler, D., and D. Kavanagh. 1975. *The British general election of October 1974.* London: Macmillan.

——— 1980. *The British general election of 1979.* London: Macmillan.

——— 1997. *The British general election of 1997.* Basingstoke: Macmillan.

Butler, D., and D. Stokes. 1974. *Political change in Britain: The evolution of electoral choice.* 2nd ed. London: Macmillan.

Carmines, E., and J. Stimson. 1986. "On the structure and sequence of issue evolution." *American Political Science Review* 80 (3): 901–920.

——— 1989. *Issue evolution: Race and the transformation of American politics.* Princeton, NJ: Princeton University Press.

Carter, D. 1996. *From George Wallace to Newt Gingrich: Race in the conservative counterrevolution, 1963–1994.* Baton Rouge: Louisiana State University Press.

Castles, S., and G. Kosack. 1973. *Immigrant workers and class structure in western Europe.* London: Oxford University Press.

Charlot, M. 1985. "The ethnic minorities' vote." In A. Ranney, ed., *Britain at the polls, 1980: A study of the general election.* Durham, NC: Duke University Press.

Clymer, A. 2002. "Divisive words: The downfall: 30-Year dream of leadership is undone by lack of allies." *New York Times* (December 21): sect. A, p. 19, col. 3.

Cohen, R. 2000. "Identity crisis for Denmark: Are we Danes or Europeans?" *New York Times* (September 10): sect. 1, p. 1.

Coleman, D. 1994. "The United Kingdom and international migration: A changing balance." In H. Fassmann and R. Münz, eds., *European migration in the late twentieth century: Historical patterns, actual trends, and social implications.* Hants, UK: Edward Elgar Pub. Co.

Cook, R. 2000. *How congress gets elected.* Washington, DC: CQ Press.

Coughlin, P. 1992. *Probabilistic voting theory.* New York: Cambridge University Press.

Crespino, J. 2002. "The ways Republicans talk about race." *New York Times* (December 13): sect. A, p. 39, col. 1.

Cuneo, P. 2001. "Ethnic minorities' economic performance." Performance and Innovation Unit, Cabinet Office, UK.

References

Daniel, W., and Political and Economic Planning. 1968. *Racial discrimination in England: Based on the P.E.P. report.* Harmondsworth: Penguin.

Danish Statistical Archive, Data Material DDA-12516: Election Survey 2001. Primary researchers: Jørgen Goul Andersen, Ole Borre, Hans Jørgen Nielsen, Johannes Andersen, Søren Risbjerg Thomsen, and Jørgen Elklit. DDA-12516 1st edition (with Henning Lauritsen, Birgitte Grønlund Jensen, and Jens Wagner). Danish Data Archive 2003. 1 data file (2026 respondents, 316 variables) with related documentation (299 pp.).

Danish Statistical Archive, Data Material DDA-4189: Election Survey 1998. Primary researchers: Jørgen Goul Andersen, Johannes Andersen, Ole Borre, and Hans Jørgen Nielsen. DDA-4189 1st edition (with Birgitte Grønlund Jensen, Jens Wagner, and Lena Wul). Danish Data Archive 1999. 1 data file (2001 respondents, 327 variables) with related documentation (249 pp.).

Dansk Folkeparti. 2004. "The party program of the Danish People's Party." Available at http://www.danskfolkeparti.dk. Accessed July 22, 2004.

Davies, P. 1999. *The National Front in France: Ideology, discourse, and power.* London: Routledge.

Deakin, N., and Institute of Race Relations, eds. 1965. *Colour and the British electorate 1964: Six case studies.* New York: Praeger.

DeLey, M. 1983. "French immigration policy since May 1981." *International Migration Review* 17 (2): 196–211.

Denny, K., C. Halmon, and M. Roche. 1997. "The distribution of discrimination in immigrant earnings—evidence from Britain 1974–93." Mimeo, University College Dublin.

Desmet, K., I. Ortuño-Ortin, and S. Weber. 2005. "Peripheral diversity and redistribution." CEPR discussion paper 5112.

Domhoff, G. 1995. "Who rules America?" In Theda Skocpol and John L. Campbell, eds., *American society and politics: Institutional, historical, and theoretical perspectives.* New York: McGraw-Hill.

Downs, A. 1957. *An economic theory of democracy.* New York: Harper Collins.

Durlauf, S. 1998. "Associational redistribution: A defense." In E. O. Wright, ed., *Recasting egalitarianism.* New York: Verso.

——— 2001. "Comments on Alesina, A., Glaeser, E., and B. Sacerdote." *Brookings Papers on Economic Activity* 2: 255–263.

Economist. 1988. "Denmark and Norway: Fear of foreigners." May 28.

——— 1999. "Testing Danish tolerance." August 28.

Edsall, T. 2002. "Lott decried for part of salute to Thurmond: GOP senate leader hails colleague's run as segregationist." *Washington Post* (December 7): sect. A, p. 6.

Edsall, T., and M. Edsall. 1991. *Chain reaction: The impact of race, rights, and taxes on American politics.* New York: Norton.

References

EIU. Various years, 1964–2001. "Country Report: Denmark and Iceland," by the *Economist Intelligence Unit*. Quarterly.

Evans, J., and P. Norris. 1999. *Critical elections: British parties and voters in long-term perspective*. New York: Sage Publications.

Feldblum, M. 1999. *Reconstructing citizenship: The politics of nationality reform and immigration in contemporary France*. SUNY series in national identities. Albany: State University of New York Press.

Fenno Jr., R. 2002. *Congress at the grassroots: Representational change in the South, 1970–1998*. Chapel Hill: University of North Carolina Press.

Fetzer, J. 2000. *Public attitudes toward immigration in the United States, France, and Germany*. Cambridge: Cambridge University Press.

Fitzgerald, M., and Z. Layton-Henry. 1986. "Opposition parties and race policies, 1979–83." In Z. Layton-Henry and P. B. Rich, eds., *Race, government, and politics in Britain*. Basingstoke: Macmillan.

Fong, C. 2001. "Social preferences, self-interest, and the demand for redistribution." *Journal of Public Economics* 81: 225–246.

Foot, Paul. 1965. *Immigration and race in British politics*. Harmondsworth: Penguin Books.

Franklin, M. 1985. *The decline of class voting in Britain*. Oxford: Clarendon Press.

Frederickson, K. 2001. *The Dixiecrat revolt and the end of the solid South, 1932–1968*. Chapel Hill: University of North Carolina Press.

Freeman, G. 1979. *Immigrant labor and racial conflict in industrial societies: The French and British experience, 1945–1975*. Princeton, NJ: Princeton University Press.

Fremskridtspartiet, FP. 1996. *Policy statement*. Available at http://www.frp.dk//foreign/engelsk.htm. Accessed July 25, 2004.

Front National. 1993. *300 mésures pour la renaissance de la France: Front national, programme de gouvernement: l'alternative nationale*. Paris: Éditions nationales.

Fryer, P. 1984. *Staying power: The history of black people in Britain*. London: Pluto Press.

Frymer, P. 1999. *Uneasy alliances: Race and party competition in America*. Princeton, NJ: Princeton University Press.

Gastaut, Y. 2000. *L'immigration et l'opinion en France sous la Ve République*. Paris: Seuil.

Gerring, J. 1998. *Party ideologies in America, 1828–1996*. Cambridge: Cambridge University Press.

Geweke, J. 1996. "Monte Carlo simulation and numerical integration." In H. Amman, D. Kendrick, and J. Rust, eds., *Handbook of Computational Economics*. Vol. 1. Amsterdam: Elsevier Science.

Gilens, M. 1999. *Why Americans hate welfare: Race, media, and the politics of antipoverty policy*. Chicago: University of Chicago Press.

References

Giles, M., and K. Hertz. 1994. "Racial threat and partisan identification." *American Political Science Review* 88 (2): 317–326.

Gish, O. 1968. "Color and skill: British immigration, 1955–1968." *International Migration Review* 3 (1): 19–37.

Glaser, J. 1996. *Race, campaign politics, and the realignment in the South.* New Haven, CT: Yale University Press.

Glover, S., et al. 2001. "Migration: An economic and social analysis." RDS Occasional Paper no. 67, Home Office, UK.

Goldey, D., and R. Johnson. 1988. "The French presidential-election of 24 April–8 May and the general-election of 5–12 June 1988." *Electoral Studies* 7 (3): 195–223.

Greene, W. 2000. *Econometric Analysis.* 4th ed. New York: Prentice Hall.

Griffin, R. 2001. "No racism, thanks, we're British: How right-wing populism manifests itself in contemporary Britain." In Wolfgang Eisman, ed., *Rechtspopulismus in Europa: Analysen und Handlungsperspektiven.* Graz: Czern-Verlages.

Hainsworth, P., and P. Mitchell. 2000. "France: The Front National from crossroads to crossroads?" *Parliamentary Affairs* 53 (3): 443–456.

Hall, P. 1986. *Governing the economy: The politics of state intervention in Britain, France, Europe, and the international order.* New York: Oxford University Press.

Hansen, R. 1999. "The Kenyan Asians, British politics, and the Commonwealth Immigrants Act, 1968." *Historical Journal* 42 (3): 809–834.

———— 2000. *Citizenship and immigration in post-war Britain: The institutional origins of a multicultural nation.* Oxford: Oxford University Press.

Hansen, R., and D. King. 2000. "Illiberalism and the new politics of asylum: Liberalism's dark side." *Political Quarterly* 71 (4): 396–403.

Hargreaves, A. 1995. *Immigration, "race," and ethnicity in contemporary France.* London: Routledge.

Harris, T. 1999. "The effects of taxes and benefits on household income, 1997–8." *Economic Trends,* no. 545, Office for National Statistics, UK.

Hartley-Brewer, M. 1965. "Smethwick." In N. Deakin and Institute of Race Relations, eds., *Colour and the British Electorate 1964: Six case studies.* New York: Praeger.

Hausman, J. 1981. "Labor supply." In Henry Aaron and Joseph Pechman, eds., *How taxes affect economic behavior.* Washington, DC: Brookings Institution.

Heath, A., G. Evans, and J. Martin. 1993. "The measurement of core beliefs and values: The development of balanced socialist/laissez faire and libertarian/authoritarian scales." *British Journal of Political Science* 24: 115–158.

Heath, A., R. Jowell, and J. Curtice. 2001. *The rise of New Labour: Party policies and voter choices.* London: Oxford University Press.

References

Hicks, J., and G. Allen. 1999. "A century of change: Trends in UK statistics since 1900." House of Commons Research Paper 99/111, House of Commons, UK.

Himelstein, J. 1983. "Rhetorical continuities in the politics of race: The closed society revisited." *Southern Speech Communications Journal* 48: 153–166.

Hiro, D. 1991. *Black British, white British: A history of race relations in Britain.* London: Grafton.

Hollifield, J. 1992. *Immigrants, markets, and states: The political economy of postwar Europe.* Cambridge, MA: Harvard University Press.

Home Office. 2001. "Community cohesion: A report of the Independent Review Team chaired by Ted Cantle."

——— 2003a. "Home Office Research Study 259—An assessment of the impact of asylum policies in Europe 1990–2000."

——— 2003b. "Asylum Statistics United Kingdom 2002."

Hotelling, H. 1929. "Stability in competition," *Economic Journal* 39, 41–57.

Huckfeldt, R., and C. Kohfeld. 1989. *Race and the decline of class in American politics.* Chicago: University of Chicago Press.

Hughes and Tuch, 2000. "How beliefs about poverty influence racial policy attitudes." In D. Sears, J. Sidanius, and L. Bobo, eds., *Racialized politics: The debate about racism in America.* Chicago: University of Chicago Press.

Husbands, C. 1983. *Racial exclusionism and the city: The urban support of the National Front.* London: Allen & Unwin.

——— 1991. "The support for the Front National—analyses and findings." *Ethnic and Racial Studies* 14 (3): 382–416.

Hussain, A. 2001. *British immigration policy under the Conservative government.* Aldershot: Ashgate.

INSÉE (Fabienne Daguet and Suzanne Thave). 1996. La population immigrée: Le résultat d'une longue histoire. Paris: Département de la démographie, INSÉE.

Jamieson, K. 1996. *Packaging the presidency: A history and criticism of campaign advertising.* New York: Oxford University Press.

Jensen, B. 1999. "Thirty years of press debate on 'the foreigners' in Denmark." In David Coleman and Eskil Wadensjö, eds., *Immigration to Denmark: International and national perspectives.* Aarhus, Denmark: Aarhus University Press.

Kalyvas, S. 1996. *The rise of Christian Democracy in Europe.* Ithaca, NY: Cornell University Press.

Karacs, I. 2001. "The politics of hate and fear flourish in suburbia." *The Independent.* November 24.

Katznelson, I. 1973. *Black men, white cities: Race, politics, and migration in the United States, 1900–30 and Britain, 1948–68.* London: Oxford University Press.

References

———— 2005. *When affirmative action was white.* New York: W. W. Norton.

Kaye, R. 1999. "The politics of exclusion: The withdrawal of social welfare benefits from asylum seekers in the UK." *Contemporary Politics* 5 (1): 25–45.

Kellstedt, P. 2000. "Media framing and the dynamics of racial policy preferences." *American Journal of Political Science* 44 (2): 245–260.

Key, V. 1950. *Southern politics in state and nation.* New York: A. A. Knopf.

Kinder, D., and T. Mendelberg. 2000. "Individualism reconsidered: Principles and prejudice in contemporary American opinion." In D. Sears, J. Sidanius, and L. Bobo, eds., *Racialized politics: The debate about racism in America.* Chicago: University of Chicago Press.

Kinder, D., and L. Sanders. 1996. *Divided by color: Racial politics and democratic ideals.* Chicago: University of Chicago Press.

Kinder, D., and D. Sears. 1981. "Prejudice and politics: Symbolic racism versus racial threats to the good life." *Journal of Personality and Social Psychology* 40: 414–431.

King, A. 1985. "Thatcher's first term." In A. Ranney, ed., *Britain at the polls, 1983: A study of the General Election.* Durham, NC: Duke University Press.

Kitschelt, H. 1994. *The transformation of European social democracy.* New York: Cambridge University Press.

———— 1995. *The radical rights in western Europe: A comparative analysis.* Ann Arbor: University of Michigan Press.

Kuklinski, J., M. Cobb, and M. Gilens. 1997. "Racial attitudes and the 'New South.'" *Journal of Politics* 59 (2): 323–349.

Laver, M., and W. Hunt. 1992. *Policy and party competition.* New York: Routledge.

Layton-Henry, Z. 1992. *The politics of immigration: Immigration, 'race' and 'race' relations in post-war Britain.* Oxford: Blackwell Publishers.

Layton-Henry, Z. 1986. "Race and the Thatcher government." In Z. Layton-Henry and P. B. Rich, eds., *Race, government, and politics in Britain.* Basingstoke: Macmillan.

Leeke, M. 2003. "UK election statistics: 1945–2003." House of Commons Research Paper 03/59, House of Commons, UK.

Le Gallou, Jean-Yves, and Club de l'Horloge. 1985. *La préférence nationale: Réponse à l'immigration.* Paris: A. Michel.

Lequin, Y. 1992. "L'invasion pacifique." In Y. Lequin, ed., *Histoire des étrangers et de l'immigration en France.* Paris: Larousse.

Lindbeck, A., and J. Weibull. 1987. "Balanced budget redistribution as the outcome of political competition." *Public Choice* 52: 273–297.

Lipset, S. 1996. *American exceptionalism: A double-edged sword.* New York: Norton.

References

Lipset, S., and G. Marks. 1997. *It doesn't happen here: Why socialism failed in the United States*. New York: Norton.

Luttmer, E. 2001. "Group loyalty and the taste for redistribution." *Journal of Political Economy* 109: 500–528.

Marcus, J. 1996. "Advance or consolidation? The French National Front and the 1995 elections." *West European Politics* 19 (2): 303–320.

Martin, P. 2003. "L'élection présidentielle et les élections législatives françaises de 2002." *French Politics, Culture and Society* 21 (1): 1–19.

Mayer, J. 2002. *Running on race: Racial politics in presidential campaigns, 1960–2000*. New York: Random House.

Mayer, N. 1993. "Ethnocentrism, racism, and intolerance." In D. Boy and N. Mayer, *The French voter decides*. Ann Arbor: University of Michigan Press. Published with the support of the French Ministry of Culture and Communication.

——— 2002. *Ces Français qui votent Le Pen*. Paris: Flammarion.

Mayer, N., and P. Perrineau. 1992. "Why do they vote for Le Pen." *European Journal of Political Research* 22 (1): 123–141.

Mayer, N., and G. Roux. 2004. "Des votes xénophobes." In B. Cautrès and N. Mayer, eds., *Le nouveau désordre électoral*. Paris: Presses de Sciences Po.

Mayhew, D. 2002. *Electoral realignments: A critique of an American genre*. New Haven, CT: Yale University Press.

McCarthy, C. 2001. "Immigration dominates Danish election." *Financial Times*. November 14.

McCarty, N., K. Poole, and H. Rosenthal. 2003. "Political polarization and income inequality." Mimeo, Princeton University.

McWilliams, C. 1939. *Factories in the fields: The story of migratory farm labor in California*. Boston: Little, Brown and Company.

Mendelberg, T. 2001. *The race card: Campaign strategy, implicit messages, and the norm of equality*. Princeton, NJ: Princeton University Press.

Messina, A. 1989. *Race and party competition in Britain*. Oxford: Oxford University Press.

——— 2001. "The impact of post-WWII migration to Britain: Policy constraints, political opportunism, and the alteration of representational politics." *Review of Politics* 62 (2): 259–285.

Miles, R., and M. Brown. 2003. *Racism*. 2nd edition. London: Routledge.

Miller, W. 1980. "What was the profit in following the crowd? The effectiveness of party strategies on immigration and devolution." *British Journal of Political Science* 10 (1): 15–38.

Money, J. 1997. "No vacancy: The political geography of immigration control in advanced industrial countries." *International Organization* 51 (4): 685–720.

Moore, R. 1975. *Racism and black resistance*. London: Pluto Press.

MORI (Market and Opinion Research International). 2001. "What's worrying Britain?" A UN sponsored European-wide survey on social concerns.

Myrdal, G. 1944. *An American dilemma*. New York: Harper & Row.

Nash, J. 1950. "The bargaining problem." *Econometrica* 18: 155–162.

Neubeck, K., and N. Cazenave. 2001. *Welfare racism: Playing the race card against America's poor*. New York: Routledge.

Nielsen, Hans Jørgen. 1999. "The Danish election 1998." *Scandinavian Political Studies* 22 (1): 67–81.

Office of National Statistics. *Population Size* 2001. Available at: http://www.statistics.gov.uk /cci/nugget.asp?id=273.

Oliver, J., and T. Mendelberg. 2000. "Reconsidering the environmental determinants of white racial attitudes," *American Journal of Political Science* 44 (3): 574–589.

Pagan, A., and A. Ullah. 1999. *Nonparametric econometrics*. New York: Cambridge University Press.

Patterson, S. 1969. *Immigration and race relations in Britain, 1960–1967*. London: Oxford University Press.

Paul, K. 1997. *Whitewashing Britain: Race and citizenship in the postwar era*. Ithaca, NY: Cornell University Press.

Pedersen, K., and J. Ringsmose. 2004. "From the Progress Party to the Danish People's Party—From protest party to government supporting party." Paper presented to the workshop "Effects on Incumbency of Organisation of Radical Rightwing Parties" at the European Consortium for Political Research Joint Session of Workshops, April 13–18.

Pedersen, Søren. 1999. "Migration to and from Denmark during the period 1960–97." In David Coleman and Eskil Wadensjö, eds., *Immigration to Denmark: International and national perspectives*. Aarhus, Denmark: Aarhus University Press.

Perrineau, P. 1997. *Le symptôme Le Pen*. Paris: Librairie Arthème Fayard.

Pettigrew, T. 2000. "Systematizing the predictors of prejudice." In D. Sears, J. Sidanius, and L. Bobo, eds., *Racialized politics: The debate about racism in America*. Chicago: University of Chicago Press.

Pierson, P. 1994. *Dismantling the welfare state? Reagan, Thatcher, and the politics of retrenchment*. Cambridge: Cambridge University Press.

Piketty, T. 1995. "Social mobility and redistributive politics." *Quarterly Journal of Economics* 110 (3): 551–584.

——— 1998. "Self-fulfilling beliefs about social status." *Journal of Public Economics* 70: 115–132.

——— 1999. "Attitudes toward income inequality in France: Do people really disagree?" CEPREMAP Working paper 9918.

References

Polakow-Suransky, S. 2002. "Fortress Denmark?" *American Prospect* (June 3): 21–25.

Poole, K., and H. Rosenthal. 1997. *Congress: A political-economic history of roll call voting.* New York: Oxford University Press.

Powell, J. Enoch, and R. Collings. 1991. *Reflections of a statesman: The writings and speeches of Enoch Powell.* London: Bellew Publishing.

Przeworski, A., and J. Sprague. 1986. *Paper stones: A history of electoral socialism.* Chicago: University of Chicago Press.

Qvortrup, M. 2002. "The emperor's new clothes: The Danish general election 20 November 2001." *Western European Politics* 25 (2): 205–211.

Randall, N. 2003. "Three faces of New Labour: principle, pragmatism, and populism in New Labour's Home Office." In S. Ludlam and M. J. Smith, eds., *Governing as New Labour: Policy and politics under Blair.* Basingstoke: Palgrave Macmillan.

Reuters. 1997. "Anti-immigration party makes impact in Danish elections." November 19.

Rich, P. 1998. "Ethnic politics and the conservatives in the post-Thatcher era." In S. Saggar, ed., *Race and British electoral politics.* London: UCL Press.

Roemer, J. 1979. "Divide and conquer: Microfoundations of a Marxian theory of wage discrimination." *Bell Journal of Economics* Autumn: 695–705.

——— 1998. "Why the poor don't expropriate the rich: An old argument in new garb." *Journal of Public Economics* 70: 399–442.

——— 1999. "The democratic political economy of progressive income taxation." *Econometrica* 67 (1): 1–19.

——— 2001. *Political competition: Theory and applications.* Boston: Harvard University Press.

Rutenberg, J., and F. Barringer. 2002. "Divisive words on the right: Attack on Lott's remarks has come from variety of voices on the right." *New York Times.* December 17, sect. A, p. 31, col. 1.

Safran, W. 1985. "The Mitterrand regime and its policies of ethnocultural accommodation." *Comparative Politics* 18 (1): 41–63.

Saggar, S. 1993. "Can political parties play the 'race card' in general elections? The 1992 poll revisited." *New Community* 19 (4): 693–699.

——— 1998. "A late, though not lost, opportunity: Ethnic minority electors, party strategy and the conservative party." *Political Quarterly* 69 (2): 148–159.

——— 2000. *Race and representation: Electoral politics and ethnic pluralism in Britain.* Manchester: Manchester University Press.

——— 2001. "The race card, again." *Parliamentary Affairs* 54: 759–774.

——— 2004. "Immigration and the politics of public opinion in Britain." Paper presented at the Workshop on Comparative Politics, Yale University.

References

Sanders, D. 1993. "Why the Conservatives won—again." In A. S. King, ed., *Britain at the polls, 1992.* Chatham, NJ: Chatham House Publishers.

Sarlvik, B., and I. Crewe. 1983. *Decade of dealignment: The Conservative victory of 1979 and electoral trends in the 1970s.* New York: Cambridge University Press.

Sauerberg, S. 1991. "The Danish parliamentary election of December 1990." *Scandinavian Political Studies* 14 (4): 321–334.

Scarman, Leslie George. 1982. *The Brixton disorders, 10–12 April 1981: The Scarman report: Report of an inquiry.* Harmondsworth: Penguin Books.

Schain, M. 1985. "Immigrants and politics in France." In J. S. Ambler, ed., *The French socialist experiment.* Philadelphia: Institute for the Study of Human Issues.

Schultz-Nielsen, Marie Louise. 2001. *The integration of non-Western immigrants in a Scandinavian labour market: The Danish experience.* Copenhagen: Rockwell Foundation Research Unit.

Schuman, H., C. Steech, L. Bobo, and M. Krysan. 1997. *Racial attitudes in America: Trends and interpretations.* Cambridge, MA: Harvard University Press.

Sears, D. O., Colette Van Laar, Mary Carrillo, and Rick Kosterman. 1997. "Is it really racism?: The origins of white Americans' opposition to race-targeted policies." *Public Opinion Quarterly* 61 (1): 16–53.

Sears, D., J. Sidanius, and L. Bobo, eds. 2000. *Racialized politics: The debate about racism in America.* Chicago: University of Chicago Press.

Shields, J. 1995. "Le Pen and the progression of the far-right vote in France." *French Politics and Society* 13 (2): 21–39.

Sigelman, L., and S. Welch. 1991. *Black Americans' views of racial inequality.* Cambridge: Cambridge University Press.

Silverman, B. 1986. *Density estimation for statistics and data analysis.* New York: Chapman and Hall.

Simmons, H. 1996. *The French National Front: The extremist challenge to democracy.* Boulder: Westview Press.

Sniderman, P., and T. Piazza. 1993. *The scar of race.* Cambridge, MA: The Belknap Press of Harvard University Press.

Solomos, J. 1993. *Race and racism in Britain.* 2nd edition. New York: St. Martin's Press.

Spencer, I. 1997. *British immigration policy since 1939: The making of multi-racial Britain.* London: Routledge.

Stimson, J. 1999. *Public opinion in America: Moods, cycles, and swings.* 2nd edition. Boulder: Westview Press.

Studlar, D. 1978. "Policy voting in Britain: The colored immigration issue in the 1964, 1966, and 1970 general elections." *American Political Science Review* 72 (1): 46–64.

References

Sundquist, J. 1983. *Dynamics of the party system: Alignment and realignment of political parties in the United States.* Washington, DC: Brookings.

Tapinos, G. 1975. *L'immigration étrangère en France: 1946–1973.* Paris: Presses Universitaires de France.

Teixera, R., and J. Rogers. 2000. *America's forgotten majority: Why the white working class still matters.* New York: Basic Books.

Thränhardt, D. 1995. "The political uses of xenophobia in England, France and Germany." *Party Politics* 1 (3): 323–345.

Triest, R. 1990. "The effect of income taxation on labor supply in the United States." *Journal of Human Resources* 25 (3): 491–516.

U.S. Committee for Refugees (USCR). 1998. Country Report: Denmark. Available at www.refugees.org/world/countryrpt/europe/1998/denmark.htm. Accessed July 27, 2004.

——— 1999. Country Report: Denmark. Available at www.refugees.org/world/countryrpt/europe/1999/denmark.htm. Accessed July 27, 2004.

——— 2003. Country Report: Denmark. Available at www.refugees.org/world/countryrpt/europe/2003/denmark.htm. Accessed July 30, 2004.

Van de Hei, J. 2003. "Dean crafts own 'Southern Strategy.'" *Washington Post.* December 8, sect. A, p. 6.

Verbunt, G. 1985. "France." In T. Hammar, ed., *European immigration policy: A comparative study.* Cambridge: Cambridge University Press.

Virdee, S. 1999. "England: Racism, anti-racism, and the changing position of racialized groups in economic relations." In G. Dale and M. Cole, eds., *The European Union and migrant labour.* New York: Berg.

Von Drehle, D., and D. Balz. 2002. "For GOP, South's past rises in tangle of pride, shame." *Washington Post.* December 15, sect. A, p. 26.

Weil, P., and J. Crowley. 1994. "Integration in theory and practice: A comparison between France and Britain." *West European Politics* 17 (2): 110–126.

White, A. 2002. *Social focus in brief: Ethnicity 2002.* London: Office for National Statistics.

Withol de Wenden, C. 1991. "Immigration policy and the issue of nationality." *Ethnic and Racial Studies* 14 (3): 319–332.

Wittman, D. 1973. "Parties as utility maximizers." *American Political Science Review* 67: 490–498.

Wood, J., and J. Enoch Powell. 1970. *Powell and the 1970 election.* Kingswood, UK: Elliot.

Ysmal, C. 2003. "France." *European Journal of Political Research* 42 (7–8): 943–956.

Index

Abernathy, Ralph, 62
abortion, 84, 85, 87, 194
Abramowitz, A., 72
Adler, F., 259, 260
AFDC, 101
affirmative action, 7, 59, 60, 69, 72, 90
Africa, 2, 131, 159, 240, 241, 244
African Americans, 2, 6, 46; and Republican
    Party, 41, 42, 49, 52, 58, 61, 70, 112;
    citizenship rights of, 48, 319; stereotypes
    concerning, 48; as captured group, 49, 65,
    362n10; and Democratic Party, 49, 52, 58, 61,
    65, 70, 71, 72, 93; civil rights of, 49–50, 55, 56;
    disenfranchisement of, 51; and Roosevelt, 52;
    and Henry Wallace, 53; mobilization of, 55;
    and election of 1960, 56; and Reagan, 61, 62;
    and Clinton, 64; as pushing too fast/hard, 68,
    73, 75; voting by, 70, 71, 72; political ideology
    of, 74; work ethic of, 77, 85, 86; whites'
    attitudes toward, 78–81; aid to, 90–92, 97–101
African British, 170
African immigrants, 135, 137, 138, 139
age: in U.S., 89, 113; in Denmark, 220, 224; in
    France, 284, 285, 286, 287
Alesina, A., 7, 85, 128, 320
Algeria/Algerians, 240, 243, 244
Aliens Act of 1983 (Denmark), 195, 198
Alliance Party (UK), 159
Amin, Idi, 151
Anderson, John, 62
Anglo-Asian Conservative Society, 152

Anglo-West Indian Conservative Society, 152
antiblack affect, 68, 73, 74, 75
antisolidarity effect (ASE): defined, 5; estimation
    of, 7; and racism, 30, 309; and tax policy,
    36; and Euclidean utility function, 37–39;
    and U.S., 68, 69, 111, 117, 119, 126, 127, 128,
    315–316, 317–318; and UK, 180–190, 316,
    318; and Denmark, 212, 221, 230–235, 316;
    and France, 303–306, 317; and counterfactual
    analysis, 312
Asia/Asians, 2, 131, 159, 175
Asia Minor, 2
asylum: hostility to seekers of, 11; in UK, 130,
    131, 132–133, 159–162, 163–164, 187; in
    Denmark, 195, 198; in France, 241, 255. See
    also immigration; refugees
Asylum and Immigration Act of 1996 (UK), 162
Atwater, Lee, 63
Australia, 135, 137
Austria, 3, 308
Austrian Freedom Party (Freiheitliche Partei
    Österreichs), 131

Baker, Kenneth, 160–161
Bakke v. Regents of the University of California, 69
Balladur, Édouard, 255, 257
Bangladeshis, 139, 170
Barnes, Clifford, 63, 200
Barre, Raymond, 250
Bartels, L., 108
Belgium, 3, 239

Index

Bell, D., 260, 262
Ben-Tovim, G., 149, 152
Benyon, J., 156
Bible, 84, 85
Billig, M., 161
Birmingham (UK), 141
Black, Earl, 50, 52, 65; *The Rise of the Southern Republicans*, 50–51
Black, Merle, 50, 52, 65; *The Rise of the Southern Republicans*, 50–51
blacks (UK), 170, 171, 175. *See also* ethnic minorities; people of color (UK)
blacks (U.S.). *See* African Americans
Blair, Tony, 162–164, 189
Blake, C., 155
Blundell, R., 174
Blunkett, David, 163
Bobo, L., 365n10
Borre, O., 196
Bosnia, refugees from, 197, 199
Bradford riots, 163
Bréchon, P., 247, 253, 254
British Commonwealth, 141
British Empire, 141
British General Election Studies (BES), 168, 173, 175, 176, 177
British National Party (BNP), 11, 130–131, 153, 161, 163
Brixton riots, 156–157
Brown, M., 135
Brubaker, R., 248, 249–250
Bryder, T., 199
Buchanan, Patrick, 65
Burnley riots, 163
Bush, George H. W., 58, 59, 62–64, 68
Bush, George W., 6–7, 41, 65
business (France), 251, 256, 262
busing, 7, 59, 60, 61
Butler, D., 146, 147, 150, 152, 162

Canada, 135, 137
Caribbean British, 170
Carlsen, Erik, 201
Carmines, E., 43, 49, 50, 54, 56, 57, 361n4
Carter, Dan, 59, 61, 62, 63, 66
Carter, Jimmy, 55, 62, 68, 86
Castles, S., 139
Catholics (France), 237, 240, 243
Catholics (U.S.), 86

Center Democratic Party (Denmark), 194, 206, 208, 234
Center Right Party (France), 248, 249, 254, 255
Charlot, M., 152
Chevènement, Jean-Pierre, 261
Chinese (UK), 171
Chirac, Jacques, 243, 249, 250, 251, 254, 255, 257, 260, 262, 378n49
Christian Democratic Party (Denmark), 234
Christian People's Party (Denmark), 194, 206, 208
Christians (U.S.), 86
citizenship: in UK, 137, 148, 155; in Denmark, 191, 203; in France, 243, 249, 250, 251, 255, 376n16
Citizens of the United Kingdom and colonies (CUKC), 148, 151
civil rights: policy on, 4; movement promoting, 6, 89, 113, 307; and parties, 43; and Democratic Party, 49–50, 53, 54, 56; and Roosevelt, 52; and Republican Party, 53, 54, 113; and Truman, 53, 54; increased support for, 55; and white backlash, 58–59; and Reagan, 62; and George H. W. Bush, 63; and conservative Protestants, 86
Civil Rights Act of 1964 (U.S.), 43, 50, 57, 59, 62, 63, 66
civil unrest (UK), 143
Civil War (U.S.), 44, 46, 47, 66
class: in U.S., 42, 44–45, 49, 66, 313; in UK, 131, 134, 146, 153, 158, 168, 169, 171, 183, 187, 190; in France, 299–300
Clinton, Bill, 64–65
Clinton-Gore ticket, 65, 118
Cobb, M., 59
cold war, 55
Coleman, D., 145, 151, 158
colonialism, 3, 11, 135, 136, 137, 155, 239, 241
Commonwealth Immigrants Act of 1962 (UK), 144–145, 147, 148
Commonwealth Immigrants Act of 1968 (UK), 148, 150
Communist Party (Denmark), 194
Communist Party (PCF) (France), 243, 245, 250, 261
compassion, for the poor: and political ideology, 72, 73, 74, 75, 76, 78, 81, 82–84, 86, 88, 90; and Republican Party vote shares, 112. *See also* poverty

Index

Compromise of 1877 (U.S.), 49

conservatism, 73, 74, 75

Conservative Party (France), 243

Conservative Party (UK): and racism, 131, 160, 187; and immigration, 134, 139, 140–141, 143, 144, 145, 146, 148, 150, 153, 158, 159, 163, 164, 187; and xenophobia, 134–135, 158; factions of, 140–141; internal divisions in, 147; race policy of, 147, 158, 172; and Commonwealth Immigrants Act of 1968, 148; and voters, 148, 150, 169, 170, 171, 181, 182, 187–188; and Race Relations Act of 1968, 149; and Powell, 149–150; and Ugandan Asian crisis, 151; and minority vote, 152, 159; and Race Relations Bill of 1976, 152; and Thatcher, 153–155; liberals in, 155; and urban riots, 156; and economic reform, 157–158; and election of 1992, 159, 160–161, 371n30; and asylum issue, 159–160, 161–162, 163, 164; corruption in, 162; and quantitative analysis, 166; as Right, 166; seat shares of, 167, 172; vote share of, 167, 172; and middle class, 168; membership of, 172, 181, 182, 183, 184, 187–188; and public sector size, 172; and tax policy, 183, 313–314; and PUNE values, 184

Conservative People's Party (Denmark), 194, 195, 198, 202, 204, 206, 208, 234, 373n2

Consumer Price Index, 98, 104

Contract with America, 65

Copenhagen riots, 200

corruption (France), 266, 267, 268

Coughlin, P., 8

counterfactual analysis: and PUNE model, 7, 311–312; and logarithmic utility function, 35–36; of American policy, 114; of British policy, 179, 185; of Danish policy, 221, 231; and French policies, 283–289, 303, 304

craftsmen (France), 251, 262

Crespino, J., 42

Cresson, Edith, 254

Criddle, B., 260, 262

crime: in U.S., 63–64; in Denmark, 193, 197, 198, 199, 200, 201, 203, 209; in France, 246, 247, 248, 261, 267, 288, 300. See also violence

culture (France), 238, 255

Cypriots, 12

Daniel, W., 142

Danish Election Survey, 205

Danish People's Party (Dansk Folkeparti, DF), 192, 195, 197, 198–199, 200–203, 204, 206, 207, 208, 234, 235

Danish Social-Liberal Party (Denmark), 234

Davies, P., 246

Deakin, N., 144, 145

Dean, Howard, 42

defense, spending on (U.S.), 83, 85

definition, party-unanimity Nash equilibrium (PUNE), 16, 270

DeLay, Tom, 65

DeLey, M., 240, 241, 244

Democratic Party (U.S.): and racism, 2, 46, 96, 119, 313; race policy of, 4, 6, 53, 54, 64–65, 66, 124, 126; and redistribution policy, 4, 6; in the South, 43, 45, 50, 51, 52, 53, 54, 55, 56, 57, 58, 65, 71; in the North, 45, 47, 49, 50, 52, 53, 54, 55; platforms of, 45; two-thirds rule in, 45, 54; and whites, 46, 50, 57, 64, 66; and Civil War, 47; postbellum racial appeals of, 47–49; and Compromise of 1877, 49; and civil rights, 49–50, 53, 54; and sectional interests, 50; and African Americans, 52, 58, 61, 65, 70, 71, 72, 93; and election of 1932, 53; and election of 1948, 54; defection from, 55, 87, 88, 89, 90, 121; and party identification, 55, 71, 87; and racial equality, 55; as Left party, 56; and quantitative analysis, 68; vote shares of, 69, 70, 71, 72, 118; and libertarianism, 86; membership of, 93, 96, 107, 108, 119–122; and PUNE values, 115; and tax policy, 115, 116, 117, 118, 127, 312; and minority voters, 169; and Dixiecrats, 307–308; and policy-bundle effect, 316

Denmark: immigration in, 3, 11, 191–204; constitutional structure of, 194; Aliens Act of 1983, 195, 198; quantitative analysis of, 205–236

desirability effects, 59

Desmet, K., 320

d'Estaing, Giscard, 243

discrimination: in U.S., 73; in UK, 140, 142, 144, 147, 148, 149, 152, 160, 163, 370n25. See also racism; segregation; xenophobia

distribution effects, 3–4

distribution issue, 5

distribution policy, 4. See also redistribution

distribution strategy (UK), 157

Dixiecrats, 6, 41, 49–56, 307–308

Index

Domhoff, G., 44
Downs, A., 8
Downsian equilibrium, 8, 17, 27, 359n5
Downsian model, 8, 9, 92, 128, 308, 310, 319. *See also* Hotelling-Downs model
Dreux, city of, 253
Dukakis, Michael, 63–64

East African immigrants, 139, 147–148
Eastern Europe, 136
economic issues: and socialism, 1; and colonialism, 3; and immigration, 3. *See also* fiscal policy; income; public sector size; tax policy; wages
economic issues (Denmark), 194, 198, 207, 208, 209, 210–211, 212, 213, 214, 215, 222, 224
economic issues (France): and immigration, 241; and Mitterrand, 244; and Dreux elections, 247; and election of 1988, 250; and elections of 1993, 254; voter concern for, 254–255, 266, 267, 268, 273–275, 278–279, 280–281, 283, 284, 285, 286, 287, 288, 289, 299–302; and Le Pen, 255; and elections of 2002, 260; and liberalism, 273, 274; and counterfactual analysis, 284, 285, 286
economic issues (UK), 131, 157, 181
economic issues (U.S.): and Republican Party, 3, 4, 112; and Democratic Party, 4; and racism, 4, 5, 119; in United States, 43, 47, 49; and political ideology, 88; and voter types, 313
Economic Recovery Tax Act of 1981 (U.S.), 102
education, level of: in U.S., 74, 76, 88, 112; in Denmark, 220, 224; in France, 252, 284, 286, 287
education issues: in U.S., 81, 82, 84, 85, 86; in UK, 130, 145, 162, 164, 187; in Denmark, 209; in France, 253, 255, 263, 266, 267, 268, 376n15
Eisenhower, Dwight D., 55
EIU (*Economist* Intelligence Unit), 196, 197
eldercare (Denmark), 199, 208, 209
election years, in Denmark: **1973,** 194, 196; **1994,** 197, 198; **1998,** 197, 199, 200, 205, 206, 207, 208, 209, 210, 211, 212, 213, 215, 216, 217, 218, 219, 220, 221, 222, 223, 224, 225, 226, 227, 228, 229, 230, 232, 233, 234, 316; **2001,** 197, 200, 202–204, 205, 206, 207, 208, 210, 211, 212, 213, 215, 216, 217, 218, 219, 220, 221, 222, 223, 224, 225, 226, 228, 229, 230, 232, 233, 234, 316; **2005,** 234

election years, in France: **1983,** 246; **1986,** 248, 249; **1988,** 250–252, 254, 258, 265, 266, 273, 274, 275, 276, 277, 278, 279, 280, 281, 282, 283, 284, 286, 287, 288, 289–293, 296, 299–301, 305; **1993,** 254, 255; **1995,** 255, 256–259, 265, 266, 274, 275, 276, 277, 280, 282; **2001,** 259; **2002,** 259–263, 265, 266, 274, 275, 276, 277, 278, 279, 280, 281, 282, 283, 284, 286, 287, 288, 289–291, 294–295, 300, 305
election years, in UK: **1945,** 167; **1950,** 167; **1951,** 167; **1955,** 167; **1959,** 167; **1964,** 145, 147, 167, 169; **1966,** 146, 147, 167, 169; **1970,** 146, 150, 167, 169; **1974,** 152, 167, 169, 170; **1979,** 154, 166, 167, 169, 170, 171, 172, 173, 175, 177, 179, 180, 184, 186, 189, 316; **1980,** 158–159; **1983,** 158, 167, 169, 170, 172, 173, 175, 177, 179, 180, 184, 187, 189, 316; **1987,** 159, 167, 169, 170, 172, 173, 175, 177, 179, 180; **1992,** 159, 160–161, 166, 167, 169, 170; **1997,** 162, 163, 166, 167, 168, 169, 170, 171, 172, 173, 174, 175, 176, 177, 179, 180, 183, 184, 185, 186, 187, 188, 189, 316; **2001,** 163, 164, 167; **2003 (local),** 130
election years, in U.S.: **1932,** 52–53, 67, 362n14; **1944,** 54; **1946 (midterm),** 54; **1948,** 49–50, 54, 55, 67; **1952,** 50, 55, 71; **1956,** 50, 71; **1960,** 50, 56, 69, 70, 71; **1964,** 43, 44, 50, 56–61, 67, 69, 70, 71, 362n14; **1976,** 55, 62, 71, 74, 75, 93, 94–95, 100, 101; **1968,** 59, 67, 71; **1972,** 61, 71, 93; **1980,** 62, 71, 93, 94–95; **1984,** 62, 64, 71, 93, 94–95, 100, 101; **1988,** 63–64, 67, 71, 93, 94–95; **1992,** 64–65, 67, 71, 74, 75, 93, 94–95, 100, 101; **1994 (midterm),** 65; **1996,** 71; **1984–1988 (pooled),** 96, 97, 99, 106, 112–113, 114, 115, 117, 118, 120, 121, 122, 125, 126, 312, 313; **1988–1992 (pooled),** 96, 97, 99, 106, 112–113, 117, 118, 119, 121, 122, 124, 125, 127, 312; **1976–1980 (pooled),** 97, 99, 106, 112–113, 117, 118, 121, 122, 312; **1980–1984 (pooled),** 97, 99, 106, 112–113, 117, 118, 119, 121, 122, 124, 312
electoral system (UK), 131, 140
employers (France), 245, 250, 257
employment: in U.S., 54, 89, 112, 123; in UK, 131, 138, 139, 144, 145, 147, 149, 157, 163; in Denmark, 192–195, 201, 208, 209, 224; in France, 238, 239, 240, 241, 243, 245, 246, 250, 254, 255, 257, 258, 260, 261, 262, 266, 267, 281, 286, 288. *See also* labor; workers
Engels, Friedrich, 1

Index

environmental issues: in U.S., 81, 82; in Denmark, 208, 209, 214, 220; in France, 266, 267, 268

equality, 29, 30, 45, 48, 55, 59, 69, 123

ethnic minorities: in UK, 131, 136, 152, 155, 156, 160, 163, 168–171, 175, 367n3; in Denmark, 191

ethnocentrism, 3; in France, 238, 252, 260–261, 262–263. *See also* xenophobia

Euclidean utility function: characteristics of, 28, 36–39, 309, 310, 314–318; and UK, 28, 40, 166, 178–180, 184–190, 314, 316, 318; and U.S., 28, 40, 68, 92–93, 96, 123–127, 314, 315–316, 317–318; and Denmark, 40, 210, 232, 233, 314; and France, 40, 305, 306, 314–315, 316; and counterfactual analysis, 311; advantages of, 314; limitations of, 319

Europe, 2, 3, 6, 7, 11, 195, 239, 260, 320

European Community, 257

European Convention on Human Rights, 159

European Economic Community, 193

European Parliament, 259

European Union, 162, 198, 199, 209

exclusion (France), 266, 267

Extreme Right parties (France): and three-party model, 27, 268, 269; and citizenship debate, 248–249; and election of 1988, 251; and working class, 258; vote share of, 265; membership of, 269, 270, 298–299; and voters, 283; PUNE values for, 290, 296, 298, 299, 300, 301, 302, 303, 317; economic policies of, 314–315

factional bargaining powers, 22–27

factions, 8, 9, 10, 14–15, 16, 39, 114, 309, 310, 311. *See also* Guardians faction; Militants faction; Opportunists faction; Reformists faction

Family Expenditure Survey (FES), 168, 173

family issues (Denmark), 208, 209

family values (U.S.), 6, 7

Faroe Islands, 194

Far Right parties (Denmark), 200, 201, 202–204

Feldblum, M., 249

feminism: and political ideology, 72, 73, 74, 75, 76, 77, 78, 81, 82–84, 86, 88, 90; and Republican Party vote shares, 112. *See also* women

Fetzer, J., 240, 241

Figaro, Le, 247

fiscal policy: analysis of, 18, 30; in U.S., 69, 104, 107–108, 119, 127, 312; in UK, 174. *See also* economic issues; tax policy

Fitzgerald, M., 160

Folketing (Denmark), 194, 200, 202

Foot, Paul, 141, 144

Ford, Gerald R., 58

Forth, Eric, 164

France: racism in, 11; quantitative analysis of, 27–28, 265–306; xenophobia in, 237–264; Commission Nationale Consultative des Droits de l'Homme (CNCDH), 261

Franco-Maghribins, 248, 249, 253

Frederickson, K., 52, 54, 55, 362n11

Freedom Party (Austria), 308

Freeman, G., 240

French Electoral-Panel (2002), 265–266

Front National (FN) (France), 11, 131, 237–238, 246–247, 249–250, 251, 253, 254–263, 308; *Être Français, Cela se Mérite*, 248; *300 mesures pour la renaissance de la France*, 256

Fryer, P., 138, 147

Frymer, P., 45, 50, 59, 64

Gaitskell, Hugh, 144

Gastaut, Y., 245, 246, 248, 253

General Worker's Union (Denmark), 201

Germany, 136, 192, 239, 308

Gerring, J., 46

Gilded Age, 46

Gilens, M., 59

Gingrich, Newt, 65–66, 204

Glaeser, E., 7, 85, 128, 320

Glaser, J., 44–45, 51–52, 55, 67

Glistrup, Mogens, 195, 200

Goldey, D., 250, 251

Golding, P., 161

Goldthorpe-Heath class classification, 168

Goldwater, Barry, 43, 50, 56, 57–58, 62, 63, 65, 362n14

government (U.S.), 73, 74, 75, 81, 82, 90, 123

Great Depression, 52, 239

Greenland, 194

Green Party (France), 261

Griffin, Nick, 11–12, 131

Griffiths, Peter, 145–146

Guardians faction, 24, 25

guest workers (Denmark), 192–195. *See also* employment

Gulf War (1991), 253

Index

Habitats à Loyer Modéré (HLMs), 245, 247
Hague, William, 131
Hainsworth, P., 256
Hall, P., 157
Hannigan, Robert F., 53
Hansen, R., 143, 150, 155, 159
Hargreaves, A., 245, 248
Harris, T., 173
Hausman, J., 104–105
Haut Conseil à l'Intégration, 254
Hayes, Rutherford B., 49
headscarf affair, 252–253, 263–264
health issues: in UK, 130, 163, 164, 178, 187; in Denmark, 199, 208, 209; in France, 256, 266, 267
health sector (UK), 138, 162
Heath, Edward, 149, 150, 151, 152
Herzegovina, refugees from, 197
Hiro, D., 142, 143, 156
Hollifield, J., 240, 241
homosexuality, 86
Hoover, Herbert, 52
Hopwood v. Texas (1996), 69
Horton, Willie, 63–64
Hotelling-Downs model, 8. *See also* Downsian model
housing: in U.S., 63; in UK, 142, 145, 147, 149, 152, 161–162; in Denmark, 193; in France, 244–246, 247, 248, 254, 256, 257
Howard, Michael, 161
Hue, Robert, 261
Humphrey, Hubert, 56
Humphrey-Biemiller resolution, 54
Hunt, W., 2
Husbands, C., 151, 153, 154, 252
Hussain, A., 151, 155

Ilford North, 154
immigration: in Europe, 2; movements against, 2, 11; as competition to workers, 3; and workers, 3; policy on, 4, 7; and citizenship, 7; and Euclidean utility function, 28, 36, 37; and logarithmic utility function, 28, 309; voter concern with, 28, 30; effects of, 308–309; and model limitations, 318, 319. *See also* asylum; race; refugees
immigration (Denmark): and politics, 11, 205; increases in, 191–193, 194; of family members, 193, 195, 197, 201, 203; voter concerns over,

194, 196–197, 198, 207, 208, 209, 211–212, 214, 215, 224–225; sentiments against, 195, 201; restrictions on, 196, 199; and residence permits, 197, 198, 203; opposition to, 198–199; and deportation, 200, 201; and violence, 200; and workers, 201; and election of 2001, 202; age restrictions on, 203; tightening of, 203; perceived platforms on, 208; and vote shares, 216, 217, 218, 219, 220, 221, 222, 223; and social rights, 221, 222; and citizenship, 319
immigration (France): growth of, 237, 238; history of, 238–243; and labor, 239, 241, 244, 245; and work permits, 240; and family reunification, 241, 243, 244, 247; guest-worker, 241; and settlement, 241; population of, 242; and family expansion, 243, 255; and repatriation, 243, 246, 247, 248; and residency regulations, 243; restrictions on, 243, 255; politicization of, 243–246; and education, 244; voter concern for, 244, 254, 255, 264, 266, 267, 268, 269, 273, 276–280, 281, 282, 283, 284, 286, 287, 288, 300, 305; and voting rights, 244, 247, 250–251; and Le Pen, 246; rhetoric against, 246, 249, 253, 254; and crime, 247, 267, 288, 300; and assimilation vs. multicultural insertion, 248; and law, 249, 250; and deportation, 250; and economic issues, 254; and state services, 256, 257; and election of 1995, 257; and Le Pen voters, 258; and election of 2002, 260; and public sector size, 261; policy toward, 268; and work ethic, 281, 287; in counterfactual analysis, 283, 284, 286, 287, 288; and employment, 288; and poverty, 305; and citizenship, 319
immigration (UK): and Thatcher, 131, 154; early policy toward, 134; and labor needs, 135, 136, 137, 138, 141, 142, 145, 369n13; history of, 135–138; political responses to, 138–148; policy of silence on, 139, 140, 143, 145–146; control of, 139–140, 143–145, 147; movements against, 140; and race, 140–141; and communities, 141, 145; local impact of, 141–144; and repatriation, 143, 151; of family members, 144, 369n13; growth in, 144, 145; and Powell, 149–150; and patrials vs. non-patrials, 150–151; and settlement rights, 155, 369n13, 370n21; and Conservative Party, 158, 164, 187; and voter positions, 158, 164; and

Labour Party, 164; silence on, 164; in policy space, 166; and racism estimations, 175; quotas for, 370n21. *See also* ethnic minorities

Immigration Act of 1971 (UK), 150, 151

Immigration and Asylum Act of 1999 (UK), 372n38

income: analysis of, 30, 31, 32, 33, 36, 37; in U.S., 88, 94, 97, 121, 128; in UK, 173–174, 177; in Denmark, 220, 224; in France, 273, 274, 275, 280, 285, 286, 287. *See also* wages

income tax, 30, 31, 36, 312, 313

Indians, 135, 137, 138, 139, 152, 170, 171

indifference curve, 18, 19, 114, 218, 219

individualism, 62, 72, 77, 85

Indochina, 239

industry: immigrant competition in, 3; in UK, 135, 138; in France, 239, 240

integration: in UK, 140, 150; in France, 243, 244, 254, 263

Iran, 195

Iraq, 195, 197

Ireland/Irish, 12, 61, 135, 144

Islam, 237, 253, 263, 320. *See also* Muslims

Italian Americans, 61

Italian Social Movement/National Alliance, 131

Italy, 239, 240

Jackson, Jesse, 63, 64, 65

Jamieson, K., 63

Jensen, B., 193, 195, 196

Jews, 12, 61, 86, 192

Jim Crow racism, 46, 49, 50, 68

Johnson, Lyndon, 43, 50, 56, 58, 66, 69, 362n14

Johnson, R., 250, 251

joint density function, 28

joint probability distribution, 29

Jospin, Lionel, 257, 260, 262, 378n49

Kalyvas, S., 2

Karacs, I., 202

Katznelson, I., 149, 319

Kavanagh, D., 152, 162

Kaye, R., 162

Kennedy, John F., 56, 69

Kenyan Asian crisis, 147–148, 151

kernel density estimation, 323–325; for U.S., 98, 99, 106, 107, 124; for UK, 174, 175, 176, 179; for Denmark, 231; for France, 296, 297

Key, V. O., 54

Kinder, Donald, 58, 63, 77, 365n10; *Divided by Color,* 57

King, A., 157, 159

King, Martin Luther, Jr., 60

Kinnock, Neil, 160

Kitschelt, H., 2

Kjærsgaard, Pia, 198–199, 200

Kolmogorov-Smirnov similarity statistic, 97, 326

Kosack, G., 139

Krysan, M., 365n10

Kuklinski, J., 59

Ku Klux Klan, 12

labor: in U.S., 12, 53; in UK, 135, 136, 137, 138, 141, 142, 145, 162–163, 368nn6, 9; in Denmark, 192–195, 200–201; in France, 239, 244, 245, 286. *See also* employment; wages; workers

labor supply, 3, 29, 30, 31, 32, 104–105, 174, 312

Labour Party (UK): and racism, 131, 180, 187; and immigration, 134, 139, 140, 141, 143, 144, 145, 146, 148, 160, 164; and Griffiths campaign, 146; internal divisions in, 147; race policy of, 147, 172; and antidiscrimination laws, 148, 149; and Commonwealth Immigrants Act, 148, 150; and East African Asians, 148; and voters, 150, 169, 170, 181, 182, 187–188; and election of 1974, 152; and urban riots, 156; and minority vote, 159; and asylum issue, 161, 162–164; as Left, 166, 189; seat shares of, 167; vote share of, 167, 172; and working class, 168; and ethnic minorities, 168–169; and whites, 169; membership of, 172, 181, 182, 183, 184, 187–188; public sector size policy of, 172; conservatism in, 173, 190; and tax policy, 183, 313, 314; and PUNE values, 184; and antisolidarity effect, 316; and election of 1992, 371n30

Laffer curve, 105, 106, 107, 111, 174, 175

Lagrangian multipliers, 19, 23, 113, 273, 290

Laver, M., 2

law: on immigration, 4; in U.S., 52, 53, 54; in UK, 136, 143–144, 147; in Denmark, 193, 195, 197, 198, 199, 200, 202–203; in France, 241, 243, 244, 246, 248–249, 250

law and order: policy on, 4; in Europe, 6; in U.S., 57, 60, 63–64; in UK, 157, 158, 163; in Denmark, 199, 209, 220; in France, 238, 246, 255, 256, 260, 267, 300. *See also* security

Index

Layton-Henry, Z., 136, 141, 143, 147, 148, 150, 151, 152, 155, 156, 157, 159, 160
Left parties, 1, 9, 307
Left parties (Denmark), 194, 205, 206, 207, 216, 217, 218–219, 226, 227, 228, 229–230, 232, 233, 234
Left parties (France): and three-party model, 27, 268, 270; and Front National, 237, 247; and immigration, 243, 246; and multiculturalism, 249; and headscarf affair, 253; and election of 2002, 261, 262; vote share of, 265; membership of, 269, 270, 290, 298–299; PUNE values for, 290, 291, 296, 297, 298, 299, 300, 301, 302
Left parties (UK), 166
Left parties (U.S.), 41, 50, 54, 56, 61
Le Gallou, Jean-Yves, 256
Le Pen, Jean-Marie, 2, 11, 131, 257–259, 302–303, 306; rise of, 237, 238, 246–247; influence of, 248, 249–250, 254, 255, 263; and election of 1988, 251; voters supporting, 251–252, 262–263, 265; and headscarf affair, 253; as anti-establishment candidate, 256; and election of 2002, 259, 260–261, 262, 300–301, 317; and public sector, 299–300; economic policies of, 314–315; and racism, 360n10
Le Pen, Marine, 263
Lequin, Y., 239
Liberal Democrats (Denmark), 206, 208
Liberal Party (Liberal Democrats) (UK), 146, 148, 166, 167, 172
Liberal Party (Venstre) (Denmark), 194, 198, 202, 204, 206, 208, 234, 235
libertarianism: and political ideology, 4, 72, 73, 74, 75, 76, 77, 78, 81, 82–84, 85, 88, 90; and conservative Protestants, 86; and Republican Party vote shares, 112
Lilley, Peter, 161–162
Lincoln, Abraham, 6, 49, 50, 51, 52, 53, 56, 58, 65, 66
Lindbeck, A., 8
Lipset, S., 44
Liverpool riots, 156–157
Lodge, Henry Cabot, 56
logarithmic utility function: and UK, 28, 39–40, 166, 173–178, 180–183, 312; and U.S., 28, 39–40, 68, 92, 94, 113–122, 126, 312; characteristics of, 28–36, 39, 309, 310, 312–314; and Euclidean utility function, 37
London, 141

Lott, Trent, 41–42, 65
Luttmer, E., 7

Macmillan government, 144
Maghribins, 243, 248, 253, 254
Major, John, 160, 166
Malawi Asian immigrants, 153
Mamère, Noël, 261
Manchester, 141
Marcus, J., 258, 259
Marks, G., 44
marriage/marital status, 28, 29, 30, 31, 32, 33, 34, 360n5; in U.S., 74, 76, 79, 89, 104, 112
Marseilles, 240, 253
Martin, P., 262
Marx, Karl, 1
Mayer, J., 56, 58, 60–61, 62, 64, 258
Mayer, N., 252, 255, 258, 262–263
McCarthy, C., 197, 202
McGovern, George, 61
median voter, 9
median-voter theorem, 8
Meghir, C., 174
Mégret, Bruno, 259, 360n10
men: and voter types, 28; and labor supply, 29; and wages, 32, 360n3; in U.S., 74, 104–105, 112; in UK, 174, 177; in France, 251, 262
Mendelberg, Tali, 43, 48, 50, 55, 57, 58, 60, 365n10
Messina, A., 141, 143, 144, 145, 149, 157–158
middle class (UK), 141, 168
Midwest, the (U.S.), 74, 89, 113
Miles, R., 135
Militants faction: and PUNE model, 9, 15, 17, 18, 19, 28, 309, 310; and Nash bargaining solution, 22, 23, 24–26; as Guardians, 24; and Wittman equilibrium, 27; and Euclidean utility function, 39; in U.S., 96, 124; in UK, 177, 184, 185, 189, 190; in Denmark, 226, 227, 228, 231, 235; in France, 283, 290, 296
Miller, Angela, 63
Miller, W., 140, 150, 154
Minority Party (Denmark), 234
Mitchell, P., 256
Mitra, S. K., 247, 253, 254
Mitterrand, François, 243, 244, 250, 251, 254
Moderate Right parties (France), 255, 257
Moore, R., 142
MORI (Market and Opinion Research International), 162, 163, 164

Index

Morocco, 243
Mouvement National Républicain (MNR), 259
multiculturalism (France), 238, 248, 249, 253, 264
Muslims, 198, 200, 202, 240, 243, 252–253, 263. See also Islam

Nash, John, 22
Nash bargaining solution, 22–24
Nash equilibrium, 9, 10, 17
National Assistance Act of 1948 (UK), 162
National Election Studies (NES), 68, 69, 72, 77, 81, 82, 92, 107, 123, 168, 176
National Front (NF) (UK), 131, 151, 153, 154, 308
nationalism, 11, 131, 246, 360n9
nationality (France), 246, 248–249, 250
Nationality Act of 1948 (UK), 137, 148
Nationality Act of 1981 (UK), 155, 156, 158, 159
Nationality Code (France), 249, 250, 251, 255, 376n16
nationalization (UK), 178
national sovereignty (France), 238
Nazi Aryanism, 11
neoliberal economic reform, 157, 158
Netherlands, the, 3
New Commonwealth (NCW) countries, 135, 137, 142, 155, 159
New Deal, 52, 53, 108
New Deal coalition, 52, 55, 56
New Labour (UK), 162–163, 166, 173, 189
New Right faction (UK), 141
New Right parties, 3, 307–308
New Zealand, 135, 137
Nielsen, Hans Jørgen, 197, 201
Nixon, Richard, 56, 59, 60, 61, 64, 65
nonmanual workers (UK), 168, 169, 171
non-Standard Metropolitan Statistical Areas (SMSAs), 98
North, the (U.S.): Democratic Party in, 45, 47, 49, 50, 52, 53, 54, 55; equality appeals in, 55; segregation in, 55; civil rights legislation in, 59; support for George Wallace in, 60; whites in, 61
North Africa, 11, 239, 240
Northeast, the (U.S.), 74
Norway, 192, 308
Nottingham, 143
Notting Hill, 143
Nouvelle Droite, 11

Office for National Statistics (UK), 173
Office of National Immigration (ONI) (France), 240, 241
Old Commonwealth, 137
Oldham riots, 163
One Nation Forum, 152
Opportunists faction: and Downs model, 8; and PUNE model, 9, 15, 17, 18, 19, 28, 309, 310, 360n2; and Nash bargaining solution, 22, 23, 24–26; and Downsian equilibrium, 27; in U.S., 116; in UK, 190; in Denmark, 229; in France, 290, 296, 304
Ortuño-Ortin, I., 320

Pagan, A., 98
Pakistanis (Denmark), 193
Pakistanis (UK), 137, 138, 139, 170
Panel Study of Income Dynamics (PSID), 68, 92, 98, 105, 107, 168
Paris, 245
parties: and racism, 4; constituencies of, 8–9, 10, 14, 15, 17; internal bargaining of, 9–10; in PUNE model, 14, 309; in U.S., 55, 70, 107, 108, 119–122
party coalitions: in Denmark, 11, 199, 202, 216, 217, 218, 220; analysis of, 15; in France, 27, 249, 255, 265, 266, 270, 283; in U.S., 52, 55, 56, 60, 61, 109
party competition, model of, 7–11
party entrepreneurs, 9
party identification (U.S.), 55, 65, 87, 121
party-unanimity Nash equilibrium (PUNE): and other models, 8, 308; definition of, 16–17, 270; as system of equations, 17–20; and factions, 22–27; and three-party model, 27–28; and logarithmic utility function, 28–36; and Euclidean utility function, 36–39, 40; and U.S. policies, 113–127; and British policies, 180–190; and Danish policies, 226–236; and French policies, 270–273, 289–303, 317; conceptual innovation of, 310
party-unanimity Nash equilibrium (PUNE) model, 9–10, 14–40, 309–312, 318–319
Pasqua, Charles, 250, 262, 378n44
Pasqua laws of 1986 (France), 250, 254
Pasqua-Méhaignerie law, 255
Patterson, S., 145
Paul, K., 136
Pedersen, K., 201
Pedersen, S., 191, 192, 195, 197, 198

people of color (UK), 131, 136, 155, 160. *See also* blacks (UK); ethnic minorities

Perrineau, P., 251, 252, 253, 256, 258

petty bourgeoisie (UK), 168, 169, 171

Pierson, P., 157

Polakow-Suransky, S., 202

Poland, 239

policy-bundle effect (PBE): characteristics of, 5, 6; estimation of, 7, 8; and logarithmic utility function, 35–36; and Euclidean utility function, 37–39; and U.S., 111, 117, 119, 126, 127, 308, 315–316, 317–318; and UK, 180–190, 186, 187, 188, 316, 318; and Denmark, 230–235, 316; and France, 303–306, 316–317; and racism, 309; and counterfactual analysis, 311, 312

policy platform, 9–10

policy space: two-dimensional, 4, 8, 43; multidimensional, 8, 9, 10, 359n5; as data, 10–11; and PUNE model, 14, 18, 28, 309, 310; and model limitations, 319

Poole, K., 50, 128, 362n14; *Congress*, 46–47

Poor Laws (UK), 162

Populationnistes, 240, 241–242

populism, 60, 197, 198

Portugal, 240

Post-Electoral Survey (1988), 265–266

Post-Electoral Survey (1995), 265–266

poverty: in U.S., 73, 74, 75, 81; in UK, 157; in Denmark, 201; in France, 245, 250, 252, 254, 257, 286, 305. *See also* compassion, for the poor

Powell, Enoch, 149–150, 153; "Rivers of Blood" speech, 131, 149

P-PUNEs, 125, 185, 186, 231, 232, 303–304

President's Committee on Civil Rights, *To Secure These Rights*, 54

privatization: in UK, 157, 178; in Denmark, 202; in France, 273, 274

probability of victory, 14, 15, 24

probability-of-victory function, 10, 20–21

Progress Party (Denmark), 194–195, 196, 198, 199, 200, 206, 207, 208, 308

Protestantism, 85–86, 89, 113, 312

Przeworski, A., 2

public expenditures (UK), 162

public opinion: in UK, 143–144, 147, 149, 151, 154, 160, 161, 162; in Denmark, 196–197, 199, 200, 201–202, 208–209; in France, 245

public sector size: financing of, 4; in Denmark,

21, 36, 207, 208, 209, 211–212, 213, 214, 216, 217, 218, 219, 220, 221, 222, 223, 224, 235, 315, 316, 319; and Euclidean utility function, 28, 37, 309, 310; and logarithmic utility function, 28; in France, 36, 256, 257, 261, 267, 268, 269, 278–279, 280, 281, 282, 283, 284, 288, 299–302, 315, 316–317, 319; ideal, 36; and income, 36; and xenophobia, 36; in UK, 172, 179, 315, 316; effects on, 308–309; in PUNE model, 309; and counterfactual analysis, 311; and racism, 315, 316–317; in U.S., 315, 316; and model limitations, 319. *See also* economic issues

public services (France), 245

PUNE. *See* party-unanimity Nash equilibrium

Q-PUNEs, 126, 185, 186, 231, 232, 304

Qvortrup, M., 202

race: and Euclidean utility function, 28, 36, 37, 309, 310; and logarithmic utility function, 28, 309, 310; and voters, 28, 29, 30; conservatism concerning, 42, 43, 44, 50, 55, 56, 57, 62, 66–67, 86, 90, 99–100; prejudice about, 73; and model limitations, 318, 319. *See also* immigration

race (France), 241–242

race (U.K), 168–171

race (U.S.): as cleavage issue, 43, 44, 45, 46, 47, 48, 49, 50, 59, 61, 63; sectional politics of, 50; and the South, 50; avoidance of, 58; and class, 313; and politics, 361n4

race policy: in PUNE model, 18, 19; and voters, 29; and counterfactual analysis, 35–36; and Euclidean utility function, 37

race policy (UK): and election of 2003, 130; and immigration, 140–141; silence on, 146, 164; and anti-discrimination laws, 147; and local authorities, 149; and Thatcher, 154; and Conservative Party, 158, 172; and voters, 158, 163, 164; of Labour Party, 172

race policy (U.S.): and law and order, 4; of Democratic Party, 4, 53, 54, 64–65, 66, 124, 126; of Republican Party, 4, 53, 56, 61, 65, 66, 124, 126; and quotas, 59, 60, 61, 77; of Reagan, 62; observed, 107; and party membership, 120–121; and voter types, 313

Race Relations Act of 1965 (UK), 147

Race Relations Act of 1968 (UK), 149

Race Relations acts (UK), 164

Index

Race Relations (Amendment) Act of 2000 (UK), 372n39

Race Relations Bill of 1976 (UK), 152

racism: effects of, 3–4, 308–309; and parties, 4; in Europe, 7; and political equilibrium, 7; appeals to, 11; and language, 11; and xenophobia, 11; against colored minorities vs. whites, 12; and working class powerlessness, 12; and antisolidarity effect, 35, 36; and policy-bundle effect, 35–36; and tax policy, 36; and tax rate, 36; absence of, 38, 314; and Euclidean utility function, 38; and European New Right parties, 308; and public sector size, 315, 316–317; creation of, 360n9. *See also* discrimination; xenophobia; *race policy entries*

racism (Denmark): absence of, 210, 221, 225–226, 231, 232; and public sector size, 315, 316

racism (France): and Le Pen, 11, 251, 252, 254; movements against, 249; and economic growth, 261; absence of, 283, 288–289, 304, 305; and public sector size, 315, 316–317

racism (UK): as wedge issue, 131; appeals to, 135, 145–146, 149, 160–161, 162, 164, 165; and immigration, 143; and voters, 147, 159; and British Nationality Act of 1981, 155; and Thatcher, 155; and Conservative Party, 160, 187; and distribution effects, 166; and xenophobia, 175; estimation of, 175–176; absence of, 177, 179, 180, 185, 186; and class, 183, 190; effects of, 183, 186–187, 190, 313–314; and tax policy, 183; and PUNE values, 185; and Labour Party, 187; and public sector size, 315, 316

racism (U.S.): and Democratic Party, 2, 46, 96, 119, 313; in United States, 2, 6, 7, 11; coded/implicit appeals to, 4, 42, 43, 44, 54, 56, 57, 58, 59, 60, 61, 62, 63–64, 65–66, 67, 364n6; and economic issues, 4, 5, 119; and the South, 6, 59; of Thurmond, 41; and Lott, 41–42; and Republican Party, 41–42, 112, 119, 313; explicit, 44, 54, 55; and Goldwater, 57; biological, 69; and political ideology, 72, 73, 74, 75, 76, 78, 81, 82–84, 88, 90; as latent variable, 73; absence of, 74, 77, 81, 96, 123, 124, 126; and income, 77, 81; singular importance of, 77; and government spending, 81; and aid to African Americans, 90–92, 93, 97–101, 112; effect on redistribution of, 118, 119, 190, 313; and Euclidean function

approach, 123–127; and tax policy, 127–128; salience of, 307–308; and public sector size, 315, 316

Radical Liberals (Denmark), 194, 199

Raison, Timothy, 155

Randall, N., 163

Rasmussen, Anders Fogh, 235

Rasmussen, Poul Nyrup, 201

Rassemblement pour la République (RPR), 255; *Une Stratégie de Gouvernement,* 248

Read, John Kingsley, 153

Reagan, Ronald, 42, 56, 58, 59, 60, 61–62, 65, 68, 107

Reagan administration, 102

Reconstruction (U.S.), 46, 47, 49, 50, 51

redistribution: and universal suffrage, 1; in Europe, 2, 4; in U.S., 2, 4, 6, 47, 81, 308; and voter racism, 7, 47; prevention of, 43–44; and racism, 118, 119; in UK, 178–179; in France, 265, 305

Reformists faction, 9, 15, 17–18, 26–27, 28, 309, 310

refugees: in UK, 163; in Denmark, 192, 193, 195–198, 199, 202, 203, 208, 211–212, 214; in France, 241, 283. *See also* asylum; *immigration entries*

religion: in U.S., 6, 7, 85–86, 87, 320; in France, 252–253

Republican Party (U.S.): conservative positions of, 4; race policy of, 4, 6, 53, 54, 61, 66, 124, 126; and redistribution policy, 6; southern strategy of, 6, 42, 61, 308; and African Americans, 41, 42, 49, 52, 58, 61, 70, 112; and racism, 41–42, 49, 112, 119, 313; racial appeals of, 42, 47–48; as antislavery, 47; progressiveness of on racial issues, 48; and Compromise of 1877, 49; in the South, 49, 50–52, 55, 58, 61, 65, 66; domination by, 51; and election of 1932, 53; and racial equality, 55; and whites, 55, 62; and civil rights, 56, 113; racial conservatism of, 56, 64, 65, 66–67; as Right party, 56; and George Wallace, 60; and working class, 62; and Clinton, 64; and Congress, 65; vote shares of, 69, 70, 112, 118; and conservative Protestants, 86; and libertarianism, 86; defection from, 88, 89, 90, 121; membership of, 107, 108, 119–122; and PUNE values, 115; and tax policy, 115, 116, 118, 127, 312; and policy-bundle effect, 316

Rich, P., 152, 158, 159, 161

Index

Right parties, 9, 11

Right parties (Denmark), 197, 199, 201, 205, 207, 216, 217, 218–219, 220, 226, 227, 228, 229–230, 232, 233. *See also* Far Right parties (Denmark)

Right parties (France): and three-party model, 27; and Front National, 237; vote share of, 265; membership of, 269, 270, 271, 290, 298–299; PUNE values for, 290, 291, 296, 297, 298, 299, 300, 301, 302. *See also* Center Right party (France); Extreme Right parties (France); Moderate Right parties (France)

Right parties (UK), 166

Right parties (U.S.), 41, 50, 53, 56

Ringsmose, J., 201

riots: in UK, 135, 143, 156–157, 158, 163; in Denmark, 200; in France, 359n8. *See also* violence

RMI (French welfare program), 256, 280–281

Rockefeller, Nelson, 57

Roemer, J., 8, 18

Roosevelt, Franklin, 52

Rosenblatt-Parzen kernel density estimation method, 98

Rosenthal, H., 50, 128, 362n14; *Congress,* 46–47

Roux, G., 255, 263

Sacerdote, B., 7, 85, 128

Safran, W., 244

Saggar, S., 153, 154, 158, 159, 161

salariat (UK), 168, 169, 171

salience parameter γ, 217–221

Sanders, Lynn, 58, 63, 77; *Divided by Color,* 57

Sauerberg, S., 196

Scarman, Leslie George, 156–157

Schain, M., 245

school prayer, 84, 85, 86. *See also* education issues

Schultz-Nielsen, Marie Louise, 191, 201

Schuman, H., 365n10

sectionalism (U.S.), 45, 49, 50, 51, 52, 55

secularism (France), 252–253, 263

security, in France, 243, 248, 253, 260, 261, 262, 263, 266, 267, 300. *See also* law and order

segregation: in U.S., 53, 54, 55, 57, 58; in France, 244, 245. *See also* discrimination

September 11, 2001, attacks, 202

Shadow Cabinet (UK), 149

Shields, J., 258, 259

shopkeepers (France), 251, 262

Sigelman, Lee, 12

Sikhs, 153

Simmons, H., 247, 248, 250

Sister Souljah, 64

slavery, 45–46, 47, 51

Smethwick episode, 145–146, 147

Social Democratic Party (SDP) (Denmark), 194, 197, 198, 199, 200, 201–202, 205, 206, 208, 234, 373n2

social expenditure (France), 256

socialism, 44, 307

Socialist Party (France), 243, 244, 247–248, 254, 256, 257, 258, 260

Socialist People's Party (Denmark), 194, 206, 208, 234

social problems (Denmark), 208, 209

social protection (France), 266, 267

social security (France), 250, 257, 261, 273

social services (UK), 178

solidarity, 5, 274, 280

Solomos, J., 135

Somalia, 197, 199

South, the (U.S.): racism in, 6, 55, 59; Democratic Party in, 43, 45, 50, 51, 52, 53, 54, 55, 56, 57, 58, 65, 71; solid, 43; race in, 45; and Compromise of 1877, 49; Republican Party in, 49, 50–52, 55, 58, 61, 65, 66, 113; racial politics in, 50; whites in, 51; and election of 1932, 52; and Truman, 53; segregation in, 55; and Goldwater, 57–58; civil rights legislation in, 59; Nixon in, 61; political realignment of, 65; and political ideology, 74, 89; and Willie Horton story, 363n19

South Africa, 137

Southall incident, 153

South Asians, 11, 170, 171

southern strategy, 6, 42, 61, 308

Spain, 239, 240

Sprague, J., 2

Sri Lanka, 195

SSI (Supplemental Security Income), 101

Standard Metropolitan Statistical Areas (SMSAs), 98

state-funded agencies (Denmark), 202

state services (France), 256, 257

states' rights, 42, 48, 54, 57, 60, 62, 63

States' Rights Democrats. *See* Dixiecrats

Statistical Abstracts of the United States, 107

Steech, C., 365n10

Stevenson, Adlai, 55, 56

Stimson, J., 43, 49, 50, 54, 56, 57, 361n4

Stokes, D., 146, 147, 150

Studlar, D., 150
suffrage, universal, 1, 307, 320
Sundquist, J., 50
Survey of Economic Opportunity (SEO), 98
Survey Research Center (SRC), 98
Swamp 81 operation, 156
Sweden, 192
Switzerland, 3, 239
Symons, E., 174

Tapinos, G., 239, 240
Taubira, Christiane, 261
tax policy: in U.S., 4, 30, 48, 53, 54, 61–62, 101–
  104, 107–108, 114, 115–119, 124, 127–128;
  in PUNE model, 18; voter concern with, 29;
  in UK, 30, 154, 157, 173, 178, 183, 313, 314;
  ideal, 35, 36, 37, 217, 218; and antisolidarity
  effect, 36; and racism, 36; and Euclidean
  utility function, 37; in Denmark, 194, 195,
  202, 203, 209, 230; in France, 250, 256, 267,
  303–304
tax rate, and logarithmic utility function, 28, 29,
  31, 36, 312
Tax Reform Act of 1986 (U.S.), 102
Thatcher, Margaret, 119, 131, 148, 152, 153–155,
  156, 157, 158, 160, 165, 166, 204
Thatcher period, 168, 180
Thränhardt, D., 251
three-party model, 27–28, 40, 268–273
Thurmond, Strom, 6, 41, 42, 50, 54–55
Tory Radicals (UK), 140–141
Toxteth riots, 156
trade unions: and universal suffrage, 1; and
  immigration, 3; in U.S., 73, 74, 75, 83, 89, 112;
  in UK, 157; in Denmark, 193, 201
Traditional Right faction (UK), 141
transfer payments, 30, 31, 34, 94, 101–104
Trente Glorieuses, 239–240
Triest, R., 104–105
Trotskyites, 261
Truman, Harry S., 50, 53, 54, 55, 62
Tunisia, 243
Turkey, 193
two-dimensional policy space, 268, 309
two-party model, 14, 40, 205, 236
two party system (U.S.), 45
Tyndall, John, 11

Ugandan Asian crisis, 151
Ugandan Resettlement Board (UK), 151
Ullah, A., 98

unemployment: in UK, 136, 154, 156, 157, 163,
  370n27; in Denmark, 193, 201; in France, 238,
  239, 243, 245, 246, 250, 254, 255, 257, 258,
  260, 261, 266, 267, 268
Union pour la Démocratie Française (UDF), 255
United Kingdom: racism and xenophobia in,
  130–165; Royal Commission on Population,
  136; Nationality Act of 1948, 137, 148;
  Commonwealth Immigrants Act of 1962,
  144–145, 147, 148; Race Relations Act
  of 1965, 147; White Paper of 1965, 147;
  Commonwealth Immigrants Act of 1968,
  148, 150; Race Relations Act of 1968,
  149; Immigration Act of 1971, 150, 151;
  Race Relations Bill, 152; Nationality Act
  of 1981, 155, 156, 158, 159; Asylum and
  Immigration Act of 1996, 162; National
  Assistance Act of 1948, 162; Race Relations
  acts, 164; quantitative analysis of, 166–
  190; Immigration and Asylum Act of 1999,
  372n38; Race Relations (Amendment) Act of
  2000, 372n39
United Left Wing Party (Denmark), 206, 208
United Nations Convention Relating to the
  Status of Refugees, 192
United Nations High Commissioner for
  Refugees, 201, 203
United Nations refugee convention of 1951, 201
United States, 135, 192; racism in, 2, 6, 7, 11,
  41–67; Civil Rights Act of 1964, 43, 50, 57,
  59, 62, 63, 66; Voting Rights Act of 1965, 50,
  57, 59, 62, 66; Fair Employment Practices
  Committee, 53; quantitative analysis of, 68–
  129; Economic Recovery Tax Act of 1981, 102;
  Tax Reform Act of 1986, 102; and analysis of
  UK, 173, 174, 176, 178
United States Congress, 45, 46–47, 51, 55, 65
United States Constitution, 45, 48
United States Supreme Court, 46
Unity List—Red-Green (Denmark), 234
urban areas (UK), 141, 142, 157
urban unrest (U.S.), 83, 85

Van Buren, Martin, 45, 46
VAP (Veterans Administration Pension), 101
Verbunt, G., 239, 245
Vietnam, 195
Villiers, Philippe de, 257, 262, 378n44
violence: in UK, 143; in Denmark, 196, 209,
  373n3; in France, 246, 253, 261. See also crime;
  riots

Index

Virdee, S., 12

Vitry, 245–246

von Neumann-Morgenstern (vNM) axioms, 8

von Neumann-Morgenstern utility functions, 22

voter family, 28, 29

voters: utility functions of, 8; indifferent, 20; and probability-of-victory function, 20; uncertainty about, 20; and coalition-formation, 27; as sincere, 27–28, 319; as strategic, 27–28; and immigration, 28, 30; and race, 28, 29, 30; and tax policy, 29

voters (Denmark): and immigration, 194, 196–197, 198, 207, 208, 209, 211–212, 214, 215, 224–225; and economy, 198; Left-Right identification of, 207; issue concerns of, 208–209; analysis of traits of, 210–216; party identification of, 226; types of, 229, 231; stable preferences of, 235; reliable data on, 236

voters (France): and immigration issues, 244, 254, 255, 264, 266, 267, 268, 269, 273, 276–280, 281, 282, 283, 284, 286, 287, 288, 300, 305; crime concerns of, 246, 247, 248, 261, 267, 288; and election of 1988, 250; and Le Pen, 251–252, 257–259, 262–263; and economic issues, 254–255, 266, 267, 268, 273–275, 278–279, 280–281, 283, 284, 285, 286, 287, 288, 289, 299–302; and election of 2002, 260, 261; concern for work time sharing, 266, 267; concerns of, 266, 267, 273–283; and law and order, 267; and public sector, 267, 278–279, 280, 281, 282, 283, 288, 299–302; in equilibrium model, 268, 269; and welfare programs, 273, 274, 280–281, 286, 287; counterfactual analysis of, 283–289; PUNE values for, 299–300

voters (UK): immigrant, 145; anti–immigrant sentiment of, 146–147; and Conservative Party, 148, 150, 169, 170, 171, 181, 182, 187–188; working class, 151, 153; minority, 152, 153, 159; upper- and middle-class, 152; and class, 153, 158, 168, 169, 171; and Ilford North election, 154; and tax policy, 154; and immigration issues, 158, 164; and race policy, 158, 159, 163, 164; racism of, 159, 180, 181; conservatism of, 161, 171–173; and asylum issue, 163; and health issues, 163, 164, 266, 267; and law and order, 163; and education issues, 164; and race/ethnicity, 168–171; and Labour Party, 169, 170, 181, 182, 187–188; ethnic minorities as, 170; and wages, 173, 174,

177; and economic issues, 181; and PUNE values, 185

voters (U.S.): and race, 4–7, 43, 59–60; and racism, 47, 68, 226; and split tickets, 55; nonrich white, 69, 70, 71, 72; and aid to African Americans, 93; types of, 97–101; and public sector size, 315–316

voter types: as data, 10; and PUNE model, 14, 39, 309; and logarithmic utility function, 28–35, 309; joint distribution of, 36; in U.S., 69, 92, 97, 99, 105, 108, 119, 121, 123, 126, 128, 129, 313; in UK, 180, 181, 185, 186, 188; in Denmark, 210, 214–216, 218, 229–230, 231, 232; in France, 268, 269, 280, 282–283, 298–299, 303, 304, 305; and model limitations, 318

vote share: and PUNE model, 21, 39; and Euclidean utility function, 38; in U.S., 69, 70, 71, 72, 107, 112, 113, 118; in UK, 167, 172, 180, 189–190; in Denmark, 205–207, 216–217, 218, 227–228, 234; in France, 265–266, 271, 300–302; and counterfactual analysis, 311

Voting Rights Act of 1965 (U.S.), 50, 57, 59, 62, 66

wages: and PUNE model, 28, 29, 31, 309, 310, 360n3; in U.S., 94, 98–99, 104, 107, 112, 121; in UK, 173, 174, 175, 177; in Denmark, 194; in France, 240, 245. *See also* income; labor

Walker, Gordon, 146

Walker, I., 174

Wallace, George, 59, 60, 61

Wallace, Henry, 53, 54

Weber, Max, 85

Weber, S., 320

Weibull, J., 8

Welch, Susan, 12

welfare: in U.S., 59, 64, 65, 66, 73, 74, 75, 101; in UK, 142, 145, 161–162; in Denmark, 192, 199, 201, 203, 209, 214, 223, 225, 235; in France, 245, 255, 256, 261, 273, 274, 280–281, 286, 287

welfare queens, 42, 60, 62, 77

welfare state: in U.S., 7, 72; in UK, 166; in Denmark, 194, 195, 198, 205, 209, 214; in France, 248, 260; and Nordic social democracies, 320

West, the (U.S.), 74, 89, 113

West Africa, 135

408

Index

West Indian immigrants, 11, 135, 136, 137, 138, 139, 143
West Midlands (UK), 141
West Yorkshire, 141
Whig Party, 46, 47
white backlash, 42, 67
White Paper of 1965 (UK), 147
whites (France), 237, 241, 243, 253
whites (UK): anti–immigration sentiments of, 142, 143; and election of 1964, 145; and Thatcher, 158; and Labour Party, 169; voting patterns of, 170, 171
whites (U.S.): political ideology of, 4–5, 74, 75, 76, 77–81, 87; and Republican Party, 6, 55, 62; backlash from, 42, 58, 59, 61, 67; and Democratic Party, 46, 50, 57, 64, 66; racial appeals to, 49, 54; in the South, 51; in the North, 61; voting by, 69, 70, 71, 72; educated, 70; uneducated, 70, 72; and aid to African Americans, 97, 100
Wilson, Harold, 145, 147
Wilson government, 148, 149
Withol de Wenden, C., 248, 249
Wittman, D., 8
Wittman equilibrium, 9, 17, 27
Wittman model, 8–9
women: and voter types, 28; and labor supply, 29; and wages, 32, 360n3; in U.S., 74, 86, 89, 104–105, 112; in UK, 174, 177; in Denmark, 220, 224; in France, 262, 286, 287. *See also* feminism

women's liberation movement, 73, 74, 75
Wood, J., 150
workers: in Europe, 3; immigrant competition to, 3; in U.S., 61, 65; in Denmark, 193, 200–201; in France, 244, 245, 251, 257, 262. *See also* employment; labor
working class: and socialism, 1; in U.S., 2, 6; income of, 3; powerlessness of, 12; and Republican Party, 62; in UK, 141, 146, 151, 154, 158, 168, 169, 171; in Denmark, 235; in France, 245, 247, 257–258, 262
World War I, 239
World War II, 55, 134, 135, 238, 239

xenophobia: in Europe, 2, 3; and political equilibrium, 7; and racism, 11; and antisolidarity effect, 35, 36; and public sector size, 36; and tax rate, 36; in UK, 131, 134–135, 144, 146, 147, 148, 149, 150, 151, 158, 164, 165, 175; in Denmark, 196, 197–202, 213, 225, 234, 316; in France, 237, 238, 246, 247–250, 251, 252, 255, 283, 284, 286, 288, 299, 300; and European New Right parties, 308. *See also* ethnocentrism; racism

Ysmal, C., 260
Yugoslavia, 193, 197

409